WITHDRAWN

The Rise and Demise of Democratic Kampuchea

About the Book and Author

The Rise and Demise of Democratic Kampuchea
Craig Etcheson

This study traces the rise of Kampuchean communism from its inception in 1930 to the present. The author analyzes the socioeconomic and political conditions that brought Cambodia to an explosive stage in 1970 and documents the cataclysmic transformation that followed. The protagonist in this ongoing historical drama is the revolutionary movement known as the *Khmer Rouge,* or "Red Khmers." Their revolution was so ultraradical that even the communists were appalled. The Soviets studiously ignored it, the Chinese vainly tried to moderate it, and the Vietnamese ultimately destroyed it. In an attempt to explain the Khmer revolution—one of the most violent in modern political history—the author focuses on the ideology created by a key group of *Khmer Rouge* leaders.

The theoretical and historical significance of the Khmer revolution and the state of Democratic Kampuchea has received little attention from scholars, and far too much of what has been written has been motivated by a bewildering array of ideological and geopolitical interests. This book is one of the first to apply a systematic analytical framework to the creation, growth, and destruction of Democratic Kampuchea.

Craig Etcheson is a research associate with the Institute for Transnational Studies at the University of Southern California, where he teaches in the School of International Relations.

The Rise and Demise of Democratic Kampuchea

Craig Etcheson

Westview Press • Boulder, Colorado
Frances Pinter (Publishers) • London

This volume is included in Westview's Special Studies on South and Southeast Asia.

Map 6.2 adapted from map by Dick Sanderson in *White House Years* by Henry Kissinger (Boston: Little, Brown and Company, 1979), p. 248. Copyright © Henry A. Kissinger. Used by permission.

"Sheep" lyrics, Chapter 7, copyright © 1977, 1978 by Pink Floyd Music Publishers Ltd., London. Published and administered in the U.S.A. by Unichappell Music, Inc. International copyright secured. All rights reserved. Used by permission.

All rights reserved. No part of this publication may be reproduced or transmitted in any form or by any means, electronic or mechanical, including photocopy, recording, or any information storage and retrieval system, without permission in writing from the publisher.

Copyright © 1984 by Westview Press, Inc.

Published in 1984 in the United States of America by Westview Press, Inc., 5500 Central Avenue, Boulder, Colorado 80301; Frederick A. Praeger, President and Publisher.

Published in 1984 in Great Britain by Frances Pinter (Publishers) Limited, 5 Dryden Street, London WC2E 9NW.

ISBN (U.S.) 0-86531-650-3
ISBN (U.K.) 0-86187-362-9

DS
554.7
E85
1984

Printed and bound in the United States of America
5   4   3   2   1

For Mary

"What then?" I said. "Do you agree that the things we have said about the city and the regime are not in every way prayers; that they are hard but in a way possible; and that it is possible in no other way than the one stated: when the true philosophers, either one or more, come to power in a city, they will despise the current honors and believe them to be illiberal and worth nothing. Putting what is right and the honors coming from it above all, while taking what is just as the greatest and the most necessary, and serving and fostering it, they will provide for their own city."

"How?" he said.

"All those in the city who happen to be older than ten they will send out to the country; and taking over their children, they will rear them—far away from those dispositions they have now from their parents—in their own manners and laws that are such as we described before. And, with the city and the regime of which we were speaking thus established most quickly and easily, it will itself be happy and most profit the nation in which it comes to be."

"That is by far the quickest and easiest way," he said. "And how it would come into being, if it ever were to come into being, you have, in my opinion, Socrates, well stated."

—Plato, *Republic* (540c–541b)

From this mélange of North Vietnamese determination, Cambodian rivalries, and American internal conflicts, everything followed with the inevitability of a Greek tragedy until there descended on that gentle land a horror that it did not deserve and that none of us have the right to forget.

—Henry A. Kissinger (1979)

Contents

List of Illustrations xi
Preface xiii
Abbreviations xv

1 *Mise en Scène* 1
    Notes 3

2 **Cambodian Politics, Society, and Economy** 5
    Echoes of Empires 6
    The Magic Kingdom That Never Was 8
    Prelude to Pandemonium 14
    Notes 22

3 **Evolution of *Khmer Rouge* Political Thought and Behavior** 27
    Roots of Ideology 27
    Components of Political Thought 33
    Stages of *Khmer Rouge* Behavior 35
    Notes 36

4 **Gestation (1930–1960)** 39
    The Early History 39
    Sihanouk and Cambodian Communism 41
    Emergence of the KCP 45
    Notes 52

5 The Early Revolutionary Stage (1960–1967) 55

The Identity of the Party................................. 55
The Deterioration of the Center........................... 61
The Strategy of Revolution 66
Samlaut... 69
Notes... 72

6 The Late Revolutionary Stage (1968–1975) 75

Guerrilla Warfare (1968–1970) 79
The *Coup* 86
The U.S. Role 89
The Kissinger-Shawcross Controversy....................... 95
Combined Warfare (1970–1975) 103
The Components of Victory 124
Notes.. 137

7 Consolidation and Society Building (1975–1978).......... 143

Utopia Wrought 143
To Kill Two Kings 149
The Transformation of Consciousness...................... 157
The Struggle Within 162
Notes.. 180

8 Utopia and Pandemonium................................. 185

The Postregime Stage (1979–1983) 185
The "Precious Model": Implications of the
  Classless Society..................................... 200
Did They Keep Their Promises? 212
Denouement 216
Notes.. 217

Appendixes

A. The Constitution of Democratic Kampuchea............ 221
B. A Chronological History of Kampuchea................ 229

Selected Research Bibliography................................ 253
Index.. 273

Illustrations

Tables

2.1	Changing Land Use in Cambodia, 1954–1965	14
2.2	Landownership and Cultivation Trends, 1930–1962	15
2.3	Cambodian Rural Population Density	18
2.4	The Erosion of Purchasing Power in Cambodia, 1953–1966	20
2.5	Critical Economic Indicators, 1955–1966	22
4.1	KCP Leadership Profile	48
6.1	Disbursement Schedule: U.S. Military Assistance Program, Khmer Republic	94
6.2	U.S. Airborne Bombardment in Cambodia, 1969–1973	101
7.1	Death in Kampuchean War and Peace	148

Figures

2.1	Cambodian Demographic Trends, 1900–1980	13
2.2	Food Prices in Cambodia, 1949–1980	19
4.1	Emergence of the Kampuchean Communist Party	46
6.1	Evolution of KCP Ties—The Rise and Fall of *Angkar Loeu*	78
7.1	Idealized Representation of *De Facto* KCP Structure, 1973	169

Maps

6.1	U.S. Airstrikes in the ARCLIGHT Series, 1973	100
6.2	U.S. Airstrikes in the MENU Series, 1969	102
6.3	Geo-Military Situation, January 1970	104
6.4	Geo-Military Situation, June 1970	105
6.5	FANK Strategic Concepts for Defense of the Khmer Republic	109
6.6	Geo-Military Situation, March 1971	112

xii *Illustrations*

6.7   The Decisive Engagement 113
6.8   Geo-Military Situation, May 1972 116
6.9   Geo-Military Situation, December 1973–June 1974 120

Photographs

6.1   *Khmer Rouge* Leaders Plot Final Assault
      on Phnom Penh 122

Preface

The sole great truth in politics is that there is no objective Truth in politics. Politics is a world of compromise and doublecross, of alliance and comparative political advantage, of redeemed villainy and corrupted ideals, of victory and sudden death. More is at stake than the survival of particular forms of political institutions.

On the surface, this is a tale of war and death. As many as three million or more human beings perished as a result of the events examined in this study. Frankly, this story is still somewhat beyond my comprehension, too fantastically macabre to understand fully even after long study. Yet, it is important to try to do so, for beneath the glossy, somehow unreal surface sheen of megadeath, there lies another story. Indeed, it is the story of a search for Utopia, and the discovery of something quite different.

This study originated as a paper for a seminar on guerrilla movements in the Third World, under the direction of Gerald Bender at the University of Southern California's School of International Relations in the spring of 1980. My thanks for their comments go to members of the seminar, including Neil Scarth, Kevin McDonnough, Al Zapanta, Leslie Gunn, Ary Aryania, Jason Chao, Shobana Kokatay, Menelek Sessing, Mohamed Diakite, Bernard Wilhelm, Mohammed Mariri, Fesseha Wolde-Emanuel, Sadiq Mehros, Sarah Fishman, and Gorden Townsend.

The bulk of the research and writing for this study was done during the summer of 1981, while the author was employed as a research associate at the University of Southern California's Institute for Transnational Studies. A debt of gratitude is owed to the institute's director, James N. Rosenau, for arranging work schedules flexible enough to permit this "extracurricular" activity, and to the institute's administrative coordinators, Liz Nelson and Carole Gustin, for generous secretarial assistance and unflagging cheerfulness in the face of a summer's worth of exhaustion-induced impatience.

I gratefully acknowledge a special intellectual debt to Neil Scarth, who was my original research partner during the seminar. Our discussions and parallel research efforts both during and after the seminar influenced in no small way the entire direction of the present study. Moreover, Neil has generously allowed me to draw heavily on his unpublished paper, "A Comparative Analysis of Kampuchean Economic Program and Performance." The second section of Chapter 8 ("The 'Precious Model': Implications of the Classless Society") very much reflects Neil's research on comparative models of economic development.

The study was completed in the spring of 1983, and I had a lot of help. Thanks are in order to the School of International Relations at the University of Southern California and to its director, Dr. Michael Fry, for a grant from the Von Kleinsmid Endowment to assist in the final preparation of the manuscript, and to the School of International Relations Machine Laboratory for computing resources used to process the final draft and produce the tables. Michelle Raymond assisted in the preparation of the tables using the Scribe Document Preparation System and a Xerox 2700 Laser Graphics Printer. Maps 6.2 through 6.9 were produced by Engineering Associates, Inc., of Los Angeles.

I would also like to acknowledge helpful comments, criticisms, and contributions by Michelle Raymond, Dan Garst, Jung Il-Hwa, Peter Berton, Stanley Rosen, Jonathan Aronson, James Rosenau, Kanthati Suphamongkhon, Constance Lynch, Gerard Chaliand, Heidi Hobbs, Douglas Pike, William Shawcross, Laura Summers, Walter Aschmoneit, Ben Kiernan, and Chanthou Boua. Special thanks go to Lynn Sipes and Janice Hanks of USC's Von Kleinsmid Library for research assistance above and beyond the call of duty. Thanks also to the editors and anonymous reviewers at Westview Press for helpful input.

Incisive criticism and commentary from David P. Chandler improved the manuscript at many points, and the author is most grateful.

Saving the best for last, I most appreciatively acknowledge the support of Dr. Gerry Bender, whose extensive comments on various drafts of this study proved to be of crucial importance. Without his constant encouragement and advice, this study would not have happened.

Although each of these persons and institutions, and many yet unnamed, improved the final product in some way, they were unable to remedy all of the work's deficiencies. The author alone is solely responsible for those.

Craig Etcheson
Los Angeles, California

Abbreviations

AAPSO	International Conference on Solidarity with the Khmer People
ADKW	Association of Democratic Khmer Women
ARVN	Army of the Republic of Vietnam (South Vietnam)
ASEAN	Association of Southeast Asian Nations
CCNL	Cambodian Committee for National Liberation
CCP	Communist Party of China
CECUF	Central Executive Committee of the United Front
CIA	Central Intelligence Agency
CIDG	Civilian Irregular Defense Group
CLF	Cambodian Liberation Front
COSVN	Central Office for South Vietnam
CPK	(See KCP)
CPSU	Communist Party of the Soviet Union
DCI	Director, Central Intelligence Agency
DRV	Democratic Republic of Vietnam (North Vietnam)
FANK	*Force Armée Nationale Khmer*
FARK	*Force Armée Royale Khmer*
FLLPK	*Front Nationale de Libération du Peuple Khmer* (see KPNLF)
FUNK	National United Front for Kampuchea
GRUNK	Royal Government of Khmer National Unification
ICA	Indochinese Communist Alliance
ICC	International Control Commission
ICP	Indochinese Communist Party
IMR	Infant Mortality Rate
KCP	Kampuchean Communist Party
KFF	Khmer Freedom Front
KNLC	Khmer National Liberation Committee
KNUFNS	Khmer National United Front for National Salvation
KPLC	Khmer People's Liberation Committee

KPNLF	Khmer People's National Liberation Front
KPP	Khmer People's Party
KPRP (1951)	(See KPP)
KPRP (1981)	Kampuchean People's Revolutionary Party
KSA	Khmer Students' Association
KSU	Khmer Students' Union
MAAG	Military Assistance Advisory Group
MACV	Military Assistance Command, Vietnam
MAP	Military Assistance Program
NEZ	New Economic Zone
NIK	*Nekhum Issarak Khmer*
NLF	National Liberation Front (South Vietnam)
NSC	National Security Council
NVA	North Vietnamese Army
PCF	French Communist Party
PFLANK	People's National Liberation Armed Forces of Kampuchea
PLCC	People's Liberation Central Committee
PRA	People's Representative Assembly
PRC	People's Republic of China
PRG	Provisional Revolutionary Government (South Vietnam)
PRK	People's Republic of Kampuchea
PYA	Patriotic Youth Association
RAK	Revolutionary Army of Kampuchea
SEATO	Southeast Asia Treaty Organization
SRV	Socialist Republic of Vietnam
UFTIP	United Front of the Three Indochinese Peoples
UN	United Nations
USAF	United States Air Force
VC	Viet Cong
VCP	Vietnamese Communist Party
VRYL	Vietnamese Revolutionary Youth League
WHY	*White House Years*, by H. A. Kissinger
WPK	Workers' Party of Kampuchea
WSAG	Washington Special Actions Group
YOU	*Years of Upheaval*, by H. A. Kissinger
Yuv.K.K.	*Sampoan Yuvachun Kampuchea Pracheathibodey*, or Alliance of Democratic Khmer Youth

1
Mise en Scène

In the course of the struggle since 1970, Cambodia has developed the political consciousness of its people, begun one of the most thorough-going agrarian revolutions in history, rebuilt much of the basic infrastructure necessary to a developing economy, and quickly resumed industrial production.
—George Hildebrand and Gareth Porter, 1976[1]

The Draconian rules of life turned Cambodia into a nation-wide gulag, as the Khmer Rouge imposed a revolution more radical and brutal than any other in modern history—a revolution that disturbed even the Chinese, the Cambodian communists' closest allies. Attachment to home village and love of Buddha, Cambodian verities, were replaced by psychological reorientation, mass relocation, and rigid collectivization.
—Sydney Schanberg, 1980[2]

Revolution is a complex business, but it is not ambiguous. The bottom line is political authority. The structure of social order is at stake in a revolution because the primary functions of political authority are the allocation of societal values and the definition of social reality. Revolution entails a transformation, by definition quite a rapid transformation, of these functions. That is, revolution is a *metapolitical* activity: It is about the structure or the framework—the form of the institutions—through which daily political interactions within a society will be played out.

It is precisely with this metapolitical dimension of revolution that students of the subject may experience their greatest challenge. The challenge goes far beyond the simple elusiveness of facts of time, place, and persons. It derives from a relativity of values, such that an event can have two (or more) entirely different meanings, depending on the point of view. This is illustrated in the case at hand by the two quotations that open this introduction. For Kampuchea, this relativity has been eloquently expressed in François Ponchaud's dialectical appraisal: "A fascinating revolution for all who aspire to a new social order. A terrifying revolution for all who have any respect for human beings."³

Who were the *Khmer Rouge*? Where did they come from? What did they stand for? How and why were they able to achieve victory? Did they deliver what they promised? Why did they ultimately fail? In this study, I offer an answer to these and other questions, but a single study as brief as this cannot pretend to be either definitive or exhaustive when the subject is a historical episode so sweeping and dynamic, and while we are still so close to the events that occurred in Cambodia. A huge gap remains in the literature on revolution, for far too much of what little has been written about the Khmer Revolutions has been a search for heroes and villains motivated by a bewildering array of ideological and geopolitical interests. To be sure, there are heroes and villains aplenty in this tale, but these serve best to symbolize the deeper meaning of the revolutions.

In an attempt to gain a more objective perspective on the revolutions, it may be useful to begin by trying to give a more explicit definition to the term "revolution," or at least by looking at how others have tried to do this. As I noted at the outset, revolution has to do with the *form of the institutions* through which daily political interactions are conducted within a society. Thus, one analyst has defined revolution as "abrupt, illegal mass violence aimed at the overthrow of the political regime."⁴ This approach focuses on mass violence aimed at the destruction of the existing political institutions. Another analyst defines revolution as the act of rebuilding a society shattered by rebellion.⁵ According to this school, then, revolution is society building.

The distinction between revolution *qua* "overthrow" and revolution *qua* "society building" is clear enough in the abstract. First the old structure of political authority must be eliminated. Only then can social relations be reconstituted at the behest of the victors. As a matter of historical fact, however, the two are usually so intimately intertwined that their separation for purposes of analysis is inevitably artificial.

In the present case, for example, the *Khmer Rouge* often boasted that they were a "complete state" years before the actual founding of their state, Democratic Kampuchea, in 1976. In areas where they gained control as early as 1968, the *Khmer Rouge* experimented with forms of social organization even while the most difficult portions of their struggle lay ahead. In fact, the career of the *Khmer Rouge* or the Kampuchean Communist Party (KCP) falls into five phases or stages, none of which corresponds unambiguously with either revolution or society building. Thus, dogmatic adherence to this dichotomy could distort analysis. Nonetheless, I will at times rely on this dichotomy for the sake of analytical clarity, while attempting to remain conscious of the pitfalls associated with the distinction.

Notes

1. George Hildebrand and Gareth Porter, *Cambodia: Starvation and Revolution* (New York: Monthly Review Press, 1976), p. 3.

2. Sydney Schanberg, "The Death and Life of Dith Pran: A Story of Cambodia," *New York Times Magazine*, January 20, 1980, p. 44.

3. François Ponchaud, *Cambodia: Year Zero* (New York: Holt, Rinehart and Winston, 1978), p. xvi.

4. Mostafa Rejai, *The Comparative Study of Revolutionary Strategy* (New York: David McKay, 1977), p. 8.

5. Chalmers Johnson, *Autopsy on People's War* (Los Angeles: University of California Press, 1973), p. 8.

2
Cambodian Politics, Society, and Economy

When we had proceeded on so far, that it pleased my Guide to show me the Creature which was once so fair, he took himself before me, and made me stop, saying: "Lo Dis! and lo the place where it behooves thee to arm thyself with fortitude." How icy chill and hoarse I then became, ask not, O Reader! for I write it not, because all speech would fail to tell. I did not die, and did not remain alive; now think for thyself, if thou hast any grain of ingenuity, what I became, deprived of both death and life.
—Dante, *Inferno*[1]

One's understanding of contemporary world events is usually enhanced by taking a look back at those previous developments from which today's events flow. The present chapter offers an introductory look back at three matters essential to an understanding of the Cambodian revolutions: (1) the history of imperial and colonial institutions in Cambodia; (2) the status of Cambodia's pre-1970 image as a jungle paradise; and (3) the role the Khmer peasantry plays in Cambodian politics.

The political economy of any contemporary nation is, of course, a virtually inexhaustible topic. Nevertheless, one can use these three "minitopics" as a context to begin describing how this traditional, agrarian Buddhist country could become the laboratory within which was executed the most radical experiment in social engineering ever conceived. By briefly reviewing the history of the Khmer people, their socioeconomic conditions, and their political institutions, one may gain some insight into the long-term dynamics of the society. Such a look at Cambodian political economy rewards the viewer with glimpses of the prelude to revolution.

Echoes of Empires

For Westerners, Cambodia was, is, and probably will remain distant, mysterious, unknown. Before 1965, most Americans could not have named the continent containing Cambodia.[2] Those who had heard of it were likely to know no more about the small country (about the same size as South Dakota) than that it has an ancient temple named Angkor Wat. Yet, that famed temple is an echo of a long history of empire. In fact, it is only within the context of the rise and fall of empires—Cambodian, as well as Javanese, Siamese, Russian, Chinese, Mongolian, French, and U.S. empires (to name only the ones of immediate concern here)—that the history of the Khmer revolution from 1960 to 1978 can be properly understood.

In 802 A.D., Jayavarman II cast off the domination of the Javanese warlords and founded the Angkor Empire, becoming the first in a nearly thousand-year succession of Khmer "god-kings." The union of the Fou Nan Dynasty and the Tchen-la Dynasty, the Angkor Empire was based upon the administrative control of a vast hydraulic system of dikes and canals, enabling a marginally higher level of agricultural productivity. The increased productivity supported the religious state, the imperial armies, and the inevitable bureaucracy that went along with them. As long as the hydraulic system continued to expand, so did the power of the Khmer god-kings continue to expand. The system functioned well over some four centuries.

With time, however, the efficiency of the hydraulic system declined as maintenance failed to keep pace with floods and silt. This failure occurred in direct proportion to the clogging of the Angkor bureaucracy with extravagance. In fact, decline followed Suryavarman II's immense expenditure to build the magnificent Angkor Wat temple complex. As productivity declined and resources invested in imperial trappings increased in relation to those invested in productive projects, territorial expansion of the empire ceased. "Torn by dissension, it would become vulnerable to the 'barbarians' outside the walls, to the armies of neighboring empires, or to its own rebellious people."[3] After peaking in the twelfth century, the Angkor Empire entered a long period of decline and disintegration. This is a common pattern for societies based on the hydraulic mode of production, and it would not be the last time a Khmer regime's collapse followed agro-stagnation.

It is a catch phrase of dialectical materialism that "the present order holds within it the seeds of its own destruction." As with the hydraulic economy of the Angkor Empire, this seemed to be the case for the political economy of the Eurocentric world system of the eighteenth and nineteenth centuries. The colonial possessions sent their chosen youth to the imperial capitals to receive the enlightenment of the masters. The liberalism of Europe's Enlightenment thus impregnated the subject peoples with the seeds of independence in the form of yearning for the ideas of democracy, nationalism, and, somewhat later, socialism.

In this manner, the democratic, nationalist, and socialist ideals of the French Revolution were transmitted throughout France's colonial empire, spawning the intellectual conditions for anticolonial wars across the empire. The French (Euro-) ideals blended with each colonial political culture to produce myriad unique and rebellious hybrids. In any given colony, a particular hybrid emerged as dominant only after prolonged struggle among the many.

In Southeast Asia, French rule was imposed at a time when the remnants of the once-great Angkor Empire were in the final stages of collapse under the pressure of the numerically and militarily superior Siamese to the west and Vietnamese to the east and south. In a sense, France may have plucked the Khmer monarchy from the jaws of oblivion, but the Faustian bargain between the French and the Khmer gave the Khmer monarchs something less than a full life. The modern history of the Khmer people thus begins with the creation of "Cambodge"[4] in 1863–1864 as the Khmer "god-kings" were forcibly plunged into the Eurocentric world system.

After seventy years of struggle to establish their authority over the proud Khmer monarchy and peasantry, the French colonial authorities began in the 1930s to plant the first of the great rubber plantations around Snuol, Chup, Peancheang, Prek Kak, Chamcar Amdong, Chamcar Loeu, and elsewhere throughout the regions of Cambodia surrounding the wetlands of the Mekong Delta. Developed primarily by French and Belgian capital, rubber production was geared almost solely to the export market.

The plantations quickly came to dominate the primary sector, and hence the bulk of the preindustrial Cambodian economy. Because of the low productivity of Khmer workers, the French preferred to import Vietnamese labor to tend the plantations. The Vietnamese communities that subsequently developed around the Cambodian rubber plantations became important centers of resistance during the independence struggles of the 1940s and 1950s as well as during the civil strife beginning in the late 1960s.

Radicals charged that the net economic effect of the French presence in Cambodia was to saddle the Khmer people with the burden of supporting the French administrative apparatus, while simultaneously retarding the development of indigenous Cambodian enterprises by opening the economy to cheaper competitive imports from more developed economies. Moreover, capital formation was inhibited by special devices designed to extract surplus from the colonial economy, effecting an income redistribution favoring the parent state.

The pernicious effects of French dominance in Cambodia eventually went beyond structural economic distortions. In May 1941, France ceded to Thailand nearly one-third of Cambodian territory, including all of Battambang and Sisophan provinces, and most of Siem Riep. These provinces contained crucial economic and cultural assets, as well as large ethnic Khmer populations. The action by the French Vichy government immediately produced a number of small resistance movements in the ceded regions. These movements would become important elements in the anticolonial wars as well as in the later struggles. (See Figure 4.1, page 46.)

By the time the Cambodians finally liberated themselves from French colonialism in 1954, the Cambodian economy was in no condition to perform the tasks demanded of it. The leaders of an economy cultivated for nearly a century by France as a privileged market and rubber colony would be ill-situated to see the tiny nation survive, let alone prosper, in the rough-and-tumble environment of mid-twentieth century global capitalism.

The Magic Kingdom That Never Was

Norodom Sihanouk had as much right to rule Cambodia as anyone else. Because of his royal lineage and high placement in the line of succession, many would argue, he had perhaps more right than most. Yet, divine right was not enough, in the modern world, for the monarch to retain power for so many years. It was his own ability that would prove him the master of Cambodian politics.

But it was scarcely the exercise of his royal free will that brought Norodom Sihanouk to the throne of Cambodia in 1941. Rather, in the interest of avoiding a repetition of previous inconvenient experiences with insubordinate colonial monarchs, the French governor-general of Indochina, Admiral Decoux, passed over the heir apparent to the throne of Cambodia (the eldest son of the late king), Prince Monireth. Eighteen-year-old Prince Norodom Sihanouk was snatched from the relatively protected environment of a Saigon *lycée* and transported into a world of international intrigue, crumbling imperial rule, and court politics premised upon nearly a century of rivalry between Cambodia's two royal houses, the Norodoms and Sisowaths.

To complicate matters for the unseasoned young monarch, Norodom Sihanouk's mother was a Sisowath, and his father, a Norodom.[5]

With Cambodia apparently united behind the traditionally "supreme" monarchy at independence in 1954, most outside observers portrayed internal Cambodian politics as remarkably cohesive until 1970. Although there were frequent dissolutions of the national assembly and numerous changes of government, political change appeared to be conducted with a certain respect for order and form over this period. For example, one-party rule was the norm between World War II and 1970. From the late 1940s until King Norodom Sihanouk's voluntary abdication in March of 1955, the Democratic Party consistently held approximately 70 percent of the seats in the national assembly. From 1955 until civil war exploded in 1970, the *Sangkum Reastr Niyum* (Sihanouk's "Popular Socialist Community" or "Buddhist Social Party") held 100 percent of the seats in the assembly.

After a reign of some fourteen years, King Norodom Sihanouk renounced the throne on March 2, 1955, so that he could take a more active and less symbolic role in Cambodian politics. He founded the *Sangkum Reastr Niyum* (or simply *Sangkum*), which proceeded to capture 83 percent of the vote and win all ninety-one seats in the assembly during the International Control Commission–supervised elections on September 11, 1955.[6] Of the seven other parties participating in the election, the Democratic Party received only 13 percent of the vote, and the *Pracheachon*, a hastily organized party formed by indigenous communists to contest the elections, received a meager 3.5 percent. The Democratic Party, which had previously always dominated electoral contests, would never again be a significant force at the polls. The *Pracheachon* never really got off the ground on a national scale.

This apparently moderate pluralism in Sihanouk's Cambodia concealed a reality of growing cleavages in Cambodian society, largely masked by the prince's disarming charisma and his dominance of the *Sangkum*. Beneath the artificial unity of the *Sangkum* political movement, competing interests simmered and struggled for representation. Untended, cleavages deepened between the ethnic Khmer majority and the various ethnic minorities, between the urban and rural economies, and among the urban elite. Far from unified and stable, according to a rigorous cross-national comparative analysis of political parties,[7] Cambodian politics "has set something of a standard for national instability."

The instability of Cambodian politics over the postwar period is expressed by the existence of a potpourri of political parties and groups shepherded by Sihanouk. Even a short list turns into alphabet soup: The *Khmer Issarak* (or Khmer Freedom Party) emerged after the Japanese were driven out, attempting to oppose the emergence of the *Khmer Rumdo*, or Sihanoukist group, which was being installed at the convenience of the French. The *Khmers Blancs*, or White Khmers, a North Vietnamese–oriented group claiming to operate in the name of Sihanouk, attempted to infiltrate and subvert the changing coalitions constituting the independent Cambodian communist groups, which in the 1960s received from Prince Sihanouk the appellation the *Khmers Rouges*, or "Red Khmers." All the while, a group Sihanouk referred to as the *Khmers Bleus*, composed of various interests on the right of the political spectrum, struggled to increase Westernization and promote business and commercial interests. The *Khmer Loeu* or Upland People are a collection of traditional mountain-dwelling ethnic groups whose allegiance was eventually won by the *Khmers Rouges*. A right-wing, U.S. Central Intelligence Agency–supported mercenary army, the *Khmer Serei* (Free Khmer), harassed both the government and the communists while living off the land, the people, and foreign patrons.[8]

In spite of the internecine rivalry within the tiny Cambodian elite, the Khmer monarchy itself has been relatively nonmilitaristic throughout recent history, at least since the eclipse of the Angkor Empire after the twelfth to fourteenth centuries.[9] The wane of Angkor's power was concomitant with the spread of Buddhism after its introduction by King Jayavarman VII in the twelfth century.[10] Jayavarman VII's Buddhism was that of the *Mahayana* or Greater Vehicle. Austere and militant in its precepts, it was easily accepted by the Vedic Brahmans who populated the god-king's court, but never achieved a mass following.

Among the peasants, the "soft" branch of Buddhism took root and spread. Emphasizing moderation and humility, the *Hinayana* or Lesser Vehicle gradually became the dominant normative force in Khmer society. It developed beyond the point of merely being the official state religion when the Khmers adopted a practice established by King Lu Thai,[11] providing that all young Khmer men enter the monkhood for a time.

In this regard, French colonial mythology reinforced the indigenous Khmer myths about Khmer society. Louis Finot once described Cambodia's version of Buddhist theology as "a sweet religion whose doctrines of resignation are marvelously suited to a tired peoples . . . a moral religion whose precepts assure peace of the soul and social tranquility. The Khmer people accepted it . . . without repugnance and laid down the crushing burdens of their glory." Norodom Sihanouk thought this description so apropos that he reportedly recounted it frequently to visitors.[12]

Indeed, Theravada Buddhism is decidedly ill-suited to the imperial mentality. Its spread contributed greatly to the docility of the ruling class (royalty and Buddhist priests and bonzes), and in part helped make the Khmers a target for more aggressive peoples. They have been subject to the will of strong powers since the fourteenth century. Nonetheless, as the king was the mode through which imperialist powers usually sought to control the Khmer people, the throne continued to symbolize authority for the common peasantry.

The symbolic unity represented by the Khmer monarchy combined with the gentility of Theravada Buddhism to give an air of plausibility to the image of Cambodia first projected by the French colonial authorities, and later adopted by the Khmers themselves. Part of the French colonial legacy surrounding Cambodia was the general image of a sort of jungle paradise. This impression seems to have been widespread, in much of the outside world as well as throughout the upper reaches of Cambodian society. Cambodia was pictured as a "gentle land," a peaceful place in the sun where poor but contented peasants passed their days in sensual meditation against a background of ancient splendor. After independence was achieved in 1954, the continued emphasis on this idyllic image served the purposes of Prince Sihanouk's political ambitions, and probably reflected his true belief. For example, in responding to leftist criticism of government policy in 1960, the official organ of Sihanouk's *Sangkum* political movement asserted that significant deprivations were not suffered by any segment of Cambodian society. On the contrary, the journal *Neak Cheat Niyum* argued, Prince Sihanouk's leadership of the *Sangkum* and of the nation was responsible for "unparalleled progress and prosperity" in both the social and economic arenas of Cambodian life.[13]

Historians and other sympathetic observers have suggested that the apparent contrast between the prewar image of an idyllic jungle paradise and the grim wartime reality of wildly brutal fratricide flows more from Western ignorance about Khmer history and society than from any inherent mystery about the Khmer people. The Kampucheans are a people who have been largely unimportant to the Western powers except for their economic and strategic value. Referring to regions of northwestern Cambodia (Battambang and Siem Riep),

David Chandler has cautioned against overenthusiastic generalizations concerning the alleged tranquility of antebellum Khmer society:

> We know very little, in a [sic] quantitative or political terms, about the mass of Cambodian society, many of whom, for most of their history, appear to have been slaves of one sort or another. The frequency of locally-led rebellions in the nineteenth century—against the Thai, the Vietnamese, the French and local officials—suggests that Cambodian peasants were not as peaceable as their own mythology, reinforced by the French, would lead us to believe.[14]

Nonetheless, the rebelliousness before imperial authority so common in Cambodian history is one thing, and the vicious fratricide of the civil war and after is quite another. One sees very little suggestion of such intense intraethnic conflict in existing narratives on Khmer history. Apparently, we have much to learn about Khmer politics and society.

If the idyllic image of Cambodia was ever accurate, it certainly was a misleading representation of conditions there in the post–World War II period. Yet, the tendency to portray Cambodia as untroubled by socioeconomic problems before 1970 was so deeply ingrained that it has carried over even into critical and scholarly analysis years after strong evidence to the contrary has become available. For example, William Shawcross noted in his 1979 book that "living standards in much of the country were certainly low, malaria was prevalent in many areas, (and) infant mortality was high." Yet, he concludes, "90% of the peasants owned some land and the burdens of rural debt of which Khieu Samphan, Hu Nim and others complained were not insupportable."[15] Shawcross offered no evidence on peasant debt or landownership.

In fact, convincing evidence suggests that the economic position of the Cambodian peasantry *and* the urban elite had been deteriorating for at least two decades before the civil war. A more complete analysis than that presented here might demonstrate that the post–World War II deterioration was merely a continuing collapse in an 800-year decline from imperial supremacy. The next and final section of this chapter will examine in some detail the economic deterioration of Cambodia after independence, in order to set the stage for explanation of the subsequent political events in Cambodia.

FIGURE 2.1
CAMBODIAN DEMOGRAPHIC TRENDS, 1900-1980

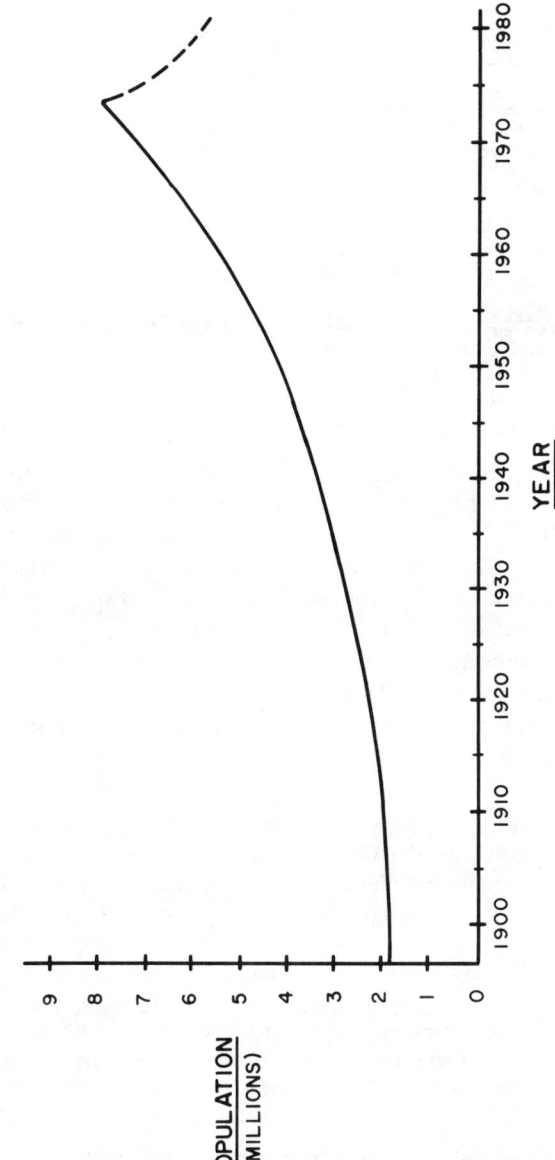

TABLE 2.1
CHANGING LAND USE IN CAMBODIA, 1954-1965

Use	1954	1965
Arable and Orchard	17.1	16.2
Meadow and Pasture	2.9	n.a.
Forest and Woodland	45.7	73.9
City, Waste, Other	34.3	n.a.
	100.0%	90.1%

Note: "n.a." indicates data not available.

Source: Compiled from data in the Oxford Economic Atlas of the World, 4th ed. (London: Oxford University Press, 1972), p. 132. Used by permission.

Prelude to Pandemonium

Very few extant analyses of the Cambodian revolutions take note of Cambodia's population explosion after World War II. Yet, Cambodia's baby boom was a major factor in the modern economic history of the nation, and hence in the political history of Cambodia. Perhaps a lack of attention to Khmer demography should not be surprising, however, for population densities have always been relatively low in Cambodia. In fact, one Indian analyst summarized the weak "radical" component in the independence struggles through the period of French colonial dominance (1863–1955) by reference to this point, adding an ominous note:

> Although, in theory, the king was the sole proprietor of land, in practice, however, the peasant could claim the right to a piece of land if he brought it under cultivation. Since there is plenty of virgin soil available, there are no landless peasants and, consequently, there is no agrarian discontent. Tenancy and share-cropping practices are almost absent. Obviously, therefore, Cambodia could hardly be the soil for radical views to take root on. However, a peasant, if ever in financial distress, had to take recourse to a moneylender, who invariably charged a high rate of interest. "Once in debt, and saddled with an interest rate that often reaches 100 percent, the peasant is seldom free of it."[16]

Although this may have been a fair description of Cambodia in the colonial days, the situation was changing rapidly in the postcolonial days. The rate of population growth climbed ever higher, a growth fueled both by a relatively stable social milieu (i.e., no war) and an

TABLE 2.2
LANDOWNERSHIP AND CULTIVATION TRENDS, 1930-1962

SIZE OF HOLDING	1930		1956		1962	
	% of Rural Pop	Their % of Cultivated Land	% of Rural Pop	Their % of Cultivated Land	% of Rural Pop	Their % of Cultivated Land
<1 ha.	43	25	55	25	31	3
1-5 ha.	51	44	37	40	55	49
>5 ha.	6	31	8	35	14	46

Note: One hectare (ha.) equals approximately 2.47 acres.
Source: Ben Kiernan, "Introduction," in Ben Kiernan and Chanthou Boua, eds., Peasants and Politics in Kampuchea 1942-1981 (New York: M.E. Sharpe, 1982), p. 6; used by permission.

ever larger population base (see Figure 2.1). At the same time, the amount of arable land fell (see Table 2.1).

The pressure exerted by a growing population and a declining acreage of arable land was further accentuated by the dynamics of land distribution in the country. While there was increasingly less land to go around, the number of large landholdings grew so that the few had more of what little there was. In Cambodia as a whole in 1930, there were indeed very few landless peasants, though a significant fraction—two-fifths—owned one hectare or less. (See Table 2.2.) By 1956, some 55 percent of the Khmer peasantry owned less than one hectare. Two short years after independence, more than half of the Cambodian population shared about a quarter of the land. Over the next six years, a dramatic transformation took place. By 1962, 31 percent owned less than one hectare, and together this poorest third of the population shared no more than 5 percent of the total arable land.

This means that in the early years following independence, many Khmer peasants were forced off their land, into tenancy or even vagrancy. In 1965, Hu Nim estimated that 8 percent of the rural peasants had become landless over the previous thirty-two years. Thus there was created "a class of rootless, destitute rural dwellers *with very few ties to the land.*"[17] As Kiernan notes, such a class would have nothing to lose in a revolution.

Moreover, because one hectare is not enough to support a family, many other peasants were forced to rent additional land.[18] Over this same period, the number of rich peasants (those owning more land than one family could cultivate, i.e., five hectares) grew from less than 6 percent of the rural population to more than 14 percent. The rich peasants would in turn rent their land to those less fortunate. Thus, in Cambodia, there was a growing cleavage between rich and poor peasants.

Most of the peasants being squeezed into tenancy and partial tenancy found it necessary to borrow from one of the Chinese rice brokers or millers, or the landlord, who might often happen to be a Cambodian of Vietnamese ethnic origin. A study by the Office of Credit in 1952 showed that 75 percent of all Cambodian farmers were seriously in debt.[19] Fourteen years later, a survey of 420 farmers in fourteen villages of Kandal Province found that 80 percent of them had contracted large debts during the previous season alone and that 67 percent had not repaid them.[20] A vicious cycle of debt, driven by annual interest rates typically reaching from 100 percent to 200 percent, accelerated the pauperization of the lower strata of the Khmer peasantry. Creditors, by and large, were not ethnic Khmer. Ethnic differences increasingly became salient factors in the developing maelstrom.

Buddhist ethnic Khmers composed about 80 percent of the Cambodian population in prerevolutionary days. Of the remaining 20 percent of a total population of about 7.2 million (plus or minus 10 percent) in 1970, perhaps half were Brao and Montagnard, or Cham, Por, Taupuon, Lao, Stieng, Thai, and Jarais peasants, and the other half were of Vietnamese or Chinese extraction.[21] Of the entire population, some 85 to 90 percent were subsistence-level agrarian peasants largely spread among small villages distributed along the rivers and in the lowlands of the Mekong Delta. Traditionally, Khmer peasants organized themselves into cooperative labor groups for the rational exploitation of the rice-lands.[22] In the twentieth century, however, the trend was predominantly to smaller operations organized around nuclear or extended family systems.

The end of French colonial dominance brought increased opportunities for Cambodians of all ethnic origins to play larger roles in the Cambodian economy. But, of the ethnic groups, only the Vietnamese and the Chinese showed much inclination to organize capitalist enterprises. Particularly in Battambang Province, where large private landholdings were the most extensive, many of the larger tracts were owned by ethnic Cambodians who had emigrated from southern

Vietnam in the 1930s and 1940s. The larger landowners increasingly turned to sharecropping, and some to wage labor, in order to exploit the productive potential of their property.

In Cambodian capital markets, ethnic Chinese came to play a dominant role. In a bad year, when crops fell below the level required to pay taxes and rent *and* stay alive, the landless or land-short peasant would have to turn to the moneylenders, who more often than not were not ethnic Khmer. These ethnic differences heightened the visibility of absentee landlordism and exploitative usury, and contributed to a general rise in peasant discontent among the ethnic Khmer while at the same time providing a convenient lightning rod for that discontent. Over the course of the late 1950s and early 1960s, this source of racial tension accumulated into a not inconsiderable "underground" reservoir of social tension scarcely visible to some perceptive Cambodian elites, much less foreign observers. The right wing of the urban elite would exploit this antiforeign sentiment to considerable advantage during and after the 1970 *coup*, much as some factions of the *Khmer Rouge* would attempt to do, though with less success, after 1975.

The average Cambodian across the course of the entire twentieth century could anticipate owning a smaller amount of property than that owned by his or her parents. Beyond the increasing concentration of landholdings, another factor contributed to the trend. Table 2.3 shows that in the period between 1913 and 1965, the Cambodian agrarian population increased by more than three and one-half times. The area under cultivation did not grow as fast, and after 1955 actually began to fall. Thus, the size of the individual holding would have declined even if the increasing concentration had not occurred, catalyzing the process of parcelization.

On the one hand, as V. M. Reddi's analysis reminds us, Cambodia did for many years show a remarkable capacity to provide new land for an increasing population. On the other hand, through the twentieth century the expansion of paddy lands did not keep pace with population growth. After 1955, this process of parcelization accelerated, probably because of the increase in large holdings as well as the aggregate decline in cultivated acreage. The productivity of the Khmer peasants has traditionally been low, and the falling size of the average holding translated into a further loss of efficiency.

In addition to the social tensions related to the shrinking average landholding, the attendant inefficiency contributed to a more serious problem: food shortages. Between 1958 and 1966, rice production for domestic consumption rose from around 1,910,000 tons to about

TABLE 2.3
CAMBODIAN RURAL POPULATION DENSITY (INDEXED TO 1913)

YEAR	Agrarian [X] Population (in millions)	[Y]	Cultivated Area (in square miles)	[Z]	Density Index (X/Y = Z)
1913[a]	(100) .95 × 1.5 = 1.4		(100) 2508		1.00
1950[a]	(249) .87 × 4.0 = 3.5		(203) 5093		1.23
1955	(339) .85 × 4.7 = 4.0[b]		(269) 6753[c]		1.26
1965	(361) .83 × 6.1 = 5.1[b]		(255) 6398[c]		1.41

Note: Agrarian population calculation is: (percent rural population) times (total population) equals (agrarian population).
Sources:
[a] All area and population figures for 1913 and 1950 are adapted from page 38 of Khieu Samphan, *Cambodia's Economy and Industrial Development* [Laura Summers, trans.] (Ithaca, N.Y.: Southeast Asia Program, Department of Asian Studies, Cornell University, 1979).
[b] Estimates by author; total population figures are based on an assumed annual population growth rate of 3.5 percent from a base of 4.0 million in 1950. Decreasing percent rural population reflects increasing urbanization.
[c] From data in Royaume du Cambodge, *Annuaire Statistique Retrospectif du Cambodge, 1937-1957* (Phnom Penh, 1958), p. 163; cited in V. M. Reddi, *A History of the Cambodian Independence Movement, 1863-1955* (Tirupati, India: Sri Venkateswara University, 1970), p. 6.

2,210,000 tons, an increase of approximately 16 percent. This increase was inadequate to keep up with that in population, which rose some 22 percent from around 5.1 million to around 6.2 million. The increasing scarcity of foodstuffs in the domestic market drove the already rising price of food up more quickly yet, contributing to a 350 percent leap in food prices between 1950 and 1970 (see Figure 2.2). For the Khmer people, these abstract figures translated into empty stomachs, and empty stomachs are angry stomachs, more easily politicized.

In another manifestation of the serious difficulties in the Cambodian economy, the purchasing power of the average Cambodian fell between 1953 and 1966. (See Table 2.4.) It was easy enough for enthusiasts in Long Boret's Finance Ministry to point to impressive rises in national income, and even in *per capita* income. But because of serious

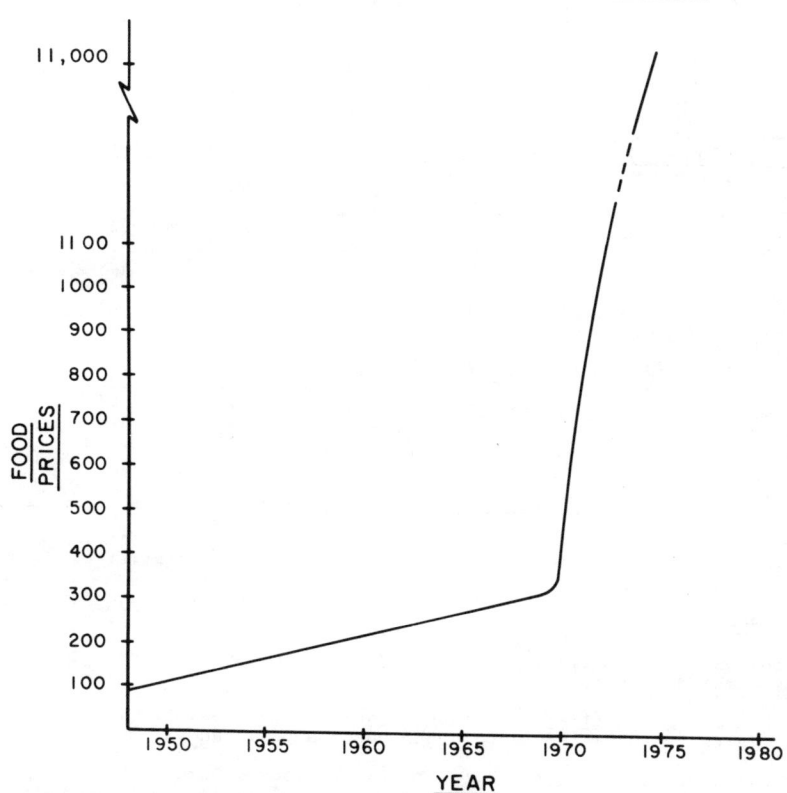

FIGURE 2.2

FOOD PRICES IN CAMBODIA, 1949-1980 [1949=100]

SOURCE: ADAPTED FROM RAW DATA IN AGENCY FOR INTERNATIONAL DEVELOPMENT REPORT AS CITED BY WILLIAM SHAWCROSS, IN SIDESHOW (NEW YORK: SIMON AND SCHUSTER, 1979), P. 221.

inflation felt by the Cambodian economy, net purchasing power trends did not present an encouraging picture.

Food shortages and high prices, falling purchasing power, high interest and rents, rising taxes, declining productivity and land availability, increasing population density—all these problems plaguing peasants in the post–World War II period were but symptoms of a general economic malaise. Except for a few very narrowly defined fractions of the urban elite (e.g., bankers, landlords, and importer-exporters), Cambodians did very well between 1954 and 1967 if they simply maintained their standard of living at a stable level; however,

TABLE 2.4
THE EROSION OF PURCHASING POWER IN CAMBODIA, 1953-1966

Year	National Income Millions of 1956 riels [a]	Population (millions) [b]	Per Capita Income (PCI)	Consumer Price Index (CPI) [c]	Purchasing Power (PCI)/(CPI)
1953	11.6	4.2	2.76	100	.0276
1954	13.0	4.3	3.02	108	.0279
1955	11.5	4.4	2.61	127	.0205
1956	12.8	4.5	2.84	127	.0223
1957	14.5	4.6	3.15	127	.0248
1958	14.3	4.7	3.04	135	.0225
1959	14.6	4.8	3.04	141	.0215
1960	16.1*	5.4	2.98	151	.0197
1961	17.6*	5.4	3.25	161	.0201
1962	19.1	5.7	3.35	164	.0204
1963	21.4	5.9	3.62	174	.0208
1964	23.2	6.1	3.80	177	.0214
1965	24.7	6.1	4.04	183	.0220
1966	26.2	6.2	4.22	181	.0233

Note: All figures for this period reflect official statistics, and should be viewed with some suspicion of overstatement.

Sources:
[a] United Nations Statistical Yearbook, various volumes, except where noted by (*), indicating estimate by author.
[b] UNESCO Statistical Yearbook, various volumes, for 1959-1966; estimates by author for 1953-1958, based on 2.7% annual growth.
[c] United Nations Statistical Yearbook, various volumes; indexed to 1953 = 100, for all consumer goods combined. Table 2-4 is adjusted from original data to reflect common index year.

most experienced significant declines. Thus, in general, the urban elite suffered along with the rural masses. As one analyst put it, "Business was probably suffering the most from the contraction in commerce."[23]

The low demand generated within the tiny, depressed Cambodian economy provided little capital for investment, and structural problems grew unchallenged. And, as radical Cambodians hastened to point out, imported goods supplied many urban needs, thus transferring the multiplier effect abroad.

Another complication within the Cambodian private sector was the rise in the late 1950s and early 1960s of a species of speculators. Dealing in currency, gold, land, rice, alcohol, opium, salt, beef, tobacco, or any other commodity that offered a chance to make a quick buck, speculators helped catalyze inflation, create supply crises, imbalance foreign accounts, and deprive the government of revenue.

The private sector in Cambodia was not alone in the increasingly hot economic water. The public sector both contributed to and suffered from the economic crisis following independence. A stagnating economy meant depressed revenues for the government, and in the early 1960s an already growing debt (both foreign and domestic) was complicated by a liquidity crisis. The Sihanouk government's solution was classic: Simply print more money. Minister of Commerce Khieu Samphan correctly argued that "use of a budget deficit to finance public spending rather than productive investment would promote inflation."[24] But such sober and decidedly unrevolutionary assessments from leftists like Khieu, and others without his radical credentials, went against the tide.

In 1963, in a series of attempts to cope with the escalating national economic crisis, Sihanouk's government instituted a number of policies designed to reverse the general decline. In conjunction with the presentation of the budget, the government proposed a series of austerity measures, prominent among which were acts aimed at reducing the quantity of imported luxury goods and simultaneously augmenting state revenues by means of a luxury tax. These measures were loudly and vigorously opposed by Cambodia's urban elite, most of whom acted out of immediate self-interest, but a few of whom were opposed in theory to state intervention in the domestic economy. If the luxury taxes and other austerity measures announced at the beginning of 1963 disturbed many members of the Cambodian elite, they would be shaken to the roots later in the year when Sihanouk announced a series of blows to their interests, including the outright renunciation of U.S. military aid, and the nationalization of banking and foreign trade.

The combined effects of the 1963 economic reform measures produced for Cambodia in 1964 the first balance of trade surplus in a decade. The next two years saw some other promising signs: National savings reversed their steep decline, and purchasing power began to climb more strongly. Yet, it can plausibly be argued, it was a case of too little, too late. Although national accounts did begin to show some meager progress, it is more difficult to show that the lot of the peasant masses had also begun to improve. And, at any rate, by this time the tensions within Cambodian society brought on by ubiquitous economic hardship were beginning to translate into political conflict. The accumulating frustrations would drive that conflict into an escalating spiral of cleavage and violence, culminating in peasant

TABLE 2.5
CRITICAL ECONOMIC INDICATORS, 1955-1966

Year	Rice Production (1000 tons)	Rice Exports (1000 tons)	Balance of Trade (million riels)	National Bank Deposits (million riels)
1955	1,490	n.a.	- 265	n.a.
1956	1,790	50	- 697	n.a.
1957	1,990	200	- 239	n.a.
1958	2,120	210	- 759	n.a.
1959	2,080	190	- 343	2.613
1960	2,330	320	- 879	2.346
1961	2,380	240	-1,175	1.892
1962	2,040	140	-1,681	1.468
1963	2,620	370	- 635	0.895
1964	2,760	490	+ 200	0.667
1965	2,500	490	+ 87	0.714
1966	2,380	170	-1,532	0.809

Note: This data is mostly from official sources, notably unreliable in the 1960s.
Source: Reproduced from page 13 of Laura Summers, "Translator's Introduction," in Khieu Samphan, Cambodia's Economy and Industrial Development [Data Paper No. 111] (Ithaca, New York: Southeast Asia Program, Department of Asian Studies, Cornell University, 1979); used by permission of Laura Summers.

rebellion in 1966 and 1967, insurgency in 1968 and 1969, and, finally, wide-open civil war after 1970.

Notes

1. Dante's "icy chill" resulted from his having been conducted to the ninth circle of Hell, that lowest and coldest domain, where those "who have done violence against their kindred," "who have been guilty of treachery against their native land," and "who betrayed their masters" receive their eternal rewards. Dante, *The Divine Comedy* [John Aitken Carlyle, Thomas Okey, and Philip Henry Wicksteed, trans.] (New York: Random House, 1950), Canto XXXIV, p. 182.

2. In 1980, an intermediate undergraduate class in international political economy was given a current events quiz that included the query, "Where is Kampuchea?" Of twenty-three students at this prestigious southern California university, only six responded correctly.

3. Anthropologist Marvin Harris has revised the hydraulic theory of culture first presented by Karl Wittfogel, and the conception of Angkor presented here draws heavily on Harris's formulation. See Wittfogel's *Oriental Despotism: A Comparative Study of Total Power* (New Haven: Yale University Press, 1957);

and Harris's *Cannibals and Kings: The Origins of Cultures* (New York: Random House, 1977). The quotation is from Harris, p. 239.

4. "Cambodge" in English is Cambodia, from the French derivation of the transliteration from the traditional native term, "Kambuja," of which the contemporary pronunciation is "Kampuchea." All four terms are used interchangably here.

5. For a fuller account of the Cambodian royal lineage and Sihanouk's ascension, see V. M. Reddi, *A History of the Cambodian Independence Movement 1863-1955* (Tirupati, India: Sri Venkateswara University, 1970), especially Chapter 3.

6. For an in-depth view of the events of this period from the unique perspective of the prince, see Wilfred Burchett, ed., *My War with the CIA: The Memoirs of Prince Norodom Sihanouk* (New York: Random House, 1972). While this volume is predictably skewed, it is useful for the insight it gives into the mind of the central figure of postwar Cambodian politics.

7. See Kenneth Janda, *Political Parties: A Cross-National Survey* (New York: Free Press, 1980). Janda's rigorous data-based analysis, which includes for Cambodia data covering the turbulent 1970s, finds Cambodian politics highly unstable over the entire post–World War II period. Even if data for the 1970s had been excluded from Janda's analysis, the instability factor for Cambodia would still be quite high.

8. See Donald Kirk, "Revolution and Political Violence in Cambodia: 1970-1974," in J. J. Zasloff and M. Brown, *Communism in Indochina: New Perspectives* (Lexington Mass.: D. C. Heath, 1975), p. 218. For more on the CIA–Khmer Serei connection, see M. Osborne, *Politics and Power in Cambodia* (Victoria: Longman Australia, 1973) especially Chapter 9; and T. D. Allman, " 'Fred,' the CIA Stirrer in Cambodia," *The Bulletin* (Sydney) 21 (August 1971).

9. Useful general histories of Cambodia include the following. The period of French dominance is well documented by John F. Cady, *The Roots of French Imperialism in Eastern Asia* (Ithaca, N.Y.: Cornell University Press, 1954); Milton E. Osborne, *The French Presence in Cochinchina and Cambodia: Rule and Response (1858-1905)* (Ithaca, N.Y.: Cornell University Press, 1969); V. M. Reddi, *A History of the Cambodian Independence Movement;* and Donald Lancaster, *The Emancipation of French Indochina* (New York: Octagon, 1961, 1974). The Khmer emperors are treated in Bernard-Philippe Groslier, *The Art of Indochina* (New York: Crown Publishers, 1962); Lawrence C. Briggs, *Ancient Khmer Empire* (Philadelphia: American Philosophical Society, 1951); M. L. Jumsai, *History of Thailand and Cambodia* (Paragon, 1970); and Chris Pym, *The Ancient Civilization of Angkhor* (New York: NAL/Mentor, 1968). Also of interest are George Coedès, *The Making of Southeast Asia* (Berkeley: University of California Press, 1967); John F. Cady, *Southeast Asia: Its Historical Development* (New York: McGraw-Hill, 1964); and D.G.E. Hall, *A History of Southeast Asia* (London: Macmillan, 1955).

10. G. Coedès, *The Indianized States of Southeast Asia* [W. F. Vella, ed.; S. B. Cowing, trans.] (Honolulu: University Press Hawaii, 1968), p. 173.

11. Trevor Ling, *Buddhism, Imperialism and War: Burma and Thailand in Modern History* (London: George Allen and Unwin, 1979), p. 19.

12. Quoted in John P. Armstrong, *Sihanouk Speaks: Cambodia's Chief of State Explains His Controversial Politics* (New York: Walker and Company, 1964), p. 30.

13. Cited in Laura Summers's introductory essay to her translation of Khieu Samphan, *Cambodia's Economy and Industrial Development* [L. Summers, trans.], Cornell University Southeast Asia Program, Data Paper No. 111 (Ithaca, N.Y.: Cornell University, 1979), pp. 11, 12, nn. 17, 18.

14. Cited in Noam Chomsky and E. S. Herman, *After the Cataclysm: Postwar Indochina and the Reconstruction of Imperial Ideology* (Boston: South End Press, 1979), p. 213; the quotation is taken from Chandler's testimony before the U.S. Congress, House Subcommittee on International Organizations, May 3, 1977, published as *Human Rights in Cambodia* (Washington, D.C.: USGPO, 1977), p. 64.

15. William Shawcross, *Sideshow: Kissinger, Nixon, and the Destruction of Cambodia* (New York: Simon and Schuster, 1979), p. 246. The arguments presented by Shawcross in this volume will be examined in more detail in Chapter 6.

16. V. M. Reddi, *A History of the Cambodian Independence Movement*, p. 7.

17. Ben Kiernan and Chanthou Boua, eds., *Peasants and Politics in Kampuchea 1942–1981* (New York: M. E. Sharpe, 1982), p. 7, emphasis added; also in this volume, see Hu Nim, "Land Tenure and Social Structure in Kampuchea," pp. 69–86, especially p. 74.

18. W. E. Willmott notes an important caveat when he points out that because Khmer inheritance is bilateral, many families owned more than one parcel. He argues that usury was the greatest problem in antebellum Cambodia, much more serious than rents or wage-labor problems. See his "Analytical Errors of the Kampuchean Communist Party," *Pacific Affairs* 54:2 (Summer 1981), pp. 218–221. This hypothesis is convincingly supported in Kiernan and Boua, *Peasants and Politics in Kampuchea*.

19. This refers to debts of 1000 riels or more; according to Kiernan ("Social Cohesion in Revolutionary Cambodia," *Australian Outlook* 30:3 [December 1976], p. 381) this figure originally appeared in a *Le Figaro* report of February 7, 1970; according to Willmott ("Analytical Errors of the Kampuchean Communist Party," p. 222) the original citation is attributable to Jean Delvert, *Le Paysan Cambodgien* (Paris: Mouton, 1961), p. 519ff.

20. Kiernan and Boua, *Peasants and Politics in Kampuchea*, p. 9.

21. See François Ponchaud, *Cambodia: Year Zero* (New York: Holt, Rinehart and Winston, 1978), p. 167. In addition, there were numerous smaller ethnic groupings; for geographical distributions, see maps diagramming population density and ethnic patterns inside the rear cover of Malcolm Caldwell and Lek Tan, *Cambodia in the Southeast Asian War* (New York: Monthly Review Press, 1973). For detailed ethnographic data on some of these groups, see *Minority Groups in the Republic of South Vietnam*, Ethnographic Series, Department of the Army, Pamphlet #550-105, 1966.

22. George Hildebrand and Gareth Porter, *Cambodia: Starvation and Revolution* (New York: Monthly Review Press, 1976), p. 69.
23. Laura Summers, "Introduction," in Khieu Samphan, *Cambodia's Economy and Industrial Development*, p. 14.
24. *Ibid.*

3
Evolution of *Khmer Rouge* Political Thought and Behavior

A (true) Brahman goes scatheless, is free from sorrow and remorse though he have killed father and mother, and two kings of the warrior caste, though he has destroyed a kingdom with all its subjects.
—The *Dhammapada* XXI:294[1]

Roots of Ideology

In 1888, the French governor introduced the concept of private property to Cambodian society, thus challenging the centuries-old tradition of feudal ownership and peasant free-tenancy. Prince Yukanthor denounced this action as an unmitigated evil: "You have established property—you have created the poor!"[2] Yukanthor thus alluded to something far more fundamental than material poverty. As Buddha teaches in the Path of Virtue, spiritual poverty is the reward of earthly lusts: "By his thirst for riches, the foolish man destroys himself as if he were his own enemy."[3]

Elements of this traditional disposition have survived down to the present day and are expressed in the ideology of the Cambodian communist movement. Although the Kampuchean Communist Party (KCP) has never explicitly elaborated a single, coherent political ideology, a substantial image of its ideology can be gleaned from its various documents and broadcasts. Ideology can also be inferred on the basis of behavior. It is instructive to compare what the KCP *said* with what it *did*, and so it is important to distinguish between what will be referred to as "declaratory ideology," based on political statements, and what will be called "operational ideology," based on political behavior. The importance of making this distinction was well stated by Karl Marx: "As in private life one differentiates between what a man thinks and says of himself and what he really is and does, so in historical struggles must one distinguish still more phrases and fancies of parties from their real organism and their real interests, their conception of themselves, from their reality."[4]

Declaratory ideology (phrases and fancies) may in the final analysis be no more than an image of the mental states of political leaders and those in control of the propaganda organs. "Actions speak louder than words," it is said. Yet, as will be shown, the collective ideals expressed in a declaratory ideology can provide an explanatory vehicle of considerable power when one turns to the question of why a certain group behaves as it does. Operational ideology can never be identical to declaratory ideology, although operational ideology (real organism and interests) is in great measure derived directly from those things declared and believed to be both just and proper.

The declaratory ideology of the KCP can be described as a combination of three elements twisted together almost beyond recognition in a creative, organic synthesis: sociocultural values and dispositions from traditional Khmer culture, certain strands of communist revolutionary thought, and traces of radical Parisian Jacobinism. Because Khieu Samphan, Hu Nim, Hou Yuon, Saloth Sar, Ieng Sary, and the other leaders of the KCP selected political goals from abstract concepts, and then brutally wrenched Cambodian society in an attempt to realize their vision of society, many analysts have concluded that they broke totally with the past, eradicating all hints of the life and society that had come before.[5] This is only partially true. The KCP leaders wished to reorganize Khmer existence along the lines of an extremely chauvinistic conception of a "pure Khmer" society, obliterating only those aspects of Khmer culture that they regarded as having been borrowed from or influenced by foreign cultures. The tragedy was that the Khmer people have always been great borrowers, and thus almost everything was "contaminated."

Although the social, economic, and political relations of Cambodian society were indeed radically restructured by the KCP, some elements of KCP doctrine, such as the aforementioned emphasis on communal ownership, communal production, and a society based almost exclusively on rice cultivation, can be traced directly to the Kampuchean past. Perhaps even the influence of religion can be seen in KCP doctrine. Some elements emphasized by the KCP, such as personal humility, may reflect the traditional religious values embedded in the *Hinayana*.[6]

As a theoretical matter, it seems inconceivable that a terrestrial human culture could "break" totally with its own historically derived nature, to the point of discontinuing those facets of culture that find their roots in intrinsic human-environmental relationships, such as geopolitical and geoecological elements. The reliance on rice cultivation as the foundation of Khmer society is an example of such an ecological factor in culture, and this indeed is one natural continuity to be observed between Democratic Kampuchea and the historical regimes of the Khmer people. Other realities, such as the fact that the mode of production is critically dependent upon the level of technology in any given society, also militate against the possibility of a "total break" with what has come before. Yet, as a practical matter, it must be admitted that the KCP came about as close as can be imagined to just that: a total or near-total break with the past. Most of the dominant features of Khmer life, unchanged though they had been for a thousand years, were summarily eliminated in the KCP's urgent efforts to purify the race and sanitize the country.

A second central component of KCP thought derives from the long tradition of Marxist political theory. Many of the great ideas in this tradition turn up in KCP doctrine. The Marxist theory of history, using class analysis as the central theoretical construct, was the lodestar of KCP doctrine, albeit in a manner never envisaged by Marx himself. Lenin's theory of imperialism and his concept of "stage-leaping" were revised and extended by two of the KCP's chief theoreticians, Khieu Samphan and Hou Yuon. Stalin's concept of autonomous socialist development or "socialism in one country" also was a central element of Khieu's theoretical system. Mao Tse-tung's "stages" of revolution, and his "people's war," plus Lin Piao's and Vo Nguyen Giap's elaborations of "people's war," can all be seen in the KCP doctrine. These ideas are all expressed in both the KCP's declaratory and its operational behavior, though in a "creative" rather than a dogmatic manner.

Karl Marx argued that all history is the story of class struggle, and therefore that in the analysis of class relations lie the true answers to the great questions of politics and history. Projecting the ideals of reason and democracy to their logical extremes, Marx predicted that one day the masses of humanity would cease meekly to carry out the self-interested dictates of the ruling few, and would seize the levers of economic power and political authority for themselves. When this occurred on a global scale, the natural harmony of the majority of humankind—the toilers—would prevail. Political competition for economic surplus would fade, and along with it the vehicle of that struggle, the state, would "wither" and cease to exist. This withering was to become one of the central goals of Democratic Kampuchea. If there were no classes, there could be no politics, and hence there would be no need for the coercive state apparatus. That was the theory, at least.

Vladimir Lenin, building on earlier works by Rudolf Hilferding, John A. Hobson, and others, extended Marx's work in a number of important ways, two of which are directly reflected in KCP doctrine. Both can be summarized as Lenin's replacement of Marxian determinism with Leninist voluntarism. Lenin argued that the historical progression from primitive communism, to feudalism, through capitalism and socialism, and finally to communism was not an objective necessity. It might be possible under certain circumstances to "skip" a stage in the historical progression.

Second, Lenin argued that it was not necessary for the proletariat to be the dominant force in society in order for the revolutionary transformation from capitalism to socialism to occur *if* a properly motivated "vanguard party" existed to provide leadership and focus to the energy of the masses. Thus, the full terrors of bourgeois development could be avoided by "stage-leaping" over the unpleasant period of capitalist accumulation, directly into the period of the harmonious dominance of the many. Cambodia's vanguard, the KCP, would attempt the leap from a precapitalist, quasi-feudal socioeconomic system directly into pure communism. Some KCP leaders, as we shall see, had advocated stage-leaping ideas as early as 1955.

Joseph Stalin was forced to deal with the continuing ability of the capitalist nations to stave off their ever-imminent collapse. If the revolution failed to occur spontaneously on a global scale, then the Russian revolution must be preserved to await the Second and Final Coming. This would occur, Stalin declared in his inimitable fashion, because the objective factors so indicated. Stalin's famous doctrine of "socialism in one country" asserted that the autonomous development of socialist forces in a single country—as opposed to the entire, decadent world system—would precede the emergence of a unifed, global communism. This notion is expressed in both the operational and the declaratory behavior of the *Khmer Rouge*, and it dovetails with their emphasis on national autarky.

The frustration apparent in Stalin's formulation was extended from the passive to the active mode by Lin Piao and Vo Nguyen Giap.[7] In a revolution, Mao Tse-tung had written, the "national-democratic stage" must precede the "socialist stage." In the first stage, however, the structures of mass oppression—labor unions, police, courts, etc., as well as myths, religion, and so on—become so deeply entrenched in social formations as to inhibit and delay the second stage, true socialism. Lin Piao argued that "people's war" would crush these structures of oppression, and overcome the power of reactionary elements who would support the anachronistic ways. It would succeed by drawing on the strength of the masses, in turn inflaming them against their masters by revealing their respective true self-interests. "The revolutionaries are to the masses as the fish are to the waters." In the troubled waters of Kampuchea, the KCP cadres would seek to become indistinguishable from the masses.

Drawing upon this heritage of Marxist-Leninist-Maoist political theory, the leaders of the *Khmer Rouge* fashioned an ethos of political purpose. Latent within this purpose was a strategy of revolutionary action. The key element in the derivation of strategy from theory is a norm that encourages pragmatic behavior. Political theory is by definition general in nature. On the other hand, specific revolutionary situations invariably dictate a logic of their own. The political theory must be "creatively extended" to fit the actual circumstances with which the revolutionaries find themselves confronted. In the process, unique new generalizations will be extrapolated from the original theory, and thus "the identity of the ideology emerges. Ideology is," as Zbigniew Brzezinski has argued, "the link between theory and action."[8] Once the ideology has crystallized into an ideographic form, it becomes "a part of reality and an autonomous existing factor conditioning behavior."

Thus, beginning with subjective goals defined by theory in terms of abstract values, a creative leadership will confront its actual social situation and, guided by norms originating in the theoretical premises, modify the strategy of political action to suit the dictates of the moment while simultaneously advancing toward the ultimate goals. Imperceptibly, of course, the objective, operational ideology is skewed away from the declared ideal goals by the compromise of exigency, and the hybrid ideology takes on a unique form while evolving gradually with the social situation. Such has been the case with *Khmer Rouge* economic and political doctrine, in a rather classic manner.

The third basic precursor of KCP ideology resulted from the fact that as leading students in the Cambodian school system, the individuals who eventually emerged as members of the Central Committee of the Kampuchean Communist Party were among the Khmer youth sent to Paris for their postsecondary education. It was there, during the 1950s, that eight of the men and two of the women who would conceive and direct an incredible human transformation studied, and that two of them took doctorates: Khieu Samphan in economics and Hou Yuon in economics and law. Their initial exposure to communism occurred in France, but they absorbed much more than just communism from the rich French cultural heritage.

The great French Revolution symbolized the equality of men and women against a monarchical sociopolitical class structure, and struck a deep and responsive chord in the young (ages twenty to twenty-five) students who resented the political dominance of Cambodia by Prince Sihanouk and the economic dominance of Cambodia by French colonial operations. Maximilien Robespierre led the second Committee of Public Safety through the Reign of Terror with the maxim that revolutionary government "is subject to no constant laws, since the circumstances under which it prevails are those of a storm. . . ."[9] In the French Revolution, this sentiment was taken to an extreme perhaps foreshadowing the *Khmer Rouge* by a group of radical leftists calling themselves the "Conspiracy of Equals." Their "Manifesto of Equals," published in 1796, asserted the end-justifies-all principle: "We consent to everything for its (the revolution's) sake, to make a clear board, that we may hold it alone. Perish, if it must be, all the arts, provided real equality be left us!"[10]

Although no hard evidence can be offered to substantiate the claim that these Cambodian youths were directly influenced by these works, there can be little doubt that they would have been affected by a heritage so closely paralleling their own historical situation.[11] The radical Jacobinist current of French liberalism thus reinforced and intellectually institutionalized the communist ideal of the end of history, a classless society of equal beings, created and sustained by terror and violence.

Contact with French communists by the Khmer students during the 1950s is an interesting matter in that French communist dogma of this particular period stressed the injustice of inequalities structured into French society. Under the leadership of Secretary General Maurice Thorez, the French Communist Party suffered intense internal discord as it weathered the storms of "de-Stalinization" in the Soviet Union and Eastern Europe through the late 1950s. Attempting to carry on in the image of Stalin, his patron and fallen hero, Thorez tried to make class differences and class conflict the premier issues of radical French politics. The closely held principle of "democratic centralism" was severely tested by dissent within the party as Thorez defended himself against bitter charges of "personalism." This spectacle may have influenced the Cambodian students in Paris, who later would cling tightly to the precepts of "democratic centralism," and would end by abusing it even more vigorously than had Thorez twenty-five years previously. That class difference was to be the central icon shattered by the KCP leaders is not to say that their ideas necessarily derived entirely from their observations of Thorez and his French Communist Party, but it does suggest an interesting historical parallel in communist doctrine.[12]

One final and central element of KCP doctrine that must be mentioned is its extremely intense nationalism. The sources of this aspect are undoubtedly manifold, and will be discussed throughout this analysis.

Components of Political Thought

Up to this point, we have been primarily concerned with the *content* of Kampuchean Communist Party ideology in a general way. In addition to discussing the origins of specific beliefs constituting the ideology, it will prove useful to make some further distinctions about ideology. To better understand the role played by ideology in revolutionary struggle, one should consider four additional characteristics of ideology: structure, functions, loci, and scope.[13] After a brief introduction to these concepts, we will be prepared for a concrete historical exposition of *Khmer Rouge* behavior.

Structure can be discussed in terms of two categories. "Interrelatedness" refers to the extent to which specific ideas constituting the doctrine cluster together, and to which the clusters are logically or normatively linked. "Stability" refers to the integrity of these linkages, and their resistance to decoupling in the face of challenges and contradictions arising in the environment.

The functions of ideology are numerous and varied. They include social, personal-social, organizational, and transmutational functions. Social functions refer to the legitimation of political authority, that is, the right to rule. Personal-social functions refer to the justification of revolutionary acts by reference to doctrine, both *a priori* and *ex post facto*. Further, they include the more general function of explaining or rationalizing personal life conditions and actions. Organizational functions include such things as the derivation of bureaucratic standard operating procedure from ideological precepts (e.g., cadre relations as a function of an insistence on equality) as well as the provision of guidelines for policy-making based on appropriate social and political values. Transmutational functions are instrumental. In various systems of thought, particularly in most schools of Marxist political philosophy, ideology is seen explicitly as a *tool* for the waging of political struggle. It is a most important tool, in fact, for it affects the hearts and minds of people. It can persuade peasants, for example, that a revolutionary cause is both just and achievable.

The fourth and fifth relevant characteristics of ideology are closely related. Loci refers to the degree of adherence to the political doctrine exhibited throughout the various classes and strata of the target population. Loci concerns the horizontal spread of ideas over a population. In contrast, scope deals with the "vertical" spread, so to speak, of the doctrine in the mind of a given individual. The depth of understanding of and commitment to doctrinal ideals is a function of the degree to which those ideas are associated with other nonpolitical elements in an individual's belief system (e.g., religious, social, and economic values).

The concepts introduced here—the content, functions, structure, scope, and loci of an ideology—will be used throughout this analysis to help elaborate the role played by ideology in the operational behavior of the *Khmer Rouge*. For example, the structure of Khmer communist thought was extremely unstable, evolving continuously over a thirty-year period. However, the interrelatedness of the structure of Khmer communist ideology grew progressively more coherent and concrete with time. The means regarded as acceptable modes of political expression began with "casual" political agitation (e.g., writing letters to prominent officials) and personal commitment, moved into active electoral competition and political organizing, at first overt and then increasingly covert, and then escalated into armed struggle, beginning with guerrilla-type sabotage and terror, and finally ending in conventional warfare. The ends to be achieved began as rather amorphous, generalized goals (i.e., end Cambodia's peripheral-dependent relationship to the world economy and become autonomous and self-sufficient) and slowly became more substantial in the form of emergent policy proposals, finally finding concrete expression as an existing social structure in Cambodia.

The interrelatedness of KCP doctrine, as well, increased over time. From inauspicious beginnings as a few marginally related ideological abstractions concerning social, political, and economic relations, KCP doctrine became integrated to an extent sufficient to provide the basis for the organization of an entire social order, organizing all aspects of Khmer life in terms of the dominant set of beliefs.

Perhaps the best way to explore the functions, scope, and loci of the Kampuchean communists' thought is to examine their actual political behavior. This will also help fill in the picture on certain aspects of the content and the structure of the ideology. We will see how the purpose of the movement was justice and equality for the

Khmer people. We will see what would be required of the people in order to build "the only true communism," a communism "better than in Russia or China, where there are still classes. . . ."[14]

Stages of *Khmer Rouge* Behavior

The active political life-cycle of the *Khmer Rouge* communist movement can be described as a five-phase progression beginning at gestation and ending with death or at least eclipse. Similarly, the evolution of *Khmer Rouge* economic and social thought can be usefully described in terms of this five stage life-cycle: the gestation, early revolutionary, late revolutionary, regime, and postregime stages or phases.

The gestation phase stretches from the first glimmerings of organized communism in Indochina with Ho Chi Minh's establishment of the Indochinese Communist Party (ICP) in 1930 to an intermediate period between the founding of the *Pracheachon* in 1954 and the "founding congress" of the KCP in 1960. During this period, a lack of organizing skills and political legitimacy hampered effective action by the relatively tiny collection of groups classifiable as communist.

With the *Pracheachon*, the Cambodian communists began participation in the legitimate Cambodian political system, and with the KCP they inaugurated carefully organized clandestine political activity in the cities and the countryside. Thus, the second stage, or early revolutionary phase, begins with the first KCP congress in 1960 and lasts until the 1967 rural peasant rebellion. Although the KCP probably was not the main cause of the 1967 rebellion, this revolt stimulated a government purge of leftists participating in government and civil service offices, driving the movement from the institutionalized political process into clandestine armed resistance.

Beginning with the initiation of guerrilla warfare in 1968, the third stage lasted until April 1975 and was characterized by military operations culminating in total victory for the KCP. This late revolutionary phase had two parts, the first of which spanned 1968 and 1969, involving harassment with guerrillas and advancing work on infrastructural organization among the rural and urban populations. Although the political work among the masses may have been difficult because of a lack of legitimacy on the part of the revolutionaries, it did not compare with the difficulties of conducting guerrilla warfare with virtually no modern armaments.

The second part of the late revolutionary phase began with the watershed event of the entire revolution, the Lon Nol–Sirik Matak *coup* of 1970. The overthrow of Prince Sihanouk was the spark for a dual strategy of internal/external and political/military united front. Politically, this included the united front tactic both internally, when the communists joined with the Sihanoukists in the National United Front of Kampuchea (FUNK), and externally, when the FUNK joined Vietnamese and Laotian communists on the "single battlefield" to struggle against "U.S. imperialism" under the banner of the United Front of the Three Indochinese Peoples (UFTIP). Militarily, this entailed combined military operations—that is, guerrilla, conventional or proxy military action as was expedient and/or possible—conducted from "liberated" rear areas of the country.

The fourth stage was the regime phase, during which the victorious communists set about razing what little was left of Cambodian society and began to erect a Utopian vision of social order, as one might play with wooden blocks. This "power" phase lasted only three and one-half years, until the abrupt termination of KCP rule via the Vietnamese invasion of December 1978, culminating in defeat for the KCP on January 7, 1979.

The final phase—oblivion and impotence—is noteworthy for the tragicomic spectacle of a "united front" between the toppled *Khmer Rouge* and the CIA-supported *Khmer Serei*. This "final" scene features both Khieu Samphan's pathetic pleas from Peking for aid from the formerly despised imperialist nations to "stop Vietnamese and Soviet expansionism,"[15] and Norodom Sihanouk's renewed alliance with the defeated KCP in hope of regaining a position of leadership in Kampuchea.[16]

Notes

1. The *Dhammapada* is a section of the *Hinayana* canonical scriptures that is attributed directly to Buddha himself. I have employed the Irving Babbitt translation (New York: Oxford University Press, 1936; and New Directions Publishing Corporation, 1965), p. 45.

2. G. Hildebrand and G. Porter, *Cambodia: Starvation and Revolution* (New York: Monthly Review Press, 1976), p. 69.

3. The *Dhammapada* XXIV:335, p. 53.

4. Quoted in N. I. Kapchenko, "Foreign Policy and Ideology," *International Affairs* (Moscow) 11 (1970), p. 80.

5. As one example, see the testimony of John Barron before the House Subcommittee on International Organizations, *Human Rights in Cambodia* (Washington, D.C.: USGPO, 1977). "The purpose here," Barron said of *Khmer Rouge* actions, "was to obliterate every vestige of Cambodian culture as it

existed prior to April 1975" (p. 9). I hope to show that this is a common but fundamental misunderstanding of *Khmer Rouge* goals.

6. See the section of this study titled "The Transformation of Consciousness," in Chapter 7, for more on possible links between traditional Buddhist values and Khmer communist doctrine.

7. One of Vietnamese General Vo Nguyen Giap's most important contributions to KCP behavior came in the form of his organizational model for revolutionary armed forces, adopted by the Cambodian revolutionaries in 1970 and implemented with advice and assistance from Giap himself. This will be treated in Chapter 6. Giap's other contributions to KCP behavior will be discussed in Chapter 8.

8. Zbigniew Brzezinski expounds the relationship between political theory and political action at some length in his *Ideology and Power in Soviet Politics* (New York: Praeger, 1967). Quotations are from pp. 131 and 135.

9. From Maximilien Robespierre, "Report on the Principles of a Revolutionary Government," reproduced in *Introduction to Contemporary Civilization in the West*, A Sourcebook Prepared by the Contemporary Civilization Staff of Columbia College, Columbia University, 3rd ed. (New York: Columbia University Press, 1961) 1:51.

10. Also reproduced in *Introduction to Contemporary Civilization in the West*, 1:59.

11. Some observers have noted, however, that the young *Khmers Rouges* were attracted to French literary and political writings. François Ponchaud (*Cambodia: Year Zero* [New York: Holt, Rinehart and Winston, 1978], p. 155) says that Saloth Sar and Ieng Sary spent more time reading and studying these writings, and publishing political tracts of their own, than at their studies. J. J. Zasloff and M. Brown (*Communist Indochina in U.S. Foreign Policy* [Boulder, CO: Westview Press, 1978], p. 129) say much the same thing, but give no documentation for the assertion. Their phraseology leaves the impression that Ponchaud is the source. In turn, Ponchaud gives no citations, but *his* phraseology and foci leave the impression that his primary source for the material was François Debré, *Cambodge: La Révolution De La Forêt* (Paris: Flammarion, 1976). Here the citation trail grows cold. Another observer has noted the apparent similarity between *Khmer Rouge* ethics and the philosophy of Georges Sorel. See Kenneth M. Quinn, "The Origins and Development of Radical Cambodian Communism" (Ph.D. diss. University of Maryland, 1982), pp. 208–211. See also Georges Sorel, *Reflections on Violence* [T. E. Hulme, trans.] (New York: Collier Books, 1950).

12. J. J. Zasloff and M. Brown (*Communist Indochina*, p. 133) assert that the controversy surrounding Thorez's alleged "personalism" "must have made a strong impression on the future Cambodian revolutionary leaders. . . ." In fact, this is most probable, because four of the young Khmer students became members of the French Communist Party (PCF) in the early 1950s, and perhaps as many as a dozen young Cambodians joined the PCF through the 1950s. See Debré, *La Révolution De La Forêt*, pp. 83, 84. An excellent

history of the French Communist Party is Annie Kriegel, *The French Communists: A Profile of a People* [E. P. Halperin, trans.] (Chicago: University of Chicago Press, 1972); also see François Fejtö, *The French Communist Party and the Crisis of International Communism* (Cambridge, MA: MIT Press, 1967).

13. For an excellent theoretical discussion of ideology, see David Minar, "Ideology and Political Behavior," *Midwest Journal of Political Science* 5:4 (November 1961), pp. 317–331. Many of the categories used in the present analysis are drawn from the Minar article.

14. From an official *Khmer Rouge* radio broadcast, quoted in John Barron and Anthony Paul, *Murder of a Gentle Land* (New York: Readers Digest Press, 1977). This volume is good on radio broadcasts from Democratic Kampuchea, but is generally messianic in tone and lacking in care with respect to regional differences.

15. Keyes Beech, "Cambodian Foes Reportedly Unite to Fight Vietnamese," *Los Angeles Times*, October 18, 1979.

16. See, for example, "Sihanouk Shelves Plans to Join Cambodian Rebels Against Hanoi," *Los Angeles Times*, February 28, 1981; also see Ramtanu Maitra, "Alex Haig OK's Plans to Bring Back Cambodian Mass Murderer Pol Pot," *New Solidarity*, March 5, 1981; F. A. Moritz, "S.E. Asia hopes for Reagan help against Vietnamese," *Christian Science Monitor*, March 16, 1981; and "Sihanouk Announces United Front," *Christian Science Monitor*, April 30, 1981; Keyes Beech, "Cambodia's Mythical United Front," *Los Angeles Times*, May 24, 1981; Robert Keatley, "Bleak Prospects for Cambodia's Anti-Hanoi Coalition," *Wall Street Journal*, March 15, 1982; three articles by Colin Campbell, all in the *New York Times*, including "3 Cambodian Groups Forming Coalition" (June 21, 1982), "3 Cambodian Groups Form Exile Regime" (June 23, 1982), and "3 Unlikely Cambodian Allies Map War on Vietnam" (July 9, 1982); and Bob Sector, "3 Factions Oppose Vietnamese Occupiers," *Los Angeles Times*, January 19, 1983.

4
Gestation (1930–1960)

"The only result of this," he answered, "will be that while I try to cure others of madness, I myself will rave along with them. If I am to speak the truth, these are things I must say. Whether a philosopher can speak falsely, I do not know, but I certainly can't. Though my advice may be exasperating to them, I do not know why it should seem presumptuous to the point of absurdity. If I should advocate policies such as Plato describes in his Republic or as the Utopians actually practice in their country, policies which are certainly much better than those I have urged, they would, I admit, be out of place. For in those commonwealths all things are held in common, while property here is privately owned. But what have I said that might not or should not be said anywhere? Of course my discourse cannot please those who rush headlong the opposite way; it checks them and shows them their dangers."

—Sir Thomas More, *Utopia*[1]

The Early History

The early history of communism in Indochina revolves almost entirely around various Vietnamese groups resisting French colonialism. In 1930, under the leadership of Vietnamese nationalist and communist Ho Chi Minh, three communist-oriented groups were united under the banner of the newly founded Vietnamese Communist Party (VCP). Later that same year, the VCP's name changed to the Indochinese Communist Party (ICP) at a meeting in Hong Kong. The ICP was given official status in the international communist movement a few months later, when its existence was sanctioned by the Soviet-directed Comintern. While officially a three-nation party, the ICP, at least in the first decade, was in reality quite another thing.

The Cambodian representatives to the ICP were almost exclusively ethnic Vietnamese and Chinese holding little influence within Khmer culture and society. Through the 1940s, however, the ICP managed to develop a small indigenous following of ethnic Khmers in Cambodia. Yet, the movement continued to be dominated by ethnic Vietnamese oriented toward Hanoi until the organization disbanded between 1949 and 1951. The influence of the Vietnamese in Indochinese communism carried over even after the ICP was reorganized into three smaller national parties, the *Lao Dong* in Vietnam, the *Lao Itsala* in Laos, and the Khmer People's Party (KPP) in Cambodia.

A *Lao Dong* ("Worker's Party") document dated November 1951 and titled "Remarks on the Official Appearance of the Vietnamese Worker's Party" explained the fragmentation of the ICP as a tactical move not intended to impair the essential unity of the communist movements in the three countries. In a section called "Reasons for the Division into Three Parties and for the Change in Party Name," the authors of the document asserted that "the creation of a separate Communist Party for the working class of Vietnam does not risk weakening the leadership of the revolutionary movement in Cambodia and Laos or the carrying out of Marxist-Leninist propaganda action. In addition, the Vietnamese Party reserves the right to supervise the activities of its brother Parties in Cambodia and Laos."[2]

The Vietnamese communists' fraternal solidarity with their Laotian and Cambodian brothers never wavered as long as the activities of those brothers continued to support the interests of the Vietnamese revolution, for the Vietnamese saw the outcome of their own revolution as the key to the future of all Indochina. However, in the eyes of some Cambodian communists—particularly those who were strongly nationalist—Vietnamese adherence to the dictates of proletarian internationalism seemed to be little more than thinly veiled aggressive expansionism.

Not surprisingly, the small and isolated communist movement in Cambodia failed to "take off" among the traditional Khmer peasants during the 1950s. The homogeneity of Cambodian society—the vast majority of the population consisted of ethnic Khmer Buddhist subsistence farmers in a precapitalist economy—militated against the spread of revolutionary ideas. The leisurely pace of traditional life was inherently conservative, and it would require tremendous social upheaval—in the form of years of widespread political terror and campaigns of strategic area bombing—to radicalize the peasantry and elevate their consciousness to a combustible level.

Amid these circumstances, the struggling communist movement in Cambodia was an easy target for abuse and repression by the government. Continual setbacks seemed to characterize its efforts, and several severe strategic losses virtually destroyed the movement between 1953 and 1959. At the Geneva Conference in 1954, the Vietnamese failed to win recognition for the Khmer People's Party, after which many of the Cambodian communists decamped to Hanoi where they would remain in exile for more than fifteen years. A decidedly determined segment of the KPP elected to stay behind and pursue the struggle. Of those who chose to remain, a few embittered cadres continued the armed struggle; these were to have a negligible and virtually forgotten impact on the course of events, until the beginning of the real fighting in 1967. The balance of the communist cadres remaining in the country decided to seek fulfillment of their aspirations through "legitimate" parliamentary channels. They formed the *Krom Pracheachon*, or People's Party, and continued to suffer repression at the hands of the Sihanouk government.

In the confused post-Geneva atmosphere, the communists in Cambodia were beset by faction and betrayal. After 1954, communist activities in Cambodia were directed by a committee including Sieu Heng, Son Ngoc Minh, and Touch Samouth, among others.[3] KPP leader Sieu Heng, who had been involved in independence struggles since 1944, returned from Hanoi in 1956 to take charge of the "urban committee" in Cambodia. Sieu soon came into conflict with Touch Samouth, who soon replaced him on the urban committee, prompting Sieu's move to the leadership of the "rural committee." This division climaxed in 1959 when Sieu Heng rallied to the side of the government, and it was revealed that he had been a double agent in the service of Lon Nol for five years. The division went full circle by 1970, when Sieu Heng commanded a battalion of Republican forces in the struggle against his former comrades.

By most estimates, up to 90 percent of the indigenous communist infrastructure in Cambodia had been liquidated by the end of 1959, largely because of Sieu Heng's deadly accurate information. One analyst summed it up this way: "After a few years of repression, all that was left of the pre-Geneva communist movement in many parts of Kampuchea was a handful of embittered cadres. What had been achieved with Vietnamese aid and advice up to 1954 had been lost. The losses could credibly be blamed upon what the Vietnamese had done at and since Geneva."[4] The growing legacy of bitterness between the Vietnamese and the Khmer communists originating in this period would become a central factor in later stages of the revolution.

Sihanouk and Cambodian Communism

Among the crucial setbacks afflicting the Kampuchean communists during the 1950s was King Norodom Sihanouk's successful campaign for independence from France. Cambodia's colonial status allowed both communist and noncommunist opposition to Sihanouk to argue that the king was a mere French puppet. Independence would neutralize this issue, and thus it became politically imperative that Sihanouk achieve that goal if he were to retain power amid the rising tide of nationalist sentiments.

In a desperate gamble during the final months of World War II, the Japanese had seized control of Indochina from the French colonial forces. Three days later, on March 12, 1945, King Sihanouk demonstrated his allegiance to France by proclaiming the independence of Cambodia. Sihanouk had been placed on the throne at the tender age of eighteen, the French believing that he would prove more pliable than his uncle, Prince Sisowath Monireth, who was the pretender from the Norodom's rival royal lineage.

Under Japanese tutelage a government was formed with Son Ngoc Thanh as minister of foreign affairs. One day before the Japanese surrender on August 15, 1945, Son Ngoc Thanh moved to force the resignation of King Sihanouk as prime minister and, arresting the remaining pro-French ministers, proceeded to form a new Council of Ministers with himself as the prime minister. This short-lived experiment with independence was swept away after the war when the Allies permitted French troops to reoccupy Indochina, thus reentrenching their colonial interests and setting the stage for decades of continuing struggle for independence among the Indochinese peoples.[5]

Events would soon prove, however, that the French no longer possessed adequate power to continue imposing their rule upon Indochina. With the reimposition of French control, numerous small nationalist resistance groups emerged in Cambodia, ranging across the political spectrum but generally subsumed under the cloak of the *Khmer Issarak*, or "Free Khmer." These divergent groups harassed French operations, engaged in banditry and smuggling, and generally made a nuisance of themselves to colonial authorities. Eventually, however, the mercurial King Sihanouk managed to form an alliance with some of the *Khmer Issarak* factions, adding greatly to the difficulty of France's position. Combined with Vietminh military pressures throughout Indochina, this move forced the beleaguered French to seek accommodation with Sihanouk.

Still, transfer of national control to Cambodia was a gradual and uncertain process. With the conclusion of the Franco-Cambodian Treaty of November 8, 1949, Cambodia achieved nominal (but illusory) independence as an associate state in the French Union. French commanders retained control over the main units of Cambodia's armed forces. Not until the climax of King Norodom Sihanouk's "royal crusade for independence" four years and one day after the signing of the Franco-Cambodian Treaty did Cambodia achieve genuine national independence.

Sihanouk's successful crusade transformed him from one of Cambodia's most important political figures into *the* important Cambodian political figure, and projected him into a role he would play for nearly twenty years. He had come to political maturity during his eight-year struggle against France, traversing a difficult path from schoolboy king serving at the pleasure of a foreign power to successful "revolutionary" leader of an independent, nonaligned nation.

The preservation of Cambodian independence, Sihanouk believed,[6] necessitated a cautious neutrality through which he could manage foreign threats by balancing regional and global powers against one another. His personal political independence he preserved through deft manipulation of the interplay between domestic elite factions and foreign powers, occasionally reinvigorating his mandate through appeal to Cambodia's peasant masses, who were believed to regard Sihanouk as a semidivine god-king.

Sihanouk's personal perceptions, and hence, Cambodia's destiny, were fundamentally influenced by three major international conferences following on the heels of independence: the Geneva and Manila Conferences of 1954 and the Conference of Nonaligned Nations (sometimes called the "Afro-Asian Conference") at Bandung, Indonesia in 1955. The Geneva Convention produced a set of accords providing for the evacuation of all Vietnamese forces from Cambodia, and mandated International Control Commission–supervised elections for both Cambodia and Vietnam. The Vietnamese withdrew from Cambodia and the Cambodians held their elections, but there were to be no elections throughout Vietnam.

In preparation for these elections, King Norodom Sihanouk abdicated the throne on March 2, 1955, in favor of his father, Norodom Suramarit. "Prince" Sihanouk then proceeded to form the *Sangkum Reastr Niyum* ("Popular Socialist Community") as an umbrella political organization in his highly successful effort to dominate the elections. The Democratic Party, until then the dominant political vehicle for the Cambodian urban elite and landowning classes, was decimated along with numerous smaller parties trampled in the rush to jump on board the *Sangkum* bandwagon. The *Sangkum* would remain as Cambodia's central organ of political aggregation until it dissolved into dictatorship during the late revolutionary period.

About a month after the Geneva Conference, Prince Sihanouk journeyed to Bandung, where his tendencies toward neutrality with respect to the international situation were strongly reinforced. Previous discussion with "neutral" Third World leaders such as India's Jawaharlal Nehru had predisposed Sihanouk to a policy of nonalignment. At the Afro-Asian Conference, he met with China's Chou En-lai and North Vietnam's Pham Van Dong, and mutual assurances of peaceful intent left Sihanouk with the essential outlines of a foreign policy to which he would adhere throughout his years in power.

Under the provisions established at the Geneva Conference, Cambodia, Laos, and now-divided Vietnam were to refrain from entering into military alliance with any foreign powers until elections could be held. Although this greatly pleased Sihanouk, not all interested parties were equally enthusiastic. The U.S. government had refused to participate in what it saw as the surrender of part of Indochina to communism, and U.S. Secretary of State John Foster Dulles set out immediately after the Geneva Conference to undermine the noninterference provisions. The Manila Conference in 1954 succeeded in doing just that. On September 8, the South East Asian Treaty Organization (SEATO) came into being.

Though Sihanouk was wary of this development, it mattered little if he refused to cooperate with SEATO. Article IV, paragraph 1 of the SEATO instrument states: "Each party recognizes that aggression by means of armed attack in the treaty area against any of the parties or *against any State or territory which the Parties by unanimous agreement may hereafter designate,* would endanger its own peace and safety, and agrees that it will in that event act to meet the common danger in accordance with its constitutional processes."[7]

Paragraph 2 of Article IV generously expands the definition of aggression to encompass "any fact or situation which might endanger the peace of the area." In an attached "Understanding of the United States," it is proclaimed that Article IV of the SEATO Treaty applies "only to communist aggression." The Treaty Protocol reveals that the signatories "unanimously designate for the purposes of Article IV of the Treaty the States of Cambodia and Laos and the free territory under the jurisdiction of the State of Vietnam." Through this device, the United States circumvented and subverted the intent of the 1954 Geneva Accords, and claimed the right to intervene in nonaligned states—including Cambodia—should the logic of events so dictate. Although Cambodia was never a party to SEATO, the treaty would be cited as a justification for massive U.S. intervention in Cambodia after Sihanouk, overthrown in March 1970, joined with the communist insurgents in a united front.

Emergence of the KCP

The institutional history of the communist movement in Cambodia is so twisted by purges, factionalism, and repression that it is difficult to summarize without oversimplifying to the point of misrepresentation.[8] On the other hand, it is a simple matter to identify the first mass-based political party in Cambodia to merit designation as an indigenous communist movement. It was the Khmer People's Party (KPP), founded upon the splinter of Ho Chi Minh's Indochinese Communist Party in 1951. Though it began as very much a byproduct of the Vietnamese independence movement, the KPP quickly became the dominant covert political vehicle for Cambodian communists. Most of the KPP members at this point were of Cambodia's Vietnamese minority, but this gradually changed through the early 1950s as the cadres devoted themselves to the construction of resistance bases in a number of remote areas of the country, slowly drawing in a larger indigenous Khmer following.

The KPP itself was immediately preceded by numerous small committees, and, over its lifespan, generated a number of smaller splinter organizations. The KPP maintained a shadowy yet direct relationship with the *Krom Pracheachon*, which was the overt political vehicle for leftist activities in Cambodia through the 1950s and early 1960s. The *Pracheachon* fared poorly in its electoral endeavors, winning only 3.5 percent of the total vote in 1955, and offering only one candidate at the national level in the 1958 elections. Its troubles were perhaps symbolized by a *Pracheachon* candidate from Kompong Speu by the name of Men Suon. A month after the vote in which Men Suon fared well, according to the International Control Commission, he was shot dead: "The motive appeared to be Men Suon's success in the elections."[9] Following this high point, the *Pracheachon* dwindled to a lingering extinction.

As has been previously noted, the Cambodian communist movement was weakened by several severe blows during the 1950s. The self-imposed exile of KPP cadres to Hanoi after the Geneva Conference in 1954 precipitously depleted the KPP's in-country strength. Variously estimated to have involved between 700 and 10,000 personnel (but more probably between 2,000 and 5,000), this 1954 exodus was the opening scene of the KPP's last act. It combined with merciless attacks by various Cambodian rightist groups as well as by Sihanouk's security forces to reduce the vitality of the KPP-*Pracheachon* movement to such an extent that by the time of the Second Party Conference in 1960, the stage was set for the rise to prominence within the party

FIGURE 4.1
EMERGENCE OF THE KAMPUCHEAN COMMUNIST PARTY

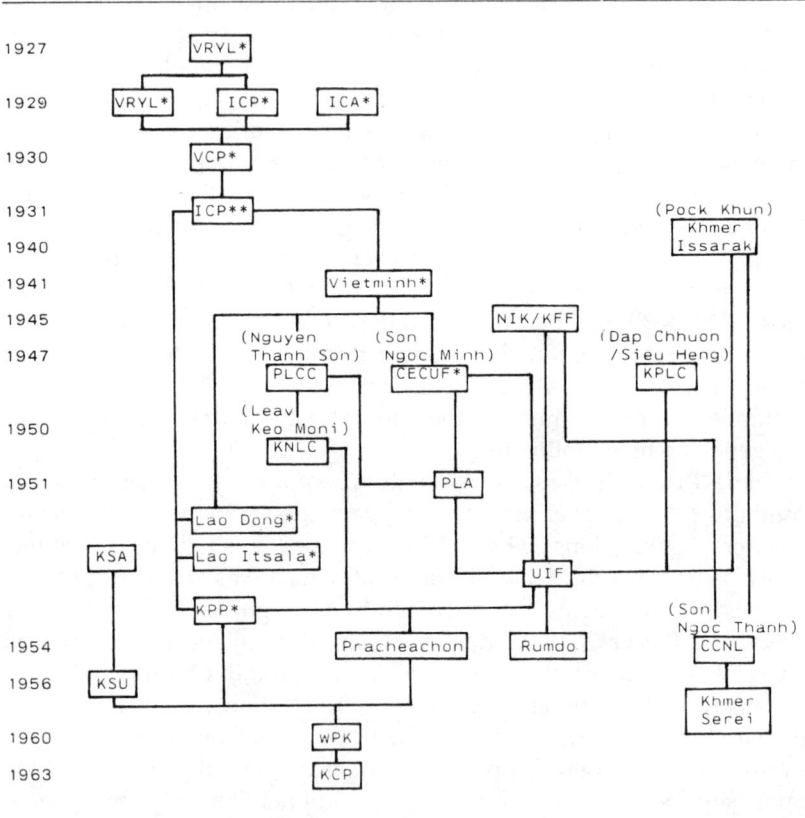

of a group that had either weak or entirely nonexistent ties to the KPP-ICP lineage.

Following what has become the conventional usage, I will refer to this latter group as the "Pol Pot faction." Later, I will also refer to this particular group as the "Stalinists" or the "politbureau." As the narrative proceeds it will be seen that the term "Pol Pot faction" is in an important sense something of a misnomer. It is clear that the Pol Pot faction has constituted the core of the Kampuchean Communist Party (KCP) over virtually the entire history of that organization. Although this faction did not achieve total supremacy within the party until sometime late in 1977, and although it at times

Key to Figure 4.1

Acronyms:

VRYL – Vietnamese Revolutionary Youth League

ICP – Indochinese Communist Party (** – Comintern Sanctioned)

ICA – Indochinese Communist Alliance

VCP – Vietnamese Communist Party

NIK/KFF – <u>Nekhum Issarak Khmer</u> or Khmer Freedom Front

KPLC – Khmer People's Liberation Committee

PLCC – People's Liberation Central Committee

CECUF – Central Executive Committee of the United Front

KNLC – Khmer National Liberation Committee

PLA – People's Liberation Army

UIF – United Issarak Front

CCNL – Cambodian Committee for National Liberation

KPP – Khmer People's Party (or Khmer People's Revolutionary Party)

KSA – Khmer Students' Association

KSU – Khmer Students' Union

WPK – Worker's Party of Kampuchea

KCP – Kampuchean Communist Party

Symbols:

Explicit Vietnamese Ties

---

controlled only a fraction of the mass membership of the movement, it controlled many of the important KCP posts after 1962, as well as the key posts in the National United Front for Kampuchea (FUNK), the Royal Government of Khmer Unification (GRUNK), and the People's National Liberation Armed Forces of Kampuchea (PFLANK) after the civil war broke out into the open in 1970.

A glance at what is known about the background of some of the important individuals who populated the KCP, prominent among whom are leaders of the Pol Pot faction, reveals some important clues as to how this group formed and why it remained so cohesive for some quarter of a century. (See Table 4.1.) Evidently, these people came to regard their own "history" as completely distinct from that

TABLE 4.1
KCP LEADERSHIP PROFILE

	SALOTH SAR	IENG SARY	KHIEU SAMPHAN	SON SEN	HOU YUON	HU NIM
BIRTHDATE	19 May 1928	1 Jan. 1930	27 July 1931	12 June 1930	1930	25 July 1932
BIRTH PLACE	Kompong Thom, Cambodia	Vinh Binh, Vietnam	Svay Rieng, Cambodia	Tra Vinh, Vietnam	Kompong Cham, Cambodia	Kompong Cham, Cambodia
CLASS ORIGIN	parents: landowners	father: landowner	father: civil servant	parents: landowners		
ETHNICITY	Sino-Khmer	Sino-Khmer	Khmer	Khmer	Khmer	Khmer
EDUCATION FIELD	radio-electronics	commerce, politics	economics, politics	letters, education	economics, law	law
EDUCATION LOCATION	Phnom Penh; Paris	Phnom Penh; Paris	Sisowath; Paris	Phnom Penh; Paris	Phnom Penh; Paris	Phnom Penh; Paris
ED LEVEL	----	B.A.	Ph.D.	B.A.	Ph.D.	Ph.D.
ALSO KNOWN AS	Sol Sat Pol Phat To Saut Pol Pot Brother #1	Kim Trang Met Vann Brother #2	Met Hem			Met Phoas

of those groups tied to the Vietnamese heritage. Not surprisingly, perhaps, they began their politically active careers during their student years.

As sons and daughters of "bourgeois" and privileged Cambodian families, they received their secondary educations in provincial Cambodian schools. By and large the members of this group were elite by birth, having been born into that fraction of the population not tied to the land by tradition and economic necessity. At least two of them are rumored to have (had) noble blood: Hou Yuon and Saloth Sar.[10] Ieng Sary, Son Sen, and Saloth Sar all came from landowning families, although Saloth Sar would later pretend that he had arisen from lowly peasant origins. Khieu Samphan's father was a minor provincial civil servant. Those who would become the masters of Cambodia's peasant revolution were not themselves peasants.

What set these young students apart from their contemporaries was the fact that they were among the select group of Cambodian students who won government scholarships for study abroad. Promising Khmer youth were sent to Paris for advanced training, and there they would be exposed to many volatile ideas—socialism, nationalism, communism, anti-imperialism, neocolonialism, and other "-isms"—that were tightly controlled back home in Cambodia. Most of the Cambodian youth in Paris became members of a nonsectarian friendship association for Paris-bound students, known as the Khmer Students' Association (KSA). Within the KSA, groups coalesced around different political persuasions. One of these groups was a radical "leftist" faction opposed to the king, the monarchy, and French imperialism. They explored various paths to nationalism, flirting briefly with Son Ngoc Thanh's *Issarak* movement.

Four members of the KSA's radical faction—Saloth Sar, Ieng Sary, Rath Samoeurn, and Sien An—joined the French Communist Party (PCF) between 1949 and 1951.[11] It was probably in their capacities as PCF members that two of them, Saloth Sar and Ieng Sary, along with another KSA radical, Thioun Mum, journeyed to East Berlin in 1951 as the KSA delegates to the Moscow-inspired Berlin Youth Festival. This appears to have been a profoundly significant event in the history of the Kampuchean revolution.

According to François Debré, when the delegation returned to Paris from East Berlin there followed a distinct change in the tenor of the discussions within the radical KSA faction. They abandoned purely theoretical discourse with their new-found understanding that "action is essential." They also abandoned their "illusions" about the democratic nature of Son Ngoc Thanh's resistance movement, concentrating now on Marxist-Leninist literature. Saloth Sar, Ieng Sary, and Rath Samoeurn set about the task of studying the techniques of subversion and revolutionary organization, earning from their colleagues the appellation, "the Stalinists." One day this would become a very appropriate label.

In 1952, the radical KSA faction scandalized Phnom Penh by publishing an open letter denouncing the king. Sihanouk had dissolved the National Assembly, the first that had ever been elected. The students branded him "the strangler of infant democracy." More than that, they went on to upbraid the king for allegedly renouncing Cambodian territorial claims to former imperial possessions, especially Cochinchina, now a province of Vietnam. (This accusation was false. In fact, in 1954, the Cambodian foreign minister would reserve the "right" to make future revanchist claims to Cochinchina.) The letter was signed by seven of the radicals: Ieng Sary, Saloth Sar, Rath Samoeurn, Hou Yuon, Khieu Thirith, Thioun Mum, and Sien An.

In spite of this incident, which was viewed with some alarm in Phnom Penh, King Sihanouk eventually learned to like at least one member of the KSA group. Hou Yuon's devotion to the people and to democracy earned a grudging respect from Sihanouk, even if he was wary of Hou's radicalism. In the late 1950s and early 1960s, this respect would be expressed in the form of a series of high-level government posts, eventually leading to Hou's appointment as secretary of state for economic planning. In Sihanouk's 1980 memoir, he would refer to Hou as a "super-intellectual." And in his 1972 memoir, Sihanouk would recall the letter incident from 1952 but would remember it as a well-intentioned constructive criticism by Hou Yuon rather than the insolent and direct attack by a committee of seven that it really was.[12] Hou Yuon was viewed by Sihanouk as a democrat. But within the radical circle of KSA students, Hou's notions of popular sovereignty did not hold sway.

Saloth Sar expressed the dominant view. Following in the footsteps of his role models, Maurice Thorez and Joseph Stalin, Saloth Sar rudely dismissed Hou Yuon's ideas as idealistic theories that would not stand a chance in the "real world" of politics: "Without a solid party structure and solid leadership, no theories can be applied, and the enemies of socialism will profit at every turn."[13] Thus, there grew a schism in the radical group of the KSA, a mirror image of the split in the French Communist Party.

When Hou Yuon objected to Saloth Sar's interpretation of democratic centralism at one study-group meeting, the young Stalinist reportedly exploded at the challenge: "It is I who will direct the revolutionary organization! I will become the secretary general, I will hold the dossiers, I will control the ministries, and I will see to it that there is no deviation from the line fixed by the central committee in the interests of the people...."[14] In 1953, however, Saloth Sar's pretensions to leadership, at least insofar as the KSA was concerned, were rudely shattered by the French police. The radical faction's enthusiasm for anticolonialism and its known history of association with Khmer "freedom fighters" had attracted the attention of French authorities, and in 1953, the French government forced the KSA to disband.

Of course, the French police could not prevent continuing informal contact among the radical students. By 1956, France had virtually forgotten her former Indochinese colonies, and, now distracted with the decolonialization of Algeria, was largely unconcerned with radicalism among the Khmer students in France. With the help of Hou Yuon, Thioun Mum and a new Khmer student in Paris, Khieu Samphan, were then able to organize the Khmer Students' Union (KSU). Unlike those of its ideologically mixed predecessor, KSU members studied Marxist political and economic theory, attempting to forge applications of a theory designed on advanced industrial economies that would be useful in the analysis of Cambodia's peasant-based economy.

Two of the radical students, Hou Yuon and Khieu Samphan, took doctorates while they were in Paris. A third, Hu Nim, completed his doctoral thesis after returning to Cambodia. These dissertations provide valuable insights into the inner workings of three profoundly revolutionary minds.

Hou Yuon's thesis, "The Cambodian Peasants and Their Prospects for Modernization" (1955), was an examination of the socioeconomic vestiges of the French colonial period that continued to impede the development of the Cambodian countryside and in many cases involved extreme exploitation of the rural peasantry by the urban elite. Arguing that it is "the peasant masses who are the real creators of the nation's wealth," Hou's thesis foreshadowed the major theoretical contributions of his later years. In a 1964 tract called "Solving Rural Problems," Hou summarized his contribution by revealing that "(o)ur purpose is to transform and develop the rural economy based on establishing the peasant as the key to the organization of production." He thus argued, contrary to the conventional western wisdom,[15] that the Khmer peasantry must play a central role in the modernization of the Cambodian economy. Hou Yuon's theories would become the intellectual foundation of the *Khmer Rouge* revolution.

Hu Nim wrote "Les services publics économiques du Cambodge" (1965), criticizing the structural evolution of the Cambodian economy.

Precious foreign exchange was being wasted providing expensive imported goods for a tiny urban elite. Moreover, the agrarian structure of the country was coming to be increasingly dominated by a small proportion of the population, eroding the economic well-being of the peasant masses.[16]

Khieu Samphan's thesis, also, is fascinating in light of subsequent policy positions he supported in Democratic Kampuchea. In his 1959 thesis, "Cambodia's Economy and Industrial Development," Khieu argued that Cambodia was "part of a whole whose center is outside the country, rather than part of a homogenous national whole."[17] Synthesizing the work of several earlier theorists, including Hou Yuon, Khieu held that only by ending Cambodia's external dependency could Cambodia develop from an agrarian to an industrial economy.

Khieu's work falls into an intellectual tradition that was just emerging when he wrote his thesis in the late 1950s. One of Khieu's colleagues in Paris, African scholar Samir Amin, has given perhaps the most systematic expression to this body of thought, generally referred to as "center-periphery relations" or more simply, "underdevelopment theory."[18] Khieu's analysis was based upon French penetration and dominance of the Cambodian economy, but by theoretical generalization it does not matter which particular imperialist nation-state assumes the role of the exploiter. Economic domination by any external entity—the United States or Vietnam, for example— would have the same result: Cambodia would remain underdeveloped and the vast majority of the population would remain impoverished. The full implications of Khieu's, Hu's, and Hou's theories would not be fully realized for almost twenty years.

Notes

1. From H.V.S. Ogden's translation of Thomas More, *Utopia* (Northbrook, IL: Ahm Publishing Co., 1949), Book I, p. 23.

2. Cited in U.S. Congress, House Committee on the Armed Services, *United States–Vietnam Relations 1945–1967*, Book 2/12, IV.A.5, Tab. 3, C.4, p. 30.

3. For detailed analyses of this murky and poorly understood period, see Ben Kiernan and Chanthou Boua, eds., *Peasants and Politics in Kampuchea 1942 to 1981* (New York: M. E. Sharpe, 1982), especially pp. 127–133 and 253; Wilfred Burchett, *The China-Cambodia-Vietnam Triangle* (Chicago: Vanguard Books, 1982), especially Chapter 4, "The Rise of the Khmer Rouge, Part 1"; Kenneth M. Quinn, "The Origins and Development of Radical Cambodian Communism" (Ph.D. diss., University of Maryland, 1982); and

Ben Kiernan, "Origins of Khmer Communism," *Southeast Asian Affairs* 1981, pp. 161-180.

4. Stephen Heder, "Origins of the Conflict," *Southeast Asia Chronicle* 64 (Sept.-Oct. 1978), p. 15.

5. For an in-depth review of events in this period see Milton Osborne, *Politics and Power in Cambodia* (Victoria: Longman Australia, 1973), Chapters 1-4; and Michael Leifer, *Cambodia: The Search for Security* (New York: Praeger, 1967), especially Chapter 2, "The Emergence of Independent Cambodia."

6. See, for example, Norodom Sihanouk, "Cambodia Neutral: The Dictate of Necessity" (1958) in M. and C. Gettleman and L. and C. Kaplan, eds., *Conflict in Indochina* (New York: Random House, 1970), pp. 237-241; also in *Foreign Affairs* 36:4 (July 1958), pp. 582-586. Also good on Sihanouk and his policies are M. Williams, *The Land In Between* (New York: William Morrow, 1970), Chapters 11, 12; J. P. Armstrong, *Sihanouk Speaks* (New York: Walker, 1964); M. Leifer, *Cambodia*, Chapters 3-9; P. A. Poole, *Cambodia's Quest for Survival* (New York: American-Asian Educational Exchange, 1969), Chapter 4; R. M. Smith, *Cambodia's Foreign Policy* (Ithaca, N.Y.: Cornell University Press, 1965), Chapters 3-6; and M. Caldwell and Lek Tan, *Cambodia in the Southeast Asian War* (New York: Monthly Review Press, 1975), Chapters 3, 4.

7. For the full text of the SEATO Treaty see U.S. Department of State, *Bulletin*, September 20, 1954, or D. D. Eisenhower, *Mandate for Change 1953-1956* (New York: Doubleday, 1963), Appendix J, pp. 600-603; emphasis added.

8. The reader is advised to bear in mind that this narrative is being presented at a very general level. For more detailed information concerning specific episodes of this period, consult the sources cited in the relevant footnotes.

9. B. Kiernan and Chanthou Boua, *Peasants and Politics in Kampuchea*, p. 21.

10. François Debré, *Cambodge: La Révolution De La Forêt* (Paris: Flammarion, 1976); on page 83, Debré says that Hou Yuon was a descendant of Prince Yukanthor. Reports of Saloth Sar's alleged royal ancestry first began to appear around 1980. In fact, it appears that he was related to a royal Khmer blood line only very tenuously; his sister was a royal concubine.

11. *Ibid.*, pp. 83, 84.

12. W. Burchett, ed., *My War with the CIA: The Memoirs of Prince Norodom Sihanouk* (New York: Random House, 1972), p. 160.

13. F. Debré, *Cambodge: La Révolution De La Forêt*, p. 86.

14. *Ibid.*

15. The conventional wisdom argues that foreign aid and foreign direct and indirect investment stimulate development in the Third World; for one of the most well-developed treatments of this perspective, see W. W. Rostow, *The Stages of Economic Growth* (London: Cambridge University Press, 1962); see also C. McMillan and R. Gonzoles, *International Enterprise in a Developing Economy* (Lansing, MI: 1964). Hou Yuon's thesis is analyzed by Laura Summers

in "The Cambodian Liberation Forces: Political and Economic Doctrine," *Indochina Chronicle*, no. 17 (July 1972). Portions of Hou's thesis are reprinted in Kiernan and Boua, *Peasants and Politics in Kampuchea*, as are parts of his essay, "Solving Rural Problems." Quotations are from pp. 67 and 147.

16. Portions of Hu Nim's thesis are reprinted in B. Kiernan and Chanthou Boua, *Peasants and Politics in Kampuchea*, pp. 69–86, under the title, "Land Tenure and Social Structure in Kampuchea."

17. Khieu Samphan's thesis has been translated into English by Laura Summers, under the title, *Cambodia's Economy and Industrial Development*, Cornell University Southeast Asia Program, Data Paper #111 (Ithaca, N.Y.: Cornell University, 1979). The quotation given here is taken from George Hildebrand and Gareth Porter, *Cambodia: Starvation and Revolution* (New York: Monthly Review Press, 1976); p. 67, n. 77 says that it was taken from page four of Khieu's thesis. The quotation is an apt capsule of Khieu's thesis.

18. See Samir Amin, *Accumulation on a World Scale: A Critique of the Theory of Underdevelopment* (New York: Monthly Review Press, 1970); also, see his "Accumulation and Development: A Theoretical Model," *Review of African Political Economy*, no. 1 (August–November, 1974); the bibliography of Khieu's thesis cites Amin's 1957 Paris thesis, "Les effets structurals de l'intégration internationale des économies précapitalists." This intellectual tradition spawned the 1960s *dependentistas* of Latin America, notably T. Dos Santos, F. Cardoso, O. Sunkel, and A. G. Frank.

5
The Early Revolutionary Stage (1960–1967)

"Lifting a rock only to drop it on one's own feet" is a Chinese folk saying to describe the behavior of certain fools. The reactionaries in all countries are fools of this kind. In the final analysis, their persecution of the revolutionary people only serves to accelerate the people's revolution on a broader and more intense scale. Did not the persecution of the revolutionary people by the Tsar of Russia and by Chiang Kai-shek perform this function in the great Russian and Chinese revolutions?
—Mao Tse-tung, November 6, 1957[1]

The Identity of the Party

Shrouded in myth, secrecy, and disinformation, the relationship between the KPP and the younger KSA-KSU student groups during the early revolutionary period is complex and poorly understood. It is important to try to penetrate this shroud of confusion, for the relationship between the veteran cadres of the Kampuchean communist movement and the young students from Paris is the key to making sense of the entire revolution. The earliest known contact between student members of the KSA and the Vietnamese-oriented KPP cadres occurred in 1951.[2] Apparently, these first contacts were positive.

According to Francois Ponchaud, when the KSA sent Thioun Mum, Ieng Sary, and Saloth Sar to the Berlin Youth Festival in 1951, there the students encountered "a delegation of Vietminh-Khmers from the National United Front" (a KPP-related front). The KSA's delegation returned to Paris with a number of prizes, including a flag and a conviction. With only minor changes, the flag was to become the official flag of Democratic Kampuchea twenty-five years later. The conviction was Ieng Sary's, and it too would come into play with only minor modifications in the years to follow. Ponchaud and François Debré say Ieng Sary became convinced in East Berlin that only armed resistance could defeat French neocolonialism. Thus began the KPP-

KCP association, a tense relationship spanning three decades and transforming a nation.

When Saloth Sar, Ieng Sary, Rath Samoeurn, and Sien An returned to Cambodia from their stints in Paris, they immediately launched themselves into political work. Saloth Sar returned in August 1953, managing to get himself assigned to the headquarters of the National Central Executive Committee at a resistance base in Kompong Cham. There he was trained in how "to work with the masses at the base, to build up the Issarak committees at the village level, member by member."[3] In 1956, Saloth Sar was assigned to the urban committee for Phnom Penh, where he worked under its chairman, Touch Samouth.[4]

Rath Samoeurn and Sien An more or less disappeared into the jungles after their return, probably going to a KPP base for training. Life in the jungles did not appeal to everyone, though. Ieng Sary, president of the KSU during the 1955–1956 school term, returned to Cambodia in 1957. He taught briefly in the public school system, and then joined the faculty of Hou Yuon's private *lycée*.

After helping set up the KSU in Paris, Hou Yuon had returned to Cambodia to found a private *lycée*, Kambuboth College. He quickly became involved in the "Committee in Defense of Neutrality," seeking to reinforce Sihanouk's policy of neutrality. This led to several official appointments in the government, culminating in his tenure as minister for economic planning in 1962.

When Khieu Samphan followed from Paris a few years after Hou, he started a French-language biweekly newspaper, *L'Observateur*, as a vehicle for leftist views. His publishing career was cut short within about a year, however, as Sihanouk's security forces closed the paper and threw Khieu into prison for a month on charges of dubious merit. After his release from prison, where he had probably been given daily thrashings in the custom of Sihanouk's somewhat overenthusiastic security people, Khieu too joined the faculty of Hou's *lycée*.

Son Sen returned to Cambodia with a teacher's certificate in 1956 after having had his scholarship revoked because of his political activities in Paris. He, like Ieng Sary, became a public school instructor, if only for a short while. In 1958, Son joined Sihanouk's *Sangkum*, thereby making himself eligible to hold public office. Thereafter he was appointed director of curriculum at the National Pedagogical Institute. Hu Nim also returned home to serve in Sihanouk's many governments in various official capacities during the late 1950s and early 1960s.

Disagreement concerning the proper political line divided the Paris students and grew more serious when they returned to political activism in Cambodia.[5] On one side, Ieng Sary, Saloth Sar, and Son Sen held to the "hard line," arguing that armed struggle against the Sihanouk regime must take the first priority in the revolutionary struggle; on the other side, Khieu Samphan, Hu Nim, Hou Yuon, and Chau Seng led the "moderate line," arguing that because U.S. imperialism was the greatest threat, therefore the party must support Sihanouk's existing policies within the existing institutions if it were to defeat U.S. designs. This division implicated external relations, as well. Vietnamese interests were with the moderate line, as long as Sihanouk continued to direct his anticommunist tendencies only towards his domestic opponents. In China, the situation was more complex: Although Chou En-lai supported the moderate line and maintained friendly government-to-government relations with the Sihanouk regime, his radical opponents within the Communist Party of China (CCP) cultivated friendly party-to-party relations through a link to the young Cambodian communists. The conflict over revolutionary tactics, strategy, and alliances transcended the KPP-KCP division and extended deep into the ranks of the Saloth Sar faction itself.

Though it is possible to trace the careers and beliefs of individual KSA-KSU students, ambiguity pervades the communist movement's shifting coalitions. In 1960, the Kampuchean communists called a party congress to assess the damage to the movement since Geneva and to propose remedial policies. However, exactly which "party" and which "congress" has become a matter of some considerable dispute. Historians had believed for many years that the 1960 event was the Second Congress of the KPP, or the Kampuchean People's Revolutionary Party, as it is sometimes called. A *Party History* issued by the KCP's eastern zone military-political service in 1973 says that the decision to "form a Marxist-Leninist Party in Kampuchea" was made at the congress, but this document refers to the 1960 event as the Second KPP Congress.[6] On September 28, 1977, some doubt was cast upon this notion when Pol Pot broadcast a speech asserting that the Kampuchean Communist Party (KCP) in fact was "really born" at the 1960 congress, making it the party's first congress.[7] Xuan Hoang further muddied the waters by claiming in a November 1980 interview with Ben Kiernan in Hanoi that the 1960 event was the founding congress of the Worker's Party of Kampuchea (WPK).[8] What is this? What happened at the congress? Reorganization? Fractionalization? Nothing more than an Orwellian attempt to rewrite history?

On September 30, 1960, twenty-one "delegates" gathered in an abandoned room at the Phnom Penh railway station compound, and for the next three days they made history, albeit a confusing history. All the delegates could agree that the struggle did not seem to be going very well. But when the seven representatives from the urban committee and the fourteen from the rural committees turned to the task of analyzing the party's recent failures, everyone came away with different lessons from the past.

Touch Samouth was a veteran with a long history of leadership in the revolutionary movement. He advocated what turned out to be the dominant position, defending the importance of solidarity with the Vietnamese and of care not to antagonize Sihanouk's foreign policy of neutralism while seeking to force domestic reform. Ieng Sary and Saloth Sar expressed the minority view, arguing that the class structure of Cambodia was intolerably anachronistic, exploitative, and, most importantly, vulnerable. The only correct policy, according to this view, was armed struggle aimed at the defeat of this unjust regime.

For whatever reasons, Touch's line won the day. The political line apparently was validated as the party adopted the name, "Worker's Party of Kampuchea," presumably showing solidarity with the *Lao Dong* (Worker's Party) of Vietnam. However, this victory may have been at the price of a compromise to mollify the young Turks in the party, providing for increased attention to "preparations" for armed struggle. As Ieng Sary later described the outcome of the 1960 congress, "We had adopted the correct stand on the necessity of armed struggle, but we still had much ideological work to do on this question. We had to educate the party members that the reform struggles—for land, democratic rights, better living standards, etc.—were very important, but that they could not give us power. Only the armed struggle, led by the Party, could put political power in our hands."[9]

Saloth Sar was elected to the number three post in the politbureau of the party, and Ieng Sary, to the number five post. But Touch Samouth and Nuon Chea, both veterans and friendly to the Vietnamese, were elected as the general secretary and the deputy general secretary at the congress. Although the KPP undertook certain administrative, tactical, and ideological changes at the Second Party Congress in 1960 in line with Touch's "moderate" anti-imperialist, pro-Vietnamese, and pro-Sihanouk policies, Saloth Sar and his associates independently determined that the main body of the communist movement in Cambodia was hopelessly incorrect both in its analysis of the Cambodian class situation and in its friendly stance vis-à-vis the Vietnamese communists. Noting any existing dissent within the KPP organization for future reference, Saloth Sar and associates proceeded after the Congress covertly to form and institutionalize the clique that became the nucleus of the KCP. Saloth's clique began to consolidate its position within the party in 1962, as is evidenced in part by the party's change of name to the Kampuchean Communist Party (KCP) in 1963.

The party as a whole probably could not avoid in 1960 the conclusion that continued agitation in the urban areas and among Cambodian elites was a necessary—but not sufficient—condition for revolutionary progress. The disastrous showings of the *Pracheachon* candidates in the 1956 local elections and the 1958 national elections were powerful evidence that serious spadework at the grass-roots level was a prerequisite to the flowering of Cambodian communism as a mass movement. Hence, the party instituted a program of mass political education and recruitment to build an infrastructure at the village level, while maintaining overt political struggle within existing Cambodian political institutions.

Cadres working at both levels, covertly and overtly, continued to be subject to repression by the Sihanouk government. In August of 1960, Khieu Samphan was publicly attacked and stripped naked in the street, then photographed by security agents.[10] Somehow these photos found their way into the subsequent National Assembly debate. As the 1962 elections approached, Cambodia's Ministry of Security intensified the harassment into a crackdown, arresting *Pracheachon* General Secretary Non Suon and thirteen of his colleagues in January after Sihanouk had forced a parliamentary confrontation with the *Pracheachon* the previous autumn. The fourteen were convicted of espionage and the next year sentenced to death, though the sentences were commuted to life in prison by Sihanouk. Some six months after the arrest of the overtly operating communists, the KPP general secretary, Touch Samouth, disappeared under circumstances that remain mysterious.[11] In this general atmosphere of terror against the left, numerous other important figures began to disappear, increasing speculation that government-orchestrated summary executions were wildly multiplying. During 1963, Saloth Sar, Ieng Sary, and Son Sen—by now all prominent figures—dropped completely from sight. In fact, many, if not most, of these "disappearances" resulted from decisions to remove key party officials from their increasingly vulnerable overt roles, and to place them in more secure covert positions in the provinces.

The political crises of 1962–1963 thus persuaded Saloth Sar, Ieng Sary, and Son Sen to continue their activities underground. Khieu Samphan, Hou Yuon, and Hu Nim would not be forced out of their overt roles until the conservative electoral victories of 1966 and the peasant rebellions of 1967. All through this period, these key figures of the Paris student group remained in close contact, and, certain tactical differences notwithstanding, progressed in their aim of displacing the influence of the older and more experienced cadres in the Cambodian communist movement.

The key beneficiary of Touch Samouth's "disappearance" was Saloth Sar. With Touch gone on July 20, 1962, the way was clear for the rise of Deputy Party Secretary Saloth Sar. At a party conclave on February 21, 1963, he was confirmed as general secretary. Ieng Sary advanced to the politbureau, with the Paris student group now holding five of the top twelve slots in the party hierarchy.[12] This watershed event marked the first ascension to internal party power by the Saloth Sar group. It was the beginning of the end of the cooperation between the old-line KPP cadres and the younger cadres organized around the Paris group. After 1962, this latter group gradually came to constitute the effective center of the Kampuchean communist movement, albeit with many rivals for party control and ideological leadership. With KPP cadres divided into several factions, defined according to various shades of opinion on pivotal issues such as the Vietnamese, Sihanouk, U.S. imperialism, and the Cultural Revolution, Saloth Sar's people began a struggle that would end in internal party supremacy late in 1977.

In the 1962 elections, Sihanouk had allowed a number of prominent leftists to run for national assembly seats. Being popular in their home districts, they won handily. The head of state then appointed several to cabinet-level posts, partly in response to harsh criticism of his domestic economic and anticommunist policies. Hou Yuon became secretary of state for economic planning, but conservative opinion reacting to a minor rebellion in Siem Riep forced his resignation within months. Khieu Samphan became secretary of state for commerce, but he was dismissed the following year in an incident concerning his refusal to take a bribe. These two appointments represented the apex of leftist success in the overt political struggle.

As part of his policy of "Buddhist socialism," Sihanouk appropriated some major elements of the leftist reform program when he nationalized foreign trade and banking. These matters will be developed at greater length in the following sections, but it is important to note for now that Sihanouk's adoption of the radical reforms had two important political effects. First, the mildly socialist measures seriously alienated significant segments of the domestic right wing. Second, and ironically, this "shrewd" political move rather disenfranchised the communists who argued for the anti-imperialist pro-Sihanouk line, as they soon found themselves on the outside looking in at a caricature of their aspirations, with their position in KCP Central Committee debates now hopelessly untenable.

The Deterioration of the Center

Two central areas of Cambodian society that need to be examined for clues about the evolution of the revolution are the urban elite and the rural peasant masses. Without the support of the urban elite, no one—neither Sihanouk nor his predecessors—had ever been able to rule Cambodia successfully. Likewise, without at least the tacit ambivalence, if not the support, of the rural masses it is an unmanageable task to govern the nation.

The number of deaths per thousand live births is the infant mortality rate (IMR), a statistic commonly used for cross-cultural comparisons of relative degrees of modernization. Low IMRs are found in relatively developed states (Hong Kong—18; Taiwan—26; Cuba—29) where modern public health and medical services are readily available to the majority of the population. The rate climbs steeply in less developed areas (Bahrain—78; Burma—126; Quatar—138).[13] At 127, Cambodia consistently maintained one of the worst infant mortality rates in Southeast Asia through the postwar period.

In part, this high IMR results from the fact that the bulk of Cambodia's people live very close to the land, relying on traditional medicine and health practices. Their welfare depends largely on good weather and the social stability required for a normal harvest. Sihanouk's *Sangkum* coalition did exert some efforts toward improving health conditions for the rural masses throughout the late 1950s. However, it relied perhaps excessively on foreign aid programs in these attempts, as it did in the establishment of health care centers to promote neonatal care and combat endemic diseases, such as malaria. Between 1955 and 1962, the Cambodian government's annual budget for public health grew from 83 million to a peak of 385 million riels.[14] After 1962, this growth leveled off and spending (in real terms) began to decline, partly because of decreases in foreign aid, but principally because more emphasis was given to more visible "status" indices of development (such as education) amid the general belt-tightening of the 1962–1963 budget crunch.

Most of the peasants remained on the periphery of these government programs. They were more likely to interact with agents of local Chinese moneylenders and absentee landlords than with public health officials from the city. The landlords and moneylenders, usually members of Cambodia's ethnic Vietnamese and Chinese minorities, are often cited as important sources of social unrest in the 1960s. With the perspective of some two decades, however, it is clear that the blame for the economic difficulties afflicting Cambodia in this period cannot be laid on Cambodia's minorities.

The elites of Cambodia, tied to urban lifestyles and cosmopolitan concerns, scarcely noticed the worsening position of the peasantry, or the fact that by the mid-1960s less than half of Cambodia's arable land was under cultivation. Sihanouk's regime, although devoted to "modernization" in some sense, tended to concentrate on symbols rather than substance. He was surrounded by phalanxes of advisors and court hangers-on who liberally indulged Sihanouk's inclination to respond favorably to favorable reports. Interviews with the former prince, as well as his various books and other publications, show that as late as 1980, Sihanouk continued to portray the image of a prerevolutionary Cambodian paradise, savaged by malevolent external forces of which he finally lost control. The reality is more like contradictory internal forces of which he gradually lost control.

In 1960-1963, Norodom Sihanouk's prestige within and control of Cambodian politics reached their zeniths. King Norodom Suramarit died on April 3, 1960, and in the succession crisis that followed, Prince Sihanouk (the king's son and former king himself) was elected by the National Assembly as Cambodia's constitutional head of state. To his roles as leader and founder of the *Sangkum* political organization, defender of the state religion, and chief patron of the arts, Sihanouk added a new title: leader of the government. From this lofty summit, there was only one direction he could possibly go, and he spent the next decade defending his position against gradual erosion.

Still, while the substance of Sihanouk's power slipped away, he fully maintained his social status, retaining his royal perquisites and his official title as head of state until the last moments of March 1970. Thus the shadows of power and status obscured to a certain extent the erosion of his influence, and so Sihanouk, consummate politician though he was, was more than a little surprised when the end of his rule seemingly came out of nowhere.

Everywhere but North Vietnam is a much closer estimate of the loci of opposition to Sihanouk, at least as far as the elites of Cambodia were concerned. In the volatile and wartorn politics of Southeast

Asia, Sihanouk's carefully orchestrated neutralism eventually alienated the left *and* the right, leaving his centrist constituency conspicuously denuded of support. His belief that Vietnam would ultimately prevail over the United States led him to seek "correct" relations with North Vietnam, even though he feared the potential power of a united communist Vietnam. But when Sihanouk wanted to apply pressure on the Vietnamese, or, more often, a lot of pressure on the indigenous communists, he always fell back on the military muscle of the domestic right.

Sihanouk could not tolerate criticism of his royal person, much less open insurrection against his royal regime, and so he kept the pressure on those members of the KPP still in armed resistance in the remote provinces, as well as any suspected of aid to the domestic subversives. While trying not to annoy the obviously superior (in power) external communists, he attempted to eradicate the relatively weak internal communists he perceived as "hard core," and to coopt those leftists who, he considered, were or could be made loyal. This complex strategy required what appeared to be a wildly inconsistent series of zigzags.

Although the members of Cambodia's right wing zealously endorsed and executed Sihanouk's anticommunist internal policies, they were not impressed with what they considered his appeasement, at best, of the external communists. This tension was aggravated by a most serious blow to Sihanouk's relations with his own military and compradore constituencies, growing out of the breaks with the United States in August 1963 and May 1965.

The United States had stuck its military foot in the Cambodian door at the very end of 1954. Modest but sustained assistance to Sihanouk's armed forces throughout the remainder of the 1950s and into the early 1960s created pockets of strong positive affect toward the United States among the Cambodian armed forces. The U.S. dollars and equipment enhanced the status and capability of key figures on the Cambodian right.[15] During the early 1960s, U.S. aid accounted for some 30 percent of Cambodia's police and military budgets, or about $12 million per year.[16] According to Sihanouk, U.S. aid between 1954 and 1963 amounted to some $300 million.[17] Thus, when Sihanouk renounced U.S. military aid in August 1963, his armed forces were seriously hurt. The slack was only partially taken up when the PRC agreed to begin supplying military aid in December 1963, largely because of the wide qualitative gap between U.S. and PRC military technologies.

The sequence of events leading Sihanouk to the renunciation of U.S. military aid, and later to a total break in diplomatic relations, symbolized Sihanouk's dilemma. This sequence was spurred by the activities of the expatriate nationalist, Son Ngoc Thanh. Thanh had been banished from Cambodia after his attempt to form a republic in the last days of World War II. From exile, Thanh had built a somewhat ragtag mercenary army, called the *Khmer Serei* ("Free Khmer"), composed of ethnic Khmers living in Thailand and South Vietnam. Eventually he was able to gain extended financial and logistical assistance from the Thai, South Vietnamese, and American intelligence services. Broadcasting from clandestine bases in Thailand and South Vietnam, the *Khmer Serei* constantly beamed anti-Sihanouk propaganda across the borders into Cambodia. These "pirate" transmissions specifically targeted Sihanouk and members of his family, showering them with biting invective. This enraged the head of state considerably, the more so because he believed, probably correctly, that these broadcasts could not continue without the cooperation of the United States. Combined with repeated violations of Cambodian territory by the Army of the Republic of Vietnam (ARVN), often in conjunction with *Khmer Serei* units, the clandestine broadcasts eventually drove Sihanouk to break relations first with Thailand and then with South Vietnam, and finally to reject U.S. military aid.

Along with these changes in foreign relations during 1963, Sihanouk ordered a number of sweeping domestic economic reform measures. These reforms, as has been previously noted, reflected the influence of leftist critics in the *Sangkum*. While his chief purpose seems to have been an economic one, these reforms also undercut the critique coming from the left. Hu Nim and Khieu Samphan had long argued that one of the primary impediments to Cambodian development was foreign penetration of key sectors of the Cambodian economy. The nationalization of foreign trade and banking implemented their critique, and took much of the wind out of their political sails.

Nevertheless, the rural masses were becoming increasingly disaffected with their economic condition, particularly in those regions where landlordism and usury were blatantly exploitative. Thus, the peasants were increasingly susceptible to the appeal of the forces on the left, who promised an end to the abuses of the "rich ones." Sihanouk explained his May 3, 1965 decision to sever diplomatic relations with the United States in terms of this political vulnerability: "It was politically imperative. . . . If I had not cut diplomatic relations, the rural populace, under the influence of the Khmers Rouges, would have become disillusioned with me and would have accused me of becoming a pro-imperialist traitor."[18]

Apparently, however, Sihanouk was not so vigilant when it came to charges from the right that he might be "becoming a procommunist traitor." To outsiders, Sihanouk's ritualistic deference to the North Vietnamese and their vassals sometimes appeared to be genuine solidarity with the international communist conspiracy. Sihanouk aroused many of his rightists when in March of 1965 he sponsored the "Indochinese People's Conference" in Phnom Penh, with representatives from communist movements in Laos, Cambodia (covertly), and North and South Vietnam prominent among those in attendance. After the plenary sessions, which ran from March 1 to March 9, the conference adopted a resolution condemning "American imperialism" and demanding an international conference to consider international guarantees for Cambodian neutrality.[19] Sihanouk did not get his international conference, but he did get a lot of flack from the Cambodian right wing.

In October 1964, the Cambodian National Assembly had threatened to break diplomatic relations with the United States if there were any further violations of Cambodian airspace by the U.S. Air Force. The last straw for some wavering Sihanouk supporters on the right came when, upon the occasion of an alleged U.S. airstrike in the "Parrot's Beak" area of Cambodia on May 1, 1965, Sihanouk seized the occasion as an opportunity to sever U.S.-Cambodian relations. As has been noted above, he later claimed that his hand had been forced by popular opinion and leftist propaganda, but it is clear that his actions were primarily motivated by his fears of the growing U.S. influence in his officer corps and business classes.

Opposition to Sihanouk and his policies from conservative critics had become so severe by the approach of the 1966 elections that in a fateful move, Sihanouk was persuaded to relinquish one of his most important political powers. In all previous electoral contests, candidacy on the *Sangkum* slate required the formal personal approval of the head of state, i.e., Sihanouk. He thus had been able to arrange the composition of the assembly, and maintain a crude balance between the domestic left and right favorable to his neutralist policy. In 1966, the prior approval requirement was relaxed, and a tide of resentment among the Western-oriented urban elite welled up and swept almost all the left-of-center elements from the National Assembly, depositing angry right-wing bodies in their places. The National Assembly, now only tenuously "controlled" by Sihanouk, immediately moved toward a more confrontational policy vis-à-vis both domestic security threats and, more significantly, the agents and suspected agents of Vietnamese communism, who by now were operating a supply line through the Cambodian port of Sihanoukville to the battle areas in South Vietnam. On October 22, 1966, the rightist victory was capped when General Lon Nol became the premier of Cambodia. It is possible that Sihanouk thought that he had the situation firmly in control, but the historical record of the subsequent events suggests another interpretation.

The Strategy of Revolution

The historical record concerning the strategy of the *Khmer Rouge* during the early revolutionary period is far from clear. Some sources claim that KCP strategy during this period was overt political struggle and covert revolutionary warfare. Others assert that the KCP was "preparing for" warfare during this period, and still others that it was not until after the repressions of 1967 that the KCP revised its tactics from political to military struggle.

The *Party History* issued by eastern zone political-military authorities (Vietnamese-oriented) in 1973 asserted that the party had conducted "politics with the support of arms" in the early revolutionary period, implying that the armed struggle had existed before, but had not been "proclaimed" until, 1968.[20] The Pol Pot people seemed to agree in their 1978 *Black Book*, which claimed that KCP strategy in the early revolutionary period was "armed struggle in combination with political struggle."[21]

The *Black Book* needed better editing, though, because the paragraph following the one just quoted appears to contradict the preceding claim, asserting that "in 1968 . . . the armed struggle movement was launched in Kampuchea."[22] Others have supported this second interpretation. Donald Kirk, for example, has argued that the pre-1968 period was characterized by the dual strategy of overt political struggle and "preparation for armed struggle."[23] This interpretation is made more credible by some additional official party sources. For example, Nuon Chea, chairman of the People's Standing Committee, made comments supporting this version in a speech on January 17, 1977.[24] A 1972 party Central Committee history also reported this version, claiming that the KPP "launched preparations for another armed struggle" in the early 1960s, and that "the events at Samlaut were prepared in advance."[25] Pol Pot himself, in contradiction with the story he would give in 1978, said in a 1975 speech that it was necessary to postpone plans for armed struggle at the time of the

Samlaut rebellion in 1967 in order to "examine and sum up the state of the contradictions and the possibility of the use of arms."[26]

A third possible version of KCP strategy in the early revolutionary period is that a decision to mount an armed struggle and abandon overt political struggle in the cities was not taken until late 1967 or early 1968. This version is also supported by official party spokespersons. In a September 1977 speech, Pol Pot said that at the time of the Samlaut rebellion "the Party Central Committee had not yet decided on nation-wide armed struggle."[27] Earlier party documents also had described the time between 1954 and 1967 as the "period of political struggle."[28]

How can one explain three different versions of KCP strategy during the early revolutionary period, all of which have been supported at one time or another by official party sources? How does one determine the facts of history? In the first place, it is clear that in some cases the divergent versions result from temporary tactical propaganda maneuvers. That Pol Pot has put forward all three versions at one time or another surely confirms this. Tactical convenience, however, cannot explain all the versions, because contradictory versions were sometimes offered by different authorities at about the same time, even in the same document, as in the case of the *Black Book*. Some of the contradictory assertions, as in the latter case, are no doubt the result of simple confusion.

To explain the varying interpretations of party history, however, one is forced to recognize the existence of Kampuchean communist factions whose objective histories are sufficiently divergent to support multiple collective memories. One clue is found in the *Black Book,* where it is confirmed that there were deep differences of opinion within the party in the analysis of the class situation in Kampuchea. The *Black Book* claims that the (Pol Pot) KCP line during the early revolutionary period held that the class situation in Cambodia demanded armed struggle, while the Vietnamese-oriented (KPP) "*Pracheachon* group" line was that the class structure of Cambodia was not ripe for revolution. This claim seems highly dubious for a number of reasons. Although the Vietnamese and the exiled KPP group in Hanoi had their own reasons for preferring to believe that the Cambodian class structure was not in a revolutionary condition, many of the KPP cadres who remained in Cambodia after 1954 had ample reason to think that armed struggle was an objective necessity. William Shawcross argues that the KPP cadres who stayed on when most of their comrades went to Hanoi after Geneva were in fact disloyal to Hanoi, believing that Hanoi and the Vietnamese communists had betrayed the Cambodian revolution.[29] Since 1954, these revolutionaries had been constantly attacked by Cambodian security forces. It is difficult to believe that all of them would renounce revolutionary violence, to which they had adhered before 1954, during the years of severe and continual repression that followed.

Some of these KPP cadres survived into the 1960s, although few in number and relatively isolated within the Cambodian communist movement. Estranged from their former comrades, regarded as unsophisticated and politically ignorant by the Paris student group, and hunted by the government, they fought a long and lonely struggle through the 1950s and 1960s. Thus when the *Black Book* asserts that the KPP eschewed armed struggle, we should understand that this is true only insofar as it applies to those who left for Hanoi in 1954 and those who took the moderate, pro-Sihanouk, anti-imperialist line in the *Pracheachon* and the KPP.

Numerous reports have indicated that the Samlaut rebellion was actually orchestrated by old line KPP cadres who had remained in the area from the 1950s. These actions occurred even as Hou Yuon and other highly visible and well-known leftists were still working aboveground in the cities. They were blamed for the uprising. It would be a little difficult to explain how the party could decide to resort to open warfare against the government when important members of the KCP Central Committee remained vulnerable in their overt roles, exposed to the reprisals of the government. These observations cast long shadows of doubt upon the sincerity, indeed upon the reality, of KCP armed struggle in the early revolutionary period.

A plausible hypothesis to unravel this confusing situation is that the Pol Pot KCP's *Black Book* represents an attempt to rewrite history by playing fast and loose with the facts, claiming that the line pursued by isolated KPP groups was their own, and assigning the line they themselves actually had followed (*viz.*, political struggle *in preparation* for armed struggle) to what they somewhat loosely refer to as the "*Pracheachon* group," clearly meant to refer to anyone who had any connection to the ICP-KPP lineage. While the leaders of the KCP, Ieng Sary and Saloth Sar, might have believed that armed struggle would eventually be necessary to break the grip of the Sihanouk regime, there is no evidence that they did anything about it before 1967, beyond propaganda and political organization.

It seems likely on the basis of fragmentary evidence that in fact fragmented KPP factions in Battambang, Siem Riep, Pursat, Koh Kong, and the eastern provinces continued to pursue a low level of armed struggle and peasant recruitment into the 1960s, while Saloth Sar's Paris student group concentrated on political struggle in the cities and the countryside. Although the KCP activities among the peasants, raising political consciousness and developing goodwill, turned into supreme assets to the Pol Pot group in the late revolutionary period, there is no convincing evidence, beyond confused and contradictory propaganda, that Saloth Sar's faction of the KCP had in fact been organized during the early revolutionary period for political violence.

By its own admission, when the KCP initiated guerrilla warfare in January 1968, there were *no modern weapons* in the provinces with which to prosecute the struggle. This would have been highly uncharacteristic for a movement as well organized as the KCP if it actually had taken up armed struggle before 1968. Most of the initial guerrilla raids were directed towards the seizure of government armories. This apparent sudden need for weapons at the beginning of 1968 would seem to be inconsistent with the assertion that the KCP had been engaged in armed struggle all through the pre-1968 period. Finally, the very fact that the Revolutionary Army of Kampuchea (RAK) was founded in the first week of 1968 would seem inexplicable had the KCP previously been engaged in armed struggle.[30]

In lieu of KCP internal party documents from this period that might definitively establish the case one way or another, there is considerable circumstantial evidence to suggest that Saloth Sar's group in fact was not prepared for armed struggle until the peasant rebellion and subsequent severe repressions of 1966 and 1967 forced it to revise its strategy of political struggle and resort to revolutionary violence. Though the leaders of the KCP may have fancied that they were preparing for armed struggle, when it came they did not seem prepared. Likewise, there are good reasons to believe that scattered remnants of the KPP group held to the line of armed struggle that they had embraced during the 1950s, but that in the 1960s, they had little effect beyond (*a*) providing for Sihanouk a convenient pretext for repression, and (*b*) providing for Saloth Sar a rudimentary heritage of armed struggle that he could appropriate as his own.

Samlaut

At the beginning of 1967, the tarnishing facade of Cambodian tranquillity was rudely shattered. It began in the province of Battambang. In Battambang, as has been previously noted, many peasants were suffering from rather severe economic dislocation associated with ever-widening disparities in wealth. Pressure on the peasants in this area increased late in 1966 when the government decided to build a sugar refinery at Kompong Kol, near Samlaut. Expropriating land needed for the project, provincial officials failed to compensate adequately the affected peasants.³¹ This failure led to an acute rise in local tensions, and set the fuse for the outbreak of conflict.

The sugar plantation project had been motivated by the desire to replace foreign exchange revenues lost by the break with the United States. This same logic led government officials to adopt a more aggressive policy of tax collection, and to this end military troops were used to collect taxes in kind from the rice storage areas in Battambang. In January, one of the collection detachments was, in the opinion of local peasants, too aggressive. The detachment was attacked by angry villagers and two members of the unit were killed.³²

At this point, the entire region seemed to rise up in rebellion. Peasants near Samlaut overran a government garrison, seized the arms stored there, and then disappeared into the jungle, triggering a massive combined police and military action aimed at pacifying the region. The order of the armory raiders strongly suggested to many that the rebellion was not entirely spontaneous. It was an irresistible opportunity to crack down on peasant discontent. In both internal and external propaganda, the government sought to convey the impression that foreign agents were the sole cause of the trouble, brushing aside any suggestion that economic hardship might be involved.

Prime Minister Lon Nol, acting as head of state while Sihanouk spent the first two and one-half months of 1967 in France, responded without mercy. In response to the raids on his armories, Lon Nol sent in paratroopers under the command of Colonel Chhay Lay. Sihanouk's brother-in-law, Secretary of State for Defense Oum Manorine, sent in units of the national police.³³ Both security forces proved enthusiastic, but of limited effectiveness. As one critic put it, "The pacification of the disturbed region was undertaken with the rude vigor peculiar to a soldiery who had been promised a monetary reward for each severed head they might forward to military headquarters in Phnom Penh."³⁴ Meanwhile, in the cities the remaining leftist figures still aboveground were collectively scapegoated, and some were arrested, with the remainder fleeing to the *maquis*.

Sihanouk returned to Cambodia in March to take personal command of the pacification operation. By the end of April, the situation had worsened to the extent that Sihanouk was able to obtain the resignation of Lon Nol as prime minister, putting Son Sann in his place. As May arrived, however, the crisis began to spread to the cities. After having been directly accused by Sihanouk of complicity in the Battambang uprising, Khieu Samphan and Hou Yuon disappeared into the *maquis*. The mood of Cambodia was such that everyone assumed, in spite of denials by the government, that these two prominent and popular leftists had been liquidated by Sihanouk's security forces. It is a measure of their popularity that some 15,000 demonstrators turned out in the streets of Phnom Penh on May 2 to protest the assumed assassinations.

The next day, the frightened head of state declared a state of emergency, and began to develop a new plan to deal with the crisis. Royal army troopers would be assisted by loyal local peasants armed with clubs (who could distinguish between friend and foe); they would enter the disaffected area and literally crush all actual and potential sources of subversion.

Although he later attempted to dissociate himself from these repressions, Sihanouk had casually noted in a 1972 interview that he "had read somewhere that 10,000 died" in the massive police action. He added the claim that his personal intervention restored peace and order.[35]

By the end of June, most of Battambang had indeed been beaten and cajoled into submission. In fact, however, the disturbance, which had previously spread to the cities, had now diffused from the city centers to the countryside in six other provinces: Pursat, Kompong Chhang, Kompong Cham, Kompong Thom, Kompong Speu, and Kampot. The harsh repression aimed at erasing the discontent had two significant effects. First, it radicalized increasingly large segments of the peasantry, making them more susceptible yet to the appeals of the *Khmer Rouge*. Second, it drove the top leadership of the *Khmer Rouge* underground, convincing any doubters that overt political struggle through existing national institutions was no longer a viable tactic in Cambodian politics. For many segments of the urban left and center-left, and virtually all KCP and KPP cadres in the overt struggle, it was a matter of physical survival: If they did not revise their tactics from overt political activism to covert political violence, they would eventually be eradicated by the Sihanouk regime. As Milton Osborne has commented, "Whatever the reasons for the actual date of the outbreak of the Samlaut rebellion, the die was cast for an accelerating contest between the left and the right of Cambodian politics, and in this contest Sihanouk increasingly appeared an onlooker rather than a participant."[36] These events heralded the end of the early revolutionary period, and the beginning of a seven-year civil war.

Notes

1. Mao Tse-tung, "Speech at the Meeting of the Supreme Soviets of the U.S.S.R. in Celebration of the 40th Anniversary of the Great October Socialist Revolution," in *Quotations from Chairman Mao Tse-tung* (Peking: Foreign Languages Press, 1976), pp. 75, 76.
2. François Ponchaud, *Cambodia: Year Zero* (New York: Holt, Rinehart and Winston, 1978), p. 157; and François Debré, *Cambodge: La Révolution De La Forêt* (Paris: Flammarion, 1976), p. 83.
3. Ben Kiernan, "Origins of Khmer Communism," *Southeast Asian Affairs* 1981, p. 175.
4. *Ibid.*, p. 176; also see Wilfred Burchett, *The China-Cambodia-Vietnam Triangle* (Chicago: Vanguard Books, 1981), p. 54; Ben Kiernan, "Conflict in the Kampuchean Communist Movement," *Journal of Contemporary Asia* 10: 1-2 (1980), pp. 7-74. This piece is an excellent history of Kampuchean communist ideology and organization; a revised version appears as Chapter 9 in Ben Kiernan and Chanthou Boua, eds., *Peasants and Politics in Kampuchea 1942-1981* (New York: M. E. Sharpe, 1982). Also see Kenneth M. Quinn, "Political Change in Wartime: The Khmer Krahom Revolution in Southern California 1970-1974," *Naval War College Review* 28:4 (Spring 1976), pp. 3-31; and Quinn's "Cambodia 1976: Internal Consolidation and External Expansion," *Asian Survey* 17:1 (January 1977), pp. 43-54. Both of the Quinn pieces are reflected in his "The Origins and Development of Radical Cambodian Communism" (Ph.D. diss., University of Maryland, 1982).
5. F. Ponchaud, *Year Zero*, p. 158.
6. B. Kiernan, "Conflict in the Kampuchean Communist Movement," p. 26; also see p. 66, n. 19.
7. *Ibid.*; the broadcast is transcribed in BBC SWB [Summary of World Broadcasts], October 1, 1977, FE/5629/C2/1 ff.
8. B. Kiernan, "Origins of Khmer Communism," p. 177.
9. Dan Burstein, ed., *Kampuchea Today: An Eyewitness Report from Cambodia* (Chicago: Call Pamphlets, 1978), p. 42.
10. There are many accounts of the affair with Khieu Samphan in August 1960, as it received wide press inside Cambodia at the time. Representative accounts are to be found in T. M. Carney, ed., *Communist Party Power in Kampuchea: Documents and Discussion*, Cornell University Southeast Asia Program, Data Paper #106 (Ithaca, N.Y.: Cornell University, 1977), pp. 63, 64; and William Shawcross, *Sideshow: Kissinger, Nixon and the Destruction of Cambodia* (New York: Simon and Schuster, 1979), p. 243.
11. It was widely assumed at the time that Lon Nol's secret police had eliminated Touch Samouth, but some speculation has been heard suggesting that he may actually have been Pol Pot's first victim. See B. Kiernan, "Conflict in the Kampuchean Communist Movement," p. 27.
12. B. Kiernan, "Origins of Khmer Communism," p. 177.

13. John W. Sewell, *The U.S. and World Development: Agenda 1978* (New York: Praeger, 1977); and F. P. Munson et al., *Area Handbook for Cambodia* (Washington, D.C.: USGPO, 1968), p. 84.

14. F. P. Munson, *Area Handbook*, p. 85.

15. Use of the broad and rather ambiguous term, "rightists," should not obscure the fact that some right-wing figures were ardent nationalists, some were democrats, and many were antimonarchist.

16. M. Caldwell and Lek Tan, *Cambodia in the Southeast Asian War* (New York: Monthly Review Press, 1975), p. 121; M. Osborne, *Politics and Power in Cambodia* (Victoria: Longman Australia, 1973), pp. 87, 88; R. M. Smith, *Cambodia's Foreign Policy* (Ithaca: Cornell University Press, 1965), pp. 125, 126.

17. Wilfred Burchett, ed., *My War with the CIA: The Memoirs of Prince Norodom Sihanouk* (New York: Random House, 1972), p. 134.

18. *Ibid.*, p. 140.

19. See, for example, M. Caldwell and Lek Tan, *Cambodia in the Southeast Asian War*, p. 131.

20. B. Kiernan, "Conflict in the Kampuchean Communist Movement," p. 29.

21. *Black Paper: Facts and Evidences of the Aggression and Annexation of Vietnam Against Kampuchea* (Department of Press and Information, Ministry of Foreign Affairs, Democratic Kampuchea, September, 1978 [rpt. New York: G. K. Ram]), p. 26.

22. *Ibid.*

23. Donald Kirk, "Revolution and Political Violence in Cambodia, 1970–1974," in J. J. Zasloff and M. Brown, eds., *Communism in Indochina: New Perspectives* (Lexington, MA: Lexington Books, 1975), p. 220.

24. BBC SWB, October 5, 1977, FE/5632/C14, cited in B. Kiernan, "Conflict in the Kampuchean Communist Movement," p. 29.

25. T. M. Carney, ed., *Communist Party Power in Kampuchea*, p. 37.

26. B. Kiernan, "Conflict in the Kampuchean Communist Movement," p. 29.

27. *Ibid.*; and BBC SWB, October 5, 1977, FE/5632/C/3.

28. See William Shawcross, *Sideshow*, p. 238.

29. *Ibid.*

30. See, for example, "The Struggle Between Kampuchea and Vietnam on the Issue of the Political Line from 1954 to 1970," in *Black Book*, pp. 26, 27.

31. F. Ponchaud, *Year Zero*, p. 162. Another French author cites an influx of Khmer Kroms (ethnic Khmers from the lower Mekong Delta region of then South Vietnam) to Sisophan and Battambang as a factor contributing to the escalation of local tensions. Sponsored by Prince Sihanouk, these refugees from the war in Vietnam were settled on land local peasants had apparently regarded as communal property. See François Debré, *Cambodge: La Révolution De La Forêt*, Chapter 7.

32. M. Osborne, *Power and Politics in Cambodia*, p. 99.
33. F. Ponchaud, *Year Zero*, p. 162.
34. Donald Lancaster, "The Decline of Prince Sihanouk's Regime," in J. J. Zasloff and A. E. Goodman, eds., *Indochina in Conflict: A Political Assessment* (Lexington, MA: Lexington Books, 1972), p. 52.
35. More precisely, Sihanouk said "j'ai lu quelque part que ces combats avaient fait dix mille morts. C'est faire beaucoup d'honneur à l'efficacité d'une armée royale . . ." (Norodom Sihanouk, *L'Indochine Vue De Peking: Entretiens avec Jean Lacouture* [Paris: Seuil, 1972], p. 90). See also M. Osborne, "Norodom Sihanouk: Leader of the Left?" in J. J. Zasloff and M. Brown, eds., *Communism in Indochina: New Perspectives* (Lexington, MA: D. C. Heath, 1975), p. 233, for a discussion of Sihanouk's denials of responsibility for the repression and deaths in Battambang and elsewhere during the 1967 rebellion and the subsequent two years of counterinsurgency war against the RAK.
36. M. Osborne, *Politics and Power in Cambodia*, p. 101; also see Ben Kiernan, "The Samlaut Rebellion and Its Aftermath 1967-1970: The Origins of Cambodia's Liberation Movement," Parts I and II, Working Papers nos. 4 and 5 (Melbourne, Australia: Monash University Centre of Southeast Asian Studies, 1976); and Ben Kiernan, "The Samlaut Rebellion, 1967-68," in Ben Kiernan and Chanthou Boua, eds., *Peasants and Politics in Kampuchea 1942-1981* (New York/London: Sharpe/Zed, 1982), pp. 166-205.

6
The Late Revolutionary Stage (1968–1975)

> Behold, a great red dragon, with seven heads and ten horns, and seven diadems upon his heads.
> His tail swept down a third of the stars in heaven, and cast them to the earth.
> And the dragon stood before the woman who was about to bear a child, that he might devour her child when she brought it forth.
> —Revelation 12:3,4[1]

In many respects, it is appropriate to refer to the "wars" in Southeast Asia between 1954 and 1975 in the singular, as the Second Indochina War. The fates of the Cambodians, Laotians, and Vietnamese were and are closely intertwined. Since 1954 Norodom Sihanouk had attempted to isolate his country from the conflicts in Laos and Vietnam, but this proved to be an impossible task for the prince.

Allied military operations in South Vietnam seemed to begin to show some meager progress after the massive U.S. troop insertions in 1965. The "clear and hold" strategy in the south had severely disrupted the infrastructure of the communist movement there, and to the U.S. command it seemed that its long efforts might at last yield some tangible political fruit. The aggressive "pacification" program was destroying the traditional village system, and their "waters" thus dried up, the revolutionary fish were left lying in the mud, to be turned to ashes by the covert U.S. counterinsurgency program, Operation Phoenix.

Before 1965, the North Vietnamese and the National Liberation Front had violated the sovereignty of Cambodia only sporadically. Violations of Cambodian territorial integrity had occurred on both sides in the conflict, by the noncommunists for purposes of reconnaissance, hot pursuit, and occasional air strikes, and by the communists for limited logistical and procurement activities, as well as for temporary sanctuary when they were retiring from action. As allied military operations in the Republic of Vietnam Military Regions II and III during 1965, 1966, and 1967 cleared out communist strongholds, however, the activities of the North Vietnamese Army (NVA) and the National Liberation Front (NLF) were pushed back from Saigon and eventually across the border into Cambodia. Particularly north and west of Saigon, where the open paddy provided little cover for communist operations, they were progressively forced to retreat across the Mekong River into Cambodia's "Parrot's Beak" and "Fishhook" areas, where their administrative and logistical facilities were rapidly expanding. During November and December 1969, for example, cement purchases on the open market in Phnom Penh rose dramatically, equaling total purchases for the previous ten months.[2] Clearly, the Vietnamese were digging in deep and hard in eastern Cambodia to implement their new long-haul strategy. Activities along the Ho Chi Minh Trail escalated, as did transshipments through the port of Sihanoukville. The escalation of North Vietnamese activities in 1968 and 1969 did not escape notice in Phnom Penh, and many Cambodians were openly alarmed at the increasing audacity of North Vietnamese operations in their country.

While the KCP struggled in the mountains, jungles, and remote villages against the authority of the Sihanouk regime, the increasing Vietnamese activity catalyzed throughout Cambodia a disagreement among the ruling elite concerning the tactics best employed to deal with the Vietnamese. This disagreement would become a very central factor, if not *the* central factor, in Sihanouk's fall from power. In turn, Sihanouk's fall proved to be the key political event of the seven-year civil war. After two years of relatively fruitless armed struggle by the KCP, Lon Nol's ascension to power was a blessing in disguise for the communists, for it gave them three most important new allies.

First, with Sihanouk and his royal prestige now associated with their movement, they had a most effective lever with which to work on the masses. Second, Lon Nol and Sirik Matak abandoned Sihanouk's centerpiece policy: Nonconfrontation with the Vietnamese was replaced by a policy of confrontation. Before 1970, the North Vietnamese and the NLF had been hesitant to aid their socialist brothers with the means to prosecute their struggle for the liberation of Cambodia. The abandoned, by and large empty Cambodian sanctuaries discovered by the U.S.-ARVN incursion forces in May 1970 were mute testimony to the abrupt change in the foreign policy of North Vietnam and the Provisional Revolutionary Government of South Vietnam (PRG). No longer were the communists able to expect any tacit cooperation from

Phnom Penh, and so the Vietnamese now threw their full support behind the Cambodian revolutionary movement.

Before 1970, the People's Republic of China (PRC), too, played both sides of the fence, offering verbal encouragement and political asylum to the Cambodian communists, while providing the Sihanouk regime with modern armaments (which the Sihanouk regime then used to kill Cambodian communists). Thus, the 1970 *coup* was a watershed event, driving the Sihanoukists, the Vietnamese communists, and the Chinese communists into the arms of the KCP. The stage was nearly set for a protracted civil war from which the KCP would emerge victorious. The only vacant role was that of friend and protector to the Lon Nol regime.

At the time of the Lon Nol–Sirik Matak *coup* in 1970, President Richard Nixon was attempting against strong domestic opposition to implement his much-vaunted "secret plan to end the war." "Vietnamization," Nixon believed, would bring "peace with honor," and his commitment to this idea seemed to be total. Nixon and his chief foreign policy advisor, Henry Kissinger, were quick to realize the value of an anticommunist regime in Cambodia for their plans in Vietnam. With a minimal commitment of personnel, the United States could create an enveloping second front against the North Vietnamese simply by arming the Republican forces in Cambodia to the teeth. In Nixon's ringing phrase, this was to be "the Nixon Doctrine in its purest form."[3] This policy would reduce the pressure on the exposed flank of the South Vietnamese government, and would perhaps allow time for the orderly withdrawal of U.S. forces and the maturation of the Vietnamization process.

A natural consequence of the resulting U.S. intervention in Cambodia after March 1970 was that the previously divided communist movement in Indochina faced a new and aggressive common enemy: "U.S. imperialism." Thus, there emerged a united front including Laotian, Vietnamese, and Cambodian communists. (See Figure 6.1.) In reality, however, the United Front of the Three Indochinese Peoples (UFTIP) was a facade behind which each of the "allied" factions vigorously pursued self-interested ends. The primary beneficiary of this liaison was the KCP, profiting in the form of substantial military assistance provided by the North Vietnamese. The North Vietnamese, too, enjoyed the benefits of this alliance, reaping substajntial propaganda advantages from this political and military liaison. The remaining three full partners in the UFTIP—the *Khmer Rumdo* (Sihanoukists), the *Pathet Lao,* and the PRG of South Vietnam—played only supporting roles in the unfolding Cambodian drama. From

FIGURE 6.1
EVOLUTION OF KCP TIES - THE RISE AND FALL OF ANGKAR LOEU

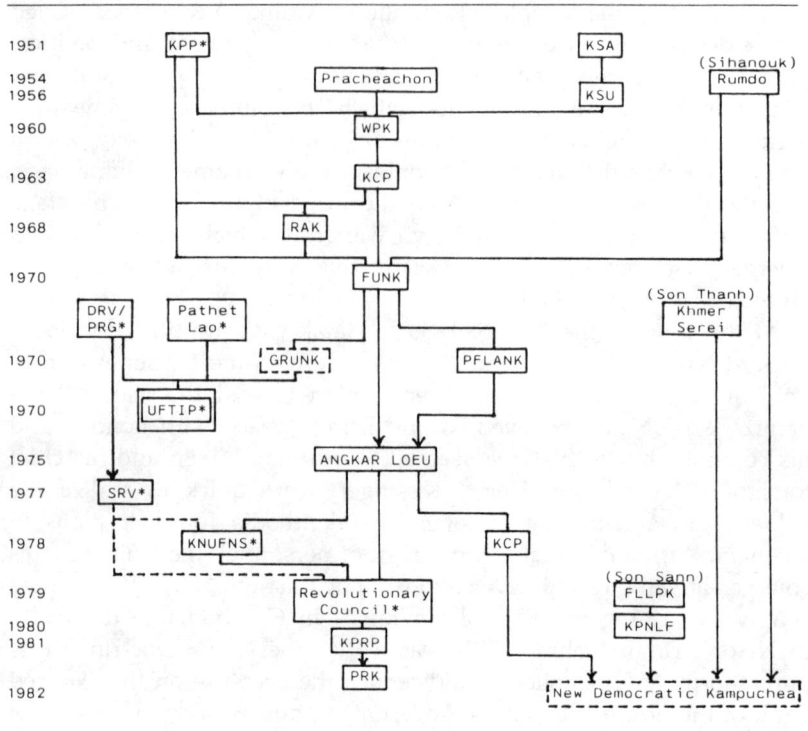

behind this unconvincing banner of unity, communism fought its way to victory throughout Indochina.

This central chapter will examine in detail the entire late revolutionary period (1968-1975). The guerrilla war being prosecuted by the KCP will serve as a background against which one may view the disintegration of Sihanouk's political regime. It is appropriate to begin with a few comments on the problems of creating revolutionary attitudes among a peasant population. As the deteriorating economic situation of Cambodian peasants and the contradictions between traditional rural and modern urban cultures provided the seed of revolution, so did the disintegration of Sihanouk's regime provide a fertile soil to nurture what would become the most radical revolution in modern political history.

Key to Figure 6.1

Acronyms:

KPP - Khmer People's Party (or Khmer People's Revolutionary Party)
KSA - Khmer Students' Association (Paris)
KSU - Khmer Students' Union (Paris)
WPK - Worker's Party of Kampuchea
KCP - Kampuchean Communist Party
RAK - Revolutionary Army of Kampuchea
DRV/PRG - Democratic Republic of Vietnam/Provisional Revolutionary Government
FUNK - National United Front of Kampuchea
GRUNK - Royal Khmer Government of National Unification
PFLANK - People's National Liberation Armed Forces of Kampuchea
UFTIP - United Front of the Three Indochinese Peoples
SRV - Socialist Republic of Vietnam
KNUFNS - Khmer National United Front for National Salvation
KCP - Ousted "Pol Pot faction" reverts to old name for two years.
FLLPK - Front Nationale de Liberation du Peuple Khmer
KPNLF - Khmer People's National Liberation Front
KPRP - Khmer People's Revolutionary Party
PRK - People's Republic of Kampuchea

Symbols:

— — — — — —   Indirect Ties

```
|‾‾‾‾|
|____|
```
Regime in Exile

☐ Organization

─────────── Direct Ties

```
| * |
```
Explicit Vietnamese Ties

▭ International Organization

Regime Formation ⟶

The rise of Lon Nol; his offensive against the North Vietnamese, and their reaction to it; the intervention of the United States; the emergence of UFTIP; the explosive growth of the Cambodian revolutionary movement—all these factors combined to create the conditions for a vicious five-year struggle out of which would rise Democratic Kampuchea. Forged in the crucible of war, the spirit of *Angkar Loeu* (the state apparatus of Democratic Kampuchea) reflected the harsh experiences of its birth by fire. The circumstances of the entire civil war, and their impacts upon the character of the emergent state, are the topics of this chapter

Guerrilla Warfare (1968–1970)

To much of the Cambodian urban elite, "nationalism" and "patriotism" referred to the maintenance and expansion of Cambodia's place in the contemporary international economic and political systems. Economic rewards generated for members of this elite through contact with "advanced" industrial and commercial powers were salient factors in their worldview. They also felt that the continued encroachments by Vietnamese communists threatened both their collective access to the Western economic system and their individual participation in it. Sihanouk not only seemed powerless to turn back the Vietnamese; his policies continued to threaten the economic position of some members of the elite.

For the rural peasants, however, who constituted some 90 percent of the population, "patriotism" and "nationalism" referred to the maintenance of traditional values, including particularly the social and economic ethics embedded in the *Hinayana*, attachment to home village and extended family, and reverence for the land and the king. Thus the peasantry remained an inherently conservative, traditional force in Cambodian society, profoundly antirevolutionary even when suffering from economic hardships. The peasants may have consciously resented some segments of the urban society, especially some agencies of the government, but it was another matter entirely for the revolution to tap this largely latent conflict and turn it into revolutionary commitment and recruitment.

Social psychological research has shed some light in this area, suggesting how individuals can become committed to a revolutionary cause. Three basic mechanisms of attitudinal and behavioral change are "compliance," "identification," and "internalization." All these processes can be observed in the case at hand, aiding in our understanding of the spreading loci of revolutionary activity in Cambodia.[4]

In compliance, an individual may conform to revolutionary behavior because of external inducements. The individual conforms not because s/he believes in the cause, but rather in order to gain certain rewards or avoid certain punishments. The degree of compliance in a given population is dependent upon the perceived *power* of the agents seeking to induce change, from the point of view of the receiver.[5] In areas under the control of the KCP, close attention was paid to the compliance of the population. Rewards for "correct thought" were widely employed to encourage compliance. These positive incentives included such things as social privileges (e.g., differential access to food rations) and social status (e.g., appointment to positions of authority). Some KCP factions, notably the Saloth Sar group, became notorious for injudicious use of negative incentives—such as execution—to encourage compliance. As the power of the revolutionary movement grew visibly, there was less need for compliance-inducing violence on the part of the revolutionaries, but by then the violent behavior patterns had become institutionalized and thus somewhat resistant to change.

A second method of attitude change is identification. Here the individual conforms to the revolutionary cause because s/he derives satisfaction from the very act of participation. Camaraderie and a feeling of belonging to a group are important in the process of identification. The extent to which identification will be important as a source of revolutionary recruitment depends upon the relative *attractiveness*—in terms of preexisting social values—of the revolutionary group as compared to the *status quo* group. In his study of the Vietnamese revolution, Paul Bernan suggested that greater than average needs for identification among peasants were related to four factors: disruption of village life, youth, uncertainty, and severe personal experiences with government and foreign troops.[6] Clearly, then, events such as occurred at Samlaut, and especially the widespread area bombing by the U.S. Air Force after 1968, would render peasants more susceptible to revolutionary recruitment. These effects upon the young people of Cambodia will be an object of particular interest.

Finally, with internalization, the revolutionary cause is or becomes congruent with the individual's value system. Ideology thus serves a personal-social function. The revolutionary ideology provides the individual with an intellectual framework through which s/he can understand and explain his or her life-conditions. The importance of internalization in revolutionary recruitment will vary with the degree of *competence* attributed by the receiver to the source of the revolutionary ideology. When the ideology is internalized, the individual believes in the moral rightness of the revolutionary cause. I shall return to the question of the competence of the message source when I have occasion to consider the problems of legitimacy faced by the incipient revolution.

Together, compliance, identification, and internalization are the processes through which an ideological program spreads across a population. Thus, these concepts describe the mechanism of ideology's transmutation function. Although the KCP was able to attract some small numbers of recruits through induced compliance and a number through identification during 1968 and 1969, its limited legitimacy among the ethnic Khmer population at large made it unlikely that the KCP would easily achieve a mass following. Committed cadres who had fully internalized the communist doctrine remained a precious resource throughout the period of armed struggle.

Amid these circumstances, the young Revolutionary Army of Kampuchea (RAK) grew only very slowly in its first two years. The social conditions of Cambodia and the political program of the KCP, as well as its administrative abilities, did not yet favor widespread success by the RAK. One analyst argues that the conditions necessary for the successful conduct of a guerrilla war are the following:

>   a) mass support flowing from the alienation of a large proportion of the population from the central government;
>   b) the ability of the insurgents to out-administer the central government in rural areas;
>   c) selective use of terror to demonstrate negative sanctions for noncompliance; and
>   d) highly visible and immediately beneficial social reforms to demonstrate the advantages of the revolutionary order.[7]

Between 1968 and 1969, none of these four conditions effectively existed throughout Cambodia. Although many of the peasants may have been becoming increasingly alienated from the Sihanouk regime (though perhaps not from Sihanouk himself), and although the RAK certainly was able to employ negative sanctions for inappropriate behavior (as well as to increase insecurity in government-held areas), its administrative abilities and sociopolitical program had not yet developed to the point where it could generate and sustain mass support on a nationwide scale.

After having been founded in the last weeks of 1967 or first days of 1968, the RAK immediately set about the task of arming itself. The Vietnamese, hoping to encourage Sihanouk's tolerant attitude, not only failed to provide armaments to the movement, but actually tried to discourage its activities. (This fact would be cited again and again by the government of Democratic Kampuchea after 1975 as evidence of the ill-will of North Vietnam toward the Kampuchean communists.) The Chinese also were of little or no help, and in fact may have been a negative factor in the struggle of the KCP. On January 4, 1968, the PRC delivered a large shipment of modern armaments to Sihanouk's military leaders (notably, Lon Nol, who had negotiated for the equipment).[8] These items included jet fighter and bomber aircraft, cargo and training aircraft, artillery, automatic weapons, ammunition, and explosives. This delivery certainly did not represent solidarity between the communists of Cambodia and those of China. Even the Soviet Union got into the act, agreeing to supply new military equipment to Cambodia in February of the same year. These blatantly anti-KCP activities on the part of well-established communist parties of the major powers in Southeast Asia convinced the leadership of the KCP that self-reliance was the only way they could prevail. Proletarian internationalism was a sham, and if the KCP was to survive, it would have to guard vigilantly against the predations of foreign parties claiming to be brothers. No one could be trusted. No one.

Thus, according to a sympathetic observer, "1968–1970 was for the [KCP] a period of isolated defiance, self-confidence and success."[9] Their success, such as it was, was very modest. Saloth Sar himself, in describing the first months of revolutionary warfare, noted that in some areas "we experienced considerable difficulties."[10] The first guerrilla raids by the RAK, as has been previously noted, were almost exclusively devoted to the capture of government armaments. This would become a common pattern of procurement for the Cambodian communists, but at first the pickings were very lean. The revolutionary cadres engaged in "armed struggle" in the eastern provinces as late as March 1968 still possessed no modern firearms, while in the north and northeast, only four guns were netted from the guerrilla raids of the first months. According to Saloth Sar, his headquarters for those early years in the mountains of the northeast where the Central Committee of the KCP was based had fewer than ten guns for the defense of the base.

In the southwest and northwest, where the military actions had first been initiated starting on January 17, the RAK had a slightly better record, capturing a few hundred arms from armory raids there. Although the territory under the control of the revolution grew slowly but surely over the period of guerrilla warfare, its bases of operation remained small, isolated one from another, and spread throughout various remote areas.

Nonetheless, Sihanouk took the RAK seriously from the very beginning. On January 27, 1968, less than two weeks after the self-proclaimed initiation of armed struggle by the KCP, Sihanouk noted that "the Khmer Communists have decided that they are going to wage war until Sihanouk and the *Sangkum* disappear."[11] The pattern was one of a steadily rising level of violent contact between government and insurgent forces. By the end of March 1968, Sihanouk's army had reported killing 182 RAK soldiers. On a single operation in April, 89 KCP cadres and soldiers were wiped out by government security forces.

Spurned by the communist parties of Laos, North Vietnam, South Vietnam, China, and the Soviet Union, misunderstood and largely ignored by the peasant population at large, and uncompromisingly tracked by Sihanouk's security forces, the KCP and its revolutionary army were unable to generate a dynamic recruitment drive. Beginning with some 2,000 regular guerrilla soldiers at the beginning of 1968, the RAK had grown to less than twice that size by the beginning of 1970.[12] Though the RAK was said to have some 50,000 "irregular" troops, these were probably confined to non-combatant support functions such as mess and billet duty. Meanwhile, the relative abundance of personnel and material channeled through Cambodia by the North Vietnamese provided additional sting to the resentment felt by the neglected KCP.

Against this background, Sihanouk was not least among those who were concerned about and resentful of the rise in Vietnamese communist activity in Cambodia. Although Sihanouk reserved his meager 35,000-man *Force Armée Royale Khmer* (FARK) for operations against the RAK and the KCP, late in 1968 he began to initiate psychological, diplomatic, and economic moves against the North Vietnamese. The tightly controlled Cambodian press began to fan public resentment against the Vietnamese presence. For some time, however, Sihanouk continued to maintain most of the official aspects of his policy of nonconfrontation. Then, in May 1969, he began to order the arbitrary seizure of cargoes being transshipped by Vietnamese communists through the port of Sihanoukville to the war staging areas along the border.[13]

Sihanouk's intent was probably simply to get the attention of the Vietnamese communists, so that he could attempt to negotiate agreements giving him more control over their activities. It was no problem to arrange for the seizure of Vietnamese war material, for FARK personnel and resources were routinely and openly assigned to assist in smoothing the complex logistics of the huge supply effort.[14] Sihanouk's bothersome interferences with the normal flow of Vietnamese supplies brought immediate diplomatic reactions from North Vietnam and the NLF.

Continuing into early 1970, similar economic pressures were turned on the North Vietnamese, but they had little effect other than to stimulate further diplomatic exchanges. The fact that these measures bore so little fruit in terms of getting the NVA/NLF to evacuate Cambodian territory only reinforced the arguments of those who had held all along for direct military action against them.

Sihanouk continued to resist this option in line with his belief that the communists would ultimately prevail in Vietnam. The 1968 Tet Offensive—so often cited in the West as the major event in the evolution of U.S. public opinion about the war—had a deep impact on Sihanouk, too. It became clear that the pacification of the population in South Vietnam was nowhere near as effective as the Johnson administration had claimed and continued to claim.

On June 1, 1969, the Provisional Revolutionary Government (PRG) of South Vietnam was created, and less than two weeks later, Sihanouk's Cambodia became the first nation to establish formal diplomatic relations with the PRG. Negotiations began immediately, and on September 25, 1969, a "Trade and Payment Agreement" was concluded, legalizing the Sihanoukville port supply operation and providing the Sihanouk regime with greater knowledge of the true extent of the supply effort. Needless to say, the trade agreement was abhorred by many of Sihanouk's conservative advisors. It may have been at this point that Lon Nol began seriously to contemplate the removal of his head of state.

The Cambodian right regarded Sihanouk's diplomatic, economic, and propaganda efforts against the North Vietnamese as totally inadequate to cope with the magnitude of the domestic security threat. Over and above the facts that the Vietnamese communists occupied a significant role in the Cambodian economy as well as a significant chunk of Cambodian territory, the domestic communists were beginning to gain some small ground, particularly among the national minorities of Cambodia. The KCP had already been successful in recruiting among the Pors, a tribe inhabiting certain parts of Battambang province. Ethnic Thais in the Cardamom Mountains in the east and the Jarai in the mountainous areas of Stung Treng had never proven to have much loyalty to Phnom Penh regimes, and they also had been good sources of recruits for the communists. Saloth Sar and his lieutenants had retreated to the mountainous and inaccessible northeastern parts of Cambodia in the early 1960s, and by early 1969 had achieved a near complete takeover of certain Montagnard tribes of the *Khmer Loeu* in the Ratanakiri and Mondolkiri areas.

The loss of the Montagnard tribes to the KCP was a key event in the sequence that led to the reestablishment of diplomatic relations between the United States and Cambodia on June 3, 1969. Still, many on the right feared that Sihanouk's actions would be too little, too late. Foremost among Sihanouk's critics was his royal cousin, First Vice-President Sirik Matak. He had been among those passed over by the French in 1941 for the throne, but this long royal rivalry was overshadowed by differences on policy. Sirik vigorously opposed Sihanouk's neutralist foreign policy and his "socialist" domestic policies, constantly working to bring change. Sirik had been instrumental in the reestablishment of relations with the United States in June, and he partly succeeded in moving some denationalization measures through the National Assembly in November 1969. This was the train of events that would eventually lead Sihanouk to retire, temporarily he thought, from the political scene in the first weeks of 1970 for his annual health-cure in the south of France.

Perhaps more dangerous to Sihanouk's political position than Sirik, however, was Lon Nol, who commanded the respect of the royal army commanders. As early as mid-1969, Lon Nol began seriously to contemplate getting rid of Sihanouk. According to an account given by Son Thai Nguyen, Son Ngoc Thanh's brother, Lon Nol met with the *Khmer Serei* leader in September of 1969.[15] Although it remains unclear whether Lon Nol actually met personally with Son Ngoc Thanh, it is relatively certain that they entered negotiations in September to consider rallying the *Khmer Serei* mercenary army to Lon Nol's defense should the royal army prove loyal to the head of state in any future confrontation.[16] The fact that Lon Nol sought an alliance with Son Ngoc Thanh confirms beyond any doubt that he had decided that a break with Sihanouk was inevitable. The *Khmer Serei*, and Son Ngoc Thanh in particular, were bitterly sworn personal enemies of Sihanouk, and the feeling was mutual. Had Sihanouk learned of these secret meetings between his military chief and his chief opponent in exile, he would most likely have launched an immediate full-scale attack on Lon Nol. But it was to be Lon Nol who would launch the first attack in the escalating power struggle among Cambodian elites.

The *Coup*

On March 17, 1970, as evening fell over Phnom Penh, armored units of the FARK took up strategic positions around the city. The international airport was closed to traffic, with a view to preventing the originally scheduled return of the prince to Cambodia on the eighteenth. The next morning, summoned to an early emergency session, delegates to the Cambodian National Assembly found their chambers under military guard. Under the watchful eye of General In Tam, the members of Sihanouk's *Sangkum* National Assembly voted 92-0 with color-coded ballots in favor of deposing their founder and head of state, Samdech Norodom Sihanouk. The prince was informed of his fall by Soviet Prime Minister Alexei Kosygin in Moscow, where he had gone to seek the help of the Soviets in pressuring the North Vietnamese.

The following day, the U.S. Department of State declared that the change of regime had been conducted in a constitutionally prescribed manner, and that therefore the question of diplomatic recognition for the new regime did not arise. It was widely assumed in foreign capitals, and to some extent in the world press, that the *coup* had been encouraged, if not actually engineered, by the Nixon administration. Sihanouk himself wrote in his memoirs that the CIA had tried to overthrow him since at least 1959, and apparently he believes to this day that it finally succeeded in March 1970.

Sihanouk was not without good reason to suspect the United States of complicity in his fall from power. In the years following his refusal to join the anticommunist Southeast Asian Treaty Organization (SEATO) in 1956, brothers Allen and John Foster Dulles (Director, Central Intelligence Agency [DCI], and secretary of state, respectively) orchestrated an international campaign to unseat Sihanouk, including diplomatic, economic, and military pressures from South Vietnam, Thailand, and Laos, as well as CIA and U.S. Army support for the anti-Sihanouk guerrilla army, the *Khmer Serei*, led by Son Ngoc Thanh.[17] Sihanouk's suspicion of the United States was heightened in 1959 when a provincial governor, Dap Chhuon, was exposed in a plot to rebel against Sihanouk. Apparently, the plot involved a widespread collection of anti-Sihanouk elements.[18] Operating from South Vietnam, Sam Sary and his small band of fighters; operating from Thailand, Son Ngoc Thanh and his *Khmer Serei;* operating in Laos, the right-wing Laotian warlord, Boun Oum—all were in league with Dap Chhuon, and the CIA had its hand in the action. CIA agent [name censored][19] was assigned to keep track of the goings-on. William Colby, who at the time was posted to the CIA station in Saigon but was to become DCI, later held that U.S. involvement in the 1959 plot was only indirect: "The Thais and the South Vietnamese were in league with Dap Chhuon and we had links with them. So Sihanouk assumed that we were *behind* them. In fact, we were urging them to desist, but as part of our intelligence coverage, we developed an agent in the Dap Chhuon entourage. We gave him a radio to keep us informed, not to encourage Dap Chhuon."[20]

Such cloak-and-dagger games only added to Sihanouk's suspicion of the United States. Things he did not know would only have reinforced his misgivings about accepting aid from the United States. In 1959, the U.S. Department of the Army contracted the production of a 471-page study called *Psychological Operations: Cambodia.*[21] This document recommended ways to influence the "middle class" and officer corps in Cambodia, creating favorable dispositions with respect to the United States, fear of communism, and respect for the power of the United States. These and similar activities, such as U.S. support of the *Khmer Serei*, continued through the 1960s. Yet, available evidence indicates that direct involvement by the United States in the 1970 *coup* against Sihanouk was negligible at most.

When Nixon was informed of the *coup*—in the past tense—he flew into a rage. "What the hell do those clowns do out there at Langley?" the President demanded of Secretary of State Rogers,[22] who could hardly be expected to know what went on deep in the heart of CIA headquarters. For its part, the CIA had been performing in classic bureaucratic style. Its candidate, Son Ngoc Thanh, was ensconced at U.S. Special Forces camps in South Vietnam along with his *Khmer Serei* mercenaries, inconveniently distanced from the real action, which was occurring in Phnom Penh. About a week before the *coup*, U.S. agents in Southeast Asia caught wind of the impending plot, and duly cabled a report to Washington. That report, which somehow got lost in the daily cable traffic and did not turn up until the very day of the *coup*, became the subject of a Special Foreign Intelligence Advisory Board investigation ordered by a chastened Nixon.[23] Henry Kissinger, in an uncharacteristic moment of candor, reported that "we neither encouraged Sihanouk's overthrow nor knew about it in advance. We did not even grasp its significance for many weeks."[24] The CIA's William Colby later reported that "Lon Nol may have been encouraged by the fact the United States was working with Son Ngoc Thanh. I don't know of any specific assurances he was given but the obvious conclusion for him, given the political situation in South Vietnam and Laos, was that he would be given United States support."[25]

Obvious, indeed, for almost immediately following the *coup*, several units of Son Ngoc Thanh's *Khmer Serei* troopers were transported from their Green Beret bases in South Vietnam to Phnom Penh and other major cities to aid in providing security for the new Cambodian regime. In addition, 3,000 to 4,000 Civilian Irregular Defense Group (CIDG) troops were transported to Phnom Penh on April 17, 1970, from their bases in South Vietnam.[26] The CIDGs had been formed under the supervision of the U.S. Special Forces in the early 1960s. These paramilitary units were manned by ethnic Khmer living in Vietnam, where almost half a million Khmer lived in the lower reaches of the Mekong Delta, holdovers from a time when Cambodian sovereignty spread far beyond its current boundaries.

Less than one month after the *coup*, Lon Nol was on the agenda for National Security Council (NSC) meetings, and Nixon was sending angry memos to his assistant for national security affairs, Henry Kissinger, complaining of Senate obstructions of his efforts to aid the struggling regime. "My immediate inclination," Nixon remembers, "was to do everything possible to help Lon Nol."[27]

President Nixon's advisors, however, were generally lined up against the proposition to intervene openly in Cambodia. Secretary of State William Rogers and Secretary of Defense Melvin Laird "strongly recommended" keeping out of the Cambodian fray on the grounds that U.S. involvement would provide Moscow, Peking, and Hanoi with a potent propaganda advantage. This fear was to be realized in the UFTIP. DCI Richard Helms argued that the Lon Nol regime did not stand a chance, supported from the United States or no. Nixon himself had some strong doubts concerning the viability of the regime. In an April 27, 1970, memo to Kissinger, Nixon said, "I do not believe he [Lon Nol] is going to survive. . . . in any event, we must do something symbolic to help him survive."[28] Lon Nol might be useful to the United States, even if he wasn't going to be around for very long.

The U.S. Role

In response to charges that the Nixon administration acted rashly in deciding to send the U.S. Army and the Army of the Republic of Vietnam (ARVN) into Cambodia in April of 1970, Henry Kissinger has argued that "the final decision . . . was not a maniacal eruption of irrationality as the uproar afterwards sought to imply. It was taken carefully, with much hesitation, by a man who had to discipline his nerves almost daily to face his subordinates."[29] Nonetheless, Kissinger had previously noted that there "had been no consideration of attacking the sanctuaries (in Cambodia) before April 21. The final decision was taken on April 28."[30] Seven days, given prior contingency planning in this computer age, would seem sufficient, perhaps, to consider and plan a major cross-border military engagement with combined forces, facing combined forces.

However, Nixon himself recalls that the entire sequence of decisions took place over the space of four and one-half days. He made the decision on April 26 to attack only *two* North Vietnamese base areas located in Cambodia, informing his surprised secretaries of state and defense as the orders were being implemented half a world away on April 28, and informing the American people in a terse nationwide televised address on the thirtieth. In this speech, Nixon justified his actions as absolutely necessary for the "peace, freedom and justice" of the world.[31]

The next morning he abruptly changed the plan. Nixon went to the Pentagon, shocking the colonels and generals there with the sudden query, "Could we take out *all* of the sanctuaries?" He was greeted with stunned silence by his top military planners. Nixon recalled the moment with obvious satisfaction: "Everyone seemed to be waiting for someone else to speak. Usually I like to mull things over, but I made a very uncharacteristic decision. I said, 'I want to take out all of those sanctuaries. Make whatever plans are necessary, and then just do it.'"[32] Such is the nature of the power available to the leader of the "free world," the president of the United States. And it is a curious sort of 'careful hesitation' displayed by Nixon, particularly for a man who had repeatedly shown the film, "Patton," during the crisis, inviting his somewhat perturbed staff to view the "inspiring" war movie on more than one occasion.[33]

The combined incursion began at the end of April, and U.S. armed forces remained on the ground in Cambodia only until the end of June, although the South Vietnamese army (ARVN) remained for more than one and one-half years before being driven out by increasing communist pressure. On the surface, it was easily possible for Nixon to go on nationwide television and announce that the entire operation was a brilliant success. Many tons of war material had been captured or destroyed. Hundreds of concrete bunkers along the Cambodian border with Vietnam, previously used to shelter their occupants from the U.S. Air Force, were blasted to pieces by the search and destroy teams.

A history of the Cambodian incursion published by the U.S. Army Center for Military History, however, contains some inconsistencies that give one cause to wonder whether Nixon's self-serving assessments of the incursion were not a bit superficial. After noting that the incursion "compelled" the NVA to "surface and commit flagrant acts of violence against Cambodia: occupying the northeastern part of the country; surrounding and threatening Phnom Penh; interdicting the Mekong River and the major land lines of communication . . . etc.," the author of this history incredibly goes on to assert in the very next paragraph of his conclusion that the incursion "effectively helped clear the enemy's initial pressure" against the Lon Nol regime.[34]

This claim is politely disputed by the man who at the time was deputy chief of the FANK's general staff. Sak Sutsakhan suggests that "on the Cambodian side, we observed that these operations (the incursion) consisted of frontal, rather than enveloping maneuvers. This gave the enemy ample opportunity for seeking refuge deeper inside Cambodia." Discreetly noting that the goals of the incursion did not take into account the welfare of Cambodia, Sak observes that "solely within the framework of Vietnamization as the U.S. command had intended it . . . it might be considered a success. . . ."[35] Indeed, Nixon claimed that the incursion had destroyed "Central Office for South Vietnam" (COSVN), allegedly that place where General Giap and Ho Chi Minh gathered by candlelight to plot their conquest of the south. In fact, however, while the incursion forces destroyed the physical plant of some important NVA/PRG base facilities, communist operations centers had already been transferred deep into Cambodia to the town of Kratie, which had been cleared of civilians to serve as the new general headquarters in view of the new aggressiveness shown by the American commanders.

One of the most important military operations of the combined U.S.-ARVN incursion into Cambodia, code-named TOAN THANG 43, occurred beginning on May 1, 1970. Units of the First Cavalry Division (the famed Airmobile Division), the Eleventh Armored Calvalry, and the ARVN Airborne Division moved from Binh Long and Tay Ninh Provinces in South Vietnam across the Cambodian border into the Fishhook area in search of the legendary COSVN. In the course of the operation, a huge facility dubbed "the city" was uncovered. It extended over some three square kilometers, and contained mess, medical, storage, training, signal, farming, and machine repair facilities. The captured and destroyed material from "the city" demonstrated the highly advanced state of Vietnamese preparations there: Eighteen permanent structures and 182 weapons caches were uncovered in the general area, containing, among other things, 1,282 individual weapons, 202 crew-served weapons, some two and one-half million rounds of ammunition, 40 tons of food, and some 30 tons of miscellaneous high explosives. Three hundred and five motor vehicles, mostly cargo trucks, were destroyed in "the city." Yet, enemy resistance in the area was generally light and diversionary.

More telling than the list of captured and destroyed material, however, were intelligence reports about the "ones that got away." According to the U.S. Army incursion history, "the number of vehicles discovered in this area represented only a small fraction of the larger fleet of trucks that the enemy used in Cambodia for supply purposes. . . . prior to the initiation of TOAN THANG 43, our observation planes had sighted several enemy truck convoys leaving the objective area; they were probably moving out part of the supplies in anticipation of our incursion."[36]

These materials were transported to more secure areas on the west side of the Mekong River, deep inside Cambodia beyond the wrath of the incursion's search and destroy teams. There they would be used to expand the small RAK into Cambodia's new fighting force, the People's National Liberation Armed Forces of Kampuchea (PFLANK). From this point on over the next two to two and one-half years, the Cambodian civil war rapidly took on the appearance of a proxy war, with foreign forces training, equipping, and fielding Cambodian armies.

In the nine months following the *coup*, the Lon Nol regime became virtually totally dependent on the United States for food, war material, and tactical and strategic air support. Nixon and Kissinger have made it clear over the years that they would have liked to intervene much more extensively yet, and would have but for Congressional interference. A staff report prepared by the U.S. Senate Foreign Relations Committee in December 1970 asserted that the "U.S. has been virtually the sole supplier of new arms, ammunition and aircraft to the Cambodian military. . . . the majority of the bombing and support strikes against the enemy in Cambodia are conducted by the United States and South Vietnamese Air Forces."[37] The U.S. role in Cambodia grew to include a variety of administrative duties normally performed by the national sovereign, including military and civilian intelligence gathering, interrogation of enemy prisoners, and "end use checks" to see that the equipment was being properly used.[38]

By 1973, the very existence of the Khmer Republic would become entirely dependent upon the continued application of U.S. B-52 airstrikes. Even though Lon Nol's defense seemed tenacious, costing the Cambodian people some one million lives (or 12 to 15 percent of the entire population), the survival of the Khmer Republic depended less on the abilities of its leadership than on U.S. military assistance. Without U.S. dollars and bombs, Lon Nol would have been less than a paper tiger, no more than a paper pussycat.

It began with symbolic shipments of both captured enemy and CIA-issue small arms and token grants of $5 million, then $10 million one month after the *coup*, directly ordered by Nixon. The American commitment grew apace until Nixon publicly pledged "all-out support" for the Khmer Republic on November 21, 1973. This personal promise from the president of the United States lapsed 10 months later with the resignation of Richard Milhous Nixon. In the words of the last head of state of the Khmer Republic, "the departure of President Nixon sealed the fate of the non-communist side in Indochina."[39]

Examining the magnitude of U.S. aid to the Lon Nol regime reveals the extent to which that regime depended on American largesse for its existence. Between 1970 and 1975, U.S. aid to the Khmer Republic totaled more than $2.3 billion.[40] Of this total, some $503 million was in the form of direct aid of various sorts, while $1.8 billion was in the form of military training and supplies. Of the $1.8 billion in training and supplies for FANK, about $1.2 billion was provided under the U.S. Military Assistance Program (MAP) for the Khmer Republic. This military aid was disbursed according to the schedule in Table 6.1.

These MAP funds, combined with other forms of aid from the United States, constituted a very large proportion of total expenditures and income in the Khmer Republic. In order to put these numbers into the proper perspective, note that in 1965 the total national income for Cambodia was $686 million.[41] In 1974, the estimated fiscal year (FY) total U.S. aid to the Khmer Republic was $688.5 million.[42] If ever one needs a definition for the term "client state," the case at hand provides a suitable illustration. In these circumstances, it was easy for the insurgents convincingly to represent the Khmer Republic as nothing more than the puppet of imperialists.

According to Hildebrand and Porter,[43] 95.1 percent of the revenue of the Lon Nol regime in 1974 was constituted by U.S. foreign assistance programs, 2.7 percent coming from other foreign aid, and a paltry 2.2 percent from domestic income sources. Of this U.S. aid during 1974, only $575 million of the estimated $688.5 million total has been directly traced, because of complex shifting of funds by the Nixon administration in its circumvention of several pieces of legislation, such as the Cooper-Church Amendment, which prohibited the use of U.S. funds for military activities in Cambodia. Of this $575 million, $325 million was in the form of direct military assistance, $175 million in food aid, and another $75 million in other economic assistance. Much of the food aid was provided under the U.S. Food for Peace Program.

Authorized under U.S. Public Law 480, the Food for Peace Program mandates two types of food aid. Title I covers grants or loans of food to governments for sale through commercial or official channels in order to generate local currency for military spending. Title II covers free donations of food for distribution to the needy.[44] Given the Congressional prediliction through the 1970s to shun military entanglements in Southeast Asia, American legislators were unwilling to subsidize Lon Nol's armory under Title I as the Khmer war began to drag on. Less than $50,000 was mandated for Cambodia under Title I over FY73 and FY74. This did not inhibit the Khmer Republic. In the first half of FY75 (July 1974 to January 1975), $72.5 million was granted under PL-480 Title II to the Khmer Republic, while only

TABLE 6.1
DISBURSEMENT SCHEDULE
U.S. MILITARY ASSISTANCE PROGRAM, KHMER REPUBLIC

FY71	FY72	FY73	FY74	FY75
$180	$220	$131	$414	$254

Note: All figures are approximate amounts in millions of current U.S. dollars per fiscal year (FY).

Source: Sak Sutsakhan, *The Khmer Republic at War and the Final Collapse* (Washington, D.C.: U.S. Army Center for Military History, 1980), p. 55.

$1 million was granted under Title I. As was widely reported in the American press at the time,[45] most of these Title II humanitarian food shipments intended to feed starving refugees were confiscated by corrupt Khmer Republic officials and sold for a personal profit—frequently to the enemy. Not for nothing did the KCP call Lon Nol its "Quartermaster."

The U.S. General Accounting Office estimated that the rake-off from padded troop rosters by FANK commanders was around $.75 to $1.0 million per month, while the *New York Times* put the figure at $2.0 million per month.[46] Corruption was not a casual thing in the Khmer Republic. It was the central occupation of the highest officials of the government. Profiteering is seen in almost all wars. In the Khmer Republic, this type of corruption reached deep into the state apparatus, and gravely imperiled what slim hope the regime had for survival. The widespread corruption and simple incompetence of many of the people Lon Nol entrusted with positions of responsibility in the Khmer Republic must be cited as a principal cause of its defeat. With such leadership, the Khmer Republic needed no enemies to achieve collapse.

The Kissinger-Shawcross Controversy

Political scientist–journalist William Shawcross has argued that part of the burden for the tragic events in Cambodia must be borne by the U.S. officials who were responsible for U.S. foreign policy during the late revolutionary period. "In Cambodia," Shawcross has written, "the imperatives of a small and vulnerable people were consciously sacrificed to the interests of strategic design."[47] He seems to agree with the conclusions of Prince Sihanouk that "Nixon and Kissinger killed lots of Americans, and many other people, they spent enormous sums of money—$4 billion—and the results were the opposite of what they wanted. They demoralized America, they lost all of Indochina to the Communists, and they created the Khmer Rouge."[48] Shawcross holds that these two men "created catastrophe. . . . Cambodia was not a mistake; it was a crime."[49]

Shortly after Shawcross published these assertions in 1979, the first volume of former Secretary of State Henry Kissinger's memoirs appeared. Presumably beneath the dignity of the body of the memoir, his vitriolic *ad hominem* counterattack on Shawcross is relegated to a footnote, where Shawcross is accused of having "excused the Khmer Rouge atrocities" by blaming them on U.S. and Cambodian efforts to resist them. Kissinger asserts,

It requires calculated advocacy, not judgment, to argue that the United States was violating the neutrality of a peaceful country when with Cambodian encouragement we, in self-defense, sporadically bombed territories in which for years no Cambodian writ had run, and which were either minimally populated or totally unpopulated by civilians, and which were occupied in violation of Cambodian neutrality by an enemy....[50]

Since Kissinger's reply in the first volume of his memoirs, this controversy has been sustained by the principals and joined by others.[51] A careful consideration of both sides reveals several serious problems.

Shawcross misses the mark in a number of respects. A minor example is his conclusion (see p. 134) that the incursion did not succeed in its purpose. In fact, the purpose of the incursion was nothing more and nothing less than to buy time for the withdrawal of U.S. troops from Vietnam with reduced harassment from the North Vietnamese Army. The incursion greatly disrupted NVA operations in eastern Cambodia, setting them back some six to nine months according to estimates by the Joint General Staff in Saigon and MACV (the Military Assistance Command, Vietnam).[52] There were some unanticipated and unintended consequences, but that it nearly led to the political destruction of its authors does not detract from the tactical achievement. And that it caused grievous damage to Cambodia, the Cambodian people, and the Cambodian government was not, as Shawcross clearly shows, really relevant to the purposes of the policy.

A related problem with Shawcross's argument is that although he indirectly accuses Nixon and Kissinger of criminal conduct, he does not adequately deal with the legal dimensions of his charges. He identifies no statutes violated by the president. He never adequately answers the Nixon administration's arguments that its actions were justified under domestic and international law, specifically mandated by Article 51 of the Charter of the United Nations (the self-defense clause),[53] Article IV of the SEATO Treaty (the collective security clause), and Article II, Section Two, of the Constitution of the United States (empowering the president as commander-in-chief). Shawcross approvingly quotes (his p. 333) the dissenting minority opinion from the House Judiciary Committee's rejection of the fourth article of impeachment against Richard Nixon (dealing with secret war in Cambodia). He also notes (p. 278) that Cambodia was never a party to SEATO. Otherwise he does not touch the administration's elaborate legal defense. Shawcross, then, is implicating Kissinger and Nixon in moral and political "crimes," but not legal ones.

A third difficulty with the Shawcross argument is that the actions of the Nixon administration by no means "created" the *Khmer Rouge*, as Shawcross strongly implies. This argument rests on the assertion that the Cambodian communists constituted an unorganized and ineffective movement that would not have prevailed had not U.S. bombings and the incursion strained the social fabric to the point of rupture, thus creating the mass base of revolution. It is untenable to assert that the KCP could not have won but for U.S. intervention. On the one hand, it does seem to be the case that between the realignment of alliance structures and the accelerated radicalization of the peasantry because of U.S. carpet bombing, U.S. actions did contribute to the ability of the KCP to recruit new members during the late revolutionary period. On the other hand, it seems highly likely that the KCP would have won anyway. What *is* open to question is just how the balance of forces within the KCP itself might have evolved in the absence of certain U.S. actions.

Fourth, Shawcross insinuates that while Sihanouk confined the war to the border regions, it was "American policy that engulfed the nation in war" (p. 396). This formulation is inaccurate. What Sihanouk *had* succeeded in doing was to confine U.S.-ARVN/NVA-PRG battles to the border regions. In the final analysis, it was the policies of the Lon Nol government—specifically the March 12, 1970 decision to give the NVA three days to "get out of Dodge"—that transformed the situation first into an NVA/FANK contest, and then into a FANK-U.S.-ARVN/NVA-PRG-PFLANK war. What the United States *did* do was to deny victory to the communists for a few years, at a very high cost. Unfortunately for the people of Cambodia, the costs charged were not the sort that could be borne by U.S. taxpayers. This bill was called due in Khmer blood.

Finally, perhaps the most serious problem with the argument Shawcross presents in *Sideshow* is inadequate attention to the domestic Cambodian sources of the civil war. The degree of peasant unrest in the late 1960s, and the extent to which the urban elite was split by cleavages—both in large measure directly attributable to the policies Sihanouk had followed—were central causal factors in the conflict. In his concern with film-making and other cultural activities, Sihanouk may have misperceived the extent of peasant distress, and when he did recognize it, he responded with harsh repression. As for the elites, Sihanouk's precarious balancing act among regional powers and superpowers necessarily contained many feints, nuances, and contradictions. These apparent inconsistencies gave ample ammunition to any and all factions desiring to take potshots at the established order.

Shawcross later amended this point when he observed in his introduction to Sihanouk's 1980 memoir that these "errors" on Sihanouk's part were the real enemy "that brought about his undoing."[54] In his haste to indict the amoral *Realpolitik* of Nixon and Kissinger in the *Sideshow* volume, however, he did not give these domestic factors enough credit for the destruction of Cambodia. In *Sideshow*, one finds statements such as, "It was to be the expansion of United States involvement in the region that precipitated Sihanouk's disappearance" (p. 63); and "[Sihanouk's] collaboration with both powers, such as it was, was intended to save his people by confining the conflict to border regions. It was American policy that engulfed the nation in war" (p. 396). Heat will not ignite a material unless it is already combustible, and indeed, the fabric of Cambodian society had been smouldering around the edges for years.

There are some serious problems with Kissinger's arguments, as well. First, the charge he makes that Shawcross "excuses" the *Khmer Rouge* is fatuous and patently false. It makes one suspect that Kissinger has not read the book. More to the point, however, Kissinger offers the following proposition: "Without our incursion, the Communists would have taken over Cambodia years earlier. That the rule of these fanatical ideologues would have been more benign under those conditions is not very likely."[55] Here, Kissinger asserts that U.S. actions did nothing to harden the policy of the KCP leadership. This argument is developed at great length in the second volume of Kissinger's memoirs, but it has a fatal and obvious flaw. Kissinger, following Kenneth Quinn's analysis,[56] argues that it was not U.S. bombing that made the KCP so vicious, but rather their own ideology. This argument has much merit, but it begs the central question: *Whose* ideology? Kissinger treats the *Khmer Rouge* as a monolithic organization with a unified, fixed political line, and he inexplicably maintains that U.S. actions could have had no impact on its internal policy debate. This line of reasoning fails to consider the relationship we now know to have existed between U.S. military intervention and the internal power struggle in the KCP. (This point will be developed forthwith.)

Elsewhere, Kissinger has stated that "the Cambodian government ... never once protested against" U.S. bombing of Cambodian territory.[57] This assertion is simply false. In fact, in the last twenty-seven months of Sihanouk's reign, the government of Cambodia filed 109 protests with the United Nations alleging violation of Cambodian territory and airspace by U.S. forces. Indeed, the House Judiciary

Committee, in considering the impeachment of Richard Nixon, felt that this was a matter of major interest. The Judiciary Committee staff assembled a file of 150 pages of selected examples of official Cambodian protest letters.[58] Kissinger's reply is simply that in 1968 Norodom Sihanouk "privately" invited U.S. air attacks on NVA sanctuaries in Cambodia, and that he then established diplomatic relations with Washington in 1969 and "warmly" invited Nixon to visit as the air raids were in progress (Years of Upheaval [YOU], p. 340). Shawcross retorts that "the issue Kissinger has consistently failed to address is" the fact that "the whims of a foreign prince are not grounds for the President to wage war" (Sideshow, p. 94).

Another serious flaw in Kissinger's argument concerns what he refers to as "sporadic bombing" of territories "either minimally populated or totally unpopulated by civilians." His choice of the term, "sporadic," and his assertion that target areas contained few or no civilians, are in retrospect open to outright refutation. The U.S. bombing programs killed many thousands of people, not merely in unpopulated zones, not merely along the border, and not merely in military installations. Kissinger knows this. Killing people was the whole idea, and as Map 6.1 shows, much of the bombing in 1973 alone occurred in some of the most heavily populated areas of the country. The very fact that these areas were in the hands of communists (both Khmer and Vietnamese), according to the Kissinger logic, automatically transformed all individuals in them into combatants.[59] Further, there was nothing whatsoever "sporadic" about the bombing (Table 6.2). It was sustained, and extremely intense, if not indiscriminate.

The fact is that the United States dropped three times the quantity of explosives on Cambodia between 1970 and 1973 that it had dropped on Japan for the duration of World War II.[60] Between 1969 and 1973, 539,129 tons of high explosives rained down on Cambodia; that is more than one billion pounds. This is equivalent to some 15,400 pounds of explosives for every square mile of Cambodian territory. Considering that probably less than 25 percent of the total area of Cambodia was bombed at one time or another, the actual explosive force per area would be at least four times this level. That Kissinger never makes a single reference in White House Years to this carpet-bombing program, code-named ARCLIGHT, greatly undermines the credibility of his entire argument. He refers only to the limited MENU campaign conducted along the border areas in 1969 and 1970.

In the second volume of his memoirs, Kissinger implicitly acknowledged that he recognized the growing seriousness of his con-

MAP 6.1
U.S. Airstrikes in the ARCLIGHT Series, 1973

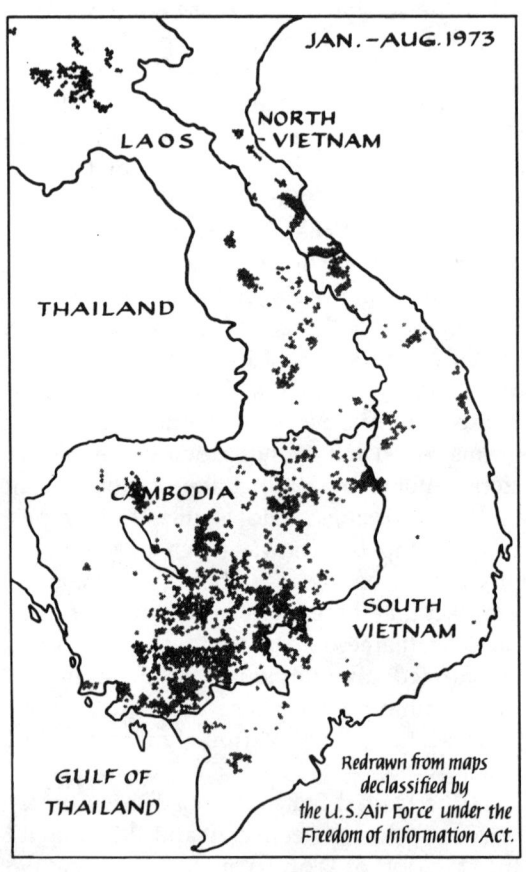

Source: William Shawcross, Sideshow: Kissinger, Nixon, and the Destruction of Cambodia (New York: Simon and Schuster, 1978), p. 267; used by permission.

troversy with Shawcross. Though Kissinger never discusses the studies, assumptions, and planning out of which the four-year long ARCLIGHT program grew in 1970, he nonetheless mounts a vigorous defense against detractors of the policy. After presenting a misleading, almost tongue-in-cheek caricature of Shawcross's arguments, Kissinger says, "It is a fevered absurdity, but it has to be dealt with" (*YOU* 336). He proceeds to devote nearly 100 pages to dealing with this "absurdity."

TABLE 6.2
U.S. AIRBORNE BOMBARDMENT IN CAMBODIA, 1969-1973

	Sorties		Munitions (in tons)	
	B-52	FB-111	B-52	FB-111+
1969	2,437	20	70,500	31
1970	2,906	13,718	74,786	19,421
1971	1,319	15,154	33,567	29,947
1972	1,855	6,702	36,899	16,513
1973	8,010	27,838	168,099	89,366
Subtotals	16,527	63,432	383,851	155,278
Totals	79,959 Sorties		539,129 Tons	

Source: Adapted from raw data in Appendix D, United States Congress, House Committee on the Judiciary, Statement of Information, Book 11: Bombing of Cambodia (Washington, D.C.: USGPO, 1974), pp. 88-108.

He performs such curious exertions as reprinting letters from Emory Swank, William Harben, Thomas Enders, and General (ret.) John Vogt (who were his deputies for Cambodia policy), denying that they engaged in any malfeasance and correcting a few minor errors in Shawcross's research. Through all of this, Kissinger fairly well finesses the question of whether U.S. policy was beneficial or harmful to Cambodia.

On balance, no clear victor emerges from the Kissinger-Shawcross controversy. Shawcross, though his research is exhaustive, is nevertheless carried away by his theme. He does a good job illustrating the pernicious effects of pure *Realpolitik* on the innocents, but he does not give the Cambodians enough credit for the genesis of their own destruction. For his part, Kissinger has done, so far at least, a poor job defending the record of the Nixon administration. As it suits the flow of his arguments, Kissinger manages to overlook, omit, or deny numerous central facts, such as the magnitude and target areas of the ARCLIGHT program, the vigorous protests against U.S. policy constantly submitted to the United Nations by Cambodian officials before 1971, and the impact of U.S. policy on the internal power struggle within the KCP. His eye ever to the judgment of history, Kissinger seems not to have caught sight of the human costs of U.S.

MAP 6.2
U.S. AIRSTRIKES IN THE 'MENU' SERIES

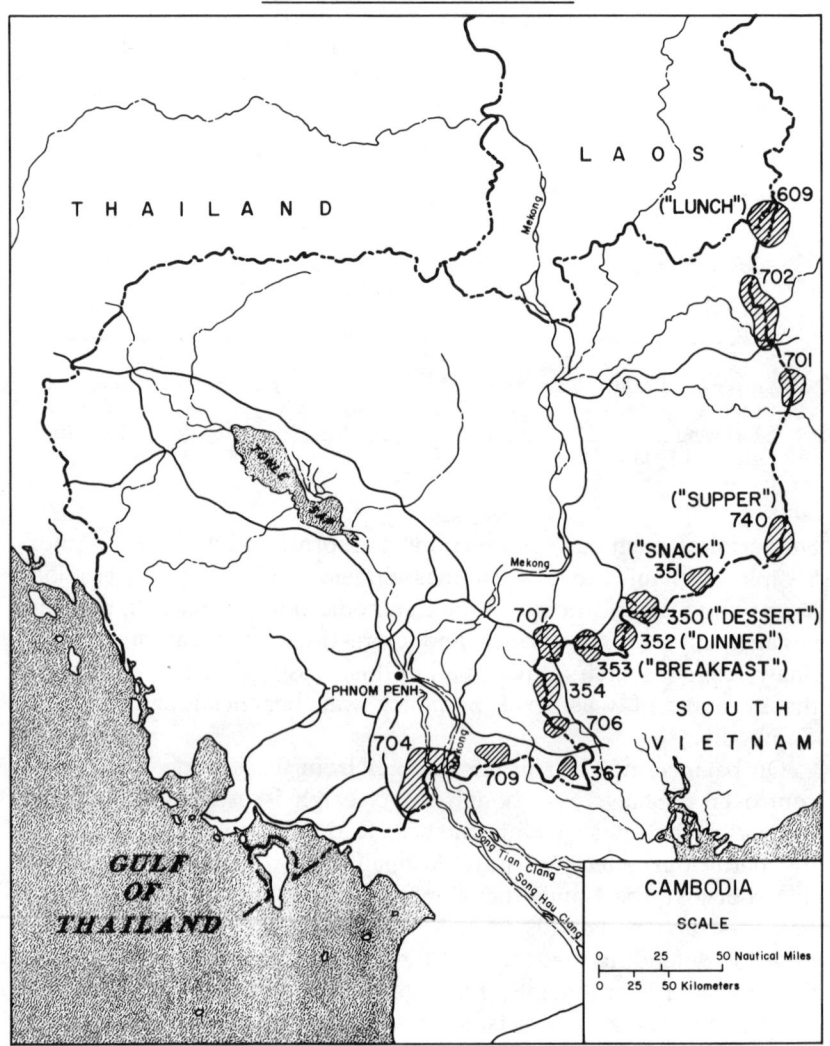

SOURCE: HENRY KISSINGER, WHITE HOUSE YEARS (BOSTON: LITTLE, BROWN AND COMPANY, 1979), p. 248. USED BY PERMISSION.

strategy. He would have history read that there were none. Ultimately, the former secretary of state implies that the Cambodians were no worse off for U.S. actions there. That is distinctly uncompelling and unconvincing. One is reminded of Thucydides's dictum: "The strong do what they can and the weak suffer what they must."

Combined Warfare (1970–1975)

After the March 18 *coup*, the war in Cambodia unfolded like the plot of a dreary seven-act play:

1. Initial Collapse (March 20, 1970–June 30, 1970)
2. Retrenchment, Counterattack, and Parry (July 1, 1970–August 20, 1971)
3. Blunder (August 20, 1971–December 3, 1971)
4. Attrition (December 4, 1971–December 31, 1972)
5. Attack and Repulse (January 1, 1973–August 15, 1973)
6. Siege (August 16, 1973–December 31, 1974)
7. The Kill (January 1, 1975–April 17, 1975)

Perhaps surprisingly, the combats that transpired were of a fairly conventional character. With considerable assistance from the North Vietnamese, the Cambodian communists conducted the shortest "war of national liberation" on record. In a word, Lon Nol was trounced.

Initial Collapse

The initial collapse of civil order in Cambodia after the March *coup* occurred in three rapidly evolving phases. First, between March 20 and March 29, the government faced massive and sometimes violent peasant protests. On March 29, 1970, the North Vietnamese Army attacked Republican positions, and for the next month Lon Nol's troops essentially retreated with heavy casualties. With the combined U.S.-ARVN incursion beginning on April 29, the third phase of the initial collapse pitted the North Vietnamese and their allies from South Vietnam, Laos, and Cambodia against the United States and the South Vietnamese and Republican Cambodian armies.

Two days after the *coup*, Prince Sihanouk announced over the radio from Peking his intention to resist his deposition. He then played his trump card, insisting that the new government was totally illegitimate. As the embodiment of national authority, Sihanouk called upon the peasant masses to rise up and strike down those who had betrayed him. The peasants responded *en masse*, and within days

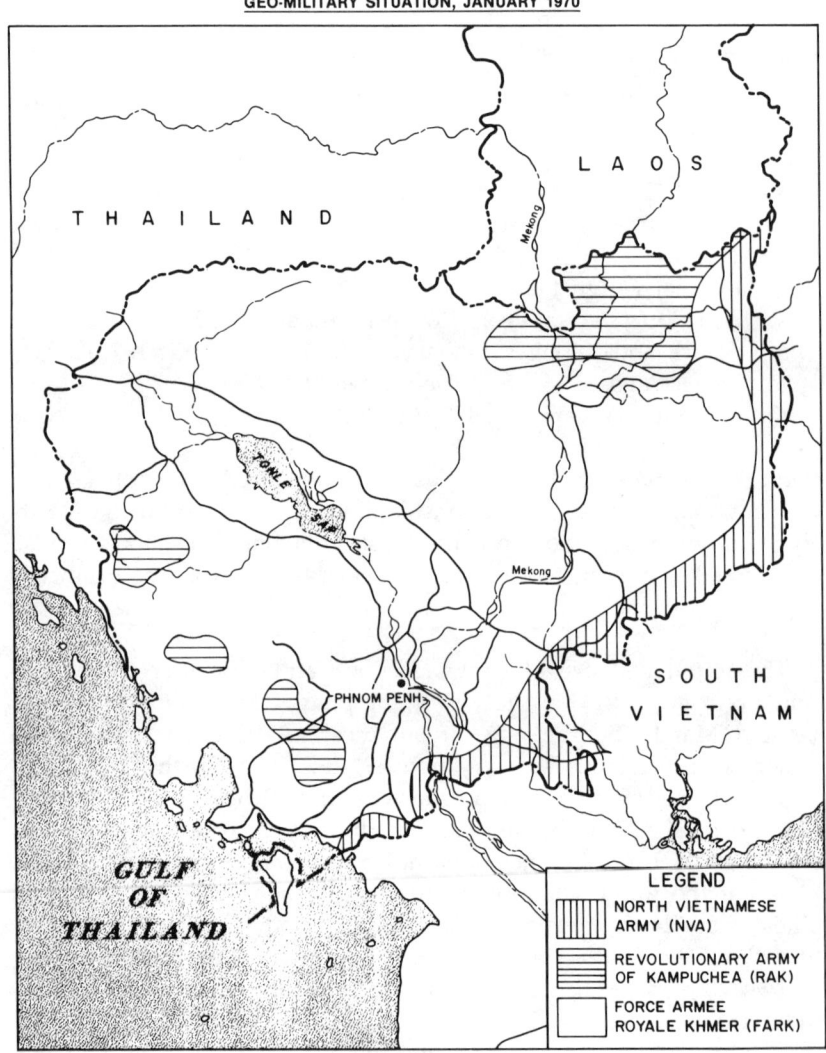

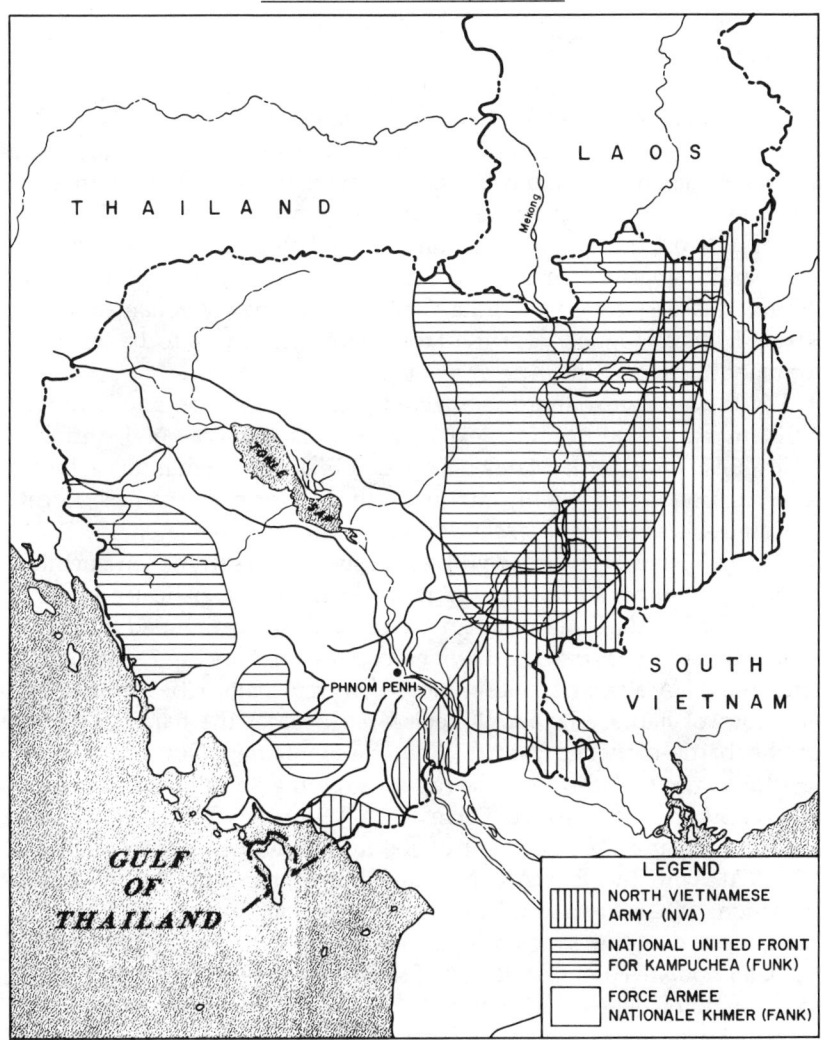

MAP 6.4

GEO-MILITARY SITUATION, JUNE 1970

LEGEND
- NORTH VIETNAMESE ARMY (NVA)
- NATIONAL UNITED FRONT FOR KAMPUCHEA (FUNK)
- FORCE ARMEE NATIONALE KHMER (FANK)

large pro-Sihanouk demonstrations were occurring throughout Cambodia.

On March 25, 1,500 villagers demonstrated peacefully at Tuol Svay Chrum, about ten kilometers south of Kompong Cham City.[61] They dispersed after asking for the return of the prince. That evening, two battalions of Green Beret–trained CIDG troopers, freshly transported from their bases in South Vietnam, were moved into the area of Kompong Cham.

On March 27, the Republican forces opened fire on peasant demonstrators in Takeo and Kompong Cham. On March 29, 1970, an estimated 40,000 Khmer and Cham peasants attempted to stage a protest march to Phnom Penh. Alarmed, the government treated the peasants as if they were an invading army. FANK and CIDG troops fell on the unarmed column long before it reached Phnom Penh and dispersed the demonstrators with heavy loss of life. Thus, during this first phase of initial collapse, the newly renamed *Force Armée Nationale Khmer* (FANK) faced down what was to be its most formidable enemy: the Khmer people.

The task of controlling the angered peasants soon became a minor problem compared to the next challenge facing Lon Nol and his colleagues. With Sirik Matak's sudden break from Sihanouk's longstanding policy of nonconfrontation with the North Vietnamese forces in Cambodia, and his *de facto* declaration of war on March 15, 1970, the North Vietnamese turned with equal suddenness from their enemies in South Vietnam to fall on the numerically and logistically inferior troops of the FANK. The Vietnamese communists responded to Sirik's ultimatum by withdrawing their embassies on March 27. Two days later, the NVA attacked, taking more than ten major cities in the first few days of battle. The FANK reeled back under the hammer blows of the battle-hardened North Vietnamese regulars, leaving behind territory to be transferred to the rapidly growing Kampuchean People's National Liberation Armed Forces (PFLANK).

The third and final segment of the initial collapse began on April 29, 1970, with the first ARVN crossborder attacks of the combined incursion. When he learned of President Nixon's speech announcing the attacks on NVA sanctuaries in his country, Secretary General of the Cambodian Foreign Ministry Prince Norodom Monissara simply said, "I don't believe it."[62] But it was true, and worse was yet to come. The secretary general's disbelief can be traced to the fact that he knew very well that a principal effect of the incursion would be to drive concentrations of NVA and PRG troops massed near the border with Vietnam deep into Cambodian territory, gravely threatening the tenability of the tottering Lon Nol regime. Units not originally committed to the attacks on the Republican government were driven perforce back from the border regions. What the foreign minister probably did not know was that in addition to being driven deeper yet into Cambodian territory, overrunning government outposts along the way, the NVA and PRG "saved" a large portion of their weapons and supply caches from loss to the U.S.-ARVN search and destroy teams by giving them to the struggling Cambodian revolutionary movement.[63]

The U.S.-ARVN incursion thus forced the NVA to accelerate the process it had already begun. Exactly what its goals were in this period remains a matter of some uncertainty. According to an NVA officer, Lt. Col. Nguyen Thanh, who was captured by the incursion forces, the NVA had intended to take Phnom Penh by May 3.[64] This information has never been substantiated by any other sources. Would the cautious NVA leaders be so optimistic? It would seem probable, at a minimum, that the NVA intended to secure its logistical facilities and lines of communications against Lon Nol and the U.S.-ARVN forces.

To achieve this end, the NVA forces proceeded on a campaign to seize the entire northeastern third of the country. As they secured an area, they would turn it over to local resistance forces for administration and then move their troops on to the next objective, thus preserving a superior balance of forces. In this manner, they rapidly overran half a dozen provinces. The FANK garrisons at Stung Treng, Sumpang, and Voeun Sai, in Mondolkiri, and in other locations were completely wiped out. Only the garrison in Ratanakiri was saved, and that because of an armored evacuation orchestrated on June 24–27, 1970, by U.S. planners.

By May 5, the NVA had set up shop in the Mekong River town of Kratie, where it had waltzed into town virtually unopposed. Kratie became a central administrative complex for communist operations, probably temporarily replacing the functions of "the city" facility in the Fishhook area, which was just then being ravaged by the incursion forces. It was now in the interests of the North Vietnamese to organize, train, and equip a Cambodian revolutionary army as quickly as possible, so as to relieve their own units, which were sorely needed in South Vietnam.

Retrenchment, Counterattack, and Parry

After U.S. ground troops were withdrawn from Cambodia at the end of June, the war settled into a low-level slugfest as all parties to the conflict regrouped, reinforced, and attempted to consolidate their positions. Lon Nol had suffered grievously, and was no longer in possession of about half of his country. In response to the strategic realities facing FANK, Lon Nol decided to adopt a "strategic defense." Drawing a line northwest from the Fishhook area to Kompong Thom, and from there straight north to the Thai border, Lon Nol ceded all territory north of the line to the communists. This was to be the "Lon Nol Line." The strategy would be implemented in three phases:

1. Phase I: Survive south of the line.
2. Phase II: Consolidate all territory south of the line.
3. Phase III: Regain lost territory north of the line.[65]

Given FANK's unenviable situation, the strategy was perhaps a good one. The Lon Nol Line was generally coterminous with Highways Six and Seven, and would have left much of the most productive agricultural land under the control of Phnom Penh. It would have, that is, if Lon Nol's forces had ever been able to progress beyond Phase I. They were unable to do so.

Educated urban dwellers generally seemed supportive of Lon Nol's declared motives. In fact, tired of the decadence of Sihanouk's court and the highly visible corruption of his family, and alarmed at his apparently casual approach to Vietnamese transgressions, the urban population did not seem especially sorry to see Sihanouk deposed. Many urban youth enthusiastically joined the FANK, and within a few months it had doubled in size to some 60,000 troops. Training was often nonexistent, and equipment was not yet abundant.

By way of comparison, over the same period the newly formed PFLANK grew by a factor of between three and five. The 3,000- to 4,000-strong RAK drew in peasants by the thousands and grew in a few months into a PFLANK of between 10,000 and 15,000 troops augmented by some 50,000 "irregular guerrillas." The RAK had been organized primarily as a classic guerrilla-style paramilitary organization, but upon being reorganized into the PFLANK, it adopted the three-tiered image of the revolutionary forces in South Vietnam. North Vietnamese General Vo Nguyen Giap's contribution to the Cambodian liberation struggle was an organizational one, and the new structure was far more suitable for the tasks that lay ahead than had been the simple structure of the old RAK.

On the "lowest" tier, local guerrillas could be assigned to conduct harassment, infiltration, and espionage missions. On the "middle" level, larger and more well-equipped regional guerrilla units were

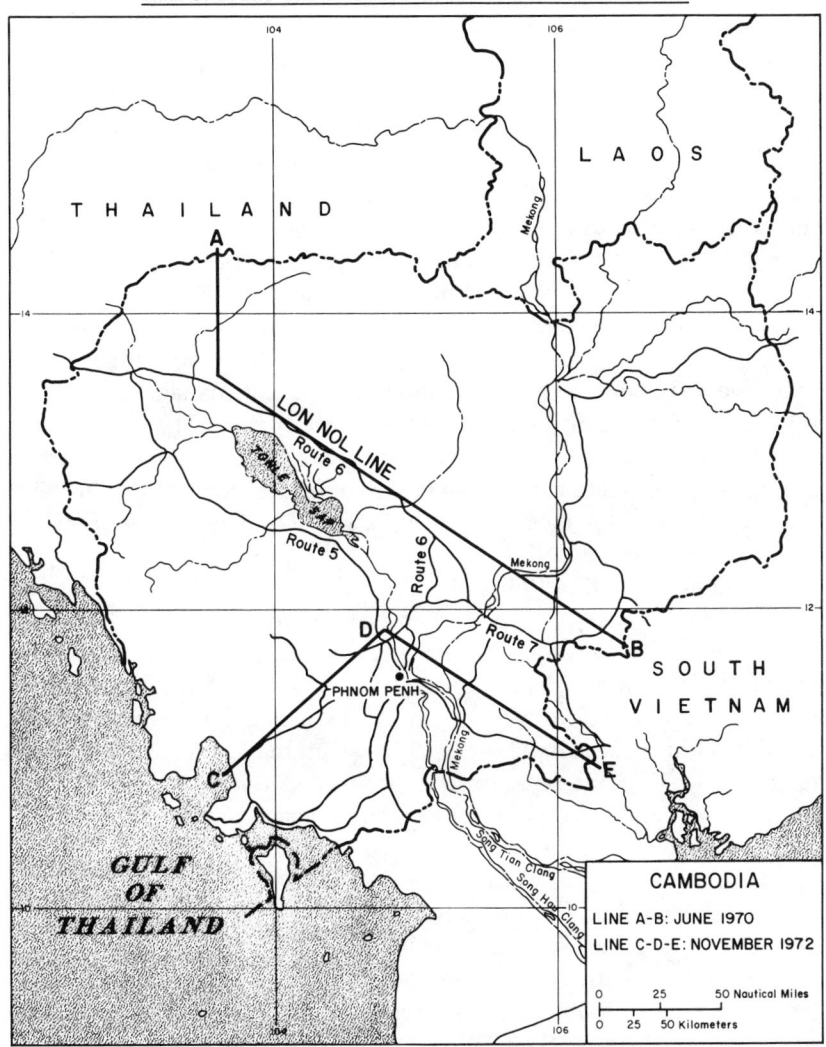

MAP 6.5

FANK STRATEGIC CONCEPTS FOR DEFENSE OF THE KHMER REPUBLIC

SOURCE: SAK SUTSAKHAN, KHMER REPUBLIC AT WAR
(WASHINGTON D.C.:U.S. ARMY CENTER FOR
MILITARY HISTORY, 1980), P.68

available to perform more complex raids and sabotage activities. At the "highest" level of the PFLANK organization, a regular army was set up for conventional military operations. In accordance with the political reality that various communist factions in Cambodia commanded the loyalty of their own units, the PFLANK command authority was distributed among the six geographical military regions, roughly corresponding to the military regions of the Republican government. With the exception of the 1973 dry season offensive, PFLANK utilized the three-tiered structure in classic fashion, harassing the enemy whenever possible to keep him off balance, avoiding engagement with superior forces on disadvantageous occasions, and striking when the odds were favorable.

In July of 1970, Lon Nol finally responded to U.S. exhortations to take the offense. Badly in need of a victory to restore flagging morale, the Republicans decided to try to reopen Highway Six, connecting the capital to the rice-rich regions around Kompong Thmar. This objective was not achieved, although FANK did manage to open a fifteen-mile stretch of Highway Six for a short time. The NVA Ninth Division was based in the area, and through constant probing was able to keep the ten to twelve battalions committed to FANK's offensive on the defensive for most of the operation. The FANK minioffensive was code-named CHENLA I.

In January of 1971, PFLANK adopted a new strategy. By hitting hard at FANK's widely dispersed and under-strength units, PFLANK could effectively tie down the Republican forces for a few days. At the same time, strikes deep into the heart of Khmer Republic enclaves would force Lon Nol to redeploy his units into defensive positions.[66] On the night of January 21–22, 1971, a commando force of approximately 100 Vietnamese guerrillas penetrated the defense perimeter of the Khmer Air Force base at Pochentong airfield near Phnom Penh. The raid almost completely destroyed the small Khmer Air Force, including all of FANK's MIG fighters. At the same time, another force attacked the naval base on the other side of the capital, while additional guerrilla units attacked several villages in the area.

The attack had the desired results. According to FANK's Lt. Gen. Sak Sutsakhan, "It was necessary for the high command to withdraw some of the units from the CHENLA column at Tang Kauk to reinforce the outskirts of the capital."[67] From this point forward, the FANK high command would be hesitant to move beyond its relatively secure urban enclaves, preferring to defend what little territory it could safely protect.

The Pochentong raid paid off with an unexpected dividend. On February 5, the "State of Emergency" was extended for an additional six months. After spending all day February 8 at the National Assembly trying to reassure the disturbed representatives, General Lon Nol suffered a serious stroke. For the next two months, Lon Nol was treated in Hawaii and his subordinates tried to hold the line at home.

Blunder

When Lon Nol returned to Phnom Penh on April 12, 1971, he immediately began preparations to take the offensive against the enemy once again. His new plan would be called CHENLA II, and this time it called for a much more ambitious set of objectives than had been unsuccessfully attempted the previous autumn in CHENLA I. The objective of CHENLA II would be to reopen the entire length of Highway Six and establish a secure line of communication between Kompong Thom and Kompong Cham. The garrison at Kompong Thom had been under siege since the previous summer, and, more importantly, the garrison there had been able to accumulate a large stockpile of rice from the surrounding paddy land. This rice was badly needed in other areas.

Within the FANK general staff, no one disputed the importance of the objectives proposed by Lon Nol, nor that his plan was in perfect accord with a strategic defense based on the Lon Nol Line. What was disputed was just how FANK was supposed to deal with two or three divisions of the NVA that were using the area as a base, plus an undetermined number of PFLANK units. To string FANK troops out along a road through unfriendly territory, some officers of the general staff argued,[68] would be to expose their flanks and turn them into easy targets. Indeed. However, Lon Nol was convinced that U.S. air power would destroy the enemy. And Lon Nol was in charge. CHENLA II went forward.

On August 20, FANK troops began moving up Highway Six. Resistance was light, and the troops advanced quite rapidly. Within slightly more than two weeks, the entire length of Highway Six had been reopened. The next six weeks were spent trying to consolidate this precarious lifeline against the intermittent harassment of small enemy units, and in the process many of the FANK units stationed along Highway Six began to experience morale problems. The men were tired, casualties had been fairly heavy, and they had never really had a chance to take a clean shot at the enemy. The NVA, the Viet Cong (VC), and the PFLANK seemed to have disappeared. Lon Nol decided that they had been destroyed by the U.S. Air Force, and he

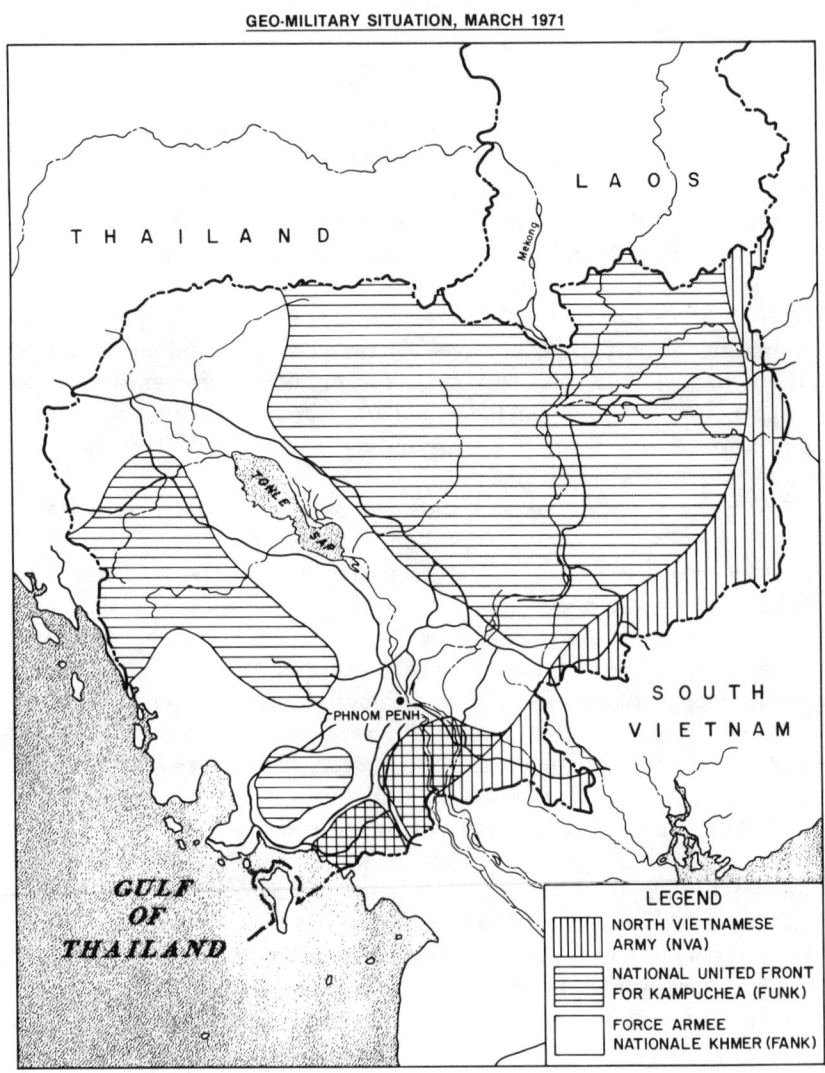

MAP 6.7
THE DECISIVE ENGAGEMENT (20 AUG. 1971 TO 3 DEC. 1971)

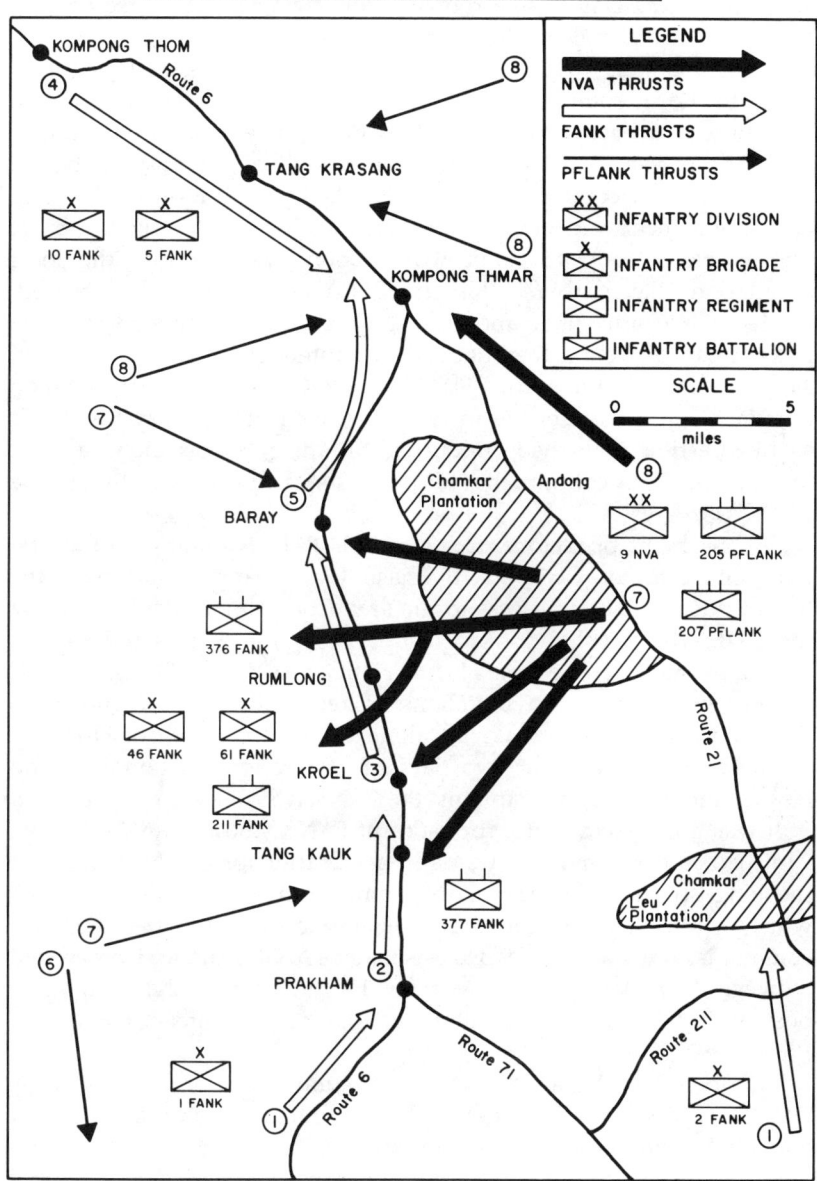

removed from his battle map the pins representing the North Vietnamese Army's Ninth Division and PFLANK's 205th and 207th regional guerrilla regiments. On October 5, Marshal Lon Nol issued an Order of the Day to his troops, emphasizing that because of their successes, the "morale of the enemy is, therefore, surely very low...."

On October 25, 1971, Lon Nol declared that the first phase of CHENLA II was complete, and a great success, at that. The troublesome map pins had been eliminated. Two days of religious and military celebrations were called, so that the troops might unwind before beginning the second phase of CHENLA II: pacification of the local population. Beer and opium were airlifted in to entertain the boys. The drunken troops did not worry about the fact that the local population, like the NVA, VC, and PFLANK, had also disappeared.

Meanwhile, the NVA and PFLANK had just completed the first phase of an operation they dubbed "Counter–CHENLA II." Between August 20 and October 25, PFLANK units had evacuated the civilian population along the entire forty-mile stretch of Highway Six. Their small guerrilla units had conducted hit-and-run operations against the CHENLA II column, but did not seriously attempt to oppose FANK's progress.

On the night of October 26–27, 1971, PFLANK initiated the first move of "Counter–CHENLA II Phase Two." Sapper units blew the main bridge providing access to the area from Phnom Penh, isolating the CHENLA II column from resupply, reinforcement, and retreat. The same night, the entire North Vietnamese Ninth Division, augmented by at least two battalions of regional PFLANK guerrillas, launched a simultaneous assault along the whole length of Highway Six held by FANK. After two days of celebrations in honor of Lon Nol's great victory over map pins, the FANK troops were not prepared.

It was a massacre. Entire brigades of FANK's best infantry literally vanished into the mud. It was an easy matter for the NVA to chop the long string of exposed FANK units into isolated little chunks, which could then be gobbled up without difficulty. Battalion-size communist units surrounded the isolated FANK units and proceeded to wear them down. On November 13, 1971, the FANK command post at Rumlong fell, signaling the end of "Counter–CHENLA II Phase Two."

"Counter–CHENLA II Phase Three" commenced on November 14. Having successfully fragmented the CHENLA II column, PFLANK and NVA regrouped into division-sized units. These concentrations were then systematically directed at the remaining besieged command posts along Highway Six, which fell one by one to the superior force.

On December 3, "Counter-CHENLA II" was concluded as the last FANK outpost was crushed. FANK Lt. Gen. Sak Sutsakhan assessed the damage to his forces: "There was never an exact count, but the estimate was on the order of ten battalions of personnel and equipment lost plus the equipment of an additional ten battalions."[69] PFLANK Commander-in-Chief Khieu Samphan was the big winner in CHENLA II. "Of about 20,000 Lon Nol troops thrown into this operation," Khieu boasted, "we killed, wounded or captured over 12,000. Not a single battalion escaped without severe losses."[70] It was a decisive defeat. Never again did Lon Nol launch a major offensive, and the stranglehold on the urban enclaves of the Khmer Republic grew tighter and tighter.

Attrition

Over the course of 1972, the PFLANK emerged as an independent fighting force. Following the communist triumph in CHENLA II, the NVA considered Lon Nol and company a dead letter, and turned back to concentrate on its war in South Vietnam. Its base areas and lines of communication now completely secure on the ground following the withdrawal of ARVN from eastern Cambodia in the first part of the year, the NVA had good reason to be pleased with the rapid development of the PFLANK. Although not yet a fully coordinated fighting organization, the PFLANK was now able to assume the role of primary opponent to the Khmer Republic. By mid-1972, most estimates put PFLANK strength at 40,000 to 50,000 regular troops plus on the order of 80,000 to 100,000 irregular guerrillas.[71]

Against this force, the badly demoralized and poorly trained, if now well-equipped troops of the FANK continued to attempt to implement Phase I of Lon Nol's grand strategy of defense. Yet, FANK was unable even to hold its own in the cities, let alone actually consolidate the countryside in the strategic defense zone south of the Lon Nol Line. By November 1972, the Khmer Republic was forced to establish another line of strategic defense, now representing its attempts to establish control over the southern tip of Cambodia. Even this sliver of Cambodia, only about 15 percent of the country, could not be secured by the FANK. (See Line CDE on Map 6.5.)

Ineffective attempts to clear the Mekong River for friendly traffic and to retake the Angkor Wat temple complex during the first three months of 1972 gave way to a fall-back defense of Phnom Penh in April, May, and June. Thus, the PFLANK strategy of countering FANK initiatives with attacks on Phnom Penh continued to be effective, always forcing FANK back into defense of the heart of the Khmer

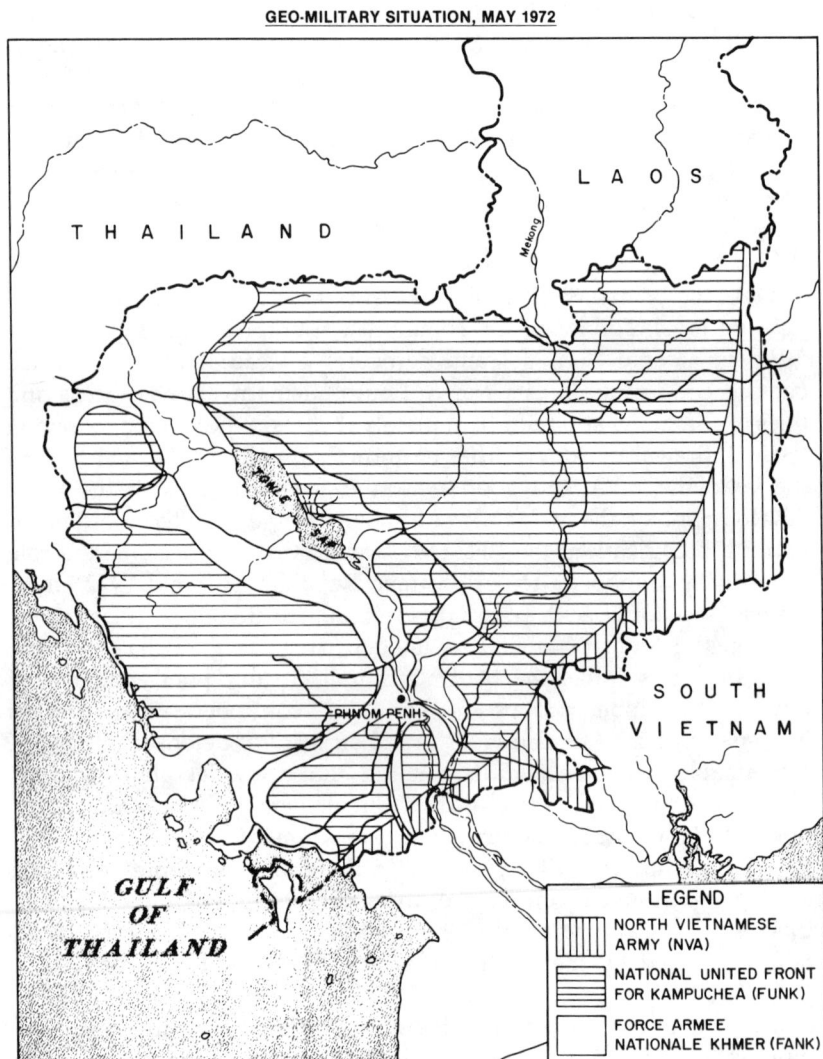

MAP 6.8
GEO-MILITARY SITUATION, MAY 1972

Republic, and progressively eliminating lines of communication between isolated enclaves and with the outside world.

The second half of 1972 was highlighted by desperate attempts by the FANK, with heavy assistance from the U.S. Air Force, to clear the Mekong corridor and keep open Phnom Penh's river lifeline. The two main operations dedicated to this objective, known as SORYA I and SORYA II, were exploited by the PFLANK with the combined use of guerrilla and conventional styles of warfare. FANK was harassed by guerrillas whenever it advanced in strength, and overrun by battalions whenever it attempted to hold objectives with less than brigade-sized units.

Attack and Repulse

In early January 1973, PFLANK launched its first full-scale "solo" offensive. The 1973 dry season offensive turned out to be a pivotal event in the conflict, despite the absence of any significant military gains by PFLANK. The military significance of this offensive itself was less than decisive. In fact, the PFLANK suffered extremely heavy casualties in the process of securing only minor strategic objectives. The primary military achievement of the offensive was simply to inflict further attrition and demoralization upon the FANK. The real significance of this offensive was political. Its importance lies in the impact of the offensive upon the dynamics of KCP internal party power and control.

First, the intensity of the U.S. bombing attacks strengthened the political position of the "hardliners" in the KCP Central Committee. After July 1973, a political solution to the conflict became impossible, for now it was too difficult to oppose the Saloth Sar line that any "compromise" with the imperialists—obviously evil after the heavy bombing—would constitute betrayal of the cause. The cease-fire agreement in South Vietnam would not extend to Cambodia.

The PFLANK command structure had yet to be fully consolidated, and coordination among the units operating in the six military regions during 1973 was haphazard at best. Their inability to synchronize their attacks left whichever unit happened to be attacking at a particular time fully exposed to the deadly U.S. Air Force FB-111 attacks. With these attacks, combined with a new boldness in using B-52s to attack enemy concentrations located very near friendly positions (just how near remains a closely guarded secret, but possibly as close as 400 feet), the U.S. Air Force inflicted horrendous casualties on the PFLANK.

At this point, PFLANK was still basically organized into battalion-sized units, but was beginning to form into regiment-sized units; the

FANK operated mainly with brigade-sized units, but was beginning to implement a division-sized structure. PFLANK strength at the beginning of 1973 was estimated at about 175 battalions. The first five months of 1973 had been characterized by heavy and relatively continuous pressure on major Khmer Republic lines of communication and provincial capitals. Siem Riep fell, was retaken, fell again, and so on. Takeo, Kompong Thom, Kompong Cham, and the Mekong corridor between the capital and the South Vietnamese border were all areas of heavy action.

In June, PFLANK turned fatefully to Phnom Penh. Approximately 75 of its 175 battalions were committed to the assault on Phnom Penh. At around 340 men—and women—per unit, the assault force was on the order of 25,000 strong.[72] PFLANK units to the south, west, and north of Phnom Penh were commanded primarily by cadres who were in the KPP tradition, both those who had been struggling ineffectually since 1954, and those who had returned from exile in Hanoi in 1968 and 1970. These PFLANK units advanced on Phnom Penh in ill-coordinated assaults, suffering in the process incredibly high casualty levels.[73]

East of Phnom Penh lay units directly under the command of GRUNK Minister of Defense and PFLANK Commander-in-Chief Khieu Samphan. Observing the carnage being meted out by the U.S. Air Force on the units assaulting the capital from the north, west, and south, Khieu prudently held back and preserved his own units relatively intact. These particular units were led by cadres loyal to the Saloth Sar faction.

The attackers were decimated. According to General John Vogt, commander of the U.S. Seventh Air Force, some 16,000 enemy soldiers were killed by U.S. air power in the early stages of the 1973 dry season offensive against Phnom Penh.[74] Distributed across all the units committed to this battle, this would represent a killed-in-action level of more than 60 percent. (It is generally assumed that casualty levels above 10 percent can cause psychological damage to the surviving troops.) Because PFLANK battalions to the north, west, and south of Phnom Penh bore the brunt of these casualties, the effective casualty rates for the PFLANK units loyal to the KPP tradition were probably well above 60 percent. Most of these units were rendered useless, and many of them, nonexistent.

Meanwhile, Khieu Samphan and his Saloth Sar battalions bided their time, waiting for a more propitious opportunity to strike the Khmer Republic. Anyone observing the domestic scene in the United States could not help but see which way the wind was blowing. Yet,

The Late Revolutionary Stage (1968–1975)   119

crouched in their bunkers as U.S. aerial bombardment of Cambodia escalated to a level of intensity unprecedented in the annals of warfare, they must at times have known flickers of a terrible doubt. This paroxysmal crescendo of airborne destruction climaxed in July and early August, and the balance of forces among the factions of the *Khmer Rouge* was forever transformed. At 5:00 A.M. on August 15, 1973, U.S. air power was withdrawn from the Cambodian war.

Siege

After the 1973 dry season offensive had been beaten back by U.S. air power, levels of military activity in Cambodia fell off as both sides crawled home to lick their wounds. For PFLANK, "home" consisted of the vast majority of the country. For FANK "home" was a few dozen besieged cities.

By reason of its control of the majority of the population and almost all the agricultural acreage, PFLANK was able not only to replace lost personnel but also to continue its growth. Eighty thousand regular troops and some 100,000 irregulars were in the field under the banner of PFLANK by the end of 1974, and these units were by now almost entirely composed of ethnic Khmer.

Without question, the tactics used by the U.S. Air Force until August 1973 and by FANK and ARVN throughout the Cambodian war contributed to the ability of the FUNK and PFLANK to recruit new personnel. As one analyst has commented concerning U.S.-ARVN-FANK tactics,

> Adapted from conventional tactics, these actions would include aerial attacks and the fire of artillery and even heavy individual weapons such as mortars and bazookas to "pacify" an area or village where insurgents had been spotted. Utilization of this "defensive" strategy, however, aids the guerillas in their prime objective of discrediting the government and its allies and alienating the population by destroying any sense of personal security. . . . American participation contributed, then, to an employment of the most dysfunctional and destructive counter-guerilla strategy available.[75]

As Norodom Sihanouk put it, "With his bombs [President Nixon] performed the miracle of turning our people into revolutionaries within weeks."[76]

On the other side, FANK's ability to replenish its losses continued to decline as eligible bodies in its enclaves became increasingly scarce.

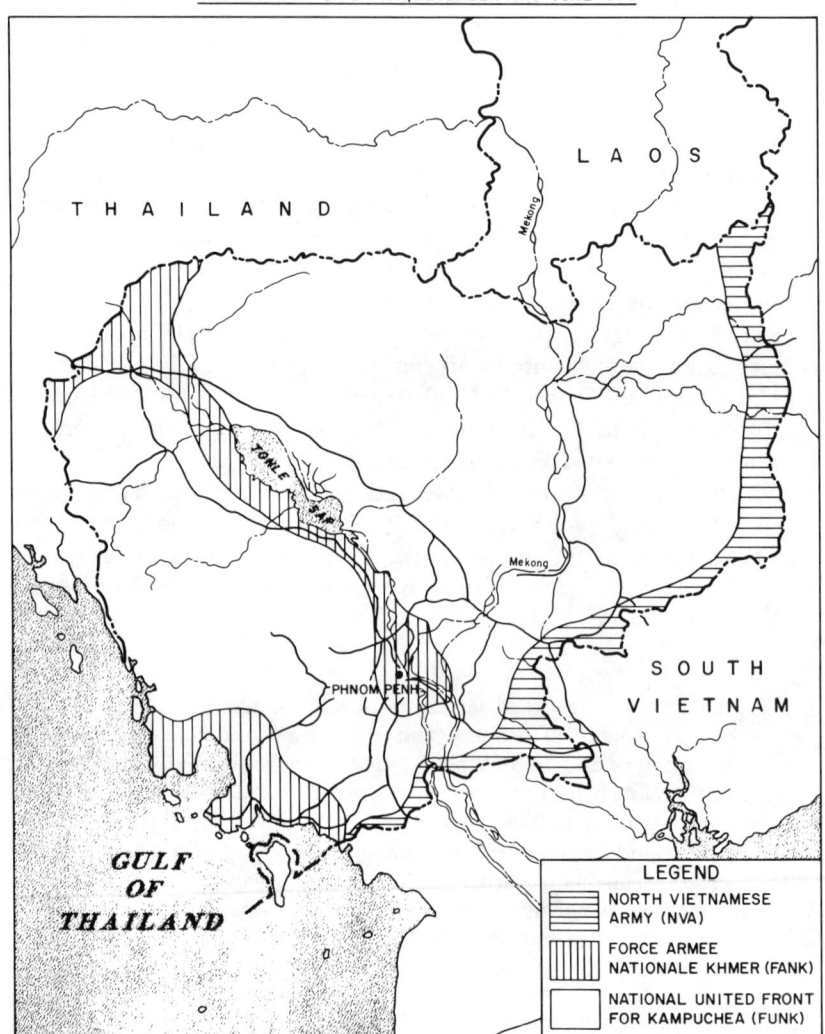

MAP 6.9

GEO-MILITARY SITUATION, DECEMBER 1973-JUNE 1974

The Late Revolutionary Stage (1968-1975) 121

As early as the first half of 1972, this process had been observed by GRUNK Defense Minister Khieu Samphan:

> All enemy plans aimed at encroaching into our liberated areas, at pillaging the people's economy, at conscripting manpower into the Lon Nol army and thus changing the balance of forces in their favour, have been successfully repulsed. The enemy cannot get fresh recruits because of his failure to seize and "pacify" liberated territory. His existing forces have been severely weakened, the morale of the remainder drastically lowered by a long series of defeats unrelieved by a single victory.[77]

Defended by demoralized and under-strength units, Phnom Penh grew more chaotic as the flow of women, children, elderly people, and wounded refugees into the capital continued to mount. The enemy tightened the siege.

After steady deterioration of FANK's lines in the second half of 1973, the new year and the new dry season brought another PFLANK offensive. Now the assaults were becoming more coordinated, and this indicated growing internal consolidation of both the PFLANK's and the KCP's command authority. While keeping up the pressure on provincial capitals, the communists began the 1974 dry season offensive by closing in on Phnom Penh. January and February were marked by pitched battles in the northeast and northwest suburbs, but by the beginning of March FANK managed to push the Khmer Republic security perimeter out a few kilometers beyond the city. In March, Oudong, the old royal capital about twenty-five kilometers northeast of Phnom Penh, was destroyed in a series of see-saw battles. In May, the nearby Lovek Logistic and Training Facility was wiped out.

Although activity generally fell during the wet season, PFLANK managed to sustain the offensive for the remainder of 1974. The number of convoys successfully running the Mekong River gauntlet dwindled precariously, and the U.S. airlift operations to supply the Khmer Republic became all-important. The tenor of the war at this point is indicated by the fact that the only notable defeat suffered by the PFLANK during the second half of 1974 occurred when three PFLANK regiments failed to take a high piece of ground northeast of the capital in November.

The Kill

On January 1, 1975, PFLANK launched the final assault, known as the "Mekong River Offensive." Phnom Penh was completely

122   *The Late Revolutionary Stage (1968-1975)*

PHOTOGRAPH 6.1
KHMER ROUGE LEADERS PLOT FINAL ASSAULT ON PHNOM PENH

(Left to Right:) PFLANK Commander-in-Chief Khieu Samphan, PFLANK Chief-of-Staff Son Sen, and PFLANK "Deputy Commander Thouch" (a.k.a. Vorn Veth) discuss the battle situation during the last week of March 1975 at forward headquarters on the Phnom Penh front.

Source: From photo preface to Fighting Cambodia: Reports of the Chinese Journalists Delegation to Cambodia (Peking: Foreign Languages Press, 1975); reproduced by kind courtesy of the People's Republic of China Foreign Languages Press.

surrounded. PFLANK held both sides of the Mekong River, and quickly consolidated its stranglehold on Phnom Penh's umbilical cord. The entire length of the river between Phnom Penh and the border with South Vietnam was secured in the first two weeks of the offensive, making the critical resupply convoys nearly impossible. A regimen of daily shelling settled in on the capital, concentrating on the air base at Pochentong. On February 5, 1975, the communists completed the laying of mines in the Mekong River, and now river traffic was out of the question. On February 16, the United States

The Late Revolutionary Stage (1968–1975) 123

began an intensive aerial bridge that would keep the besieged city alive until both the air bridge and the city were terminated at the end of the second week of April.

On March 12, 1975, Lt. Gen. Sak Sutsakhan assumed the role of commander-in-chief of FANK. Sak later recalled his thoughts on the day he took office:

> The picture of the Khmer Republic which came to mind at that time was one of a sick man who survived only by outside means and that, in its condition, the administration of medication, however efficient it might be, was probably of no further value. ... the general military situation throughout Cambodia consisted of little more than defeats everywhere, due to various reasons: the lack of resupply; inefficiency; misunderstandings; and discontent, provoked by the conduct of certain senior officers.[78]

The Congress of the United States concurred with Sak's assessment.

On March 1, the Mekong River ferrytown of Neak Luong fell, and from there the end came quickly. In spite of the fact that Phnom Penh was surrounded and defended by four divisions and three brigades of the best troops FANK had left, the PFLANK closed in on all sides. Far outnumbered, running out of ammunition, and unable to deal with their own skyrocketing casualties, the FANK positions were overrun and turned into pockets of doomed soldiers. On April 1, ex-President Lon Nol fled the country. On April 12, the U.S. mission evacuated the capital, taking Acting President Khoy with them. On the thirteenth, newly appointed President Sak Sutsakhan futilely tried a last-ditch peace offer. On the fourteenth, U.S. President Gerald Ford caved in to congressional pressure; the aerial bridge supply line was terminated. The next day the air base fell, and on the sixteenth FANK abandoned the defense perimeter around the capital of the Khmer Republic.

On the morning of April 17, 1975, Saloth Sar's troops were the first to enter the city. Shortly before noon, FANK General Mey Sichan came on Radio Phnom Penh, requesting all troops to lay down their arms and hoist the white flag. But before he could finish his sentence, one of Saloth Sar's men was heard to interrupt Mey with the cry, "We come as victors, as masters, and not as negotiators!"[79]

The Components of Victory

Leadership

Previous sections have discussed the purely military aspects of the Kampuchean civil war. But revolution is a fundamentally political affair. What factors can be adduced with regard to the political dimensions of the KCP's victory? Saloth Sar has suggested four:

1. "The efficient and correct leadership" of the KCP.
2. "Our people are very courageous . . . and especially they have been organized into cooperatives . . . since 1973."
3. "Of secondary significance (was) increased production and supply of food to [sic] the rear areas."
4. "Not to be forgotten though it is only of secondary significance (is) the support we received from the world."[80]

For the political chieftain of the KCP, then, leadership was the most important single element contributing to the victory.

Ben Kiernan, Malcolm Caldwell, and many others have pointed out that a small group of individuals cannot successfully make a revolution (as opposed to a *coup d'état*) in the absence of the requisite socioeconomic and political conditions. Peasants don't change unless there is a highly compelling reason for them to do so. Conversely, it is equally true that in the absence of leadership, social discontent will not take the form of coordinated revolutionary action. Indeed, without leaders, it is not likely to be considered more than amorphous insurrection.

It can be argued that before 1970, the necessary social conditions for mass-based revolution did not yet exist in Cambodia, and hence that no degree of leadership could have achieved revolution. After 1970, events conspired to provide a social milieu within which a creative vanguard party could foment mass-based revolution. For their part, the *Khmers Rouges* were well aware of the importance of leadership. In January 1972, Ieng Sary argued that "in order for the revolution to triumph, it is indispensable that at each echelon there be a leadership core composed of men who are firm on principles and who know how to apply our political line in concrete national conditions creatively and with precise aims."[81]

The Central Committee of the KCP was dominated by an unusually close-knit group. The organizational skills and capacity for strategic thought of this tiny clique are manifest in the fact that the band of a half-dozen or so individuals achieved for a time unchallenged supremacy over an entire nation. This could be accomplished only by creating an instrument of revolutionary action fanatically loyal to the leadership, and in control of an effective coercive apparatus. The task was greatly complicated by the need to ally with some enemies at certain times in order to gain a tactical advantage, and then be able to turn suddenly and destroy the allied enemy. This can be quite difficult unless one's troops are totally unquestioning of orders.

Khieu Samphan, Hu Nim, Hou Yuon, Son Sen, Khieu Thirith, Khieu Ponnary, Ieng Sary, and Saloth Sar. They were dominant among the people who created and controlled the myriad organizational entities over the stretch of the five stages in the rise and fall of Democratic Kampuchea. In the early 1960s under the leadership of Saloth Sar (secretary general of the Central Committee of the Kampuchean Communist Party, 1963–1981, and prime minister of Democratic Kampuchea, 1976–1979), the KCP divided the country into five tactical regions for the development of a political infrastructure.[82] This early work on the development of attitudes among the peasantry favorable to the cause of the revolutionaries, perhaps in a way analogous to the development of a candidate's "name recognition" by political strategists in Western electoral campaigns, laid the groundwork for the radicalization of the masses in the periods of revolutionary violence between 1968 and 1975. It is in this sense that the KCP had been "preparing for armed struggle" through the early revolutionary period.

The importance of competent cadres during the early phases of revolutionary organization follows from one of the most well-documented findings in research on the role of ideology in political behavior. Elites tend to have belief systems that are complex and contain idea elements that are highly interrelated and logically consistent. Mass publics, on the other hand, tend to have less well-integrated cognitive belief systems in which political objects do not have a central place.[83]

Thus, although some cadres in a revolutionary movement will internalize the ideology and develop an intense commitment to the revolutionary cause based upon ideological beliefs, the rank and file of the mass organization do not tend to internalize all the complexities of the ideology. The KCP tried to combat this tendency by requiring stringent scrutiny of candidate members to the party, and a prolonged period of apprenticeship and probation before full membership was conferred.

Mass Support

However, the problem of winning the cooperation and understanding of the masses remains. Research, as well as revolutionary experience, has shown that ideology in a reduced or shorthand form—simple slogans and symbols—under certain conditions can motivate the rank and file members of a mass organization.[84] When individuals are "intensely discontented" and/or when nationalistic passions are aroused by protracted overt conflict, they tend to be susceptible to motivation by revolutionary slogans and songs.

Peasant discontent and nationalism in Cambodia became intense after 1970, and this fact contributed to the ability of the KCP to recruit and motivate the masses. One of the ways the KCP consciously developed this means of mass motivation was by encouraging the singing of revolutionary songs. More than morale builders, the songs embodied revolutionary principles couched in terms of traditional peasant experiences, the association thus performing an effective and important pedagogical function. For example, one song extolled the notion of doing battle with a hoe in one hand to tame nature and a gun in the other hand to tame the imperialists:

[Untitled]

We no longer rely on heaven in farming,
But on collective strength
And be it the dry or the rainy season,
The rice grows fragrant throughout the year!

We dig and we hoe,
To clear out stones and brush.
The Wilderness of yesterday,
Gives way to fertile fields today!

With shoulder-pole and baskets,
We do battle against nature
Defeat the stubborn U.S. imperialist foe and its lackeys,
Win a good harvest and a better life.

The rice is ripe in the fields,
It ripples gracefully in the breeze
The sun of revolution lights the land,
Shedding its golden, happy rays everywhere![85]

No doubt, it loses something in the translation. These songs were probably quite effective in reinforcing camaraderie and *esprit de corps*. The land and the harvest are central to peasant society, and the KCP revolutionary songs often focused on these images. Another song lauds resoluteness, solidarity, self-sacrifice, and hatred of the enemy:

> The Beauty of Kampuchea
> O beautiful, beloved Kampuchea,
> Our destiny has joined us together
> Uniting our forces so as not to disagree
> Even young girls get up and join the struggle.
> Pity our friends who shoulder arms.
> Thorns pierce their feet; they do not complain;
> This is an accomplishment of Khmer children
> Struggling until blood flows out to cover the ground.
> They sacrifice themselves without regret,
> They chase the Lon Nol bandits
> With swords and knives hacking at them,
> Killing them, until the Lon Nol bandits are destroyed.[86]

The function performed by these songs is better understood if viewed in the social context where they "naturally" occurred.

Organization

Sometime during the early 1970s—as early as December 1970, in the northeastern provinces according to some accounts—the KCP revolutionary planners laid out a six-tiered framework of political organization, connecting the tiny group of leaders to every individual in the liberated parts of Cambodia controlled by the Saloth Sar faction. As new areas came under the control of Saloth Sar, this political framework was applied to give the Organization control over the activities of the populace. The political framework was instituted in areas of Takeo Province "liberated" in 1972, for example, allowing the organization and implementation of "production solidarity groups" at the beginning of 1973.[87] The combination of political control and economic productivity proved to be one of the central assets of the KCP's struggle.

At the base of the KCP political hierarchy were groups of ten to fifteen nuclear families, called *kroms* or "groups." The *krom* was ruled by a tripartite committee composed of a chairman (party authority) appointed by the *Khmer Rouge*, and a vice-chairman (task allocation) and a member (social matters), drawn from the people. A varying number of groups made up a *phum* or "village," which in plurality constituted a *khum* or "canton" or "zone." A number of cantons, moving up the organizational ladder, combined into a *srok* or "sector."

From the *krom* through the *phum* and the *khum* to the *srok*, each of these four levels in the politico-administrative hierarchy was ruled in the same manner as the *krom*, with a party-appointed chair plus a vice-chair and a member. Of these four lowest levels, only the uppermost, the *srok*, coincided with the traditional Cambodian administrative districts.[88]

The fifth level, called a *damban* ("district"), replaced the traditional province (*khet*). Finally, at the apex of the administrative hierarchy, Kampuchea was divided into six *phumpheak* or "areas" plus five *svayet* ("autonomous districts"). Thus the administrative hierarchy was constructed in such a manner that the KCP Central Committee (known as the *kanak machim*) had only to communicate with the uppermost tier of the structure, the *phumpheak* and the *svayet*. The two uppermost tiers of the hierarchy were staffed entirely by military commanders. The strong social base provided by this structure was a critical asset to the KCP. With most of the country liberated in the early parts of the struggle, the KCP was able to bring large numbers of people directly into support of the revolution even if the people had no idea exactly what the "cause" was.

This creeping state apparatus gave substance to the claims and boasts of KCP leaders like Khieu Samphan, who in 1974 told the Cambodian Information Agency, "We are a complete state, totally independent, politically, militarily, and economically. We have power, an army, and sufficient finances. In brief, we have a complete administrative regime . . . without being dependent on any foreign country."[89]

The social base of mass support and the high degree of organization instituted by the KCP were central elements in its strategy of the late revolutionary period. The leaders of the KCP were convinced that this social base was a key to victory in their struggle. Saloth Sar listed it second in importance, second only to his own leadership. In reference to the victory over Lon Nol in CHENLA II during late 1973, Khieu Samphan has argued that "the total support of the people explains why our numerical inferiority, with no heavy equipment to oppose the enemy's tanks, artillery, and planes, could bring off the victory."[90]

The KCP's Use of Sihanouk

Before 1970, however, direct identification with the goals of the revolution was for most peasants an unlikely event. After all, the former king of Cambodia himself had continually denounced the Cambodian communists as worse than common bandits, as the demented agents of a foreign enemy. In this connection, identification with the revolutionary movement and internalization of the ideology of the movement are closely related to the legitimacy accorded to the efforts of the revolutionaries. In the eyes of most peasants before 1970, the communists had very little legitimacy. What was the basis upon which these "bandits" demanded that the people abandon their traditional life-styles and devote themselves to this "cause"?

Religious and social values are deeply embedded in the collective consciousness of any people, perhaps particularly so for the Khmers.[91] Revolutions must begin with this fundamental fact, and the *Khmer Rouge* were aware of it. Although it took some time, the KCP was eventually able to learn to exploit the traditional collective consciousness, linking traditional values with its cause. The revolutionary songs above are good illustrations of this tactic. The KCP's lack of long-term fidelity to the traditional value systems was a central factor in its demise.[92]

For the peasants of Cambodia, the king was the traditional locus of all political authority. Moreover, the king was the official protector of the state and national religion, Buddhism. Without linkage to this most important symbolic force, political activity in Cambodia would gain little support among the Khmer peasants at large. In the words of one Cambodia scholar, "To the Khmer people, the king *was* the state, and without him national existence itself would be threatened."[93] Although this may overstate the case, Sihanouk remained the central figure in Cambodian politics through the 1960s.

On May 5, 1970, with the founding of the Royal Government of Khmer National Unification (GRUNK) and the establishment of Norodom Sihanouk as head of state in exile, the peasants rallied around the movement *en masse*. As the traditional symbol of leadership and political and religious authority, Sihanouk endowed the entire movement with the element of legitimacy that makes the difference between passive and active support. Until the emergence and expansion of the Kampuchean National United Front (FUNK) and GRUNK, as one observer noted, "the peasants, however much they may have regretted Sihanouk's deposition, were ill-equipped to translate their feelings into action."[94] Similarly, before FUNK and GRUNK, the guerrillas of the RAK were ill-equipped to win the allegiance of the peasants. Sihanouk, deposed and exiled, had no means to resist except his prestige. Thus, FUNK and GRUNK were a marriage of convenience for all parties: "The guerillas were endowed with legitimacy by Sihanouk's endorsement, while conversely the experienced liberation cadres endowed Sihanouk's appeals with the necessary practical and tangible structure."[95]

What did this mean in concrete terms? When Sihanouk announced the formation of FUNK in Peking on March 23, 1970, he did so over a radio broadcast heard by Major Tim Niang, who was commander of the two battalions of government troops defending the key Mekong River town of Kratie. Responding to the prince's appeal, Major Tim paid his troops five hundred *riels* per head to go home. Then the Major delivered the town and with the town the entire Sixth Military Region of Cambodia into the hands of the local resistance cadres, who held it until the NVA was able to secure it on May 5.[96] Thus "liberated" on the first day of FUNK's life, Kratie became a central PFLANK and NVA headquarters for the duration of the struggle.

Similar events occurred throughout Cambodia. The key Mekong River ferry town, Neak Luong, was "liberated" for a short time following Sihanouk's broadcast appeal when local Buddhist bonzes persuaded government troops stationed there to lay down their arms and leave the area. In the west, it was the same: "In the Battambang area ... an old resistance cadre heard Sihanouk's appeal and without awaiting further instructions he went to talk things over with a company of Lon Nol's troops in his area. They followed him into the jungle where they set up an important resistance base, reinforced a few days later by groups of students from Battambang University."[97]

Sihanouk's March 23 appeal to resist the Lon Nol regime was calculated to woo the KCP, for Sihanouk badly needed an ally who had the means to fight if he ever hoped to regain power in Cambodia. His declaration was worded accordingly: "The handful of reactionary bourgeois elements and princes who were able to climb to the highest positions thanks to the Sangkum," Sihanouk began, "is leading our country straight into anarchism and war provoked by U.S. imperialism."[98] He called on all his "children" to take up guerrilla warfare in the jungles. The KCP wasted no time in accepting his invitation. Detailing three men to seduce the prince, the party released a "Statement of Support to Prince Norodom Sihanouk" over the names of Hu Nim, Hou Yuon, and Khieu Samphan. These three members of the KCP Central Committee were intimately familiar with the prince's politics and foibles. Their March 26 call for solidarity pledged loyalty to the person of the prince and the policies he had declared since 1955: neutralism on the basis of the Bandung Principles. These three key communists were received by the prince in Peking, and assumed leadership of the three most important ministries in the exile government. Khieu Samphan became vice-prime minister and minister of national defense. Khieu was nominally in charge of PFLANK, the new army Sihanouk had ordered to appear, but behind the scenes Saloth Sar quietly ran the army. Hu Nim became minister of information and propaganda, and Hou Yuon was put in the position of minister of interior, communal reforms, and cooperatives. With these three key ministries under its control, the KCP would find it a relatively straightforward albeit demanding matter eventually to seize control of the entire GRUNK apparatus by means of creeping administrative *coup*.

The segregation of the KCP factions in GRUNK from those loyal to Norodom Sihanouk was carefully orchestrated by the communists. Naturally, the PFLANK was the primary instrument of revolutionary activity, and was located wholly within Cambodia. The political bureau of GRUNK's Central Committee was evenly divided, six *Khmer Rumdo* or "Sihanoukists" and six *Khmer Rouge*. Responsibility and operational authority, however, were not evenly distributed between Sihanouk and the KCP. The Sihanouk entourage was encouraged to remain in Peking while the KCP led the struggle at home. A message of April 30, 1971, from Khieu Samphan at PFLANK headquarters in Kratie to Sihanouk in Peking expresses the flavor of this tactic of splitting GRUNK into two parts as well as anything:

> Our important victories are the result of the struggle and the perfect unity between that part of the [FUNK] which is abroad, and that part which is inside the country. It is this unity that the enemy is trying to shatter and to attain this end it would like to disperse Samdech Head of State [Sihanouk], and other [FUNK] leaders somewhere away from Peking. . . . it is therefore indispensable that leading members of [FUNK] remain in Peking.[99]

For his part, Sihanouk seemed to understand very well the role he had been accorded. This is clearly evident in many comments made by the prince. In a statement issued from Peking shortly after the *coup*, for example, Sihanouk renounced any claim to the throne, declaring that his only duty now was to defeat the Lon Nol regime. "This duty, which I will fulfill without fail till victory or my death, is a sacred duty for all Khmer worthy of the name . . . [but] from now on I belong to the past and I know this."[100] In France he was reported to have said in September 1971, "I am giving everything to the Red Khmers. They are pure. They will do what is necessary for the people. They are patriots."[101]

By June of 1973, Sihanouk began to feel the pinch of expanding KCP control, and this perception led to slightly more pessimistic estimates. That month he told Italian journalist Oriana Fallaci, "The Khmer Rouge do not like me at all, I know that. Ohh! la la! I understand quite well that they only tolerate me because without me they cannot prevail over the peasants. Without the peasant, one can make no revolution in Cambodia. It is clear to me. When they no longer need me, they will spit me out like a cherry pit."[102]

Little did he know, but Sihanouk was already in the process of being "spit out." Sihanouk had been on a tour of the liberated zones in April of 1973 to give cheer to those pursuing the struggle. Shortly after he left, the KCP began to institute a systematic campaign of "de-Sihanoukization." Meak Sam Hon, who had been chairman of a *phum* under the KCP but who fled to Thailand to escape its rule, said that at the beginning of April 1973, immediately following Sihanouk's visit to the area, "if you still use his name and support Sihanouk, then you will be taken away and you will never return. They told us to support Khieu Samphan and no others."[103]

Throughout 1973, evidence of Sihanouk's "slippage" within GRUNK and FUNK continued to mount. In June and July, he was accompanied on an East European tour by Ieng Sary, who humiliated him by continually "clarifying" statements that the head of state was making.[104] By September of 1973, the KCP was being quite open about Sihanouk's fate, at least in external propaganda. In an interview with Sylvana Foa in Peking, Ieng Sary reported that "Sihanouk is one of those aspects of Cambodian tradition, like Buddhism and the monarchy, which we believe unnecessary for the larger union. We will phase out those aspects we do not consider to be progressive and revolutionary."[105] At a press conference at the beginning of April 1974, Sihanouk was reduced to the role of interpreter for Khieu Samphan, perhaps an indication of the KCP's growing contempt for the ex-monarch.

Thus, with periodic bureaucratic reorganizations within GRUNK, administrative authority was gradually usurped by the communists, led by the Saloth Sar faction. By April 1973, the KCP felt confident enough of its control over the population of the liberated areas to begin decoupling Sihanouk from the movement in the minds of the people. In November of that same year, partly in response to charges from Lon Nol that a government in exile was unworthy of consideration for Cambodia's seat in the United Nations, GRUNK moved the political section of the provisional government to the northeastern region of Cambodia.[106] Sihanouk and his advisors stayed behind in Peking as the "diplomatic corps." Now the United Front was united only in name. From November of 1973, the KCP controlled all aspects of the situation from Cambodia. Throughout the following year, the remaining few vestiges of Sihanoukism scattered through the administrative apparatus were purged.

Yet, so effective was the KCP's use of Sihanouk to bolster its image internally and externally that even Henry Kissinger was duped for a time into believing that control of Sihanouk was the same thing as control of the left in Kampuchea. In February of 1973, Kissinger and the PRC's Chou En-lai concocted a scheme to draw GRUNK into negotiations with the Khmer Republic, a scheme that relied on Chou's ability to influence Sihanouk and Sihanouk's ability to dominate GRUNK and FUNK. In ignorance of the real balance of forces within GRUNK, Kissinger pressed the scheme to no avail. Even as he was attempting to draw Sihanouk into negotiations, the KCP was proceeding full speed ahead with the de-Sihanoukization campaign inside the country. The whole deal fell apart in mid-July 1973, when Chou realized that Sihanouk would have no voice in a "National Congress" scheduled for July 19–21 to affirm GRUNK policy. On July 18, Chou informed Kissinger that the scheme had collapsed. The next day, as the National Congress in liberated Kampuchea declared its intent to achieve "total victory" over U.S. imperialism, Kissinger summed up the failure to his staff in Washington: "Sihanouk couldn't deliver the Khmer Rouge and the Chinese couldn't deliver Sihanouk."[107] The key to the failure of this gambit was the fact that Sihanouk could never have "delivered" the KCP.

Vietnamese Support

During this same period, beginning immediately after the signing of the Paris Peace Accords on January 27, 1973, the Saloth Sar faction pressed the termination of the KCP relationship with the Vietnamese communists. It accelerated the liquidation of all ethnic Vietnamese serving in the PFLANK and the administrative structure of the emerging regime. It began to restrict the regions in which the NVA and the PRG were welcome to conduct operations in support of their activities in South Vietnam. But, at this stage of the game, these actions proved to be little more than minor sources of irritation for the Vietnamese, though they perceived themselves as having sacrificed much on behalf of the Kampuchean liberation struggle.

Thus, at the same time the Khmer National United Front (FUNK) was beginning to collapse as even an imaginary entity, the United Front of the Three Indochinese Peoples (UFTIP) was also rapidly degenerating. Though an undercurrent of anti-Vietnamese sentiment in the KCP inner circle had been evident from 1970 and before, considerable cooperation had been possible until January 1973. With the signing of the Paris Peace Accords by Le Duc Tho and Henry Kissinger on January 27, 1973, that undercurrent of KCP hostility was catalyzed to near rage.

The Khmer communists had refused to be a party to the Paris negotiations between the United States and North Vietnam, perceiving them as a Vietnamese sellout. When the U.S. bombers were finally called off Hanoi after the signing of the agreement, this fact in effect freed the entire awesome might of U.S. tactical air power in Southeast Asia to pound the Khmer communist positions. In fact, the 1973 air war against the Kampuchean communists was unprecedented in intensity. This perceived betrayal in turn intensified the KCP's long-standing hatred of the Vietnamese. As Norodom Sihanouk explained it, "Immediately after the signing of the U.S.-Vietnam peace agreement, the Khmer Rouge ordered the Vietminh and Vietcong stationed in Kampuchea out of the country, demanding that they dismantle their bases and supply routes. In this way the Khmer Rouge hoped to punish the Viets, 'whose government (Hanoi) betrayed the common cause.'"[108]

Since UFTIP had been formed in March 1970, laying the political groundwork for the military assistance program offered by the Vietnamese, the Vietnamese had indeed given much assistance to that "common cause." They had provided military advisors, some weapons, many soldiers, and, on many critical occasions, direct military support with regular NVA troops. NVA support had been crucial in the reorganization of the KCP's army, and the NVA had repeatedly saved the day for the KCP on the field of battle: in 1970 during the initial collapse of the Lon Nol regime and in the CHENLA I offensive; in 1971 during the CHENLA II offensive; and in the Mekong campaigns of 1972. Saloth Sar even admitted that the NVA provided crucial artillery support during the final offensive against Phnom Penh![109] Although there had been a long history of intrigue between the Vietnamese and Cambodian communists, the decision to begin cutting all ties and seek total, uncompromised independence was a very critical event in the history of the KCP. The beginning of the end for the Saloth Sar faction can be dated from this first grave insult to its brothers in the struggle against U.S. imperialism.

The Khmer Republic

It would be unjust to conclude an assessment of the reasons for the KCP's victory without a few words on the role played by its opponent, the Khmer Republic. That this factor is reduced to a "few words" is in direct proportion to its weight. Lon Nol's Republic was never able to build or sustain among the urban elite a sense of legitimacy comparable to that achieved by GRUNK among substantial segments of the rural population. This first requisite of victory was never really approached by the Khmer Republic. What little respect the Khmer Republic might have developed among the peasants progressively deteriorated under the pressure of FANK's often brutal tactics, the more so when it became obvious that Phnom Penh could protect them neither from its own troops, from its allies, nor from the enemy.

If a time-lapse view of the KCP's development over the late revolutionary period showed steady and rapid growth, then the time-lapse view of the Khmer Republic showed the steady disintegration of power. The internal power struggles among the Phnom Penh elite often seemed to take precedence in the minds of many influential Republicans over the struggle with the communists.

As one critic wryly put it, Lon Nol advocated the principle of all-for-one and one-for-all. Along with his brother, Lon Non, who headed the special internal security forces of the Khmer Republic and who was a well-known opium dealer, Lon Nol commanded the obedience if not the respect of most of the military. Sirik Matak, long-time royal rival to Sihanouk, and closely allied with conservative Western-oriented business interests, was the primary challenger to Lon Nol's position. Son Ngoc Thanh, leader of the repatriated *Khmer Serei* mercenary army, managed to rise through the government to the post of prime minister, a post he had held briefly some 25 years earlier. After so many years of exile, however, Son did not find it easy to cultivate a loyal constituency from among the Phnom Penh elite. General In Tam, who presided over the 1970 *coup* and held several important posts in the Khmer Republic, managed to keep alive a loyal if small and ultimately ineffective political party to back his ambitions. The list goes on, and indeed becomes rather more sordid, but the above is sufficient to give an idea of the fragmentation that beset the Phnom Penh power elite. In spite of the emergence of some capable military commanders near the end of the war, corruption, inefficiency, and just plain lack of commitment and planning had eaten the core out of what little basis the Khmer Republic had to begin with. It was too late.

Summary of Late Revolutionary KCP Strategy

The KCP strategy in the late revolutionary period was multifaceted and dynamic. It relied heavily on political violence. Beginning with the decision to supplement political struggle with armed struggle at the end of 1967, the KCP created the RAK and conducted an only moderately successful guerrilla war. The KCP did manage to hold its own and even to grow modestly until Norodom Sihanouk was deposed in March 1970. The previously fragmented insurgency in Cambodia was politically welded by the *coup*, immediately entering into internal united front with Sihanouk and KPP outliers, and external united front with the Vietnamese and Laotian communists. A new level of support was also gained from the Chinese. All of this set the stage for an explosive growth in the revolutionary movement, a growth to be assisted by the U.S. Air Force.

Military operations after 1970 were conducted in a highly flexible manner, taking advantage of combined warfare including guerrilla, conventional, and proxy modes of combat as the situation warranted. The military operations were supported by a broad array of political measures, such as complex domestic and international propaganda campaigns carefully tailored to a wide variety of target audiences. This enabled an equally complex transfer of legitimacy and administrative control from both domestic and international allies. Identification with Prince Sihanouk's royal prestige and reliance on Vietnamese revolutionary experience were phased out as they ceased to be perceived as necessary.

At the same time that the Saloth Sar KCP was directing all these "external" activities, it maneuvered for the elimination of competition for internal party power. This end was considerably advanced by its being able to arrange, by virtue of its control of the Ministry of Defense, to have old line KPP-loyal and Hanoi-KPP-loyal military units sent into some of the toughest battles. KCP politico-military strategy included also as a central element mass-based psychological, economic, and social reorganization on the civilian front, providing a sound social and economic basis for the revolutionary violence. On the military front, a strict adherence to the principles of economy of force and maintenance of the initiative was sustained, except in the case of the 1973 dry season offensive, when the former principle was deliberately violated for internal political reasons.

Clearly, then, the *Khmer Rouge* were highly skilled leaders. Multi-level united front, combined warfare, social reorganization, and administrative *coup d'état* all contributed to the KCP victory. The Saloth Sar faction of the KCP, firmly in control of the center of the organization and a highly refined coercive apparatus, emerged from the civil war in a good position to initiate the final stage of the revolution: internal consolidation of party power.

Notes

1. The Great Red Dragon, described in the Book of Revelation, was a portent of war in Heaven. Passage quoted is from the Revised Standard Version of the New Testament.
2. Douglas Pike, *Cambodia's War* (New York: American Friends of Vietnam, 1971), p. 13.
3. From President Nixon's press conference of November 12, 1971.
4. Herbert Kelman, "Compliance, Identification and Internalization: Three Processes of Attitudinal Change," *Journal of Conflict Resolution* 2 (1958), pp. 51–60; more general treatments include Harry C. Triandis, *Attitude and Attitude Change* (New York: Wiley, 1971); Gary Cronkite, *Persuasion: Speech and Behavioral Change* (New York: Bobbs-Merrill, 1969); and Charles A. and Sara B. Kiesler, *Conformity* (Reading, Mass.: Addison Wesley, 1970).
5. Harry C. Triandis, *Attitude and Attitude Change*, pp. 159, 172.
6. Paul Bernan, *Revolutionary Organization: Institution-Building Within the People's Liberation Armed Forces* (Lexington, MA: D. C. Heath, 1974), p. 237, n. 14.
7. There are many taxonomies of "prerequisites for successful guerrilla war," though this one is adequate for the present limited purposes. It is drawn from Sheldon Simon, *War and Politics in Cambodia* (Durham, NC: Duke University Press, 1974), p. 27.
8. Stephen Heder, "Kampuchea's Armed Struggle: Origins of an Independent Revolution," *Bulletin of Concerned Asian Scholars* 11:1 (1979), p. 12.
9. S. Heder, "Origins of the Conflict," *Southeast Asian Chronicle*, no. 64 (1981), p. 16.
10. S. Heder, "Kampuchea's Armed Struggle," p. 13.
11. *Ibid.*
12. *Ibid.*, p. 14; Sheldon Simon, *War and Politics in Cambodia*, pp. 49, 119. William Shawcross cites one Vietnamese cadre who said that the actual number of soldiers in the RAK was much smaller, probably around 400; see his *Sideshow* (New York: Simon and Schuster, 1979), p. 246.
13. D. Pike, *Cambodia's War*, p. 19.
14. Tran Dinh Tho, *The Cambodian Incursion* (Washington, D.C.: U.S. Army Center for Military History, 1979), pp. 21, 22.
15. See Donald Lancaster, "The Decline of Sihanouk's Regime," in J. J. Zasloff and A. E. Goodman, eds., *Conflict in Indochina* (Lexington, MA: D. C. Heath, 1972), p. 61.
16. See Malcolm Caldwell and Lek Tan, *Cambodia in the Southeast Asian War* (New York: Monthly Review Press, 1975), pp. 250, 251, citing the article by T. D. Allman.
17. For a review of events surrounding the formation of SEATO, see W. Shawcross, *Sideshow*, pp. 52–55; also, see Wilfred Burchett, ed., *My War with the CIA: The Memoirs of Prince Norodom Sihanouk* (New York: Random House, 1972). For additional comments on the so-called Bangkok Plot, see Milton

Osborne, *Politics and Power in Cambodia* (Victoria, Australia: Longman Australia, 1973), pp. 62, 63; and Michael Liefer, *Cambodia: The Search for Security* (New York: Praeger, 1967), pp. 197n. and 198n. For a more extreme view of these events, see Charles Meyer, *Derrière le Sourire Khmer* (Paris: Plon, 1971), pp. 234–236.

18. See M. Caldwell and Lek Tan, *Cambodia in the Southeast Asian War*, pp. 98–104; R. M. Smith, *Cambodia's Foreign Policy* (Ithaca, NY: Cornell University Press, 1965), pp. 163ff; and W. Shawcross, *Sideshow*, pp. 53, 54.

19. The 1982 Intelligence Identities Protection Act provides very strict sanctions against actions by scholars and journalists that might endanger U.S. intelligence assets. I am legally constrained from identifying this agent, even though this is a historical work and though the agent's identity has been previously published in many places, e.g., W. Shawcross, *Sideshow*, p. 54; and M. Caldwell and Lek Tan, *Cambodia in the Southeast Asian War*, p. 103.

20. W. Shawcross, *Sideshow*, p. 54.

21. *Ibid.*, pp. 55–58. There is some confusion regarding the date of this document. In his text, Shawcross discusses it in the context of the late 1950s and the early 1960s, and he dates it 1959. In his citation, however, the document is dated 1969.

22. Richard M. Nixon, *The Memoirs of Richard Nixon* (New York: Warner Brothers, 1978), 1:553.

23. Henry Kissinger, *White House Years* (Boston: Little, Brown, 1979), p. 464; hereafter designated WHY.

24. *Ibid.*, p. 463.

25. W. Shawcross, *Sideshow*, p. 122.

26. Tran Dinh Tho, *The Cambodian Incursion*, pp. 13, 14, and 32.

27. R. M. Nixon, *Memoirs*, p. 553.

28. *Ibid.*, p. 555.

29. H. Kissinger, *WHY*, p. 502.

30. *Ibid.*, p. 487.

31. This phenomenal address, which the author can remember first hand, is a must for students of contemporary political rhetoric. It appears as Appendix 10 in M. Caldwell and Lek Tan, *Cambodia in the Southeast Asian War;* also as pages 218–224 in U.S. Congress, House Committee on the Judiciary, *Statement of Information: Book 11—Bombing of Cambodia* (Washington, D.C.: USGPO, 1974).

32. R. M. Nixon, *Memoirs*, 1:562.

33. On the matter of viewing "Patton" at the White House during this crisis, see for example, H. Kissinger, *WHY*, p. 498; W. Shawcross, *Sideshow*, p. 135; and Roger Morris, *Uncertain Greatness: Henry Kissinger and American Foreign Policy* (New York: Harper and Row, 1977), pp. 173–174.

34. Tran Dinh Tho, *The Cambodian Incursion*, p. 182.

35. Sak Sutsakhan, *The Khmer Republic at War and the Final Collapse* (Washington, D.C.: U.S. Army Center for Military History, 1980), p. 173;

also appears in the chapter by Sak in Tran Dinh Tho, *The Cambodian Incursion*, pp. 165, 166.

36. Tran Dinh Tho, *The Cambodian Incursion*, p. 78.
37. United States Congress, Senate Foreign Relations Committee, *Cambodia: December 1970* (Washington: USGPO, 1970), p. 4.
38. M. Caldwell and Lek Tan, *Cambodia in the Southeast Asian War*, p. 345.
39. Sak Sutsakhan, *Khmer Republic at War*, p. 175.
40. See J. J. Zasloff and M. Brown, *Communist Indochina and U.S. Foreign Policy* (Boulder, CO: Westview Press, 1978), p. 143 and n. 63; also see *Background Notes: Cambodia*, U.S. Department of State Publication #7747 (Washington, D.C.: USGPO, 1977).
41. *Oxford Economic Atlas of the World*, 4th ed. (London: Oxford University Press, 1972), p. 132.
42. G. Hildebrand and G. Porter, *Cambodia: Starvation and Revolution* (New York: Monthly Review Press, 1976), p. 32.
43. *Ibid.*
44. *Ibid.*, p. 36; all figures regarding PL-480 are taken from Hildebrand and Porter.
45. For example, see *New York Times* exposé on December 27, 1972; also, *Hearing* before the U.S. Congress, Senate Subcommittee on Agriculture, Environmental and Consumer Protection Appropriations, April 25, 1974, *Agriculture, Environment and Consumer Protection Appropriations for FY75, Part 2*, for testimony of W. C. Goodfellow (director of research, Indochina Resource Center) on the failure of PL-480 in Cambodia; and *Foreign Food Assistance, Hearings* before the Senate Subcommittee on Foreign Agricultural Policy, April 4, 1974, for a review of the adequacy of the PL-480 program with respect to Cambodia and South Vietnam.
46. G. Hildebrand and G. Porter, *Starvation and Revolution*, p. 30; also, see *Report on the Payment of Phantom Troops in the Cambodian Military Forces*, Comptroller General of the United States, July 3, 1973 (Washington, D.C.: USGPO, 1973).
47. W. Shawcross, *Sideshow*, p. 396.
48. *Ibid.*, p. 391.
49. *Ibid.*, p. 396.
50. H. Kissinger, *WHY*, p. 240; see p. 1485, n. 17 for H.A.K.'s wrath. Reportedly, when the Shawcross book appeared, sections of *WHY* dealing with Cambodia had already gone to the printers, but the galleys were recalled for alteration in view of Shawcross's charges. Elsewhere, Kissinger has referred to *Sideshow* as "inaccurate and distorted." (See rear cover of the Pocket Books edition of *Sideshow*.)
51. See William Shawcross's introduction to Norodom Sihanouk, *War and Hope: The Case for Cambodia* [M. Feeney, trans.] (New York: Random House, 1980); see also Peter Rodman, "Sideswipe: Kissinger, Shawcross and the Responsibility for Cambodia," *American Spectator* 14:3 (March 1981), and the

Shawcross-Rodman exchange in *American Spectator* 14:7 (July 1981); and the second volume of Henry Kissinger's memoirs, *Years of Upheaval* (Boston: Little, Brown, 1982), hereafter cited as *YOU*.

52. Tran Dinh Tho, *Cambodian Incursion*, pp. 171-173.

53. For an explanation of the right, precedence, and scope of defensive activities under international law and the Charter of the United Nations, see W. W. Bishop, Jr., *International Law* (Boston: Little, Brown, 1971), pp. 916-933; and pp. 934-947 for U.S. State Department defense of U.S. military action in Southeast Asia based upon these laws. For an opposed view, see J.H.E. Fried, *United States Military Intervention in Cambodia in the Light of International Law* (Toronto, 1971); also see Richard Falk, *The Vietnam War and International Law*, 4 vols. (Princeton: Princeton University Press, 1968-1976), especially vol. 3, *The Widening Context* (1972).

54. See William Shawcross, introduction to Norodom Sihanouk, *War and Hope*, pp. xxxvi-xxxvii.

55. H. Kissinger, *WHY*, p. 517.

56. See H. Kissinger, *YOU*, p. 348; cf. K. Quinn, "Political Change in Wartime: The Khmer Krahom Revolution in Southern California 1970-1974," *Naval War College Review*, 28:4 (Spring 1976), pp. 3-31, n. 18. Quinn's thesis is developed in greater detail in his "The Origins and Development of Radical Cambodian Communism" (Ph.D. diss., University of Maryland, 1982).

57. Quoted in W. Shawcross, *Sideshow*, p. 395.

58. These letters constitute Part Four of the U.S. Congress, House Judiciary Committee, *Statement of Information: Book 11—Bombing of Cambodia*, pp. 443-597; also see p. 4, n. 6, as per U.N. Security Council, Supplement 2 (A/8002, pp. 101-103, 1970).

59. In 1941, the British Royal Air Force pioneered the strategic concept that holds civilian population concentrations as legitimate targets for airborne attack, for purposes of industrial/agricultural disruption and population intimidation. The concept reached its ultimate realization at Hiroshima and Nagasaki in 1945 at the hands of the United States, which has refined the concept considerably since that time. See F.J.P. Veale, *Advance to Barbarism: The Development of Total Warfare from Serajevo to Hiroshima* (Torrance, CA: Institute for Historical Review, 1979). This book was originally published under the pseudonym, "A. Jurist" (London: Thompson and Smith, 1948).

60. Anthony Lewis, "Out, Damned Spot!" *New York Times*, September 24, 1979.

61. Ben Kiernan and Chanthou Boua, *Peasants and Politics in Kampuchea 1941-1981* (New York: M. E. Sharpe, 1982), p. 206.

62. William G. Effros, *Quotations: Vietnam 1945-1970* (New York: Random House, 1970), p. 244.

63. See, for example, W. Burchett, ed., *My War with the CIA: The Memoirs of Prince Norodom Sihanouk*, p. 69.

64. Tran Dinh Tho, *The Cambodian Incursion*, pp. 69, 173.

65. Sak Sutsakhan, *The Khmer Republic at War*, p. 67.

66. See M. Caldwell and Lek Tan, *Cambodia in the Southeast Asian War*, p. 353.
67. Sak Sutsakhan, *Khmer Republic at War*, p. 72.
68. *Ibid.*, p. 74.
69. *Ibid.*, p. 79.
70. Quoted in W. Burchett, ed., *My War with the CIA*, p. 243.
71. See, for example, Sheldon Simon, *War and Politics in Cambodia*, pp. 49, 119; W. Shawcross, *Sideshow*, p. 261; Ben Kiernan, "Conflict in the Kampuchean Communist Movement," *Journal of Contemporary Asia* 10:1-2 (1980), p. 70; Donald Kirk, "Revolution and Political Violence in Cambodia, 1970-1974," in J. J. Zasloff and A. E. Goodman, eds., *Conflict in Indochina: New Perspectives* (Lexington, MA: D. C. Heath, 1972), p. 217.
72. W. Shawcross, *Sideshow*, p. 298.
73. Sak Sutsakhan, *Khmer Republic at War*, p. 120.
74. W. Shawcross, *Sideshow*, p. 298.
75. S. Simon, *War and Politics*, p. 27.
76. W. Burchett, ed., *My War with the CIA*, p. 178.
77. *Ibid.*, p. 238; from Khieu Samphan action report to Sihanouk.
78. Sak Sutsakhan, *Khmer Republic at War*, p. 155.
79. *Ibid.*, p. 170.
80. B. Kiernan, "Conflict in the Kampuchean Communist Movement," p. 20.
81. Reported in *Le Monde*, and cited in T. M. Carney, *Communist Party Power in Kampuchea: Documents and Discussions*, Cornell University Southeast Asia Program, Data Paper #106 (Ithaca, NY: Cornell University, 1977).
82. D. Kirk, "Revolution and Political Violence," p. 221.
83. See Philip Converse, "The Nature of Belief Systems in Mass Publics," in David Apter, *Ideology and Discontent* (New York: Free Press, 1964), pp. 206-261. And see Ted Gurr, *Why Men Rebel* (Princeton University Press, 1970); and Paul Berman, *Revolutionary Organization*, pp. 197-207.
84. P. Berman, *Revolutionary Organization*, p. 244, n. 6.
85. *Fighting Cambodia: Reports of the Chinese Journalist Delegation to Cambodia* (Beijing: China Books, 1975), p. 45; used by kind courtesy of the People's Republic of China Foreign Languages Press.
86. See David P. Chandler, *Early Phases of the Liberation in Northwestern Cambodia: Conversations with Peang Sophi* (Melbourne: Center for Southeast Asian Studies, Monash University, 1976); translated from Khmer by David P. Chandler and used by his permission.
87. See G. Hildebrand and G. Porter, *Starvation and Revolution*, p. 71; the economic structure of Kampuchea under the *Khmer Rouge* will be dealt with at greater length in succeeding sections of this study.
88. François Ponchaud, *Cambodia: Year Zero* (New York: Holt, Rinehart and Winston, 1978), pp. 89-95.
89. Quoted in S. Simon, "The Khmer Resistance," in J. J. Zasloff and M. Brown, eds., *Communism in Indochina: New Perspectives* (Lexington, MA: D. C. Heath, 1975), p. 201.

90. Quoted in W. Burchett, ed., *My War with the CIA*, p. 188.
91. See, for example, David E. Pfanner and Jasper Ingersoll, "Theravada Buddhism and Village Economic Behavior," *Journal of Asian Studies* 21:3 (May 1962); and May Ebihara, "Interrelations Between Buddhism and Social Systems in Cambodian Peasant Culture," in M. Nash, ed., *Anthropological Studies in Theravada Buddhism* (New Haven: Yale University Southeast Asia Studies Program, 1966).
92. Ieng Sary in effect admitted that the errors of the KCP's ultraradical policies included insufficient regard for traditional sensibilities, when he denied at a news conference in New York City on July 8, 1981, that the new KCP program was "ideological, communism or socialism."
93. M. Caldwell and Lek Tan, *Cambodia in the Southeast Asian War*, p. 24; emphasis in original.
94. M. Osborne, *Politics and Power in Cambodia*, p. 112.
95. M. Caldwell and Lek Tan, *Cambodia in the Southeast Asian War*, p. 313.
96. W. Burchett, ed., *My War with the CIA*, pp. 175, 176.
97. Wilfred Burchett, *The Second Indochina War: Cambodia and Laos* (New York: International Publishers, 1970), pp. 71, 72.
98. Both Norodom Sihanouk's March 23, 1970 appeal and the March 26 reply from Hu Nim, Hou Yuon, and Khieu Samphan are reprinted in M. Caldwell and Lek Tan, *Cambodia in the Southeast Asian War*, as Appendices Five and Six.
99. W. Burchett, ed., *My War with the CIA*, pp. 212, 213.
100. M. Caldwell and Lek Tan, *Cambodia in the Southeast Asian War*, p. 276.
101. Donald Brown, "Exporting Insurgency: The Communists in Cambodia," in J. J. Zasloff and A. E. Goodman, eds., *Indochina in Conflict* (Lexington, MA: D. C. Heath, 1972), p. 127.
102. J. Barron and A. Paul, *Murder of a Gentle Land* (New York: Reader's Digest Books, 1977), p. 56.
103. D. Kirk, "Revolution and Political Violence," p. 218.
104. M. Osborne, "Norodom Sihanouk: A Leader of the Left?" in J. J. Zasloff and M. Brown, eds., *Communism in Indochina: New Perspectives* (Lexington, MA: D. C. Heath, 1975), p. 240.
105. *Ibid.*
106. S. Simon, "The Khmer Resistance," p. 202.
107. H. Kissinger, *YOU*, p. 336.
108. Norodom Sihanouk, *War and Hope*, pp. 64, 65.
109. *Dossier Kampuchea*, Part 1 (Hanoi: Le Courrier De Vietnam, 1978), p. 8; also see Wilfred Burchett, *The China-Kampuchea-Vietnam Triangle* (Chicago: Vanguard Books, 1981), p. 143.

7
Consolidation and Society Building (1975–1978)

Bleating and babbling I fell on his neck with a scream.
Wave upon wave of demented avengers
March cheerfully out of obscurity into the dream.
Have you heard the news? The dogs are dead!
You better stay home and do as you're told.
Get out of the road if you want to grow old.
—Roger Waters, from "Sheep"[1]

For a revolutionary movement, the most severe test comes not during battle to capture the seat of national power, but rather with the moment of victory. Although military strategy tends to exert an overwhelming force during war, often overpowering even the political objectives it ostensibly serves, with victory the military aspects of a revolution must be displaced by social and political concerns if the revolution is to make good on its promise to provide a better life for "the people."

Yet, this imperative is made more difficult to satisfy by the perception that at the moment of victory, at the inception of the revolutionary regime, the newly born order is most vulnerable. Counterrevolutionary elements in the defeated regime and society must be dealt with, neutralized. Perhaps more importantly, the revolutionary movement itself must be secured against threats from within; in this process, a dominant coalition or faction emerges. Most importantly, perhaps, the revolution must be secured against external threats. These concerns form the substance of this chapter.

Utopia Wrought

In his description of the final step in the creation of a perfect city—the rustication of all inhabitants tainted by the "old ways"—

Plato seems to have meant for his readers to understand that the perfect city was beyond the realm of possibility, and that moderation was therefore the best guide for reform within the *polis*. When the *Khmer Rouge* inherited a nation on April 17, 1975, moderation did not seem to be part of the plan.

The first action of the revolutionary forces that marched into Phnom Penh that morning, virtually simultaneously with the capture of key objectives such as the FANK General Staff headquarters and the studios of Radio Phnom Penh, was to initiate a mass evacuation of the entire population of the city: rustication. Within three days, the city that had swollen to more than three million (or five times its prewar population) was totally devoid of civilian life, except for a few score foreign diplomats and journalists holed up in the French embassy. Into the jungles and paddy went bankers, shopkeepers, refugees, everyone.

There has been much speculation as to the motives for the rustication. It is now clear that there were at least five reasons for this ultraradical action. First, there was the problem of security. It would be very difficult to secure the cities against various counterrevolutionary elements, including the defeated military, foreign agents, and "depraved" and "traitorous" social elements. Second, the new authorities were faced with severe health, sanitation, and food distribution and production problems. This set of problems could be solved in the long run only by the return of the bulk of the rural refugees to productive agricultural employment. A third and perhaps more salient reason has to do with ideology. The *Khmer Rouge* political program, based upon the theories of Hou Yuon, called for the construction of a rural-based society, and Saloth Sar, whose troops were the first to enter the city on April 17, was highly dedicated to an extreme implementation of this program. This latter fact is directly connected to a fourth and possibly most important reason for the rustication of Phnom Penh: internal party power. Gaining control of the defeated urban populace was an essential step in Saloth Sar's move towards total supremacy within the party as a whole. Although this could not be achieved immediately—the evacuation immediately grew into an omnidirectional exodus, with columns of rusticants moving out from the city in a radial pattern, and many moving into zones not controlled by troops loyal to Saloth Sar—getting a leg up on agenda-setting in the postvictory period by implementing the rustication plan immediately was a shrewd move by its authors. Finally, one last possible motive that is worth mentioning, though of questionable importance, is fear of bombing of the capital. Many refugees later reported that the cadres directing the evacuation justified the action to the rusticants by claiming that the U.S. Air Force was going to attack the city. American B-52 attacks on cities taken by the communists were indeed familiar to the KCP, and, whether or not the cadres actually believed that B-52 attacks against Phnom Penh were really imminent, President Ford did in fact order some limited B-52 raids against Cambodia—although not on Phnom Penh—on May 12, 1975, less than three weeks after the revolution came to victory. Thus, fears of American air attacks against the victorious revolutionaries were not as groundless as many scholars have claimed. All five of these factors were salient to one degree or another in the rustication.

The victorious army consolidated its control of the cities, first Phnom Penh, then Battambang, followed by the few others that remained to be liberated. As news of the end/beginning filtered to the provinces, crowds of refugees in the last bastions of the Khmer Republic began to clamor for the heads of the remaining Khmer Republic officials and FANK general officers. Having stopped in Oddar Meanchey to refuel his escape helicopters, the last Khmer Republic chief of state and FANK commander-in-chief, Sak Sutsakhan, narrowly escaped being turned over to hostile crowds at one of FANK's last strongholds.[2]

Those who did not escape found themselves in the two days after the fall of Phnom Penh being separated according to rank and occupation. Military officers and high officials of the Khmer Republic were given highest priority, and many of them had chosen to remain behind to see what was going to happen. They were not kept in suspense for very long. The fate of a group of FANK soldiers from the Battambang area is probably typical of that which awaited the entire leadership of FANK and the Khmer Republic.

On April 19, 1975, more than 300 officers from Lon Nol's army who had been collected from Battambang were told to put on their finest uniforms and all their decorations, as they were going to greet Prince Sihanouk in his return to a glorious and free Cambodia. After preparing themselves as instructed, they were loaded onto trucks and delivered to a prearranged location near Kbal Damrei where they were told to unload. They were subsequently machine-gunned from all sides.[3] Two of the intended victims managed to escape this trap and eventually told their story outside Kampuchea. The reports of several refugees who saw the pile of bodies in dress uniform at Kbal Damrei, and others elsewhere as well, confirmed that the KCP acted quickly and systematically to liquidate the upper levels of the defeated military.

In general, it seems beyond serious question that the victorious communists moved efficiently and rapidly to identify and eliminate this potential source of threat, as well as certain other intensely hated groups, such as bomber pilots. What is open to serious question is just how systematically, thoroughly, and deeply the postvictory purification pogrom affected the lower levels of the civil service, intellectuals, and bourgeoisie. The very fact that many refugees reaching sanctuary in Thailand and Vietnam fell into these categories by itself is enough to raise suspicions about *Khmer Rouge* efficiency and thoroughness in eliminating the hated class enemy, if in fact this was the undisputed plan. As we shall see, it was not.

Accounts from survivors of "reeducation" camps seem gravely threatening to the arguments of those who prefer to believe that the KCP immediately instituted a uniform policy of class genocide with ruthlessly effective rationality. If the account of the former deputy chief physician at Phnom Penh's central hospital, published in Paris in 1977, is an accurate reflection of conditions throughout Kampuchea in the immediate postvictory period, then it appears that the survival of nonpeasant individuals under the new regime was dependent upon two factors: (1) the ability to represent convincingly that one had abandoned the "old ways," counterrevolutionary and bourgeois attitudes; and (2) the good fortune and good sense to conceal successfully any actual or alleged ties to people and positions of power in the Lon Nol regime.[4]

A small number of analysts have argued that the killings of government (and to a lesser degree, civilian) personnel in the immediate aftermath of the April 17 victory did not represent a policy of systematic extermination ordered by the party leadership, but rather were the result of unplanned, spontaneous excesses by a vengeful and war-crazed army of ignorant, teenaged peasant soldiers.[5] This may or may not be a reasonable description of the PFLANK, but it is difficult to explain why, if this were the case, it was a full six weeks before an order went out from the revolutionary authorities in Phnom Penh on May 28 for these actions to cease.[6] It is likely that in the chaotic wake of victory, tight central control of the revolutionary troops was impossible because of the decentralized command structure of the PFLANK and the inevitable difficulties associated with the collection of accurate information. Undoubtedly, these factors were important elements in the postvictory violence in at least some areas.

Nonetheless, these factors seem insufficient to account for either the delay in issuing the cease-slaughter order, or the high rate of attrition suffered by those associated with the defeated regime in roles of authority, unless it was the Organization's policy to kill as many people as possible from the upper echelons of the defeated leadership. Still, these facts alone do not prove that the KCP instituted a program of class genocide.

In the face of a profound lack of hard physical evidence, many observers early on in the tenure of the KCP were sufficiently persuaded by the fragmentary and often contradictory interviews with refugees from Democratic Kampuchea indicating that indeed, a deliberate, systematic, and very thorough campaign of class liquidation was in progress. Comparisons to Hitler's Nazi regime and death camps abounded. In the May 3, 1977, Hearing on Human Rights in Cambodia before the House Subcommittee on International Organizations, New York Representative Stephen Solarz hammered away on this theme, making half a dozen or so references to Nazi genocide in his questioning of witnesses.[7] In his 1980 memoir, Norodom Sihanouk asserted that Adolf Hitler was "Pol Pot and Ieng Sary's hero" and that "even Hitler had nothing on his Khmer Rouge disciples."[8]

The flood of condemnation in the Western press, reflective of true belief in the genocide theory of Kampuchean politics, remained before 1979, however, unsupported by solid, independently verifiable evidence concerned with the alleged mass atrocities. This condition changed with the Vietnamese invasion of December 1978, resulting in the KCP's fall the next month. Kampuchea began to open to outside inspection, and hard evidence of mass killings, if not of a systematic class-oriented program, began to appear in the outside world.

Barry Wain, diplomatic correspondent for the *Asian Wall Street Journal*, visited the Dangkor district south of Phnom Penh and reported what seems to have been an extermination center, "discovered" by local villagers upon their return to the area early in 1980.[9] Exploration of the site revealed 129 mass graves containing an estimated 16,000 bodies. Some of the bodies were still linked one to another by crude leg and arm shackles. Apparently sites such as the one in the Dangkor district have been discovered throughout the country.

There have been many estimates of the level of casualties during the period of consolidation and society building in Kampuchea. Table 7.1 shows a number of these estimates. A 1980 report prepared by the CIA is also revealing:

TABLE 7.1
DEATH IN KAMPUCHEAN WAR AND PEACE

War (Estimates for 1970-1975)		Peace (Estimates for 1975-1978)	
W.J. Sampson	0.2	Ieng Sary	0.03
		Time Magazine	0.60
Ieng Sary	0.6	French Foreign Ministry	0.80
		Saloth Sar	0.80
Norodom Sihanouk	0.6	Khieu Samphan	1.00
		Barron and Paul	1.20
U.S. State Department	0.6	U.S. State Department	1.20
		Amnesty International	1.40
Saloth Sar	0.8	Norodom Sihanouk	1.50
		Ben Kiernan	1.50
Khieu Samphan	1.0	Francois Ponchaud	2.30
		Lon Nol	2.50

Causes of Death	
(1970-1975)	
By Combat (combatants)	0.1-0.8
(noncombatants)	0.05-0.3
By U.S. Air Power	0.03-0.5
(1975-1978)	
By Rustication	0.02-0.4
By Disease and Hunger	0.7-2.0
By Execution	0.002-1.0
By Attempted Escape	0.02
(1978-1981)	
By Famine	>0.5

Note: This is a compilation of estimates attributed to various authorities concerning the magnitude of fatal casualties in Kampuchea during various periods. The unit of measure used here is millions of human lives lost.

The estimated decline in the Kampuchean population between 1970 and 1979 is unprecedented in any national population since World War II.... To measure the demographic impact of the social upheavals on the Kampuchean population during the 1970's, we prepared population estimates for the period 1970-1979, using the 1962 census as a base. The December 1979 population is estimated to range between 4.7 million and 5.5 million persons, with the most likely estimate 5.2 million—down from 7.1 million in 1970. Under normal demographic circumstances the population would have totaled roughly 9 million by year end 1979.[10]

None of these estimates can be considered authoritative, as the data simply do not exist. Taken together, however, the combined estimates paint a grim picture of life in the land ruled by the *Khmer Rouge*.

An article published in the Italian journal, *Famiglia Christiana*, reports that Khieu Samphan estimated during an interview at the Columbo Conference of Nonaligned Nations in August 1976 that approximately one million persons had died as a result of the war, implying that approximately one million more had been executed as "war criminals."[11] Whether or not this estimate is accurate, or even genuine, it is clear that there was much suffering and widespread death. Although it can never be known precisely how many lives were lost in *Khmer Rouge* revolution, of the approximately 7.2 million (plus or minus 10 percent) population of Cambodia in 1970 plus the approximately 1.5 million live births over the period, roughly 4.8 million (plus or minus 15 percent) Cambodians are alive today in 1983. At least a third and possibly as many as one-half of the Khmer people have perished as a result of war, disease and starvation, and political terror. In absolute magnitude of bloodiness, the Kampuchean revolution bears comparison with the Russian and Chinese revolutions. In terms of the percent of the total population lost, it is undoubtedly the bloodiest.

To Kill Two Kings

Consider the problem of revolution. Sudden and fundamental change in the historical trajectory of a society requires much more than the mere destruction of the physical manifestations of the *ancien regime*. Those physical (or "objective," or "infrastructural," or "historical") aspects of society—for example, the political apparat, including parliament building, constitutional arrangements, associated habitual behavior patterns, etc.—are inextricably linked with the metaphysical (or "subjective," or "superstructural," or "mythological") life of society.

One of the central reasons that the KCP (in the guise of FUNK) was able to achieve victory over the Khmer Republican forces of Lon Nol was that it managed to link itself, in the eyes of the majority of the peasants, to two of the pivotal sources of myth in the collective consciousness of the Khmer peasants: the monarchy and the monachy. This link once forged, and the population securely under the KCP's control, it came to be one of the central tasks associated with consolidation and society building for the KCP to usurp the power held by these traditional sources of Khmer authority. The task, then, was one of myth management.

The importance of historical myth in the life of a society should not be underestimated. You can seize the palace, and even kill the king, but still you do not have "power." This is because "power" can derive only from historically conditioned social circumstances. It is embedded in the physical and metaphysical structures of society; it flows from the interstices of social relations. To paraphrase a great philosopher, power (i.e., authority) is not something that can be passed around like a crown or a bomb. Political power grows not so much from the barrel of a gun as in the minds of men and women.

Perhaps particularly for a people who for centuries have been defeated, conquered, and colonized with a remarkable consistency, this collective mythology exerts a significant influence over the manner in which individuals perceive their reality and interpret the events that occur around them. Without this historically conditioned psychomilieu, nothing would make any sense at all. Historical mythology is composed of myriads of accumulated cultural experiences, manifest in everyday life in terms of religious (superstitious) values and rituals, in legends of national heroes and their glorious exploits in days gone by, and in the very character of daily personal interactions. This is illustrated perhaps in the Khmer case by the wide circulation during the war of rumors among the peasantry that the great heroes of the nineteenth-century peasant rebellions—Pu Kombo, A Soa, Si Votha— had been reincarnated to participate in the contemporary struggle.[12] The revolution must engulf and absorb these subjective or metaphysical aspects of social reality, turning those that can be adapted to the purposes of the revolution into tools of the struggle, and eliminating those aspects deemed unsuited to the revolution.

Relations between "church" and "state" in Cambodia had been intimate since the rise of the Angkor Empire, so intimate in fact that it is misleading in many respects to draw the conventional distinctions between them usually made in Western culture. The monarchy assumed not only temporal authority; with the king's role as "Defender of the Faith," he was invested with a measure of spiritual authority as well. Thus, the "god-kings." Likewise, the monachy had more than a spiritual role in society, wielding a degree of influence in village life amounting to a sort of adjunct temporal regime. Therefore, the problem of destroying the legitimacy and authority represented by Sihanouk was complicated by the twin necessity of destroying the legitimacy of the religious authorities.

Both the physical and the metaphysical, the temporal and the spiritual, the body and the will, then, if you will, had to be engaged in this revolution. Moreover, once both the "throne" and the "temple" had been vanquished, new ones would then have to be erected in their places. Not merely new political forms, but an entirely new historical mythology was required to displace the *ante* forms and myths. The *Khmer Rouge* had to kill not one, but two "kings." It is in this sense that some friends of the Kampuchean Communist Party in the People's Republic of China remarked that "their splendid triumph overturned heaven and earth."[13]

Theravada Buddhism was the majority religion and the official state religion in Cambodia for centuries. The basic thrust of this religion is that life is full of suffering; that one brings suffering upon oneself through evil deeds; that the suffering should be bravely endured and combated by moral righteousness and self-purification, so that one may liberate oneself from accumulated "bad Karma" and achieve "Nirvana," that sublime state of nothingness. The *Khmer Rouge* were interested neither in nothingness nor in those who sought it. There was work to be done, after all. Moreover, the official religion of the defeated order was viewed as a dangerous source of counterrevolutionary influence, not to mention a possible source of challenge against the authority of the party.

The Constitution of Democratic Kampuchea specified in Article 20 the policy of the Organization regarding religion: "Every citizen of Kampuchea has the right to worship according to any religion and the right not to worship according to any religion. All reactionary religions that are detrimental to Democratic Kampuchea and the Kampuchean people are strictly forbidden." This article would seem to provide, *prima facie*, some latitude for believers to practice their religions. But Vietnamese propaganda referred to Article 20 as a "dead letter,"[14] and in truth this was a rather charitable assessment.

Article 20 was enforced in such a manner that not only Buddhism but also Mohammedanism and Christianity—in short, virtually all the religions commonly practiced in prerevolutionary Cambodia with the exception of certain animistic belief systems held by some of the traditional hill tribes—were classified by the Organization as "reactionary" and "strictly forbidden." Places of religious worship were desecrated. There were widespread reports that pagodas had been transformed into centers for political indoctrination, storage facilities, and even torture chambers. Monks were stripped of their saffron robes and made to attire themselves in the black garb of the revolution. Apparently, in most areas, the monks were turned out of their temples and made to perform productive labor in the fields with everyone else (a sacrilegious act in and of itself). The monks were stigmatized by propaganda as "parasites who eat the rice of the people."[15]

In one of the rare glimpses into Democratic Kampuchea afforded to outsiders, Yugoslav journalist Slavko Stanic reported that on his

March 1978 guided tour of the country, he happened to meet a Buddhist monk, wearing, of course, the black revolutionary garb. According to Stanic, the defrocked monk "told us that Buddhism and communism had the same humane goals, and that there was no great antagonism between them."[16] What to make of this provocative report? It would be easy to attribute it simply to the monk's desire to sustain his belief system in the face of determined efforts by the Organization to smother it. Another possibility, much more intriguing, is that the monk's comment suggests an historical continuity between traditional Khmer beliefs and KCP teachings that is usually unrecognized or disregarded in Western analyses.

The difficulties faced by the KCP in its antireligious program were formidable, largely because of the temporal and spiritual influence held by the monachy over the peasants. Religion was a *deeply* integrated influence in Khmer society. There is fragmentary evidence to indicate that in some areas, monks were allowed to remain in their temples, though their interactions with the people were severely restricted. At present, the extent of and reason for this remains an open question. How some of the monks managed it is hard to say. Perhaps, in these areas, cadres dedicated to the more extreme aspects of the Saloth Sar program had not yet gained complete ascendancy. Perhaps the monks' hold on the people was sufficiently strong that the Organization dared not move any faster than it did. Perhaps the personal charisma of some of the aged monks intimidated the young cadres charged with their persecution. Perhaps some of the Buddhist monks were themselves revolutionaries of standing in the movement who had not yet conformed to the policy of the Central Committee. At any rate, such cases were the exception.

The mythology of Buddhism would be replaced by an "antimythical" mythology of class conflict, historical materialism, and self-reliance. This new mythology was manifest in the rhetoric of the Organization, particularly, as has been noted above, embodied and transmitted in the form of revolutionary slogans and songs. One popular slogan epitomized the replacement of the spiritual with the materialistic, of the fatalism of the *Hinayana* with the voluntarism of *State and Revolution*, of dependence by independence. The system of dikes and canals being built by the *Khmer Rouge* was an integral element of the planned self-liberation, widely symbolic of the new materialistic ideology: "In farming rely on the people and not on heaven." No longer would the Khmer people be at the mercy of the gods for life-giving rain. Their own labor power would control the waterworks upon which rice culture depends. The power of the people would bring self-redemption. So confident was the KCP that the "people" would make any sacrifice in the name of themselves that Khieu Samphan reportedly told Norodom Sihanouk, "if we are faithful to the people, it does not matter what we do to the Buddhist monks."[17]

Claiming to defend important cultural treasures from Lon Nol, the KCP set up artillery at the base of the great towers of Angkor Wat. There were two advantages to this wartime act. First, the KCP appeared to be defending things that the peasants valued. Second, the KCP knew that Lon Nol would not allow his enemy undisputed possession of so important a symbolic objective, and FANK's attacks did some of Saloth Sar's religious destruction for him. This destruction, Khieu's claim notwithstanding, contributed to the KCP's fall.

The monarchy in Cambodia has not had a constitutionally designated role in the government since the constitutional crisis following the death of King Suramarit in 1960. Yet, the supreme position of the Khmer monarchy in Khmer society over the many preceding centuries and the personal visibility and popularity among peasants of Norodom Sihanouk through the postwar period combined to ensure the symbolic importance of the monarchy as well as Sihanouk's personal political potency.

As has been discussed extensively in Chapter 6, Sihanouk willingly lent his prestige to the KCP through FUNK and GRUNK, not realizing how soon and how completely the KCP would dump him. The KCP's de-Sihanoukization campaign, which began in earnest in April 1973, however, was only the start of the KCP's efforts to combat "Sihanoukism" and "feudalism." The intricacy of the de-Sihanoukization was impressive, subtle, and sophisticated.

Ith Sarin defected from the Khmer Republic to the FUNK during the war, and then repatriated himself to the Republicans in 1973. In an intense tract called "Life in the Bureaus of the Khmer Rouge," part of a larger tract called *Regrets for the Khmer Soul*, Sarin described many aspects of KCP organization and procedure, including the educational program employed by the communists to transform into committed socialist revolutionaries those who had joined FUNK out of respect for Sihanouk. Though it requires an excessively long citation, it is worth while to quote Ith Sarin's story at length:

> The Bureau of Economic Affairs was at Phum Tang Khmau on the banks of a stream northwest of Wat Tang Khmau . . . On the east and south of the Economic Affairs Bureau many shelters were built to receive "newly arrived guests" who had just run from Phnom Penh and whose political trends agreed with those of the Front cadre

(Sihanoukism). The Organization first had to "mature the consciousness" of these "newly arrived guests" here, so they did not have as much freedom to come and go. . . .

As for members of the Military Bureau who still love King Sihanouk, they (the Organization) do not yet dare to show their true intentions. They hold only to the principles of struggle in the framework of the Front as the lesson to be taught; i.e., the principle of national revolution. . . . Bit by bit they edge into the theory of national democratic revolution and stir up class warfare, class rage, and the life and death class struggle in Kampuchea. They attack feudalists, reactionaries, and compradore capitalists. They do not attack King Sihanouk's name openly nor do they foster and praise it either. Some cadre in the ranks are openly attacking Sihanouk's "feudal traits." Those Khmer Rouge cadre who dare to praise King Sihanouk are regarded as people opposed to the revolution. . . . In political education schools the Khmer Rouge Organization uses clever tricks, uses various documents to educate according to the lines of each member (they usually say political awareness), which is to say that, for a member who still holds Sihanouk in affection (cadre of the front) and fears a socialist regime, they usually use only documents that square with the ideas of the Front for education or they let this category of member simply receive training at his bureau. Sometimes they show the road to red theory by means of various documents; there are seminal documents dealing with

- The Division of Khmer Society in Classes
- Class Struggle
- Mass View
- Criticism and Self-criticism
- Proper and Improper Pride
- Quality of Administrators
  etc.[18]

After the war ended, political education was intensified throughout the country, and with it the anti-Sihanouk and antimonarchy campaigns also intensified. Now going beyond mere theoretical suggestions concerning the role of feudal elements in class conflict, the KCP directly attacked Norodom Sihanouk and the entire long line of Khmer kings as corrupt anachronisms who had always sucked the blood of the people. As Sihanouk himself related, "Khmer Rouge radio propaganda, not unlike Lon Nol's, blamed the monarchy for all of Kampuchea's past troubles. Their visceral hatred of the monarchy extended to the great Angkor kings (Jayavarman I, Duryavarman II, Jayavarman VII, and others), denying them any share of the Angkor civilization's worldwide renown. They were not even given credit for having considerably enlarged the original Kambuja."[19]

With the demystification and vilification of the monarchy and the monachy, the Kampuchean people were dispossessed of the very substance of their social order. Within this vacuum, the authority of the party grew apace. Particularly among the very young peasants from the poorest strata of Kampuchean society, hand-picked and carefully groomed to become shock cadres, the party Organization was emerging as the locus of authority and legitimacy in Kampuchean society.

What was the basis of the KCP's political authority? *Khmer Rouge* authority can be seen as flowing from three interrelated wellsprings: just cause, mass support, and authorizing myth.

According to the KCP line, justice is constituted by equality. Because the Lon Nol regime was merely a figurehead ("puppet," "lackey," or "running-dog") through which U.S. imperialism in conjunction with the hopelessly corrupt urban elite was exploiting, even slaughtering the masses of the Kampuchean people, so the line went, the manifest inequality and therefore injustice axiomatically legitimated the revolutionary cause. When the regime's injustice was linked to the humiliation of being exploited by a foreigner, even the simplest of peasants could comprehend the justice of the cause. The extent to which patriotic sentiments were represented by and salient to the purposes of the revolutionary leaders is illustrated in a purported wartime letter to Sihanouk from Khieu Samphan, Hu Nim, and Hou Yuon:

> It is worth mentioning that all our cadres and all our fighters at all levels work and fight without taking any salaries. What is more, they have not even thought of this. The love for the fatherland and the faith in the just cause they are defending are the sole motive force propelling our cadres and fighters to devote all their physical and moral strength and even to sacrifice their lives for the liberation of our beloved fatherland (from U.S. imperialism).[20]

The southwest region's troops and cadres reportedly *did* take salaries, although nominal.[21] That Khieu's troops in the northeast region fought for the cause, while the troops under Ta Mok in the southwest fought for 135 *riels* per month (less than $1 by late 1971) salary is perhaps revealing of differences between the two regions with regard to effectiveness of indoctrination, level of commitment, and content of the ideology.

During a civil struggle, there can be a "bandwagon" effect following the attainment of some critical level of population control, and generally this effect is magnified with the fall of the defeated regime. With victory comes the "Mandate of Heaven," an oriental conception that justice and right will prevail. More precisely, it is considered that the side that was "supposed" to win will actually do so, that therefore the winners necessarily must have the "blessing of heaven." The mass support required for rule, in concert with the leadership's ability to utilize that support, necessarily confers the right to rule. This is the validation of victory, such that most Cambodians were predisposed on the face of it to accept the communist victory. Initially, at least, most probably did.

Prince Sihanouk himself seemed to be persuaded by the internal logic of this traditional touchstone of legitimacy. Toward the end of 1973, he was quoted as saying:

> Cambodia will become Communist, and it is only right that it become Communist, because the revolution that the Khmer Rouge have made in the liberated areas has succeeded . . . they have done things that I never succeeded in doing. . . . When I was head of the state, they produced a ton and a half per hectare [note: actually, closer to 0.5–1.0 ton/ha]. Now, it is two and a half tons per hectare. Or three . . . when one sees such results, one must admit that those who have obtained them have the right to govern the country.[22]

Just cause and mass support were both important sources of authority and legitimacy for the KCP. However, authorizing myth is probably the most important of the sources of political authority. Just cause begins to lose potency as a source of authority the day after the victory celebrations have ended, progressively dwindling in impact with time. Once the revolutionary authorities are in power, they suddenly become responsible for all the people's problems. Thus, neither is mass support an assured basis of authority after victory is achieved. In the long run, only an authorizing historical myth with a widespread locus and a deep scope can assure the continuity in support required to maintain the semblance of authority, as distinct from raw terror and coercion.

The institutions of society exist as purpose-fulfilling entities. An *a priori* problem in revolution, then, is the purpose, the ethos to be served. In Democratic Kampuchea, the ethos was to be constituted by the people themselves. The revolution was synonymous with justice, inasmuch as it was in the name of the "people" (an abstract entity, in fact) that the struggle was waged. The leaders of the *Khmer Rouge* were careful early on in the struggle to establish the principle that the cadres at *all* levels were to be "faithful" to the people, to be "of the people," and to be "one with the people." Cadres were constantly exhorted by the party to "live with the people and learn from the people." Distinctions between the cadres and the people were supposed to be forbidden, and the political strategy of the revolution in this sense followed the classic lines for guerrilla warfare set down by Mao Tse-tung. If successfully executed, it would provide the most secure social base for a political movement that is possible. Insofar as it was achieved, it was a truly revolutionary development in modern political history. In practice, however, distinctions grew between various levels of ideological commitment among the cadres, between the military and political cadres, between the cadres and the liberated populace, between the liberated populace and the unliberated populaces, and among certain ethnic divisions.

On May 30, 1975, Radio Phnom Penh issued a statement on the aims of the revolution: "A new Cambodia that is independent, peaceful, neutral, non-aligned, prosperous, having neither rich nor poor, will certainly be built in the very near future on the beautiful land of Angkor."[23] It would be a culturally and spiritually homogeneous nation, blessed with a land that, if prudently managed, would provide a veritable cornucopia of natural bounty far exceeding the requirements of the people. And it *would* be prudently managed, for no domestic conflict could exist in the classless society. The development strategies would be manifest, flowing from the consensual attitudes of the people. The people would be many, but of one mind; all would participate equally in all national activities, cultural, productive, and political.

This was the vision. This was the myth. Implementation of the myth would require a carefully groomed population, and it is to the process of creating the prerequisites of paradise that attention now turns.

The Transformation of Consciousness

Perhaps the most fascinating aspect of the Kampuchean revolution is the scope of the change that the KCP sought to bring about in Democratic Kampuchea. Its design penetrated far beyond the reorganization of political and economic institutions, social relations, and kinship systems, and into the very seat of human consciousness itself. This was genuine totalitarianism. The aim was to transform the grammar of thought within the culture, so that the newly restructured belief sets would produce a new understanding, and, more importantly, new behavior patterns in the new type of citizen needed to populate a virtually classless social system.

The transformation of consciousness on a mass scale with radical suddenness was bound to have a profound impact on both the individual and the social levels:

> If the revolutionaries are successful, they eliminate not only the personnel and instruments of the old order but also its *world of meaning*. Between the collapse of the old, mythically structured world and the installation of the new there is a time of utter confusion when only those who have been confirmed in the revolutionary gnosis have a conceptual scheme by which to distinguish right from wrong and link past, present and future.[24]

Given the rapidity with which the "revolutionary gnosis" was imposed on the masses in Kampuchea, it is likely that the intensity of these effects would be amplified. Most of the psychological "signposts" by which a peasant related to the social world suddenly were no longer valid: Buddhism and Buddhist values were labeled "reactionary"; the monarchy was now "corrupt feudalism"; all personal property was eliminated as an element in Saloth Sar's program, and all aspects of life were communalized. Extended family systems were fragmented by the regime, often consciously, as part of a larger design to blot out all individual distinctions, a design against traditionally strong Khmer individualism. It was rather like what the U.S. Army tries to do to the heads of young recruits at boot camp, except that the entire country was the boot camp in this case.

Individual disorientation thus resulted literally for a time in huddled, confused masses, herded about from work site to work site by the cadres—mostly very young—who had internalized the doctrine. The masses thus weakened were "easy pickings," ill-suited and/or unwilling to resist in psychological and physical combat. Although this might have been a great advantage in terms of population control, it presented significant liabilities in terms of national security. Democratic Kampuchea fell to invaders and insurgents before this situation could be fully transcended. That defeat can be traced directly to the condition of the masses:

> The disruption in the wholeness of human experience corresponds to the disintegration in culture and group solidarity. When the bases of unified collective social action begin to weaken, the social structure tends to break and produce a condition which Emile Durkheim has

termed *anomie*, by which he means a situation which might be described as a sort of social emptiness or void. Under such conditions, suicide, crime and disorder are phenomena to be expected because individual existence is no longer rooted in a stable and integrated social milieu and much of life's activity loses its sense and meaning.²⁵

The reestablishment of a stable and integrated social milieu, then, must have been a primary goal for the KCP. Without the *meaning* derived from an individual's understanding of his or her relationship to social referents, alienation is inevitable. Accordingly, an extensive program of political education was initiated at the mass level, aimed at the mass transformation of consciousness.

As part of this process, a new vocabulary emerged—often cruelly ironic—to express and entrench the new concepts. *Angkar Loeu*, literally, "High Organization," was the name given to the upper echelons of the party structure, and the party structure embodied all truth and authority (in the name of the people, of course). The political apparat in general was referred to as *Angkar* ("Organization"). The people of the land ruled by *Angkar* were referred to as *opokar*, which in the traditional literal translation is "instruments."

An integral component of the new system of political education— all traditional forms of educational institutions having perished—was an occasion known as *sneuer*, which literally means to "invite" or "ask." In the new society, people were quick to learn, *sneuer* now meant to be taken away by *Angkar* for interrogation and probable execution.²⁶

The *sneuer* was the periodic result of the frequent indoctrination sessions in which the participation of all citizens was mandatory. At these meetings, organized at the *krom* level, exhibiting excessive thoughts about prerevolutionary times would indicate a case of *chhoeu sattak aram*, literally, "memory sickness."²⁷ One particular variety of this disease was called *khael chak* ("old dandruff"), which referred to fretting about formerly owned material possessions, such as an automobile or real property.²⁸ The prescription in such cases was the *kosang*, or "construction": "A kosang was a formal and ritualistic warning to someone who had displeased Angkar Loeu. The transgressor was expected to submit to public humiliation, then to 'construct' himself or herself into a good and pure person by confessing and repenting the sin alleged."²⁹ More than two *kosangs* resulted in an invitation from *Angkar Loeu*.

Among the revolutionary slogans to become platitudes in Democratic Kampuchea was the phrase, *lot dam*, meaning "to forge a new character."[30] The institutionalized rituals of political terror used to effect this transformation were well-designed to bring quick and sincere-sounding professions of adherence to the slogans and symbols of the revolution, but they were also likely to spread fear and resentment among a large proportion of the population.

The depth of understanding of and commitment to the ideals of the revolution among the Kampuchean masses was quite probably, under these conditions, less than ideal. While the loci of the ideology were universal, then, the scope—the critical element in terms of commitment—was probably quite shallow in general.

The irony of the new rhetoric, familiar words, with twisted, unfamiliar denotations, was no doubt not lost on the new citizenry. Many Kampuchean refugees interviewed by journalists, government and international relief agencies, and researchers reported that they were confused by *Angkar* policy. Few could name concrete grievances about the Organization, but most felt that they did not belong to the new society. Although they tended by and large to believe that the revolutionaries had good intentions, also by and large they were not at all committed to helping *Angkar* realize its aims. For example, according to Peang Sophi, who fled Wat Rokar in Battambang in January 1976, contradictions between the communists' professed beliefs and their actions were troubling: "The (Khmer Rouge) theory is good," Sophi observed, but "When you ask them, 'Why do you say one thing and do another?' the answer was that 'the organization moves by leaps and bounds.' "[31]

According to another refugee, one Nou Seng, a farmer who had been held prisoner by the KCP fifty miles south of Phnom Penh before his escape in 1974, the *Khmer Rouge* were "honest" even if they did "use force, dictate and kill the people." Nou Seng added, "They have black blood because they want to kill the old men and convince the young of their ideology."[32]

Indeed, the party did favor the young, finding in them a very useful tool. With marginally integrated cognitive belief systems and immature development of normative values, the young are ideal instruments of revolution. Mature persons, more set in their ways and more resistant to the internalization of the new revolutionary values, are more problematic. The communists took advantage of this natural fact from the beginning of the early revolutionary period by organizing an intensive program of youth indoctrination and recruitment.

According to a party document from 1973 concerned with the role of youth in the revolution, a secret youth organization called the

Sampoan Yuvachun Kampuchea Pracheathibodey ("Alliance of Democratic Khmer Youth") was founded in 1962.[33] Later, probably in September or October 1972, the name of the organization was changed to *Sampoan Yuvachun Kommunis Kampuchea* (Yuv.K.K., the "Alliance of Communist Youth of Kampuchea"). The party "educated, watched, nourished and built youth as the central force in the revolutionary movement."[34] According to the document cited above, the youth corps "became the right arm of the party under the direct aegis of the party."

After the founding of FUNK in 1970, the KCP founded a youth organization known as the Patriotic Youth Association (PYA). This was an organization for "cadres of the Front," that is, for followers of Norodom Sihanouk. As was the case with the other administrative branches of FUNK and GRUNK, Yuv.K.K. and the PYA were kept strictly separate, the former being exclusively for committed young cadres in training for positions of leadership in the party, and the latter used as a recruitment pool of the unindoctrinated. Hopeful cases might graduate from the PYA to the Yuv.K.K. after a lengthy apprenticeship, but mostly the PYA provided bodies for the front lines. The KCP organized PYA training camps, which were little more than rudimentary military training and indoctrination in the cause of the revolution. After two or three weeks at a PYA training camp, "returning youngsters fiercely condemned religion and custom, rejected parental authority and showed a militant attitude with marked confidence in mechanical weapons and a rejection of the mystical."[35]

After the war ended, Democratic Kampuchea lavished special attention on the education of children. Former university student Ung Sok Choeu observed that the "only subjects the children were being taught were revolutionary thinking and the aims of the Khmer Rouge and how to detect the enemies of both."[36]

This would explain the recurrent reports that children were spying on their parents for the Organization, and turning those counterrevolutionary culprits over to the revolutionary authorities. The KCP was indeed acutely conscious of the importance of youth in the establishment of a new society. Plato had recommended in his *Republic* that those seeking to establish the "perfect city" follow these rules: "Taking over their children, they will rear them—far away from those dispositions they have now from their parents—in their own manners and laws." The leaders of the KCP took him literally.

In August 1973, the inaugural issue of the official organ of the Yuv.K.K., *Yuvachun Nung Yuvaneari Padevat* ("Revolutionary Young Men and Women"), the party described its task with respect to the youth of Kampuchea: "In all, that is, the aim is of building the reflexes of our youth toward the overall good and increasing their understanding and desire for manual activities; that is to say, changing their old worldview progressively and causing the adoption of a new, revolutionary worldview as a replacement."[37]

In his 1980 memoir, *War and Hope*, Norodom Sihanouk reported that the party drafted youngsters at the tender age of twelve. After indoctrination at training camps, the youth were integrated into the revolutionary army, whereupon they were honored with the title, *opokar phdach kar robas pak*, or the "dictatorial instrument of the party." Having attained a degree of single-minded commitment to the party, these youthful shock troops were given command over the "troops of workers," the legions of laborers created with the rustication. Sihanouk explained the fanatical commitment of these products of party discipline:

> The young Khmer Rouge soldiers were often motivated by true patriotic feeling, backed up by solid ideological indoctrination. The Khmer Rouge child-soldiers had no reason to hate Pol Pot's inhuman regime. They had never known and so could not remember what life was like under Sihanouk. They sincerely believed what they were told about the "old society": that it was despicable, contemptible, corrupt, unjust and oppressive in the extreme.[38]

Thus these young cadres occupied a special niche in the emerging social structure of Democratic Kampuchea. As a party publication expressed it, "the forces of youth . . . became the nucleus, the wick of the struggle."[39]

With a program so meticulously tailored to indoctrinate the youth of the nation, there soon emerged an extremely militant corps of youthful cadres totally committed to *Angkar*'s instructions. The corps was created and administered under the direction of Mrs. Ieng Thirith, wife of Ieng Sary. More than the "wick of the struggle against imperialism," these shock cadres became key elements of the struggle within.

The Struggle Within

The bloody struggle for internal party power in the KCP recalls Joseph Stalin's rise to power in the Union of Soviet Socialist Republics. After the death of Vladimir Lenin in early 1924, there ensued a four-year power struggle among the leading members of the Communist

Party of the Soviet Union (CPSU). Eliminating all potential rivals, Stalin emerged as the new czar. His method is interesting. Stalin's initial rise was conducted in the context of the struggle over domestic development policy: how, and how fast to industrialize.

Following in the relatively moderate heritage of Lenin, the right argued for a slower approach to socialism; the left pressed for rapid industrialization, the peasants be damned. After defeating and politically discrediting his opponents with the moderate or gradualist line, Stalin usurped the arguments of the left and turned on the right wing of the party. This he was able to accomplish because as first secretary, he had used his power of appointment to place loyal followers in positions vacated by defeated opponents and their allies. In the following decade, claiming a rising threat to internal security from external sources, he was able to defeat completely his former allies on the right.

The CPSU, the Red Army, and the entire governmental apparatus experienced deadly mass purges during the 1930s. After having been politically discredited, Stalin's defeated opponents were seized by the secret police and tortured until they made confessions, often unlikely and even absurd. For VIPs, show trials followed; then death. As Stalin's power grew to be beyond all question, the formalities became unimportant. Opponents of less stature than respected party members, however (e.g., a class of petty bourgeois farmers called the Kulaks), were always exterminated with less ceremony. With some minor modifications, all this can be seen as a rough model for what Saloth Sar did in Kampuchea.

The Major Players

Over the course of the late revolutionary period (1968–1975) and well into the period of consolidation and society building (1975–1978), there were literally scores of independent or semiindependent factions operating in opposition to the regime in control of Phnom Penh, and in opposition to each other, as well. From among these, at least six identifiable trends emerge with sufficient coherence to qualify for designation as major players. What is here referred to as a "player" does not necessarily constitute a single, unified organizational entity; rather, a "player" is meant to designate a distinct ideological grouping or alliance grouping.

Broadly united under the banner of FUNK in the eyes of most of the outside world, these six players came to regard one another as far more dangerous threats than their ostensible common enemy, the Khmer Republic. These groups had separate external patrons, separate internal constituencies and geographical bases of power, separate ideological lines, and separate conceptions of themselves as well as their respective origins. These six major groupings or factions identifiable within FUNK were as follows.

1. *The Stalinists* were the followers of Saloth Sar, and were loosely allied with the CCP right wing. They were committed to the maintenance and extension of party discipline, rapid and sustained rustication, and autarky. These elitists, the core of the KCP Central Committee, exhibited anti-Vietnamese, antimonarchist, and revanchist tendencies. Based in the northeast of Cambodia, and tracing its roots to the KSA/KSU heritage, this group included Saloth Sar (a.k.a. Pol Pot), Ieng Sary, Khieu Samphan, Son Sen, et al.
2. *The Internationalists* were former KPP cadres who decamped to Hanoi after 1954. Based in the north, southwest, east, and west of Cambodia, they exhibited pro-Vietnamese and democratic tendencies. Though the internal divisions of this group are unknown, its prominent personalities included Vorn Veth, Touch Phoen, et al.
3. *The Issarakists* were former KPP cadres who stayed after 1954 to engage in continued armed resistance, and were based primarily in the south, southwest, and west, with a few in the east. Displaying anti-Vietnamese and antimonarchist tendencies, this group included Keo Moni, Ta Mok, and former followers of Touch Samouth and Hieu Seng, et al.
4. *The Pracheachonists* were former KPP cadres who stayed after 1954 to conduct overt political activism. They exhibited democratic tendencies, but no firm tendency toward the Vietnamese. They were based in the south, southwest, west, and east, and their prominent personalities included Keo Meas, Non Suon, et al.
5. *The Maoists* were allied to the CCP left wing, stressed the peasant role, and favored partial rustication and limited autarky. A mass-based group, they exhibited anti-imperialist and democratic tendencies, but no firm tendency toward the Vietnamese. Based in the south, southwest, and north, this group included Hu Nim, Hou Yuon, Phouk Chhay, et al.
6. *The Rumdo* were the followers of Norodom Sihanouk, and this group included a broad mix of democrats, republicans, and monarchists. Allied to the CCP center, they tended to be conciliatory to the Vietnamese. Based in the north, west, south,

southwest, and east, this group was unique in that it had no independent military apparatus.

There is overlap and interchange among these "players," these somewhat loosely labeled categories, but they serve to summarize the broad outlines of this complex power struggle. Not much is known about the interactions among these groups, but a few things are fairly clear.

For example, the legendary PFLANK, the "Khmer People's National Liberation Armed Forces," was a deadly hoax. PFLANK was supposed to be composed of all "patriotic" elements in the Khmer revolutionary struggle, including all six of the players listed above. Command would of course be unified, and under the ultimate direction of the nominal mother-body, the Kampuchean Royal Government of National Unification (GRUNK).

In reality, however, top-level command was always in the hands of members of the Central Committee of the KCP. At first, PFLANK was very much like FUNK itself, a loose federation among numerous small, isolated, and autonomous regional armies. It was not until July 1975, some four months *after* PFLANK achieved victory, that the KCP Central Committee was able to achieve a significant enough degree of unity in the command structure of the army to declare it actually unified. A "high command" for PFLANK had been established in March 1972,[40] but it was more than three years before the high command was in command of all "its" units. Even then, the price of a unified command was the reorganization of PFLANK (once again given the old name, Revolutionary Army of Kampuchea or RAK) and a reportedly fierce firefight in Phnom Penh at the time of the July 1975 unification. On top of this, some suspect units were excluded from the new organization, to be dealt with later. This is not exactly a smooth way to transfer authority.

At no time from 1970 onward did Sihanoukists share significant command authority at or above the regional level. Sihanouk wistfully reminisced about the fate of followers in the struggle: "this union of Khmer Rouge, Sihanouk supporters, and Khmer Vietminh [i.e., KPP] was not to be, despite the willingness of the Vietnamese. The Sihanouk-supporting Khmer nationalists were . . . ultimately decimated, liquidated by the Khmer Rouge. The PFLANK never materialized."[41]

Nevertheless, a well-organized if decentralized revolutionary army did emerge during 1971 and 1972. By 1973, the KCP was ready to move into battle on its own, with its forces referred to as "PFLANK" only in (*a*) external propaganda, and (*b*) internal political indoctrination of the *Rumdo*. Though Sihanouk supporters were never able to reach positions of real authority in the revolution, they did make excellent cannon-fodder. Whenever possible, the Central Committee preferred to employ units composed mostly of Sihanoukists ("cadres of the Front") in battles where high casualty rates were anticipated. The Stalinists preferred to send anybody's units but their own into dubious engagements.

By 1972, the Stalinists were in firm control of the far northern and northeastern portions of the country, already instituting an early version of their ultraradical agrarian revolution in some areas. In the eastern regions bordering Vietnam, territory and population were jointly administered by NVA/PRG forces in conjunction with Internationalists, Pracheachonists, and perhaps a few Issarakists here and there. In the south and southwest, apparently, many different forces operated and cooperated without undue friction before 1973. In this area, also, the agrarian revolution started in some places as early as 1972, near Takeo for example. This fact may indicate the presence of Maoists in that area. Issarakists, Pracheachonists, Internationalists, Maoists, *Rumdo*, and even the NVA/PRG were all actively engaged in the southwest. Thus the southwest region is one of the most interesting of the revolution, both in view of the rapid advances made in the revolution there and because of the extraordinary degree of cooperation among members of the Front in that area early in the struggle. (It might have been a model for the entire revolution had not Saloth Sar succeeded in his efforts to impose iron unity, crushing the factions that there cooperated.) In the west, Pracheachonists, Internationalists, Issarakists, and the *Rumdo* worked together in another example of close cooperation among the coalitions of the revolutionary forces. Finally, the "special zone" surrounding Phnom Penh was apparently not under the undisputed, unified control of a single force until sometime in February of 1977.

The Central Committee and the Regions

At the beginning of 1973, a defector from the revolution gave a list of the members of the KCP Central Committee, supplemented here by additional information that has since become available:[42]

    Saloth Sar—Secretary General
    Ieng Sary—First Deputy Secretary
    Khieu Samphan—Defense Minister; PFLANK Commander-in-Chief
    Son Sen—PFLANK Chief of Staff

Saloth Ponnary—Chair, Association of Democratic Khmer Women (ADKW)
Ieng Thirith—Deputy Minister, Culture, Education, & Youth
Hu Nim—Minister of Information
Tiv Ol—Deputy Minister of Information
Hou Yuon—Minister of Interior (Communes)
Koy Thuon—Deputy Minister for Finance
Chou Chet—Deputy Minister for Health (SW Region Chair)
Sok Thuok—Deputy Minister for National Security (Special Region Chair)
Pok Doeuskomar—Deputy Minister for External Affairs

The first six on the 1973 Central Committee list were all closely allied behind Saloth Sar. Ieng Sary and Son Sen both had fled to the *maquis* from Phnom Penh back in 1963 with Saloth Sar, out of respect for the thoroughness of Sihanouk's secret police. The wives of Ieng and Saloth, sisters Khieu Thirith and Khieu Ponnary, followed them into the jungles a year later. Ieng and Saloth had been close since at least 1951, although it is not known precisely when Son Sen and Khieu Samphan were coopted into the Stalinist clique.

With his people filling all the top party slots, Saloth Sar had very substantial control over the Central Committee. Although it is not yet known in any detail how the internal dynamics of this group unfolded, it is clear that Saloth's clique composed a *de facto* "politbureau." Yet, control of the KCP Central Committee was a far cry from control of the entire revolutionary movement. Of the six military regions (northwest, west, south, east, northeast, and special), only the northeast was securely controlled by forces loyal to the Stalinist faction at midyear 1973.

In the course of the 1973 dry season offensive, Khieu Samphan gained at least partial control of the liberation forces in the special zone, which was at first under the leadership of Sok Thuok.[43] It appears that a struggle for control of the special zone occurred during the 1973 offensive. Effective control of the special zone surrounding Phnom Penh would be crucial to the conduct of the 1973 offensive as well as to the Stalinists' determination to conserve their forces. Perhaps a compromise and a shift of internal coalitions took place, certainly some skirmishes among regional military units, but in the end it appears that part of the apparat dedicated to the southwest zone was withdrawn deep into an area of the southwest beyond the reach of military units directly under the command of the Central Committee (the so-called Unconditional Divisions).[44] Troops of the special and southwest zones were apparently able to stave off further attacks by northeastern zone units attempting to encroach on their zones at this time. This probably gave the southwest zone a reprieve while the Stalinists sought to extend their control in other less resistant arenas, and may have been a factor in Saloth Sar's eventual decision to ally with the southwest zone in the progressive internal purges of the 1970s.

Between the end of 1973 and the end of the war in 1975, the geographical distribution of military control among the insurgent factions seems to have been more or less stable, with one notable exception. That exception was the recurring experience of having young cadres from Central Committee training centers arrive in the regions to assume positions of leadership in the regional commissariats. The regional commissariats were the ministries and administrative representatives of the provisional government, whose theoretical function was to provide political guidance to the military commanders at the regional level, thus transmitting the will of the Central Committee. Real power, however, still rested with the regional military commanders, and no doubt they jealously guarded their command prerogatives in the face of internal challenges. Nonetheless, and more and more often as the last years of the war dragged by, waves of militant young cadres from the Central Committee training schools would displace political and military personnel at the regional levels. These cadres were totally dedicated to the authority of the Central Committee. Slowly, the authority of the party line was making itself felt.

Figure 7.1 illustrates, as well as can be done given both a fluid institutional situation and inadequate information about it, the *de facto* structure of the *Khmer Rouge* forces during 1973. At the very top of the administrative hierarchy, Saloth Sar's Stalinist clique constituted a "politbureau," that is to say, a standing executive committee of the Central Committee. Whether or not there actually existed a body officially so constituted, the fact of its existence as an ongoing clique at the very apex of the party for nearly two decades suggests that it performed the executive function even if it was not so empowered by the Central Committee as a whole.

The problem facing the politbureau was how to enforce the party line (as defined by the politbureau, of course). The Central Committee was composed of a relatively diverse collection of ideologues, including Stalinists, Issarakists, Pracheachonists, Maoists, and Internationalists. Although the Central Committee in theory was the supreme body within the party structure, ideological disagreements and mutual

FIGURE 7.1
IDEALIZED REPRESENTATION OF DE FACTO KCP STRUCTURE, 1973

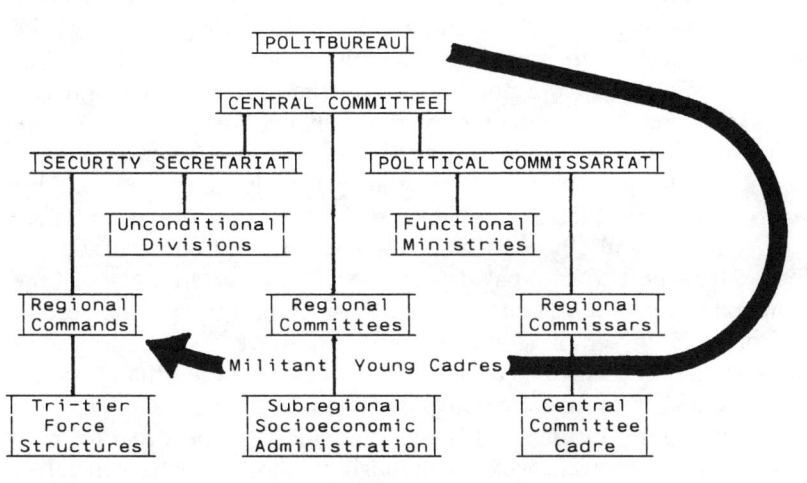

suspicion among the diverse members effectively pushed the locus of actual authority down to the regional level. At the regional level, whichever group controlled the political and especially the military cadres of the area naturally enough controlled that particular region.

Ideally, the regions were constituted by tripartite administration: the military commands, the regional party committees, and the political commissars (the latter representing the functional divisions of the ministries, e.g., communes, finance, information, health, etc.). In practice, these functions were not so clearly separated, there being administrative overlap among the offices, bureaus, and military units. By virtue of their independent power bases, the regional party committees and regional PFLANK commands were autonomous from the Central Committee. The ministers and the commissars were of a more malleable constitution: Their constituencies were dispersed to a greater degree than those of the regional committees and commands. This allowed the politbureau more discretion with the ministerial apparat, more leverage than it had with the committees and commands. By using the products of the Yuv.K.K. and the Association of Democratic Khmer Women (ADKW) to pack the staffs of the ministries and the commissariats, the core of the party was able to extend its authority slowly but surely among the regions. Eventually this encroachment would pay off in footholds in the regional committees and commands.

By the time of the "liberation" of Phnom Penh in April 1975, the Stalinists had succeeded in seeding the political infrastructure of the party organization in most regions with their spawn, young cadres totally committed to the politbureau and its directives. Though still facing challenges from ideological rivals in perhaps all areas except their base of operations in the northeast, Saloth Sar's people were able to implement their rural program virtually countrywide. This seems to indicate that the influence of Saloth Sar's people, possibly in a coalition with the Maoists, was supreme in setting the party line with respect to internal development policy at around the time of liberation. The differences among the regions through the second half of 1975 in terms of the character of the economic program's implementation seemed to be a matter of degree, rather than of kind. The amount of coercion employed against the "New People," the urban rusticants, in speeding their adaptation to the program may have been the central factor distinguishing those regions controlled by the Stalinists from those regions where their control was less than total.

In July 1975, there appears to have been a change of internal coalition composition. The much heralded refounding of the RAK that month probably represented the consummation of an alliance between the Stalinists of the northeast and the Issarakists of the southwest region. The reported firefights in Phnom Penh at this time and again in September may well have been a move by the new allies (Saloth Sar and Ta Mok) against the odd men out,[45] for the pact gave the politbureau a vastly superior balance of forces in the internal power struggle. These changes in the 1975 dry season set the stage for the remainder of the year:

> Ta Mok, secretary of the Southwest regional committee, ironically was the most powerful of the regional secretaries and controlled the largest territory, the greatest population and the most troops. It was to Ta Mok that Pol Pot [a.k.a. Saloth Sar] turned in search of allies for his purge. The deal was sealed when Duch [sic], the *nom de guerre* of a former *lycée* professor, came to Phnom Penh to serve as the chief of the secret police for the central committee. From then on Pol Pot and Ta Mok had the same chief investigator, jail warden and executioner.[46]

Hou Yuon was the minister of communes and cooperatives in GRUNK, and a Maoist who had spoken out boldly in defense of popular democracy consistently since the early 1950s. He was an instrumental figure in the design and early implementation of the rural agrarian collectivization undertaken in the liberated areas during the war. Much of the theoretical basis of the program derived from Hou's revisions of Mao's thought, stressing the leading role of peasants in constructing an Asian socialist society, and the contradictions between the urban and rural economies.

Hou Yuon was known to have differed with Saloth Sar as early as 1952 regarding the nature of democratic centralism. Hou Yuon believed in the capacity of the people to govern themselves and to develop themselves. Hou believed in the people. Saloth Sar, on the contrary, believed that among the people lurked the enemies of the revolution, and that only a vigilant vanguard could safeguard the party against counterrevolution. Saloth Sar believed in the party. In August 1975 Hou Yuon resigned in protest and then disappeared. The purge was on, and now it was feeding upon the core of the party.

In September 1975, the Stalinists and the party they were coming to control completely made another bid to further consolidate their power. A second round of massive population relocation was undertaken. It may have been in preparation for this action, because of his actual or potential opposition to it, that Hou Yuon was removed from public life and soon from all life. At any rate, through the second half of 1975, the control exercised by the politbureau continued to grow. By contrast, in the countryside dissent was beginning to appear.

A Setback for the Stalinists

The Stalinists' consolidation was dealt a severe blow in December, when the party convened for the Third National Congress in order to constitute a regime. From the middle of December the details of the constitution were hammered out, and on January 3, 1976, the Constitution of Democratic Kampuchea was ratified by the GRUNK Council of Ministers. It was promulgated two days later, and on January 5, 1976, the state of Democratic Kampuchea came into being. In the process, an entire state apparat also was brought into existence, confronting the Stalinists with a challenge of major proportions.

Critics of the Stalinists' interpretation of democratic centralism—all central and no democratic—rushed into the huge administrative vacuum of the newly constituted regime. Although the Stalinists still controlled the main military forces under the Central Committee, the Third National Congress represented a resounding defeat for them and their political line. It would take them more than a year to recoup the losses suffered at this time. The ferment within the party and the relative loss of control experienced by the politbureau at the Third Congress boiled over into the text of the constitution. Article Four of that document explicitly states: "Democratic Kampuchea applies the collective principle in leadership and work."

At the end of March, elections were held to constitute the People's Representative Assembly (PRA). One hundred and fifty persons were "elected" to represent the peasants, fifty to represent the "laborers and other working people," and fifty to represent the revolutionary army. In itself, this was a truly revolutionary achievement. As one analyst observed at the time, for "the first time, the Assembly is not dominated by princes, officials, moneylenders, district chiefs, or educated urban dwellers."[47] But then again, the assembly has never dominated Cambodian politics.

Because of their control of large portions of the armed forces, the Central Committee's Stalinists probably had an assured voting block of at least fifty, though there may have been a few chinks in this block. Exactly what happened to the KCP as an organizational entity at this time is not clear. All that is really certain is that the Stalinists were required to adopt an entirely new approach to the task of imposing revolutionary discipline on Democratic Kampuchea.

Among the fifty individuals elected to represent "laborers and other working people" was a previously unheard-of man who listed his occupation as "a representative of rubber plantation workers." He said his name was Pol Pot. In what one analyst has referred to as "secrecy unprecedented in socialist history,"[48] Saloth Sar (who had not been mentioned publicly since April 1975) changed his identity to become a simple member of the People's Representative Assembly. When Pol Pot became prime minister of Democratic Kampuchea in April, Thiounn Prasith, who at the time was a high-ranking member of Democratic Kampuchea's foreign ministry, had apparently never heard of Pol Pot. He transmitted information to the Kampuchean mission in Paris indicating, quite incorrectly, that the new prime minister was associated with a pro-Vietnamese group. As Ben Kiernan noted, "It is indicative of the closeness of the political tussle then taking place in Kampuchea that such a high-ranking cadre could have seen it as a reasonable possibility that a member of the pro-Vietnamese constituency in the Party would become Prime Minister."[49] From the midst of this struggle emerged Democratic Kampuchea.

According to the Constitution of Democratic Kampuchea, the PRA was responsible "for defining the various domestic and foreign policies" of the nation (Article seven). The "government" (presumably meaning the ministries and departments) is elected by and subordinate to the PRA, and is "responsible for giving effect to the laws and political lines laid down" by the PRA (Article eight). "Justice is administered by the people's courts," and "judges at all levels shall be chosen and appointed by the PRA (Article nine). Finally, the PRA also chooses and appoints a State Presidium (chair, and first and second vice-presidents) "responsible for representing the State of Kampuchea inside and outside the country," and also for defending the constitution and the PRA's policies (Article eleven).

Nowhere in the constitution is the structure of the "government" specified. This probably indicates that the structure remained an issue in contention even as that structure emerged. All that is specified by the constitution is that the PRA is the supreme body, indicating the extent of democratic ferment still in progress, and the extent to which the Stalinists' position had slipped.

At the beginning of April 1976, the PRA elected the government, the people's judges, and the presidium. Khieu Samphan, by now a genuine national hero, was appointed on April 4, 1976 to the post of president of the presidium, the new Democratic Kampuchean head of state. Nuon Chea was elected to chair the 10-member PRA Standing Committee. Although Chea was a veteran of the struggle, and an Internationalist, his committee was an ideologically mixed group. From this point in April, the Stalinists faced what was to be their most serious challenge to date.

On April 14, a central administration for the government was created: Pol Pot became prime minister, and his deputies were Ieng Sary (foreign affairs), Son Sen (national defense), and Vorn Veth (economic affairs). Of these, only Vorn was not a Stalinist. He controlled half a dozen cabinet-level committees, packed with his allies. At the same time, So Phim and Nhim Ros were appointed as Khieu Samphan's first and second deputies. So Phim was an Internationalist, but Nhim Ros had been named in early 1975 as a member of the "secret five-person inner leadership of the revolution,"[50] i.e., the Stalinist politbureau. Thus, in spite of widespread internal challenges, the Stalinists were well-situated in the new regime. They dominated the central administration and the presidium. Several key ministries were in friendly hands: Ieng at foreign affairs and Son at national defense, plus Ieng Thirith (Mrs. Ieng Sary) at the head of social affairs, Mrs. Son Sen at the head of culture and education, and Pol Ponnary (Mrs. Saloth Sar, or Mrs. Pol Pot) at the Association for Democratic Khmer Women (or its successor organization).

Nonetheless, with the new competition for authority over the formulation of policy, the thrust of the Stalinists' policy preferences was clearly blunted. The second half of 1976 saw the character of Democratic Kampuchea's external policies change radically from the complexion that had presented itself between April 1975 and April 1976. Diplomatic relations were established with a number of countries, and several embassies were exchanged. Border skirmishes with Vietnam declined, and border talks with the Vietnamese were explored more seriously. Groups of advisors from the PRC began to appear to reconstruct factories and communications. Limited trade relations were opened; in September, Ieng Sary was sent to Japan to negotiate a contract for 10,000 tons of steel. The following month, the Ren Fung Trading Company was established in Hong Kong to administer trade between Democratic Kampuchea and nonsocialist countries. Antimalaria chemicals were acquired on the international market, surprisingly, from that most hated of the imperialists, the United States. These developments in the external relations of Democratic Kampuchea cannot be explained without reference to external patronage.

The China Connection

The precise composition and timing of alliances between KCP Central Committee members and powerful individuals in the People's Republic of China (PRC) may never be known in any detail, because of the highly clandestine nature of such political intrigue. Yet on the basis of circumstantial evidence, it appears certain that there was a direct and key relationship between internal politics in the PRC and in Kampuchea.

Hu Nim and Phuok Chhay were leaders of the Cambodia-China Friendship Association and supporters of Chinese radicals behind the Cultural Revolution in the mid-1960s. Hu spent a month in China during 1965, just before the Cultural Revolution, and he returned to Cambodia denouncing the Soviet Union as "revisionist."[51] Around this same time, Saloth Sar and several of his associates also visited the PRC. Although it is not known whether there was any relationship between Saloth's visit and Hu's, it is believed that Saloth paid a fairly long visit to China, possibly as long as several months, during the Cultural Revolution.[52]

While these prominent KCP figures cultivated relationships among members of the Chinese Communist Party (CCP), PRC Prime Minister Chou En-lai maintained very friendly state-to-state relations with Sihanouk's regime. Through the late 1960s, the PRC was the major supplier of military hardware to Sihanouk's security forces. This hardware was used to kill KCP members, and the Stalinists would not forget Chou's favor.

In October 1967, when the KCP was in the process of deciding to ride the wave of peasant rebellion and initiate armed struggle, there may have been a brief exception to the norm of pre-1970 Sino-Khmer relations: "The Cultural Revolution was at its peak in China, and radicals who briefly seized control of the Chinese Foreign Ministry may have signaled endorsement of the armed struggle decision. Within three months, however, Prime Minister Chou En-lai regained control of the Foreign Ministry (and) withdrew support for the fledgling war on Sihanouk."[53]

The "ultraradical" ideas espoused by the KCP's theoreticians were said to disturb the Chinese moderates in control of the PRC so much that when Sihanouk was deposed, his old friend Chou En-lai helped him to set up FUNK and GRUNK. Hoping to introduce an element of moderation to counterbalance the radicalism in the KCP, Chou actually backed the very anachronistic vestige of "feudal corruption" that the KCP had resolved to destroy. It may also have occurred to him to wonder what the effect upon his own domestic political position might be should the Kampuchean faction backed by his radical opponents within the CCP prevail in its struggle.

All through the war, Sihanouk's moderate Chinese allies had supported him and provided the only real institutional power base he had. By the end of the war in 1975, however, Chou En-lai was dying, both politically and physically. The struggle between Chou's annointed successors, Teng Hsiao-p'ing and Hua Kuo-feng, on the one side, and the radical Maoists against whom Chou had long struggled, on the other side, was beginning to break out into the open.

Behind the scenes and apart from official state-to-state relations under the control of Chou and his moderate factions, radicals within the CCP had long cultivated relations on a party-to-party basis with the KCP. In internal CCP politics, the Chinese radicals, symbolically represented by Mao's widow, Chiang Ch'ing, and the three other members of the now-renowned "Gang of Four," had struggled since before the beginning of the Cultural Revolution to seize party power from the moderates. To this end, the radicals spent a decade packing local party committees and army units with militant young cadres drawn from the peasantry. By the beginning of 1976, their strength had grown to such a degree that they decided the time was right to move against Teng, who had been rehabilitated by Chou after his purge at the hands of the radicals at the height of the Cultural Revolution some ten years earlier. On April 7, 1976, Teng was squeezed out by the radicals, and he would not regain the upper hand in the internal struggle in China until the radical leaders' arrest during the first week of October. At this time, "KCP" sources (probably Maoist) reportedly labeled Teng as "anti-socialist and counter-revolutionary."[54]

Coinciding almost exactly with this action in the PRC were significant changes in Democratic Kampuchea. During the six-month period of radical dominance in China in the middle of 1976, "Vietnam and Kampuchea enjoyed their best relations for the whole of the 1975–1979 period."[55] It seems likely that this indicated that an internal alliance in Kampuchea among the Maoists, the Pracheachonists, and the Internationalists had succeeded in challenging the Stalinist-Issarakist coalition for control of Democratic Kampuchea's foreign policy.

On September 27, 1976, three days before the opening of a conference in China that would precipitate the fall of the radical faction ("Gang of Four"), Pol Pot was kicked out and replaced by Internationalist Nuon Chea as prime minister. Within a matter of days, "Kampuchea unprecedentedly attacked [Teng Hsiao-p'ing], whose sacking in Peking six months before had until then drawn no comment from Phnom Penh."[56] Clearly, internal politics in Kampuchea and China were out of sync, for just as the coalition of Maoists, Pracheachonists, and Internationalists scored a major victory in the Kampuchean internal struggle, its radical patrons within the CCP were about to be roundly crushed. By October 15, 1976, Pol Pot had regained the prime minister's portfolio. On October 22, the first official notice of the change from Nuon Chea back to Pol Pot was simply Pol's signature on a public statement issued from Phnom Penh denouncing the "counter-revolutionary Gang of Four anti-Party clique" whose political star was in rapid decline in China.[57]

Exactly what the linkage could be that could effect such an apparently direct relationship between the fortunes of the right wing in China and the Stalinists in Kampuchea is anybody's guess. It could be a simple coincidence, but that is not really a satisfying explanation. Perhaps the routing and destination of military aid shipments were controlled by whoever controlled the PRC's Foreign Ministry, and whoever received those shipments in Democratic Kampuchea thereby gained the upper hand. It is more likely that the relationship was more subtle and complex. Whatever the precise nature of this connection, as Teng's rightists staged their comeback against Chiang's radicals, Pol Pot intensified his purges. From this point on through the remainder of the history of Democratic Kampuchea, the control exercised by the Stalinist faction over the lives of the mass of the Democratic Kampuchean population would mount relentlessly. At the same time, the level of violence employed by the internal and external security apparatuses in Democratic Kampuchea also mounted relentlessly.

The Stalinists Triumphant

The fall of the Chinese radicals shattered the Maoist-Pracheachonist-Internationalist coalition, if indeed that coalition had not already disintegrated under the pressure of the Stalinists' secret purge method. Through the remainder of Pol Pot's regime, the Stalinists increasingly emphasized the issues of internal security and fidelity to the constantly evolving party line. Purges all the way down to the *phum* level in the party organization and through the ministries of the government and the ranks of the RAK progressively decimated any open opposition to Pol Pot's power. With his enemies divided and conquered, the task of control became a simple management problem: Which ones to "crush to bits" first? The answer was pro-Vietnamese of all stripes.

Now, Pol Pot and his tiny clique directed the entire revolutionary organization. Pol Pot held the dossiers. Pol Pot controlled the ministries. And Pol Pot saw to it that there was no deviation from the line fixed by the High Organization in the name of the people. In the process, hundreds of thousands were slaughtered as the party "purified" itself.

As one refugee survivor of this round of purges expressed it, "anyone they didn't like, they would accuse of being a teacher or a student or a former Lon Nol soldier, and that was the end."[58] The president of the presidium of Democratic Kampuchea stated it a little differently on April 15, 1976, some five days after the arrest of Information Minister Hu Nim: "We must wipe out the enemy in our capacity as masters of the situation, following the lines of domestic policy, foreign policy and military policy of our revolutionary organization. Everything must be done neatly and thoroughly. We must . . . constantly maintain the spirit of revolutionary vigilance and continue to fight and suppress all stripes of enemy at all times."[59]

By the time of the second Vietnamese invasion in December 1978, it had become clear to most analysts outside Kampuchea that massive purges, if not indeed a widespread genocidal policy of class extermination, were occurring in Kampuchea. Yet, there remained the problem of "hard" evidence, of documentation. Although it was easy enough to give credence to the continuing reports by refugees, the *corpora delicti* required to substantiate such a horrible suspicion simply did not exist, nor did it seem that they ever would. As analyst David

P. Chandler asserted before a U.S. Congressional subcomittee investigation of Democratic Kampuchea, "the regime doesn't have much of a documentary sense . . . we can count the number of Jews who were killed in the war because the Germans kept records of each one they killed. The Cambodians never did."[60]

Or did they? In fact, Chandler had mistaken extreme secrecy for a lack of documentation. Time has shown that the KCP cadres in charge of internal security were indeed meticulous in their "documentary sense." Everything *was* done neatly and thoroughly, just as Khieu Samphan had advised, at least with respect to important "enemies" of the party. The accumulated caches of records of what might euphemistically be termed "national security investigations" are today a treasure-trove of unmitigated horror.

One of the Stalinists' most important archives of death is located at a security center, a place called "S-21." Today it is generally referred to as Tuol Sleng. This installation was a Phnom Penh secondary school in the days of Norodom Sihanouk and Lon Nol. Under Pol Pot, it became an interrogation center, or more accurately, an elaborate torture chamber exclusively reserved for important party, government, and military personnel.

Pol Pot's chief of the secret police was a man named "Mit Deuch" ("Mit" was the required revolutionary name, meaning comrade or brother). Mit Deuch set up shop at S-21 sometime in mid- to late-1975, probably in July or August. That first six months, S-21 records reveal, the party "crushed to bits" 154 "anti-Party" enemies. "For 1976, 2,250 are recorded. The figure rises to 6,330 for 1977, and to 5,765 for the first half of 1978 only. After that the records are lost."[61] All in all, it is estimated that some 20,000 important party officers and cadres were executed at S-21, many by means of torture.

This operation was no simple madness; the torture was designed to aid in the extraction of elaborate "confessions" from the prisoners. Captives were made to write and rewrite the confessions repeatedly. This tactic was no doubt useful for identifying undetected "enemies of the party and the state and the people." It was probably also necessary in a political sense, considering the independent constituencies still held by such prominent figures as Hu Nim and Hou Yuon at the time of their arrests.

Stephen Heder argues that these purges were carried out with no open ideological debate.[62] It is indeed quite clear that many if not most of the purges were carried out secretly, with cadres called away to meetings never to return, or simply disappearing outright. Still, given the ideological differences among the various factions of the party, it is inconceivable that there was no open ideological debate. In particular, early on in the existence of Democratic Kampuchea, before the Stalinists had gained an unchallenged upper hand, almost certainly there must have been if not open debate within the *Angkar Loeu* and between *Angkar Loeu* and *Angkar*, then at least considerable dissent outside the inner circle. Perhaps a hint of this is visible in one of Hu Nim's "confessions" found at Tuol Sleng. He wrote at least seven different versions, and by the time he wrote this draft, he had been tortured for seven weeks and was beginning to "confess" some really bizarre and impossible crimes against the party. Still, moments of lucidity in between the induced lunacy of most of the confession reveal traces of the resistance to the Stalinists' party line: "Hu Nim says that he was much 'disturbed' by policy sessions run for the 'core of the organization,' about 'class positions in the new Kampuchean society . . . about materialism, about the abolition of money, about popular education . . . it disturbed and tormented most those individuals who were prone to private property, and had strong middle-class, feudalist, and capitalist standpoints.' "[63] One would think that there must have been some discussion and dissent surrounding such radical measures as those implemented by the KCP, and Hu Nim's confessions do seem to reveal a few of these issues. Hu Nim, a dedicated and professional communist revolutionary, could hardly be justly accused of "strong middle-class, feudalist, and capitalist standpoints," but any deviation from *Angkar Loeu*'s commitment to ultraradical change was labeled treason.

Whatever the extent of ideological debate within the party, Pol Pot was determined to crush it to bits. Bou Meng, one of only fourteen people known to have survived a visit to "S-21," recalled his experience: "Many nights I heard screaming . . . it was the noise of people nearly dead."[64] And the security center at Tuol Sleng was only one of a network of Kampuchean gulags. (Number 21 of . . .?)

Some of the security centers were in operation much longer than "S-21." A security center in Takeo Province in the village of Krang Ta Chan, run by one "Comrade Uncle An," was believed to have operated from 1973 to 1979. Was this "Comrade Uncle An" actually Sien An, Saloth Sar and Ieng Sary's old buddy from the KSA? Impossible to say, but records from An's security center indicate, in an undated memo, that "from when we began crushing the enemy to bits until now, we have got rid of 1,500 people."[65] No one is known to have survived a visit to this particular security center, and local peasants say that traffic through the death camp was heavy, "a thousand a day" according to one old woman who obviously had seen more people killed than she could count.

The extremely high levels of violence maintained by the Stalinists in their attempts to secure the gains of the revolution and the discipline of the party proved counterproductive on both counts. The wildly excessive internal violence emaciated the party and the people, critically weakening both at a time when the revolution could ill afford such a heavy burden.

Notes

1. Roger Waters, "Animals." Copyright © 1977, 1978 by Pink Floyd Music Publishers Ltd., London. Published and administered in the U.S.A. by Unichappell Music, Inc. International copyright secured. All rights reserved. Used by permission.

2. Sak Sutsakhan, *The Khmer Republic at War and the Final Collapse* (Washington, D.C.: U.S. Army Center for Military History, 1980), pp. 170, 171.

3. John Barron and Anthony Paul, *Murder of a Gentle Land* (New York: Reader's Digest, 1977), p. 67.

4. See United States Congress, House Subcommittee on International Organizations, Hearings of May 3, 1977, *Human Rights in Cambodia* (Washington, D.C.: USGPO, 1977, Appendix 3, pp. 59–62, where is reprinted the story of Dr. Oum Nal, "A Doctor Zhivago Among the Khmer Rouge," (from *Le Figaro* [Paris] February 11, 1977). Of the group of 397 people committed to the "reeducation" process along with Dr. Nal, apparently some 10 percent were able to meet the two requirements of survival. The objective of the program described by this physician seemed to be not the physical liquidation of class enemies so much as the *psychological* liquidation of the potentially counterrevolutionary strata of the population, often resulting in death.

5. Noam Chomsky and Edward S. Herman, in their *After the Cataclysm: Postwar Indochina and the Reconstruction of Imperial Ideology* (Boston: South End Press, 1979), do the best job of exposing the flimsy and contradictory evidence upon which pre-1979 Kampuchean genocide theories were based, although these authors do not specifically defend the argument that there was no central genocide policy, contenting themselves with demonstrating how reams of exaggeration were generated on the basis of precious little evidence. For an example of the more extreme view, see George Hildebrand and Gareth Porter, *Cambodia: Starvation and Revolution* (New York: Monthly Review Press, 1976).

6. Ben Kiernan, "Conflict in the Kampuchean Communist Movement," *Journal of Contemporary Asia* 10:1-2 (1980), p. 51.

7. See *Human Rights in Cambodia*, pp. 32–38.

8. Norodom Sihanouk, *War and Hope: The Case for Cambodia* (New York: Random House, 1980).

9. Barry Wain's report, "Cambodia: What Remains of the Killing Ground," is reprinted in the *Wall Street Journal*, January 29, 1981.

10. The U.S. Central Intelligence Agency, "Kampuchea: A Demographic Catastrophe," March, 1980; cited in Kenneth M. Quinn, "The Origins and Development of Radical Cambodian Communism" (Ph.D. diss., University of Maryland, 1982), p. 170; cf. n. 86.

11. The authenticity and/or accuracy of this alleged interview with Khieu Samphan has been challenged by a number of authorities, including William Shawcross, Gareth Porter, François Ponchaud, Noam Chomsky, and Edward Herman; for the best account, see N. Chomsky and E. S. Herman, *After the Cataclysm*, pp. 137, 138, and 172–177. Also see Gareth Porter's testimony in *Human Rights in Cambodia*, pp. 35, 36, 49, 50.

12. Ben Kiernan, "Social Cohesion in Revolutionary Cambodia," *Australian Outlook* 30:3 (December 1980), p. 374.

13. *Fighting Cambodia: Report of the Chinese Journalist Delegation to Cambodia* (Beijing: China Books, 1975), p. 1.

14. *Dossier Kampuchea*, (Hanoi: Le Courrier de Vietnam, 1978), p. 29.

15. J. J. Zasloff and M. Brown, *Communist Indochina and U.S. Foreign Policy* (Boulder, CO: Westview Press, 1978), p. 139.

16. Cited in Noam Chomsky and Edward S. Herman, *After the Cataclysm*, p. 194; originally, BBC SWB FE [Summary of World Broadcasts, Far East], 5801/B, 3–9, April 29, 1978.

17. Norodom Sihanouk, *War and Hope*, p. 49.

18. Timothy M. Carney, *Communist Party Power in Kampuchea: Documents and Discussion*, Cornell University Southeast Asia Program, Data Paper #106 (Ithaca, NY: Cornell University, 1977), pp. 45, 51.

19. N. Sihanouk, *War and Hope*, p. 54.

20. Malcolm Caldwell and Lek Tan, *Cambodia in the Southeast Asian War* (New York: Monthly Review Press, 1975), p. 352.

21. Ith Sarin in T. M. Carney, *Communist Party Power in Kampuchea*, p. 43.

22. In Khieu Samphan, "Underdevelopment in Cambodia" [L. Summers, trans. and introduction; M. Winnacker, L. Finley, and C. Falk, eds.], *Indochina Chronicle* (Berkeley), nos. 51/52 (September–November 1976), p. 17; quotation is from the *New York Times Magazine*, August 12, 1973.

23. G. Hildebrand and G. Porter, *Starvation and Revolution*, p. 94.

24. T. Weber, "Political Authority and Revolution," *Worldview* 17:5 (May 1974), p. 27; emphasis added.

25. Karl Mannheim, preface to his *Ideology and Utopia* (New York: Harcourt, Brace and World, 1936), p. xxiii.

26. Sydney Schanberg, "The Death and Life of Dith Pran," *New York Times Magazine*, January 20, 1980, p. 45.

27. J. Barron and A. Paul, *Murder of a Gentle Land*, pp. 132–205.

28. See John Barron's testimony in *Human Rights in Cambodia*, p. 7.
29. J. Barron and A. Paul, *Murder of a Gentle Land*, p. 132.
30. François Ponchaud, *Cambodia: Year Zero* (New York: Holt, Rinehart and Winston, 1978); see Chapter 8, "Uproot Three Mountains."
31. David L. Chandler, *The Early Phases of Liberation in Northwest Cambodia: Conversations with Peang Sophi* (Melbourne: Center for Southeast Asian Studies, Monash University, 1976), pp. 5, 11.
32. Donald Kirk, "Revolutionary and Political Violence in Cambodia, 1970–1974," in J. J. Zasloff and M. Brown, eds., *Communism in Indochina* (Lexington, MA: D. C. Heath, 1975), pp. 222, 223.
33. T. M. Carney, *Communist Party Power in Kampuchea*, pp. 32, 33.
34. *Ibid.*, p. 10.
35. *Ibid.*
36. J. Barron and A. Paul, *Murder of a Gentle Land*, p. 136.
37. "Manifesto of the Periodical 'Revolutionary Young Men and Women,' " in *Yuvachun Nung Yuvaneari Padevat* 1 (August 1973), pp. 1–7; reproduced in T. M. Carney, *Communist Party Power in Kampuchea*, pp. 27–29; the quotation is from Carney, p. 29.
38. Norodom Sihanouk, *War and Hope*, p. 29.
39. T. M. Carney, *Communist Party Power in Kampuchea*, p. 32.
40. *Indochina Chronicle* (Berkeley), no. 47, (Feb.–Mar. 1976), p. 11.
41. Norodom Sihanouk, *War and Hope*, p. 47.
42. T. M. Carney, *Communist Party Power in Kampuchea*, p. 44.
43. *Ibid.*, p. 43; Sok Thuok was Nuon Chea's *nom de guerre*.
44. See Ben Kiernan, "Conflict in the Kampuchean Communist Movement," pp. 30–50; and Sihanouk, *War and Hope*, p. 73, for comments on the "Unconditional Divisions."
45. On September 16, 1975, Radio Phnom Penh went off the air for two days with no explanation offered, likely indicating that a struggle for control of party propaganda and communications organs was taking place. Ieng Sary later reported what he called a "coup attempt" in September. More likely, someone entered the capital in force to demand an explanation of what was going on, and quickly found out. See B. Kiernan, "Conflict in the Kampuchean Revolutionary Movement," p. 51.
46. Stephen Heder, "Kampuchea 1980: Anatomy of a Crisis," *Southeast Asia Chronicle*, no. 77 (Feb. 1981), p. 5.
47. B. Kiernan, "Social Cohesion in Revolutionary Cambodia," p. 379.
48. B. Kiernan, "Conflict in the Kampuchean Revolutionary Movement," p. 54.
49. *Ibid.*
50. *Ibid.*
51. B. Kiernan, "Bureaucracy of Death," *New Statesman*, May 2, 1980, p. 673.
52. Several analysts have constructed "conspiracy theories" based upon these and other events, arguing that the Chinese communists were the "real"

architects and executors of Democratic Kampuchean domestic and foreign policies. Varying degrees of this line of reasoning are to be found in V. Simonov, *Crimes of the Maoists and Their Rout* (Moscow: Novosti Press Agency Publishing House, 1979); W. Burchett, *The China-Cambodia-Vietnam Triangle* (Chicago: Vanguard Press, 1981); K. M. Quinn, "Origins and Development of Radical Cambodian Communism," especially pp. 180–215, "The Chinese Connection: Radical Left Wing Chinese Communist Underpinnings of Cambodian Communism"; and Daniel Snyder, "Life After Death in the Kampuchean Hell," *Executive Intelligence Review*, September 29, 1981, pp. 19–31.

53. Heder, "Origins of the Conflict," *Southeast Asian Chronicle*, no. 64, p. 22.

54. *Ibid.*, p. 23.

55. B. Kiernan, "Conflict in the Kampuchean Communist Movement," p. 52.

56. *Ibid.*, p. 56.

57. *Ibid.*, p. 57.

58. Sydney Schanberg, "The Death and Life of Dith Pran," *New York Times Magazine*, January 20, 1980, p. 39.

59. B. Kiernan, "Bureaucracy of Death," p. 675.

60. D. L. Chandler's testimony in *Human Rights in Cambodia*, p. 52.

61. Anthony Barnett's report reprinted in B. Kiernan, "Bureaucracy of Death," p. 671; also see William Branigin's series of four articles in the *Washington Post*, titled "Cambodia: A Fragile Convalescence," August 9, 10, 11, and 12, 1981; see especially the last installment in the series, "Khmer Prison Recalls Cambodian Nightmare."

62. S. Heder, "Kampuchea 1980: Anatomy of a Crisis," pp. 4–7.

63. B. Kiernan, "Bureaucracy of Death," p. 676.

64. B. Wain, "Cambodia: What Remains of the Killing Ground," p. 22.

65. Ben Kiernan, "Kampuchea's Choices for Survival," *Southeast Asia Chronicle*, no. 77 (February 1981), p. 28.

8
Utopia and Pandemonium

Hell heard the unsufferable noise, hell saw
Heaven ruining from heaven and would have fled
Affrighted; but strict fate had cast too deep
Her dark foundations, and too fast had bound.
Nine days they fell; confounded chaos roared,
And felt tenfold confusion in their fall
Through his wild anarchy, so huge a rout
Encumbered him with ruin: Hell at last
Yawning received them whole, and on them closed,
Hell their fit habitation, fraught with fire
Unquenchable, the house of woe and pain.
—John Milton, *Paradise Lost*[1]

For some time to come, debate and division will continue concerning the circumstances surrounding the fall of Democratic Kampuchea. The quality of Democratic Kampuchea's leaders will be a central topic in this debate, for they made some hard choices: equality at the expense of liberty and efficiency; order at the expense and in the name of justice; unity at the expense of fraternity; power at the expense of peace; and independence at the expense of existence. This final chapter will examine the legacy of Democratic Kampuchea. Where does one draw the line between bad judgment and extreme prejudice? between extreme prejudice and criminal insanity? Although there are no final answers, it is beginning to become clear how the end came, and what it meant.

The Postregime Stage (1979–1983)

Historically frequent changes in the political boundaries separating the peoples and sovereignties of Southeast Asia in general and Indochina in particular have resulted from the continual ebb and flow of various empires. As a result of this history, and especially of French colonial manipulations in the last century,[2] Cambodia's borders with Thailand and Vietnam have been in dispute throughout the modern period. In part, these historical disputes were a factor in what has come to be known as the "Third Indochina War,"[3] though they seem to have been relatively minor factors compared with the attitudes taken by the primary belligerents.

As with most other aspects of the country's history, many years of careful sifting through the evidence—most of which is not yet generally available and much of which has been destroyed—will be required before historians are able to tell fully the story of the demise of Democratic Kampuchea. Eventually, this story is likely to evoke considerable interest from scholars, for the event was unprecedented in socialist history. The Third Indochina War was the first instance of a full-scale war between two avowedly socialist nations.

The rustication of the cities in Democratic Kampuchea, the uncompromising collectivization, the destruction of the monarchy and the monachy, the purges, the institutionalized violence, even, perhaps, the rejection of modern technology, all these and more can be understood as "rational" responses to the conditions existing in Kampuchea, given the goals of the regime. As ultraradical as the Democratic Kampuchean revolution seems to most observers, Marxist or otherwise, all the policies and actions undertaken by the leadership of Democratic Kampuchea can be interpreted as "rational" behavior, with one glaring exception. The only action of *Angkar Loeu* that seems not to make any sense is Democratic Kampuchea's apparent aggression against an obviously superior neighbor.

The Development of Anti-Vietnamese Aggressiveness

There are still many unanswered questions, but the balance of the available evidence indicates that the incursion into Kampuchea by the Socialist Republic of Vietnam (SRV) in late 1977 to early 1978, and then the full-scale invasion in December 1978, were primarily responses to aggression by Democratic Kampuchea against the SRV. How does one explain aggression by the weak against the strong? One must always hesitate, and carefully reassess existing evidence, before one invokes psychopathological factors as central explanatory variables in the analysis of interstate relations. Yet, it is difficult to make any sense of the Third Indochina War without attributing to the top leadership in Kampuchea a serious case of "groupthink,"[4] in which the leadership consensus was characterized by malignant paranoid schizophrenia. Here, persecutory delusions were compensated for with delusions of grandeur and power, outwardly manifest in the form of imperial revanchism.

There are many possible explanations for Pol Pot's apparent revanchist ambitions beyond reference to psychopathological factors. Some analysts have interpreted Democratic Kampuchea's aggressiveness in terms of nonpathological criteria. For example, Stephen Heder has argued that it was with a view to the consolidation and maintenance of party control that the Stalinist leadership galvanized its population with anti-Vietnamese hatred: "Were Pol Pot to admit that the problem was something more than the sinister infiltration of foreign agents, he would open up opportunities for debate on the party line in which he might be defeated and the whole party would unravel."[5] Heder's thesis attributes the Democratic Kampuchean aggression against the Vietnamese to "rational" calculations related to the perceived needs for national unity and party discipline. This interpretation is quite plausible.

Such a view is buttressed by Norodom Sihanouk, who quotes Khieu Samphan on the purposes of the aggressive anti-Vietnamese line: "to unite our compatriots through the Party, to bring our workers up to the highest level of productivity, and to make the *yotheas*' [the child soldiers'] ardor and valor in combat even greater, the best thing we could do was incite them to hate the Yuons [Vietnamese] more and more every day."[6]

The deflection of domestic dissent by focusing public attention on alleged foreign threats can be seen as a "rational" strategy. Indeed, this tactic has been employed for centuries. But when a nation of some five or six million people challenges a neighbor of some fifty to sixty million to a duel to the death, then the rationality of that move must be called into question. When the larger nation has great technological and organizational advantages to boot, then the smaller nation's aggression begins to appear a little bit "crazy."

Another view is offered by Wilfred Burchett. He too was puzzled as to how Pol Pot could possibly choose to pursue a policy of aggression against Vietnam, and he asked the deputy foreign minister of the Socialist Republic of Vietnam about it in October 1978:

> But how could Kampuchea with a population of (by then) 5–6 million dare to take on a battle-hardened Vietnam with a population of over 50 million? I asked Nguyen Co Thach. He countered with: "Why would an Israel with a population of 3 million dare to invade Egypt with its population of 35 million? Because the Khmer Rouge are assured they

have 800 million Chinese behind them, as Israel has the might of the United States to rely on."[7]

These, then, are three possible elements of an explanation of Democratic Kampuchea's aggressiveness: leadership pathology, national and party unification strategies, and Chinese stewardship. Beyond these factors, another important element motivating KCP behavior towards the Vietnamese was a deep fear of Vietnamese power and intentions. Sihanouk says that Khieu Samphan told him that "the Vietnamese will never rest until they have completely swallowed up our country," and therefore that it is "the Kampuchean's sacred duty to hate the Vietnamese more than anything. . . ."[8] This is the same message that *Angkar Loeu*'s propaganda organs constantly beamed at the Khmer population:

> Particularly since the middle of 1975, because Vietnam's goal is to swallow Cambodia's territory and force Cambodia into an Indochinese federation under its control, and because Vietnam is no longer fighting the U.S. imperialists and their lackeys and thus needs no more help from Cambodia in the form of economic assistance, food, sanctuary and transportation routes as it did during the war, the annexationist, expansionist Vietnamese have openly, continuously and wantonly encroached on Cambodia's national independence, soveriegnty and honor.[9]

The leaders of Democratic Kampuchea seem to have become convinced, on the one hand, that the Vietnamese intended to dominate their country, and on the other hand, that they themselves were capable of militarily defeating this threat while simultaneously satisfying revanchist ambitions. From the perspective of 1983, it is difficult to attribute *Khmer Rouge* fears of a Vietnamese takeover entirely to a paranoid delusion, but there is such a thing as a self-fulfilling prophecy.

In fact, however, veteran Indochina-watchers generally agree that the Vietnamese communist authorities had not publicly claimed primacy over the Kampuchean communist movement since the 1951 to 1954 period, when the successor organizations to the Indochinese Communist Party were forming.[10] Further, there is considerable evidence that Vietnam's leaders were extraordinarily sensitive to the traditional Khmer inferiority complex vis-à-vis the Vietnamese, and that they took extensive measures during and after the 1970–1975 war to encourage self-reliance and independence on the part of the Kampuchean revolutionary movement.[11] Often the efforts of the Vietnamese leaders to temper the traditional Vietnamese paternalism towards the Khmers seemed to reflect the very attitudes they were attempting to extinguish, but the sustained nature of this effort leaves little doubt as to its sincerity.

The last time Sihanouk's Cambodia had gone on record officially reserving the right to make future revanchist claims to the lower Mekong Delta and Cochinchina was the Geneva Conference in 1954. It should be recalled that in 1952, the radical faction of the Khmer Students' Association in Paris—including "Pol Pot," Ieng Sary, Khieu Thirith, and Hou Yuon—blasted Sihanouk for just this: allegedly abandoning Cambodia's claims to former Angkor territories in present-day Vietnam. Did these former students, now the leaders of Democratic Kampuchea, decide to act on this ambition, rather than simply making claims?

As has been noted above, a maze of conflicts of analyses, strategies, and interests had existed between the Vietnamese communists and some factions of the Kampuchean communist movement at least since the Geneva Conference in 1954. Along with other ideological, historical, and geopolitical animosities, this legacy of suspicion between "fraternal" communist parties resulted in the emergence and growth of an anti-Vietnamese clique covertly situated at the very apex of the Kampuchean Communist Party, and led by Pol Pot and Ieng Sary.

Even as they welcomed massive infusions of revolutionary experience and military equipment from the Vietnamese after joining the "United Front of the Three Indochinese Peoples" in 1970, the KCP's top leaders were already executing a systematic program for the elimination of all traces of Vietnamese influence from the Kampuchean revolutionary organization. As Khieu Samphan expressed it to Norodom Sihanouk in 1978, the Stalinist politbureau of the KCP "never once stopped considering Vietnam and its army as Enemy Number One."[12]

In 1967–1968, and again in 1970–1971, the exiled KPP cadres who had spent the interregnum since Geneva as "guests" in Hanoi returned to Kampuchea to assist in the development of the revolution. These "Internationalists" were considered to be hopelessly "contaminated" by their long exposure to the North Vietnamese, and, although the Stalinists claimed to have "tried to save" a few of them, most were eliminated one way or another. The liquidation of the Internationalists at the hands of the KCP inner circle was carried on during the war with the greatest of secrecy. The scope and thoroughness of this effort, however, most certainly tipped off the Vietnamese leadership. The excellent intelligence apparatus operated by the Vietnamese communists probably identified the hostility of the Pol Pot group early on. In many cases it was easy to tell something was amiss.

As early as 1970, there were reports of *Khmer Rouge* attacks on Vietnamese communist units operating in Cambodia. In September of that year, a KCP unit near Kompong Thom was reported to have fired on a North Vietnamese unit from behind as the latter was assaulting a FANK position.[13] From this point onward, the violence perpetrated against the Vietnamese and those who could be associated with the Vietnamese by their Kampuchean comrades gradually escalated. Ieng Lin, an Internationalist who defected to the Republicans late in 1971, said that "only the local Khmer Rouge [as opposed to the Internationalists] held political positions within the local organizations," and that those who had been in Hanoi since 1954 were assigned "the combat positions."[14] By 1973, the purification of the revolutionary apparatus was in full swing. By attrition and by assassination, the Internationalists dwindled in number.

From this kind of calculated extermination of "contaminated" KPP cadres during the war, violence against the Pracheachonists, the Issarakists, the Maoists, and the remaining Internationalists (not to mention the now nearly extinct Rumdo) at the hands of the Stalinists escalated after the war to widespread secret purges. The days of pluralism in Kampuchean communism were numbered.

Open Conflict Between Socialist Nations

Open fighting between the Vietnamese and the Kampucheans began even before the victory celebrations in Saigon could occur. On April 17, 1975, the very day of the victory against the Khmer Republic, the Kampuchean National United Front later announced, the Vietnamese had "seized" some contested coastal islands and "invaded" Ratanakiri and Mondolkiri Provinces. Within two weeks, fighting between the two communist forces was reported on and around the contested coastal islands. (These islands were later ceded to the Kampucheans by the Vietnamese.) In June of 1975, Saloth Sar led a high-level delegation to Hanoi in order to establish a commission to deal with the border problems. These talks proved fruitless, as did others the following year when Vietnamese party leader Le Duan traveled to Phnom Penh. Through the remainder of 1975 and into 1976, there occurred a series of charges and countercharges between the Vietnamese and the Kampucheans, both alleging aggression and atrocities along their common border.

With the establishment of the government of Democratic Kampuchea early in 1976, however, it appears that one or both of two factors caused the level of border violence to decline dramatically. The problem of reestablishing internal control after the formation of the government may have so preoccupied the Stalinists that they had inadequate military resources to spare for aggression against Vietnam. Or, possibly, the Stalinists may have temporarily lost control over part or all of the forces being used to press the Kampuchean territorial claims on the Vietnamese. Whatever the reason, 1976 was a period of relative calm between the socialist neighbors.

Following the Stalinists' gradual return to internal predominance toward the end of 1976, however, the reported incidence of border clashes again began to climb. Then, in February 1977, the Democratic Kampuchean regime reported that there had been an apparently serious attempted *coup d'état*. The Stalinists labeled the alleged act "Hanoi-inspired," and accelerated the rate of internal purge. In April Democratic Kampuchea began to turn outward again, launching division-sized attacks against the Ha Tien and Chau Doc regions of Vietnam. In the following month, there ensued fierce fighting as the Vietnamese attempted to repulse the attackers.

It was at this point, most likely, that the Vietnamese decided that the time had come to teach the Pol Pot regime a lesson. After making what he regarded as adequate preparations, Vietnamese General Vo Nguyen Giap led an incursion in September 1977 along much of the 650-mile length of the Kampuchean-Vietnamese border. Using crack elements of the NVA's elite Ninth Division in a highly mechanized action, Giap penetrated up to ten miles and more in some areas. However, reliance on heavy armor during the wet season, against an opponent well-versed in meeting superior battlefield technology, turned out to be a major miscalculation for the esteemed general. His forces met unexpectedly stiff resistance.

As the fighting continued to escalate through October and November, the Vietnamese attempted to expand their hold on Svay Rieng Province. This was the famous Parrot's Beak area, terrain intimately familiar to the Vietnamese commanders who had used it as an important base area during the war with the United States. Even so, in November Democratic Kampuchea claimed to have killed 10 percent of the Vietnamese incursion force of 20,000. By December, the Vietnamese were having such a difficult time that their high command decided to send in a reinforcement of 58,000 troops to relieve the hard-pressed Ninth Division. This fateful action persuaded the Standing Committee of the Kampuchean People's Revolutionary Army that the conflict had become a duel to the death. On December 25, 1977, the Kampuchean Revolutionary Army committed itself to all-out war.

The first week of January 1978 saw pitched battles in Takeo and Kampot Provinces between a five-division Vietnamese army of 60,000 and perhaps 30,000 soldiers and three divisions of the Revolutionary Army of Kampuchea. At this high point in the conflict, the Vietnamese apparently determined that their lesson had been adequately communicated. They began the withdrawal of their incursion forces as early as January 6, 1978. *Angkar Loeu* saw fit to interpret this action as an admission of defeat. Over the following few months, Vietnam's repeated requests for a cease-fire and negotiations were regularly rebuffed by the Kampucheans as the Vietnamese continued their withdrawal from the occupied eastern region of the country.

A Radio Phnom Penh broadcast in May 1978 seemed to reflect the general tone of *Angkar Loeu*'s internal propaganda at that point, in its projection of the requirements for the extermination of the entire Vietnamese nation:

> In terms of numbers, one of us had to kill 30 Vietnamese. . . . So far, we have succeeded in implementing the slogan of 1 against 30. . . . Using these figures, 1 Kampuchean soldier is equal to 30 Vietnamese soldiers . . . 2 million troops should be more than enough to fight the Vietnamese, because Vietnam has only 50 million inhabitants. We do not need 8 million people. [sic] We need only 2 million troops to crush the 50 million Vietnamese; and we would still have 6 million people left. We must formulate our combat line in this manner in order to achieve victory. . . . If we can use one against 30, we will certainly win, even if this fight lasts 700 years or more. . . .[15]

Chief of eastern zone security for the Stalinists was a man named Pok. After the Vietnamese pressed their withdrawal from the border regions in the first half of 1978, Pok took decisive action to deal with suspected subversion fomented in the eastern zone during the Vietnamese occupation. According to reports, Pok declared that the population there had "Khmer bodies but Vietnamese minds."[16] His security forces began the evacuation of the entire civilian population of the eastern zone of Democratic Kampuchea. The evacuees were marched to more secure areas away from the border regions, where many were subsequently executed. An estimated 50,000 people were killed in this undiscriminating pogrom. Similar repressions were reported from throughout the country.

As the purges intensified over the course of 1978, the Stalinists began to get lax, their methods a bit lazy. There were reports that they were using artillery to "wipe out traitors" in villages.[17] It became obvious to all Kampuchean citizens that *any* connection with the Vietnamese was a capital offense, even if the crime was no more heinous than to happen to reside in the border regions. The flow of Democratic Kampuchean citizens seeking sanctuary in Vietnam steadily rose. The Vietnamese were able to turn the refugee flow, at first something of a problem, into an asset. Over the course of the summer of 1978, an estimated 150,000 people fled their Khmer homeland for the safety of Vietnam. Some went out with the retreating incursion forces, some had gone out during the incursion, and others escaped alone or in small groups. Some military units defected virtually intact. Other Cambodians, such as So Phim and Heng Samrin, rebelled against the repression practiced by *Angkar Loeu*, but did not immediately fall into the arms of the Vietnamese.

Perhaps the last surviving KCP Central Committee member who was not rabidly anti-Vietnamese, Vorn Veth, led an unsuccessful revolt in the eastern zone in November 1978. Was this *coup* attempt inspired by a Vietnamese desire to dominate Kampuchea, or was it provoked by the extreme oppression of the High Organization? This is a crucial question for historians, but for the politicians of Indochina at the end of 1978, it was a moot point. The die had been cast.

On December 3, Radio Hanoi announced the formation of the Khmer National United Front for National Salvation (KNUFNS). KNUFNS was a disparate coalition of refugees. It was partly composed of non- and anticommunist elements (e.g., bourgeoisie and priests) who had fled during the period of consolidation and society building, but was mainly made up of Internationalists, Pracheachonists, and Issarakists who had escaped the purges and were disillusioned with the course of the revolution under *Angkar Loeu*. Dominated by "veterans of the struggle," these cadres shared a revolutionary heritage dating back to the anticolonial struggles of the 1940s and 1950s. These people were, by now, by and large friendly to the Vietnamese and their government.

What of the Vietnamese motives for the invasion? John Spragens, Jr., of the Southeast Asia Resource Center, reports that there appear to have been three important reasons for the full-scale Vietnamese invasion of Democratic Kampuchea in December of 1978.[18] From his analysis of internal and external Vietnamese propaganda and his interviews with Vietnamese leaders, Spragens suggests that the primary concern shown by the Vietnamese in their invasion decision was related to domestic political considerations. Specifically, Kampuchean raids into Vietnam's New Economic Zone (NEZ) areas, on land internationally considered to be Vietnamese (Cochinchinese) territory for about a century, increased in frequency and intensity after late 1977. By late 1978, the NEZ settlers felt so insecure that their fear began to translate into anger against their own government. The Socialist Republic of Vietnam faced a major internal crisis over its ability to protect its newly liberated citizens, the former residents of South Vietnam.

Of secondary but still major importance were certain strategic military considerations. Foremost here was the Vietnamese fear of facing a two-front war against the Kampucheans and the Chinese. This eventuality was realized, but was still preferable, perhaps, to the feared alternative: a prolonged border war with Pol Pot, allowing his forces access to his population for long-term casualty replacement and easy military resupply by sea from China.

Finally, according to Spragens, a third but less than decisive factor influenced the invasion decision: humanitarian considerations. Although this has been billed in Vietnamese propaganda as the most important reason for the invasion, in reality the humanitarian motive appears to have been less than causal. "Until (Democratic Kampuchea) directly attacked Vietnam, the Vietnamese were willing to consider the killings inside Kampuchea a domestic affair of the Kampucheans" (p. 10), even though the Vietnamese knew that the principal category of victims consisted of those suspected of being "soft" on Vietnam.

Norodom Sihanouk has no great love for the Vietnamese. Indeed, in his latest book, he continually refers to them using the term *Yuon*, a derogatory reference favored by the Stalinists. Yet, Sihanouk seems to see the Vietnamese motives in the invasion of the country he ruled for 25 years as primarily self-defensive:

> Each people has its honor to defend. The Vietnamese nation, conscious of its stature, could not continue to ignore the Khmer Rouge's most blatant affronts to Vietnamese honor: Khmer Rouge soldiers would rape a Vietnamese woman, then ram a stake or a bayonet into her vagina. Pregnant women were cut open, their unborn babies yanked out and slapped against the dying mother's face. The *yothea*s also enjoyed cutting off the breasts of well-endowed Vietnamese women. Vietnamese fishermen who fell into the hands of the Khmer Rouge were decapitated. Prisoners of war were tortured, then made to read speeches full of the crassest insults to Phan Van Dong, Le Duan, Truong Chinh, Vo Nguyen Giap, Nguyen Duy Trinh, and even the late Ho Chi Minh. . . .
>
> There was obviously no way Hanoi could forgive all this, and the only way it could put a stop to it was by toppling the Pol Pot–Ieng Sary regime.[19]

That regime—the "Supreme Organization," *Angkar Loeu*—was a decentralized state apparatus given what coherence it had by the fanatical devotion of the young, hardcore cadres to the directives of the Stalinist politbureau, still composed of the same core of fewer than half a dozen individuals who had come to prominence in the Kampuchean Communist Party in the early 1960s: the students from Paris. The carefully engineered apolitical nature of their organization, when combined with the sorry condition of the social fabric in Kampuchea and the general state of *anomie* deriving from the destruction of the social milieu, resulted in what may fairly be described as a very weak state. They had only a marginal ability to motivate those within the state, and no ability whatsoever to motivate positively the behavior of those outside the state.

It seems that one cannot motivate an entire people to reject the past and adopt a new identity virtually overnight. The terror that shattered the Kampuchean peasants' reality made possible the mass psychograft of an alien ideology. Yet, this graft did not cut deeply into the peasants' individual belief structures, associating with values and habits of mind acquired over a lifetime. Rather, the Kampuchean masses were required to associate with revolutionary rhetoric and institutions to the exclusion of their experience. Although committed cadres might "understand," the masses were prone to confusion. As Perlmutter and LeoGrande argue, "Although it may be possible to undertake a radical shift in value orientations within the relatively controlled environment of the hierarchically structured armed forces, civil society is much more resistant to firestorms of ideological change, even when the coercive resources of the military are devoted to promulgating them."[20] And so, for the mass of the Democratic Kampuchean citizens, confusion shaded into resentment, and resentment became a silent hatred of their own government, the pressure building toward a cathartic release.

Thus, the strategy that enabled the *Khmer Rouge* to prosecute successfully their struggle against the *ancien regime* held the seeds of self-destruction for the utopia they hoped to construct. Inexorably, the means perverted the ends, indelibly coloring the emergent strategy of society building with an oppressively violent hue: blood red. As the contrived social structure began to approximate more closely to the theoretical ideal, far more than the socioeconomic infrastructure of Kampuchea had been broken and destroyed. The spirit of the Khmer people had been broken, not to be easily or quickly restored.

Commenting on the impressive victory of the PFLANK forces over the massed power of Lon Nol and the U.S. Air Force in CHENLA

II during 1971, Khieu Samphan, then GRUNK defense minister and PFLANK commander-in-chief, concluded that the key element was the fact that his "armed forces had the support of a solid military, political and social base."[21] For precisely this same reason—the condition of its social base—the *Khmer Rouge* regime disintegrated before the Vietnamese advance in mid-December 1978 just like the illusion called a society it had created.

Sociopolitical factors relating to *Angkar Loeu*'s repression were perhaps the key elements in the collapse of Democratic Kampuchea, but strategic factors proved to be crucial in the timing and speed of that collapse. In the name of KNUFNS, the Socialist Republic of Vietnam fielded an army of 120,000 against Pol Pot's 30,000 to 40,000 troops. The end came quickly, in part because of a serious tactical error by Pol Pot. Of the nineteen "divisions" committed to the border war with Vietnam, Pol foolishly placed almost half in two of the most vulnerable areas of the country, the Parrot's Beak in Svay Rieng and the Fishhook in Kompong Cham. As Burchett describes it, "Pol Pot divisions were encircled in a massive outflanking movement, their tanks and artillery were destroyed by superior Vietnamese fire-power and accuracy, and their cadres were liquidated largely by their own troops revolting against the intolerable repression within the armed forces."[22]

On January 5, 1979, Pol Pot announced over Radio Phnom Penh that the Revolutionary Army of Kampuchea would achieve "certain victory" over the Vietnamese invaders. The Chinese thought otherwise, and were hurriedly evacuating diplomatic personnel, technicians, military advisors, and dependents. On January 6, Norodom Sihanouk escaped to Peking aboard the last flight out of Phnom Penh. On the seventh, Phnom Penh belonged to Vo Nguyen Giap.

After the Fall

What then of the future? It is premature to speak of the *Khmer Rouge* strictly in the past tense. As Giap and the KNUFNS took Phnom Penh, the top personnel of the government of Democratic Kampuchea retreated with the rump of their army to well-prepared strongholds in the vast expanses of forest. They linger in the northeastern hills near Laos, in northwestern areas along the border with Thailand, in the far southwest, and in a number of other remote locations, waging a guerrilla war against the Vietnamese in hope of regaining power. This would seem unlikely, although Pol Pot's tenacity is amply demonstrated by the continued existence of some 180,000

Utopia and Pandemonium 197

to 200,000 Vietnamese troops protecting the People's Republic of Kampuchea against a Stalinist strength of no more than 30,000 troops. Despite years of attempts, the Vietnamese have been unable to eradicate the Stalinists. This is not for want of effort on the part of the Vietnamese. The destruction of Pol Pot's forces has been among the premier goals of their entire foreign policy since 1979, and their exertions have indeed been prodigious. Their military effort has included the employment of sophisticated chemical and possibly even biological weapons. According to U.S. State Department reports,[23] there were at least sixteen documented chemical warfare attacks against Kampuchean guerrillas by the Vietnamese army in the first six months of 1982, including several attacks alleged to have involved the use of mycotoxin weapons. Yet, the Stalinists persevere, even though their population base—a most crucial consideration in the conduct of guerrilla warfare—is estimated at no more than 60,000.

How can one explain the continued existence of the *Khmer Rouge* as a political, diplomatic, and military force, in the face of their several disadvantages? Again, reference to the international situation is required. The geopolitical realities in Southeast Asia provide the structure for a strange game that has been played, with various participants, for centuries. The game is called, "Who Encircles Whom?"

If Vietnam (on China's southeastern flank) is allied with the Soviet Union (on China's northern flank), and if Vietnam dominates Laos and Cambodia (on China's southwestern flank), then China will be "encircled" by hostile forces. On the other hand, if Kampuchea (on Vietnam's western flank) is allied with China (on Vietnam's northern flank), then Vietnam will be "encircled" by hostile forces. Thus, so long as the Vietnamese and Chinese take it upon themselves to sustain mutual disapprobation, there is a contradiction between regional security for China and regional security for Vietnam. Kampuchea is the keystone binding this contradiction, the central pawn in the ongoing struggle. Add to this alignment the policy of the United States, which is to oppose the Soviet Union whenever possible, and this sum yields the dynamic that sustains the *Khmer Rouge*.

On October 9, 1979, former Cambodian Prime Minister Son Sann crossed over the border from Thailand into Cambodia, and there declared the existence of the Kampuchean People's National Liberation Front, the KPNLF. With an estimated 6,000 troops, Son wanted to offer himself as a viable "third force," providing the Western powers an option besides supporting either the new Kampuchean regime or the old *Khmer Rouge*. Norodom Sihanouk immediately set about the task of forming a coalition with Son's KPNLF.

After a year and a half of on-again-off-again attempts to form such a coalition, Sihanouk and Son signed a "declaration" for "common action against the Vietnamese" at the beginning of September 1981. This action appeared to freeze out the Stalinists, with whom Son had refused truck. But Son Sann, with an estimated 6,000 poorly armed troops, and Sihanouk, with no troops, together seemed to pose little threat to the People's Republic of Kampuchea.

This argument was no doubt employed by the Chinese in their discussions with Son Sann and Norodom Sihanouk. In support of its interest in seeing the conflict in Kampuchea sustained, the PRC has assisted the *Khmer Rouge* in reviving the united front tactic. Through 1980 and into 1981, the Chinese pressured the Stalinists to modify their program sufficiently to render themselves acceptable partners in an anti-Vietnamese coalition with Son Sann and Norodom Sihanouk. The Stalinists began the construction of a new and "moderate" image by making public some of their self-criticism. Khieu Samphan reportedly noted that they may have "forced the people to do manual labor which was too harsh for some people."[24] Ieng Sary noted that some "political errors were made." Among the "errors" mentioned by Ieng were the rustication of the cities, the suppression of religion, and the destruction of family networks, traditional educational institutions, and the monetary economy. Pol Pot, his name now synonymous with mass murder, has discreetly stepped out of the limelight, with Khieu Samphan in his place as the front man for the Stalinists. The first week of March 1982, Khieu claimed that "Pol Pot will bow to the orders of the government elected by the people."[25] However, reports emanating from Thailand as late as the middle of 1983 indicate that Pol Pot still controls the main force of the Stalinists' guerrillas,[26] and thus the people of Kampuchea might be forgiven if they doubt the sincerity of Pol Pot's sudden conversion into a humble servant of the people.

These actions did not satisfy Son Sann, and he continued to refuse to join a coalition with the Stalinists. In New York attending a United Nations conference on Kampuchea in July 1981, Ieng Sary defined the political program of his movement as "not ideological, not socialism or communism." At this same news conference, he asserted that a united front with Son Sann was not possible. The Chinese disagreed with this assessment, and by the end of the year Chinese Premier Zhao turned up the pressure on the Stalinists by suggesting that Son Sann and Norodom Sihanouk would make better leaders of the Kampuchean resistance movement than would Khieu Samphan and his associates.[27] The pressure was effective. In December 1981, the

Kampuchean Communist Party announced that it was officially dissolving itself. This dramatic if suspicious action opened the door for the establishment of a coalition among the three Kampuchean resistance factions. On June 22, 1982, Sann, Sihanouk, and Samphan signed the papers creating the new "Democratic Kampuchea," and setting the stage for continued warfare in Kampuchea through 1983 and beyond. The success of this coalition depends upon the hope that the Khmer people have very short memories, and will soon forget the nature of their existence under the leadership of Pol Pot and his followers.

But the Kampuchean people are not likely to forget, even if they could, which is doubtful, for the new regime installed by the Vietnamese has been careful to make the "boundless evil of the genocidal Pol Pot–Ieng Sary clique" the centerpiece of the new mythology. There are constant reminders of what has come before and what they could expect with Pol Pot's return. The new regime has moved quickly to pick up the scattered pieces of Kampuchean society. Within a year after the defeat of Democratic Kampuchea, KNUFNS formed a "Revolutionary Council," charged with the responsibility of restoring some normalcy in a society almost totally destroyed by a decade of war and revolution.

The first priority, as always, was agriculture. The retreating Stalinists sabotaged some of the irrigation system, and thus reconstruction of the poorly designed and war-ravaged hydraulic works, as well as the revival of phosphate fertilizer production, was among the initial efforts undertaken by the new regime. Internal communications and transportation systems are being rebuilt with Vietnamese and Soviet aid. The PRK has reestablished a monetary economy, aiding in the return of internal trade. Medical facilities closed by the KCP have been reopened by the PRK, and new provincial health centers have been established along with an aggressive campaign to train paramedical personnel.

Programs to restore the cultural heritage of Kampuchea have been established by the new regime. The remnants of the monachy are being assisted in the revival of Buddhism among the peasantry, as uncommunist as it may seem. This policy is tempered by the fact that the new regime discourages young people from joining the priesthood. Restoration of the damaged and denigrated architectural treasures of Kampuchea has been planned, highlighted by international appeals to the Western countries for technical assistance in the rebuilding of such monuments as the Angkor Wat temple complex.

Significantly, the Vietnamese have hurried to help establish and equip a new national army for the People's Republic of Kampuchea, keenly aware that their welcome is already running out among some of the Khmer people. Until the new army is capable of defending the regime against the guerrilla threats posed by the KPNLF and the Stalinists, however, the Vietnamese are likely to see themselves as having little choice other than to continue their occupation.

Yet, the probability seems to be fairly high that the new regime will survive its own formidable internal challenges as well as the hostility displayed by the United States, the People's Republic of China, and the members of the Association of Southeast Asian Nations (ASEAN). This probability is enhanced by the "simple" things that the government of the PRK has done for the war-weary Kampuchean people. Heng Samrin described this aspect of the regime's efforts: "The revolutionary power has also ensured for all citizens a joyful life, a reunited family, free marriage, the right of movement, the right to education and medical care. Therefore, all Kampucheans are now attached to the new regime."[28] Democratic Kampuchea was an easy act to follow.

If the PRK proves itself capable of bringing a permanent end to the famine introduced after years of warfare, in addition to continuing to permit the normal amenities of life that had been cut off by the KCP, then it is very difficult to imagine a set of circumstances wherein the Kampuchean people would countenance a return to power by the Stalinists. Yet, the nature of the geopolitical struggle that continues to rage in Southeast Asia leaves little optimism that the people of Kampuchea will soon know any respite from the conflict that has haunted their world for generations.

The "Precious Model": Implications of the Classless Society

The section, "Roots of Ideology," in Chapter 3 discussed some of the developments in the evolution of Marxist-Leninist-Maoist theory that influenced the KCP's central leaders. Although theoretical tracts from Kampuchean Communist Party working sessions are unavailable to substantiate the claim definitively, it is nonetheless clear that the Kampuchean experience has provided the world with a new "model" of socialist development in the great tradition of the Soviet, East European, and Chinese models.

Marx believed that peasants were elements of a feudal culture, totally alien to the very concept of socialist society.[29] Lenin revised this tenet of Marxism, arguing that, in league with the industrial proletariat, the peasantry could make positive contributions to socialist revolution. Stalin agreed in his own way, and greased the path to industrialism with the blood of Russia's peasantry. Mao Tse-tung once more revised this tenet of Marxism-Leninism, holding that the peasantry could be the leading force in bringing about an Asian socialist revolution. Finally, in the logical culmination of this tradition in Marxist-Leninist-Maoist thought, Hou Yuon went all the way: The peasantry could stage-leap itself (or be staged-leaped by a vanguard party) over the periods of capitalist accumulation and socialist construction without the inconvenience of the intermediate historical stages. Prolonged class struggle would only burden this process, and since one class was really the ultimate goal anyway, why not start that way? The peasants already constituted 85 to 90 percent of Khmer society, so the transition to a single class should be easy to accomplish. The party embraced this idea even as it eliminated the author.

Although the left in China may have applauded this development, the more powerful moderates and right-wingers of the CCP were skeptical, and tried to caution the KCP against going through with this ultraradical approach. In 1975, as Chou En-lai was dying in a Peking hospital, Khieu Samphan, Ieng Thirith, and Norodom Sihanouk paid a courtesy visit to the fading leader's deathbed. Although Norodom Sihanouk was there to give homage to his friend and patron, Khieu and Ieng had other purposes. Sihanouk described this scene, surely one of the most poignant episodes of the entire drama:

> I heard him advise Khieu Samphan and Ieng Thirith not to try to achieve total communism in one giant step. The wise and perspicacious veteran of the Chinese revolution stressed the need to move "step by step" toward socialism. This would take several years of patient work. Then and only then should they advance toward communist society. Premier Chou En-lai reiterated that China itself had experienced disastrous setbacks in the fairly recent past by trying to make a giant leap forward and move full speed ahead to pure communism. The great Chinese statesman counseled the Khmer Rouge leaders: "Don't follow the bad example of our 'great leap forward.' Take things slowly: that is the best way to guide Kampuchea and its people to growth, prosperity and happiness." By way of response to this splendid and moving piece of almost fatherly advice, Khieu Samphan and Ieng Thirith just smiled an incredulous and superior smile. . . .
>
> Not long after we got back to Phnom Penh, Khieu Samphan and Son Sen told me that their Kampuchea was going to show the world that pure communism could indeed be achieved at one fell swoop. This was no doubt their indirect reply to [Chou En-lai]. "Our country's

place in history will be assured," they said. "We will be the first nation to create a completely communist society without wasting time on intermediate steps."[30]

Thus, the leaders of Democratic Kampuchea saw themselves as presenting to the world a new alternative, what can be called the "Kampuchean Model" of socialist economic development. What is this "Kampuchean Model," and how does it compare with other models?

Given the radical nature of the *Khmer Rouge* economic program, meaningful comparative analyses are difficult. Even within the restricted subset of communist regimes, a great many amazingly different systems are included under the labels "socialist" and "communist." A comparison of Czechoslovakian and Kampuchean economic programs would be tantamount to a comparison of apples and widgets because of the vast differences in their respective degrees and modes of agricultural and industrial production. This divergence is ultimately a reflection of varying economic, cultural, and social structures and antecedents, precisely the structural differences to which Mao Tsetung alluded in condemning the applicability of Soviet-style communism to developing Asian nations.

A far more suitable comparative set would be composed of nations that had espoused and ostensibly implemented a non-Eurocentric, rural brand of communism based on the "broad shoulders" of the peasantry rather than the urban proletariat. The two foremost examples of this style, of course, are the People's Republic of China (PRC) and the Socialist Republic of Vietnam (SRV, née Democratic Republic of Vietnam, or DRV). Another interesting dimension in a tripartite comparison of Democratic Kampuchea, the PRC, and the SRV lies in the fact that the latter two nations were the major Asian influences in the development, the implementation, and, ultimately, the destruction of Democratic Kampuchea's regime and economic program.

The Vietnamese were responsible for much of the impetus behind Kampuchean communism, commencing with the integration of Cambodian elements in the Indochinese Communist Party in 1930. Despite traditional Vietnamese-Cambodian antagonism and the division of the ICP into national components, the Vietnamese continued to wield considerable influence in the Kampuchean communist movement if only by virtue of the fact that many of the Kampuchean cadres were trained in Hanoi. This influence was manifest until the closing chapters of the *Khmer Rouge* saga, when in the wake of what may have been Vietnamese-inspired *coup* attempts and the associated purges within the Kampuchean Communist Party, outright warfare between the two states eliminated any illusions of common interest or socialist solidarity.

The Chinese Communist Party and state have also given long-standing support to various Kampuchean communist factions. Gradually the PRC assumed the mantle of the fledgling party's and nascent regime's mentor. Chinese support was extended to ever increasing degrees, from moral support ranging through extensive financial and military aid and finally to an actual invasion(s) designed to "punish" former ally Vietnam for incursions into Democratic Kampuchea. The Chinese commitment to Democratic Kampuchea has been very impressive, despite the misgivings of moderate and rightist Chinese leaders over *Khmer Rouge* tactics. The PRC risked incurring the wrath of the Soviet Union (Vietnam's new mentor), and to some extent, the United States, as well as the ASEAN countries. With this history of sometimes intimate and always complex relations among Democratic Kampuchea, the PRC, and the SRV, it seems appropriate to consider the similarities and differences among their respective economic development strategies. This discussion will provide a basis upon which to define what is unique about the "Kampuchean Model."

> The basic principle for the economic construction of the People's Republic of China is to develop production and bring about a prosperous economy through the policies of taking into account both public and private interests benefiting both labor and capital, of mutual aid between city and countryside, and circulation of goods between China and abroad. The state shall co-ordinate and regulate the state owned economy, co-operative economy, the individual economy of the peasants and handicraftsmen, private capitalist economy and state capitalist economy in their sphere of operation, supply of raw materials, marketing, labor conditions, technical equipment and policies of public and general finance.
> —Common Program of the PRC, Article 26[31]

> The political power in our country is a democratic power of the people, that is, of the workers, peasants, petty bourgeoisie, national bourgeoisie and patriotic and progressive personages and landlords. . . . while special attention must be paid to the development of agriculture, we must develop industry, handicrafts and home trade. . . . with regard to the national bourgeoisie, our Party encourages, assists and guides it in its enterprises.
> —Platform of the Vietnam Lao Dong Party[32]

> The State of Kampuchea is a state of workers, peasants and all other working people. All important means of production are collective

property of the people's state and of the people's collectives. Property for everyday use remains in private hands.
—Constitution of Democratic Kampuchea, Article 4[33]

One way to begin a comparison of the economic programs instituted by Kampuchean, Chinese, and Vietnamese communists is to refer to the documentary claims made by each of these nations when they first set about their national revolutions. Although these documents were part propaganda, part planning, and part preliminary projections anticipating future transformation, they do provide a starting point for a comparison of the three economic models. It would be tempting to try to compare the advanced stages of the PRC and SRV development models to that of Democratic Kampuchea, but impossible, because the *Khmer Rouge* program did not last long enough to reach an advanced stage.

There exist a considerable number of immediately obvious differences in the degree of explanation among the stated economic goals of the Kampucheans, Chinese, and Vietnamese. But the actual differences extend far beyond those evident in this rhetoric, for Democratic Kampuchean documents are generally not reliable guides to the regime's behavior. A realistic comparison necessitates an overview of actual policies in Democratic Kampuchea, whether enunciated or not, juxtaposed against the Vietnamese and Chinese documents that were relatively good indicators of policy, and considered in view of the later evolution in Chinese and Vietnamese policies. This survey of comparative developmental plans will focus on a number of specific areas, including agricultural land ownership and agrarian reform, industry, trade, finance, technology, property ownership, and social structure.

Agricultural Land Ownership and Agrarian Reform

Even after the revolution in 1949 the basic mode of land ownership in the PRC was small private peasant-owned plots. The land holdings of the landlords were entirely confiscated, although, significantly, any nonagricultural productive enterprises they also owned were left intact in the first stages of the revolution. The holdings of middle peasants and even some rich peasants were apparently sacrosanct, but the land distribution program was far-reaching. Over 115 million acres were reallocated for the benefit of 300 million poor or landless peasants.[34] Even former landlords and enemies of the state were offered a stake in the new society; they too would be allocated land in accordance with their needs if they were willing to work. One of the most interesting aspects of the Chinese agrarian reform was the documentation of land ownership. After the redistribution was complete, title deeds were issued to all land owners who were then free to buy, sell, or rent their land as they saw fit, subject to rent ceilings and the possibility of being branded as bourgeois if their acquisitive instincts ran unbridled. Interest rates were lowered.[35]

Vietnamese agrarian reform also strjessed private ownership of land by the peasants. Vietnamese treatment of landlords, however, varied from that of the Chinese. The holdings of the French and of "traitorous" landlords were subject to immediate confiscation without compensation. "Patriotic" landlords were permitted to keep their land and collect rent in accordance with the law controlling rents,[36] despite the exploitative aspect of this practice. Any land that was expropriated from patriotic landlords was to be paid for in the form of 10-year, 1.5 percent interest bonds.[37] The holdings of middle peasants were protected as in China, as well as those of rich peasants. Former enemies were granted an opportunity to atone for their past sins. Landlords and minor traitors, those sentenced to less than five years' imprisonment, were eligible for small plots. The land of merchants and industrialists in North Vietnam was protected in the early stages of the reforms with a view to encouraging production. Agricultural rents and interest rates were subject to strict ceilings.

As has been previously noted, Kampuchean land ownership and agricultural production were characterized by total and immediate collectivization on or before April 17, 1975. Within two years, the collectivization was universal and so total as to extend to such implements as those necessary for personal hygiene. This collectivization made no concessions whatsoever to private ownership. The means of production lay entirely within the sphere of the state, and the collectivization of both land and labor in Kampuchea's essentially unisectoral economy was pervasive and complete. Such archaic concepts as rent and interest rates were rendered obsolete in the wake of this profound structural realignment of the economy. *This realignment bears no comparison to the programs in China and Vietnam, neither in conception, nor in implementation, nor in results.*

Land redistribution and the emancipation and mobilization of the peasantry have "traditionally" served as the chief attractions and dominant economic themes in both the theory and the practice of Asian communism. Variations on the Chinese model have been implemented in Vietnam, Laos, Mongolia, and North Korea. Yet, the close contact between the central theorists and practitioners of revolutionary Kampuchean economics and their counterparts in Vietnam and China evidently had little impact upon Democratic Kampuchean agricultural policy, except insofar as the Vietnamese and Chinese economic models may have been perceived as negative exemplars. In its evolution and implementation, Democratic Kampuchea's agricultural program diverged indisputably and radically from those in Vietnam and China, though it shared common theoretical antecedents with them. The Chinese and Vietnamese tolerated, and even encouraged in some cases the continuation and development of a class structure; *Angkar Loeu* sought to begin from the start with a perfectly homogeneous economic class structure.

Industry

The Chinese plan for industrial development was succinctly stated by Article 35 of the Common Program. It called for the "systematic rehabilitation of the development of heavy industry such as mining, the iron and steel industry, the power industry, machine-making industry, electric industry and the main chemical industries."[38] At the time when the Common Program was adopted, the Chinese were obviously influenced by the Soviet model, in which heavy industrial development serves as the vanguard of economic development, at least in the urban areas. This approach has the obvious advantage of simultaneously providing the military capability required to consolidate the gains of the revolution. Although the growth of and priority accorded to Chinese industrial development has ebbed and flowed over the decades in response to both ideological convulsions and economic constraints, industry has continued to grow and is presently expanding under the pragmatism of the post-Mao leadership.

Because of its insatiable thirst for massive capital infusions, heavy industry has remained the exclusive domain of the national bourgeoisie and state capitalism in the PRC. At the other end of the industrial spectrum, the "individual economy of handicraftsmen," small merchants, and traders was also encouraged, if not consistently, then at least recurrently. Thus it appears that the Chinese envisioned the development of an integrated industrial structure ranging from cottage industry through heavy industry and secondary sectors.

Although accorded a less important role than in the Chinese developmental model, industrialization was not neglected in Vietnam. The Manifesto of the Vietnam Worker's Party acknowledges the primacy of agricultural development, but also specifically articulates the goal of developing both heavy and cottage industry.[39] The underlying ideological sources of these differences have been articulated by Stephen Heder:

> the theory and practice of the Vietnamese revolution [exhibited] relatively high degrees of class caution and traditionalism. In practice, this is manifested in a preference for administrative measures rather than relatively violent mass movements [as in Democratic Kampuchea and the PRC] in resolving social contradictions. In theory, it is manifested in an emphasis on the forces of production (i.e., science and technology) rather than the relations of production (i.e., class struggle and conflict) in the post-liberation stage of socialist construction.[40]

Little detail regarding which industries were to be developed was specified in the Vietnamese Worker's Party documents. Though practices were altered in later stages of reform by redefinition of the term, "patriotic elements," the legitimate role of the national and petty bourgeoisie, merchants, and small workshop owners in the development process nonetheless is made explicit in the Manifesto.

There is hardly any reference to industry in the Kampuchean Constitution. Ironically, this is one of the few instances in which that document serves as a reliable guide to actual *Khmer Rouge* behavior. What little industry existed in Kampuchea was immediately deactivated by the KCP's rustication of the urban areas. Whether deindustrialization was a specific objective of the leadership or merely a function of the rustication program remains unclear. Out of necessity, given the autarkic nature of the economy, some industry was reactivated on a limited scale during the regime's brief tenure, along with a concomitant if partial repopulation of the cities. This served partly to support the agricultural sector, which remained the preeminent sector of the economy throughout the reign of *Angkar Loeu*. A principal aim of the limited revival of industry, however, appears to have been related to military procurement. This very limited reindustrialization was an inevitable concession to economic and political realities by a leadership that had apparently rejected urban industrial society as bourgeois and reactionary.

The differences between the Chinese and Vietnamese industrial strategy, on the one hand, and the Kampuchean lack of industrial strategy, on the other hand, are even more striking than differences in the agricultural sector. Although similarities among the respective agricultural programs did not extend beyond the existence of that sector in all three nations, there is greater basis for comparison there than in the industrial sphere. In both Vietnam and the PRC, industry was accorded a definite role in the economic development scheme. In Kampuchea, by contrast, industry was unilaterally neglected.

Trade

Unlike the Soviet Union and some other East European states, the PRC rejected autarky as a development strategy. Article 26 of the Common Program calls for "mutual aid between city and countryside and circulation of goods between China and abroad."[41] The objective of regional trade within China and internationally was evidently achieved as Chinese international trade exceeded $1 billion (US) as early as 1950.[42]

The platform of the Vietnam Lao Dong Party also specifies the need to develop international and home trade.[43] In spite of the severe dislocations and structural distortions associated with the war and reunification, Vietnam's international trade had reached approximately $1.2 billion (US) by 1978.[44]

The virulent nationalism that underscored the success of the *Khmer Rouge* expressed itself in economic policy through the adoption of a program for "autonomous national development," a euphemism for complete autarky. As in the case of industrial policy, this initial policy of extremism was tempered by the passage of time. Internally, domestic trade was hampered by the abolition of a monetary economy. In its place lay only a clumsy agrarian barter system. Externally, between 1976 and 1978 a limited amount of trade was conducted although it was never a significant component of the Kampuchean economy. Most of the international trade that did occur appears to have been in the form of a military aid program conducted by the Chinese. This nearly total reliance on domestic economic production stands in sharp contrast to the Vietnamese and Chinese experiences.

Finance

Article 39 of the Chinese Common Program delegates to the state-owned bank the responsibility of issuing currency, regulating foreign economic flows and rates, and presumably, monitoring and setting interest rates.[45] Although no direct reference to banking is made in the Vietnamese documents, the monetary economy was maintained in Vietnam. This economy would necessitate a state-owned bank, fulfilling functions similar to those of its Chinese counterpart.

The abolition of the monetary economy in Democratic Kampuchea eliminated the need for banking and any other financial institutions and devices. This backward transition not only deviates from common practices of the Chinese and Vietnamese revolutions, but is unparalleled anywhere in modern history. Finance was irrelevant in Democratic Kampuchea.

However, there were indications that shortly before the fall of Democratic Kampuchea, the leaders may have been contemplating the reintroduction of a monetary economy. According to one Thiounn Chhum, interviewed by Swedish anthropologist Jan Myrdal at a Democratic Kampuchean resistance base in 1979, he and other "financial specialists" were called to Phnom Penh in August 1978: "My assignment was to be the organization of the country's finances and the preparatory work for the introduction of money. Production had increased to such a degree that barter no longer sufficed. We were going to have a market economy, and for that we needed both coins and banknotes, but above all, a planned economy. The banknotes were already ordered and printed."[46] A planned market economy? It should be stressed that this somewhat incongruous report is an anomaly, and as yet there has been no independent confirmation of Myrdal's interview. If in fact the reintroduction of finance was impending at the fall of Democratic Kampuchea, the structure of the system that was to have emerged remains unknown.

Technology

The acquisition of technology, in recognition of its role as a major engine of modern economic growth, was specified as a responsibility of the state in Article 26 of the Chinese Common Program.[47] Technology is vital to any program of industrial development, and therefore its development must have been an important, if unstated goal of the Vietnamese leadership as well. Obviously, a country such as Vietnam, which fought incessantly against relatively advanced technological powers for more than a generation, could not have been averse to technological transfers. This is particularly the case in the military sphere, where the Chinese, and later the Soviets, served as technologically advanced benefactors to the Vietnamese. The Soviets had of course served this function for the Chinese for about a decade.

Once again, Democratic Kampuchea chose to steer an uncharted course with respect to technology. By inflicting an extremely high casualty level on the educated classes, and filling engineering, medical, and economic positions with untrained ignorant peasant children, the *Khmer Rouge* wrought a largely atechnical society. As Nou Seng, a peasant refugee, put it, "the people who do not know how to write are appointed as Khmer Rouge chiefs because the Khmer Rouge believe they are honest men. The people who have no knowledge, no education must always be the chiefs."[48] This represents yet another unparalleled economic and social strategy. Pol Pot was reliably reported to have "spoken well" of those zones "where they use no machinery at all, only labor."[49] The sole exception to this atechnical orientation was the military sphere, where *Angkar Loeu* seemed anxious to obtain such modern technology as it could lay its collective hands on. The atechnical approach to development, along with monetary abolition, complete autarky, and classlessness, was among the most radical elements in Democratic Kampuchea's economic program.

Ownership

At least in print, the prerogatives of ownership were zealously guarded in the PRC. Despite the general principle that the state should own the means of production, land ownership—the country's foremost means of production—remained private until the more advanced stages of the revolution in the late 1950s. This represented a gradual approach. Article 3 of the Common Program stresses that the state "must protect the economic interests and private property of workers, peasants, the petty bourgeoisie and the national bourgeoisie."[50] Apparently the Chinese did not view having both state and private capitalist sectors in their economy as contradictory to the achievement of socialist society. Private economic activities would be regulated by the state until such time as they were transformed during the actual transition to genuine socialism. Article 30 of the Common Program specifies that the state will encourage the operation of private economic activities "beneficial to national welfare and will assist in their development."[51] Although the wording of this document leaves considerable scope for government intervention in private economic activity, it unequivocally indicates that the rise of the communist party in China did not necessarily signal the total elimination of private property.

A similar situation existed in Vietnam. In addition to guaranteeing rights of land ownership for peasants, the regime permitted certain landlords to retain their lands and charge rent subject to government guidelines.[52] Both the petty and the national bourgeoisie were permitted to retain their property and were to be assisted and guided in the development of the economy. With the exception of the much-hated French and of prisoners of war, the lives and property of foreigners were guaranteed in the Democratic Republic of Vietnam.

In contrast to Vietnam and China, Democratic Kampuchea tightly and immediately embraced the notion of state ownership of *all* the means of production. As the Constitution specified, only items of everyday use were to remain in private hands. This proved to be no empty rhetoric; indeed, toward the end of *Angkar Loeu*'s reign even items of everyday use were collectivized. Democratic Kampuchea underwent the most rapid and comprehensive collectivization ever witnessed. The Vietnamese and Chinese sought to transform the sociopolitical structure of the villages and cities gradually, by degrees, envisioning the evolutionary and dialectical emergence of a socialist infrastructure; the *Khmer Rouge* nullified the existing social structure, and created *ex nihilo* a "socialist" infrastructure.

Social Structure

In the orthodox Marxist *Weltanschauung*, social structure is a reflection of the current mode of production. The class components of these three societies after their respective revolutions would accordingly be expected to reflect the differences in their approaches to economic development.

In both China and Vietnam, society was officially composed of four groups: workers, peasants, petty bourgeoisie, and national bourgeoisie. The existence of the latter two classes testifies to the continuation of private ownership and the state-sanctioned role of private capital in the economy. Although the national bourgeoisie and particularly the landlords were cast as villains in the Chinese revolution, their position in society in the aftermath of the revolution indicated the willingness of the government to reeducate or integrate these former adversaries into the new society. This was particularly the case in Vietnam, where much of the anger and propaganda during the revolution was directed against foreign forces, first the French and then the Americans.

In the Kampuchean case, the situation was radically different. As Stephen Heder has explained, the *Khmer Rouge* faced opponents, first Sihanouk and then Lon Nol, who had impressive nationalist credentials and could make a case proclaiming a commitment to certain types of progressive social reform:

> In launching a revolutionary movement against such a state, the Communists could not rely on simple nationalist and reformist themes to build up a popular base. Rather, they had to emphasize class struggle against a deeply rooted indigenous enemy with strong nationalist credentials, and the [KCP's] nationalist line had to outdo Sihanouk's. These tendencies toward radical class struggle and nationalism became integral elements of the Kampuchean communist movement. . . . [53]

In a September 1977 broadcast, Pol Pot defined prerevolutionary Kampuchean society in terms of five classes: workers, peasants, bourgeoisie, capitalists, and feudalists. According to the leader of Democratic Kampuchea, "Among all the [class] conflicts, the most outstanding was the one between the peasants and the landlords. . . ." However, Pol Pot continued, in prerevolutionary days "the peasants suffered oppression by *all* other classes."[54] In a sense, Democratic Kampuchea was the wrath of the poorest strata of the peasant masses.

According to the Constitution of Democratic Kampuchea, Kampuchean society was composed only of workers, peasants, and soldiers. The bourgeoisie, the capitalists, and the feudalists officially ceased to exist with the creation of Democratic Kampuchea; they were simply eliminated as classes. No second chance existed.

Overall, the economic and societal structure of Democratic Kampuchea bore only a superficial documentary resemblance to those of the PRC and the DRV/SRV. Thus, even when viewed against the backdrop of the two most similar nations, Democratic Kampuchea stands out as radically different in almost all characteristics of development planning and methodology. Agrarian reform, agricultural land ownership, industry, trade, finance, technology, property ownership, and social structure as they existed in Democratic Kampuchea varied greatly from their counterparts in the People's Republic of China and the Democratic Republic of Vietnam.

The "Kampuchean Model" of economic development stands as an alternative exemplar for future revolutionaries. Indeed, Pol Pot saw his movement as providing just such an example: "In a word the great victory won by our people and revolutionary army under the leadership of the Communist Party of Kampuchea has become a precious model for the world's people, the world's revolutionary movement and the international Communist movement."[55] Whether any other revolutionary movement will ever choose to implement Pol Pot's "precious model" of atechnical, nonmonetary, autarkic, antiindustrial, and classless economic development remains a question for future history.

Did They Keep Their Promises?

It is difficult to ascertain the extent to which the *Khmer Rouge* kept the promises they made to their people because their promises and their goals tended to evolve continuously over the course of the revolution. Although hints of the autarky policy are found in Khieu Samphan's doctoral dissertation, and clear indications of the primacy to be accorded the peasants are evidenced in Hou Yuon's thesis, the actual policies of Democratic Kampuchea were far more radical than anything envisioned by the revolutionaries as young students.

The FUNK Political Program is an unreliable guide to the KCP's intentions because it was composed in coalition with the Sihanoukists in Peking in 1970.[56] Perhaps fittingly, almost exactly one-half of the goals specified in the Political Program of the National United Front for Kampuchea were achieved in Democratic Kampuchea: Six of thirteen political promises, eight of sixteen economic promises, and five of ten educational and cultural promises were implemented in a recognizable albeit radical form.

The Constitution of Democratic Kampuchea is in many respects even more problematic than the Political Program. As has been previously noted, the Constitution was in large part the product of a moment of political balance in the ongoing political struggle during the emergence of the regime in the wake of victory. It is extremely vague and general, and as often as not, as in the case of the "people's judiciary," represented an idealization of nonexistent conditions.

Despite the shortcomings of documentary analysis in assessing the achievements of the *Khmer Rouge* revolution, it will be seen that there are two areas where the Kampuchean revolution seems to have done a fair job of making good on its promises. These two areas concern food and privilege. Though these "promises" were merely implicit in much of the *Khmer Rouge* rhetoric and doctrine, they represented the fundamental basis of the entire revolution's legitimacy.

Food

Perhaps as much as anything else, the rustication program represented the KCP's recognition of the most elemental of facts: food is the first priority. In view of the tribulations suffered by both the land and the people during the long, destructive war, what little evidence there is indicates that a not inconsiderable amount of progress was made in raising the level of agricultural production. In 1974–1975, the *Khmer Rouge* announced a bumper crop, and reportedly the eastern zone was even able to export some small amounts of rice to aid the Vietnamese. Through 1976, the KCP appeared to be capable of supporting those people it chose to support at around a subsistence level. As the *Far Eastern Economic Review* stated, this was "no mean achievement given that Washington estimated that one million Cambodians would starve."[57] Perhaps fewer than 25 percent of that number actually starved in 1975–1976.

In 1977, however, man and heaven conspired to make conditions more difficult for the Kampuchean people, the former contributing through shoddy engineering, and the latter, by weather patterns. The majority of the workers, cadres, and project planners were unskilled peasants. The impressive and essential irrigation system that the regime began constructing in 1972 was progressively rendered nonfunctional and structurally unsound by a profound ignorance of engineering principles on the part of planners and leaders. In 1977, the bad engineering combined with a 100-year flood to reduce the size of the crops to 20 to 25 percent less than the 1976 level, and the 1976 level had been subsistence. Daily per capita consumption dropped to a dangerously low 125 grams of rice, compared to 200–300 grams per day in 1976.[58] The government claimed that a recovery was made in 1978 to the extent that the food problem eased considerably. Information regarding rice production in Democratic Kampuchea between 1975 and 1980 is still subject to dispute, but the country's ability to feed itself over this period likely improved, if only because there were progressively fewer people to feed.

Privilege

In terms of economic leveling and the creation of a classless society, Democratic Kampuchea was far more advanced than such ostensibly socialist yet comparatively class-ridden societies as the USSR and the PRC. For years, the People's Republic of China served Western liberal anticommunists as the paradigm of all the terrible things that happen to the wealthy under communism. Democratic Kampuchea must now fill that role. Unlike their counterparts in China and Vietnam, rich and middle Kampuchean peasants did not escape the economic leveling. All were entirely dispossessed. In fact, in some areas such as Battambang, rich peasants were in many cases executed. Privileges normally associated with property ownership were erased in an attempt to eliminate those status differences that define class.

Nonetheless, perfect classlessness was not achieved in several significant social and economic senses. First and most interestingly, members of the Revolutionary Army, having suffered extraordinarily and sacrificed valiantly during the war, after the war found themselves apart from the people. They lived in their own camps, and they developed a distinctive warrior-caste *ethos*. Their influence in Democratic Kampuchean society was sufficient for one-fifth of the seats in the People's Representative Assembly to be allocated to their representatives. The Revolutionary Army enjoyed significantly higher rations than the general population, at least after liberation. Many of the troops grew their own crops, in addition to their share from the common stocks. Also, of course, they no doubt enjoyed the social status inherent in their authoritative role as enforcers of the will of the party. It was considered to be a distinct privilege, the ethics of the *Hinayana* notwithstanding, to be among the killers as opposed to the killed.

Even within the Revolutionary Army, there appear to have been significant distinctions in status. (All Sihanouk supporters and pro-Vietnamese elements in the PFLANK and the RAK, of course, were just out of luck.) The so-called Unconditional Divisions or superdivisions (i.e., those personally loyal to Pol Pot and company, the Praetorian Guard as it were) enjoyed a special place above the remainder of the regular army. The "Unconditionals" enjoyed choice duty in their capacity as the internal security apparatus, and were more or less exempt from purges, unlike the rest of the army.

There were additional societal stratifications beyond those involving the military. Enshrined in the Constitution of Democratic Kampuchea and embodied in the structure of the People's Representative Assembly along with the civil-military distinction was another distinction, that between worker and peasant. In practice, however, it appears that this social distinction was negligible. One possible exception is indicated by recent reports that some factory workers in Phnom Penh were able to arm themselves and ward off attacks by the Stalinist forces until after the Vietnamese arrived at the beginning of 1979.[59]

A more significant social cleavage in Democratic Kampuchea was that created by the rusticants, the "new people," as they were called. These people had been taken from the cities into the jungles at the end of the war, and were treated as second-class citizens, potential sources of counterrevolution and subversion. This, in spite of the fact that some four-fifths of those who were in the urban enclaves at the end of the war had been simple peasants before the war drove them from the surrounding countryside. It was the "new people" who were repeatedly relocated in the massive population movements orchestrated by the Stalinists. These people received lower food rations, and they formed the bulk of the refugees seeking sanctuary in Thailand and Vietnam during the reign of *Angkar Loeu*.

Even taking into account these several sources of social cleavage, however, it is still clear that Democratic Kampuchea retains the title as the closest thing to an absolutely egalitarian society in modern history. Because of this close approximation of a one-class society, the state did indeed begin to "wither" in at least two senses. First, with the abolition of the monetary economy and the implementation of a decentralized agrarian barter system, the central control of the state over economic interactions became somewhat dispersed. Second, to the extent that there was a single class guided by a single party—and this state of affairs was attained in late 1977 and persisted through 1978—social relations within Democratic Kampuchea did for a time lose their political character, as is supposed to happen in the "perfect," final stage of communism. In this sense, the revolution in Democratic Kampuchea was truly revolutionary, an unprecedented event in political history.

Beyond any "promises" concerning food and equality, and beyond any implicit or explicit promises embodied in declaratory and operational political behavior, however, there exists an ultimate responsibility. This imperative was admirably expressed by Premier and Chairman Pol Pot himself in an address on September 27, 1977, when he set forth three central "revolutionary tasks":

1. "Defense of Democratic Kampuchea";
2. "a continuing improvement of the socialist revolution"; and
3. "the paying of close attention to the building of socialism in the country."[60]

In terms of this fundamental set of goals, the leadership of Democratic Kampuchea has failed utterly. Utopia remains elusive.

Denouement

Ends and Means. The fundamental ideals expressed in the ideology of the *Khmer Rouge* embodied many of the most humane and universal aspirations in the history of human civilizations. Altruism, humility, equality, self-reliance, and industriousness were expressed again and again in KCP doctrine and practice. For championing these lofty ideals, the *Khmer Rouge* had a right to collective pride.

Yet, the contrast between the goals of the revolution as a whole, on the one hand, and the methods employed by the tiny clique of leaders who eventually dominated Kampuchean politics, on the other hand, could not be more striking. The diabolical cruelty displayed by *Angkar*'s security apparat boggles the mind, the more so because that cruelty appears to have been not merely tolerated or endorsed by the Stalinist leadership, but actively cultivated, particularly after 1973. When in 1978 Vietnamese propaganda called Pol Pot's Kampuchea a "Hell on Earth," most serious observers were inclined to point out that the two nations were very nearly at war, so hyperbolic rhetoric might well be expected. By 1981, most serious observers were inclined to the opinion that the Vietnamese assessment was perhaps not entirely inaccurate. The details of how and why the "total victory" of April 17, 1975, could in three and one-half dreadfully long years be transformed into total defeat will be debated for decades to come, but it is an inescapably tragic fact that the *Khmer Rouge* revolution failed, and failed spectacularly.

At the outset of this study, two general approaches to the problem of revolution were outlined. Political revolution has been defined as "abrupt, illegal mass violence aimed at the overthrow of the political regime as a first step toward overall social change."[61] Another analyst defines revolution as the act of rebuilding the society shattered by "rebellion" ("the violent spontaneous act of ordinary people saying No! to conditions") in accordance with an ideology.[62]

In point of fact, successful revolution entails *both* the overthrow of the old order *and* the construction of the new. In reality, these are one and the same act, merely appearing distinct when abstracted as threads drawn from the seamless fabric of social evolution. The *Khmer Rouge* were masters at making the first part of revolution, but for the very reasons they succeeded in the first part of their endeavor, they failed in their second, and primary task: creating a new life for their people. In the end, the group of Khmer students from Paris were like the angels who were ejected from heaven; they promised Utopia and they were delivered unto Pandemonium.

Notes

1. John Milton, *Paradise Lost* [Maurice Kelley, ed.] (New York: Walter J. Black, 1943, Book VI.

2. See Stephen Heder, "The Border Dispute on Land," *Southeast Asia Chronicle*, no. 64 (Sept.–Oct. 1978), pp. 36–38.

3. For examples, see William Shawcross, "The Third Indochina War," *New York Review of Books*, April 4, 1978; David Elliot, *The Third Indochina Conflict* (Boulder, CO: Westview Press, 1981); Serge Thion, "The Cambodian Solution to the Third Indochina War," *Cornell Review*, Summer 1979; and William Turley and Jeffrey Race, "The Third Indochina War," *Foreign Policy*, no. 38 (Spring 1980).

4. See Irving L. Janis, *Victims of Groupthink: A Psychological Study of Foreign Policy Decisions and Fiascoes* (Boston: Houghton-Mifflin, 1972), on the tendency of isolated decision-making groups to drive for consensus at the cost of alternatives.

5. Stephen Heder, "Kampuchea 1980: Anatomy of a Crisis," *Southeast Asia Chronicle*, no. 77 (February 1981), p. 6.

6. Norodom Sihanouk, *War and Hope: The Case for Cambodia* (New York: Random House, 1978), p. 92.

7. Wilfred Burchett, *The China-Cambodia-Vietnam Triangle* (Chicago: Vanguard Press, 1981), especially Chapter 10, "The Frontier War"; the quotation is from p. 149.
8. Norodom Sihanouk, *War and Hope*, p. 99.
9. Phnom Penh Domestic News Service, January 26, 1978, in FBIS for January 27, 1978; cited in J. J. Zasloff and M. Brown, *Communist Indochina and U.S. Foreign Policy* (Boulder, CO: Westview Press, 1978), pp. 66, 67.
10. See L. Finley, "The Propaganda War," *Southeast Asia Chronicle*, no. 64 (Sept.–Oct. 1978), p. 33; and R. M. Smith, *Cambodia's Foreign Policy* (Ithaca, NY: Cornell University Press, 1965), pp. 154, 155; and my Chapter 4.
11. From Ben Kiernan's discussion of a number of documents captured by the U.S. Army from Vietnamese communist troops in 1970, "Conflict in the Kampuchean Communist Movement," *Journal of Contemporary Asia* 10:1–2 (1980), pp. 30–34.
12. Norodom Sihanouk, *War and Hope*, p. 18.
13. B. Kiernan, "Conflict in the Kampuchean Communist Movement," p. 36; W. Shawcross, "The Third Indochina War."
14. B. Kiernan, "Conflict in the Kampuchean Communist Movement," p. 35.
15. L. Finley, "Propaganda War," p. 33; cites FBIS Daily Report, Asia and Pacific, May 12, 1978, pp. H-2, 3; also see Sihanouk's comments on this line, which was drilled into the populace during 1978 (*War and Hope*, p. 62).
16. Ben Kiernan, "Kampuchea's Choices for Survival," *Southeast Asia Chronicle*, no. 77 (Feb. 1981), p. 29.
17. See the story told by a district chief of the Heng Samrin regime, about how the use of artillery to deal with "traitors" convinced him that "this revolution has gone mad," inducing him and others to join the anti–Pol Pot resistance; in Paul Quinn-Judge, "Chamcar Loeu: A Gradual Recovery," *Southeast Asia Chronicle*, no. 77 (Feb. 1981), pp. 23–26.
18. John W. Spragens, Jr., "Don't Forget the Practical Problems," *Southeast Asia Chronicle*, no. 79 (Aug. 1981), p. 10.
19. Norodom Sihanouk, *War and Hope*, pp. 91, 92.
20. Amos Perlmutter and W. M. LeoGrande, "The Party in Uniform: Toward a Theory of Civil-Military Relations in Communist Political Systems," *American Political Science Review* 76:4 (Dec. 1982), p. 782.
21. W. Burchett, ed., *My War with the CIA* (New York: Random House, 1972), p. 243.
22. W. Burchett, *The China-Cambodia-Vietnam Triangle*, p. 207.
23. See Table 3, p. 7, of U.S. Department of State, *Chemical Warfare in Southeast Asia and Afghanistan: An Update*, Report from Secretary of State George Shultz, Special Report No. 104, November 1982; also see U.S. Department of State, *Chemical Warfare in Southeast Asia and Afghanistan*, Report to the Congress from Secretary of State Alexander M. Haig, Jr., Special Report No. 98, March 22, 1982.
24. See W. E. Willmott, "Analytical Errors of the Kampuchean Communist Party," *Journal of Contemporary Asia* 11:2 (1981), p. 217.

25. William Branigin, "Cambodian Guerrilla Admits Viet Gains," *Los Angeles Times*, March 11, 1982.
26. Personal communication from Kanthati Suphamongkhon.
27. From excerpts of a Zhao/Hua press conference, February 1, 1981, reprinted in *Journal of Contemporary Asia* 11:2 (1981), p. 258.
28. Heng Samrin interview, September 23, 1980, excerpted in *Journal of Contemporary Asia* 11:2 (1981), pp. 256–259.
29. In his "The Eighteenth Brumaire of Louis Bonaparte," Marx observed of the French small-holding peasants that they "form a vast mass," but "their mode of production isolates them from one another instead of bringing them into mutual intercourse." Therefore, "in so far as there is merely a local interconnection among these small-holding peasants and the identity of their interests begets no community, no national bond, and no political organization among them, they do not form a class. They are consequently incapable of enforcing their class interest in their own name . . ." (cited in *Introduction to Contemporary Civilization in the West*, edited by the Contemporary Civilization Staff of Columbia College, Columbia University [New York: Columbia University Press, 1961], p. 755]). This passage points directly to Lenin's revision, wherein through alliance with the industrial proletariat and urban intelligentsia, the class interests of the peasantry might be "enforced." Other relevant citations here include J. Stalin, "The Foundations of Leninism" (*Essential Works of Marxism* [New York: Bantam Books, 1961], pp. 209–296); Mao Tse-tung's "Analysis of the Classes in Chinese Society" (pp. 13–21) and "How to Differentiate the Classes in Rural Areas" (pp. 137–140), both in *Selected Works of Mao Tse-tung*, vol. 1 (Peking: Foreign Languages Press, 1965); Truong Chinh and Vo Nguyen Giap, *The Peasant Question (1937–1938)* [C. P. White, trans.], Cornell University Southeast Asia Program, Data Paper #94 (Ithaca, NY: Cornell University, 1974); and Hou Yuon, "La Paysannerie du Cambodge et Ses Projets de Modernization," of which portions are reprinted in English translation in Ben Kiernan and Chanthou Boua, *Peasants and Politics in Kampuchea 1942–1981* (London: Zed Press, 1982).
30. Norodom Sihanouk, *War and Hope*, p. 86.
31. Solomon Adler, *The Chinese Economy* (New York: Monthly Review Press, 1957), p. 239.
32. Robert F. Turner, *Vietnamese Communism: Its Origins and Development* (Palo Alto, CA: Hoover Institution Press, 1975), pp. 344–346.
33. See Appendix A for the Constitution of Democratic Kampuchea.
34. S. Adler, *The Chinese Economy*, p. 28.
35. From Article 30 of the *Agrarian Reform Law of the People's Republic of China* (Peking: Foreign Languages Press, 1955), p. 13.
36. R. F. Turner, *Vietnamese Communism*, p. 339.
37. *Agrarian Reform Law* (Hanoi: Foreign Languages Press, 1955), p. 15.
38. S. Adler, *The Chinese Economy*, p. 242.
39. R. F. Turner, *Vietnamese Communism*, p. 346.

40. Stephen Heder, "Origins of the Conflict," *Southeast Asia Chronicle*, no. 64 (Sept.–Oct. 1978), p. 4; bracketed inserts are added, and those in parentheses are in the original.
41. S. Adler, *The Chinese Economy*, p. 239.
42. *Ibid.*, p. 210.
43. R. F. Turner, *Vietnamese Communism*, p. 346.
44. National Foreign Assessment Center, *The World Factbook* (Washington, D.C.: USGPO, 1981), p. 214.
45. S. Adler, *The Chinese Economy*, p. 242.
46. Jan Myrdal, "Why Is There Famine in Kampuchea?" *Southeast Asia Chronicle*, no. 77 (Feb. 1981), p. 18.
47. S. Adler, *The Chinese Economy*, p. 239.
48. Donald Kirk, "Revolution and Political Violence in Cambodia, 1970–1974," in J. J. Zasloff and M. Brown, eds., *Communism in Indochina: New Perspectives* (Lexington, MA: D. C. Heath, 1975), p. 223.
49. Ben Kiernan, "Bureaucracy of Death," *New Statesman*, May 2, 1980, p. 676; from one of Hu Nim's "confessions," where he discusses his deviations from the correct Party line as defined by "Brother Number One" (a.k.a. Pol Pot).
50. S. Adler, *The Chinese Economy*, p. 239.
51. *Ibid.*, p. 240.
52. R. F. Turner, *Vietnamese Communism*, p. 339.
53. S. Heder, "Origins of the Conflict," p. 4.
54. From B. Kiernan, "Conflict in the Kampuchean Communist Movement," p. 22, emphasis added; originally BBC SWB, October 4, 1977, FE 5631/C2/2.
55. B. Kiernan and Chanthou Boua, *Peasants and Politics in Kampuchea*, p. 234; from BBC SWB, October 1, 1977, FE 5629/C2/1 ff.
56. See the "Political Program of the National United Front of Kampuchea," in *Beijing Review*, no. 20, May 15, 1970.
57. See the *Far Eastern Economic Review*, October 29, 1976.
58. Karl Jackson, "Cambodia 1978: War, Pillage and Purge in Democratic Kampuchea," *Asian Survey*, January 1979, p. 83.
59. See, for example, S. Heder, "Kampuchea 1980," p. 6.
60. J. M. van der Kroef, "Political Ideology in Democratic Kampuchea," *Orbis*, Winter 1979, p. 1010.
61. Mostafa Rejai, *The Comparative Study of Revolutionary Strategy* (New York: David McKay, 1977), p. 8.
62. Chalmers Johnson, *Autopsy on People's War* (Los Angeles: University of California Press, 1973), p. 8.

Appendix A
The Constitution of Democratic Kampuchea

On the basis of the sacred and fundamental desires of the people, workers, peasants, and other laborers as well as those of the fighters and cadres of the Kampuchean Revolutionary Army; and

Whereas a significant role has been played by the people, especially the workers, poor peasants, lower-middle-class peasants, and other strata of laborers in the countryside and cities, who account for more than ninety-five percent of the entire Kampuchean nation, who assumed the heaviest responsibility in waging the war for the liberation of the nation and the people, made the greatest sacrifices in terms of life, property, and commitment, served the front line relentlessly, and unhesitatingly sacrificed their children and husbands by the thousands for the fight at the front line;

Whereas great sacrifices have been borne by the three categories of the Kampuchean Revolutionary Army who fought valiantly, day and night, in the dry and rainy season, underwent all sorts of hardship and misery, shortages of food, medicine, clothing, ammunition, and other commodities in the great war for the liberation of the nation and the people;

Whereas the entire Kampuchean people and the entire Kampuchean Revolutionary Army desire an independent, unified, peaceful, neutral, non-aligned, sovereign Kampuchea enjoying territorial integrity, a national society informed by genuine happiness, equality, justice, and democracy, without rich or poor and without exploiters or exploited, a society in which all live harmoniously in great national solidarity and join forces to do manual labor together and increase production for the construction and defense of the country;

And whereas the resolution of the Special National Congress held on 25, 26, and 27 April 1975 solemnly proclaimed recognition and respect for the above desires of the entire people and the entire Kampuchean Revolutionary Army;

Source: Foreign Broadcast Information Service, Daily Report (Asia and Pacific), January 5, 1976, pp. H2–H5; edited by author.

The Constitution of Kampuchea says:

Chapter One

The State

Article 1

The State of Kampuchea is an independent, unified, peaceful, neutral, nonaligned, sovereign, and democratic State enjoying territorial integrity.

The State of Kampuchea is a State of the people, workers, peasants, and all other Kampuchean laborers.

The official name of the State of Kampuchea is "Democratic Kampuchea."

Chapter Two

The Economy

Article 2

All important general means of production are the collective property of the people's State and the common property of the people's collectives.

Property for everyday use remains in private hands.

Chapter Three

Culture

Article 3

The culture of Democratic Kampuchea is of a national, popular, forward-looking, and healthful character such as will serve the tasks of defending and building Kampuchea into an ever more prosperous country.

This new culture is absolutely opposed to the corrupt, reactionary culture of the various oppressive classes and that of colonialism and imperialism in Kampuchea.

Chapter Four

The Principle of Leadership and Work

Article 4

Democratic Kampuchea applies the collective principle in leadership and work.

Chapter Five

Legislative Power

Article 5

Legislative power is invested in the representative assembly of the people, workers, peasants, and all other Kampuchean laborers.

This Assembly shall be officially known as the "Kampuchean People's Representative Assembly."

The Kampuchean People's Representative Assembly shall be made up of 250 members, representing the people, the workers, peasants, and all other Kampuchean laborers and the Kampuchean Revolutionary Army. Of these 250, there shall be:

Representing the peasants	150
Representing the laborers and other working people	50
Representing the revolutionary army	50

Article 6

The members of the Kampuchean People's Representative Assembly are to be elected by the people through direct and prompt general elections by secret ballot to be held throughout the country every five years.

Article 7

The People's Representative Assembly is responsible for legislation and for defining the various domestic and foreign policies of Democratic Kampuchea.

Chapter Six

The Executive Body

Article 8

The administration is a body responsible for executing the laws and political lines of the Kampuchean People's Representative Assembly.

The administration is elected by the Kampuchean People's Representative Assembly and must be fully responsible to the Kampuchean People's Representative Assembly for all of its activities inside and outside the country.

Chapter Seven

Justice

Article 9

Justice is administered by people's courts, representing and defending the people's justice, defending the democratic rights and liberties of the people, and condemning any activities directed against the people's State or violating the laws of the people's State.

The judges at all levels will be chosen and appointed by the People's Representative Assembly.

Article 10

Actions violating the laws of the people's State are as follows:

Dangerous activities in opposition to the people's State must be condemned to the highest degree.

Other cases are subject to constructive reeducation in the framework of the State's or people's organizations.

Chapter Eight

The State Presidium

Article 11

Democratic Kampuchea has a State Presidium chosen and appointed by the Kampuchean People's Representative Assembly once every five years.

The State Presidium is responsible for representing the State of Democratic Kampuchea inside and outside the country in keeping with the Constitution of Democratic Kampuchea and with the laws and political lines of the Kampuchean People's Representative Assembly.

The State Presidium is composed as follows: a president, a first vice-president, and a second vice-president.

Chapter Nine

The Rights and Duties of the Individual

Article 12

Every citizen of Kampuchea enjoys full rights to a constantly improving material, spiritual, and cultural life.

Every citizen of Democratic Kampuchea is guaranteed a living.

All workers are the masters of their factories.

All peasants are the masters of the rice paddies and fields.
All other laborers have the right to work.
There is absolutely no unemployment in Democratic Kampuchea.

Article 13

There must be complete equality among all Kampuchean people in an equal, just, democratic, harmonious, and happy society within the great national solidarity for defending and building the country together.
Men and women are fully equal in every respect.
Polygamy is prohibited.

Article 14

It is the duty of all to defend and build the country together in accordance with individual ability and potential.

Chapter Ten

The Capital

Article 15

The capital city of Democratic Kampuchea is Phnom Penh.

Chapter Eleven

The National Flag

Article 16

The design and significance of the Kampuchean national flag are as follows:
The background is red, with a yellow three-towered temple in the middle.
The red background symbolizes the revolutionary movement, the resolute and valiant struggle of the Kampuchean people for the liberation, defense, and construction of their country.
The yellow temple symbolizes national traditions of the Kampuchean people, who are defending and building the country to make it ever more prosperous.

Chapter Twelve

The National Emblem

Article 17

The national emblem consists of a network of dikes and canals, which symbolize modern agriculture, and factories, which symbolize industry. These are framed by an oval garland of rice ears, with the inscription "Democratic Kampuchea" at the bottom.

Chapter Thirteen

The National Anthem

Article 18

The national anthem of Democratic Kampuchea is the "Dap Prampi Mesa Moha Chokchey" ["Glorious Seventeenth of April"].

Chapter Fourteen

The Kampuchean Revolutionary Army

Article 19

The three categories of the Kampuchean Revolutionary Army—regular, regional, and guerilla—form an army of the people made up of men and women fighters and cadres who are the children of the laborers, peasants, and other Kampuchean working people. They defend the State power of the Kampuchean people and of independent, unified, peaceful, neutral, nonaligned, sovereign, and democratic Kampuchea, which enjoys territorial integrity, and at the same time they help to build a country growing more prosperous every day and to improve and develop the people's standard of living.

Chapter Fifteen

Worship and Religion

Article 20

Every citizen of Kampuchea has the right to worship according to any religion and the right not to worship according to any religion.

Reactionary religions which are detrimental to Democratic Kampuchea and the Kampuchean people are absolutely forbidden.

Chapter Sixteen

Foreign Policy

Article 21

Democratic Kampuchea fervently and earnestly desires to maintain close and friendly relations with all countries sharing a common border and with all those near and distant throughout the world in conformity with the principles of mutual and absolute respect for sovereignty and territorial integrity.

Democratic Kampuchea adheres to a policy of independence, peace, neutrality and nonalignment. It will permit absolutely no foreign country to maintain military bases on its territory and is resolutely opposed to all forms of outside interference in its internal affairs, and to all forms of subversion and aggression against Democratic Kampuchea from outside, whether military, political, cultural, social, diplomatic, or humanitarian.

Democratic Kampuchea refuses all intervention in the domestic affairs of other countries, and scrupulously respects the principle that every country is sovereign and entitled to manage and decide its own affairs without outside interference.

Democratic Kampuchea remains absolutely within the great family of nonaligned nations.

Democratic Kampuchea strives to promote solidarity with the peoples of the Third World in Asia, Africa, and Latin America, and with peace- and justice-loving people the world over, and to contribute most actively to mutual aid and support in the struggle against imperialism, colonialism, neo-colonialism, and in favor of independence, peace, friendship, democracy, justice, and progress in the world.

APPENDIX B
A Chronological History of Kampuchea

This chronology can assist the reader by providing a sequential descriptive record to help lend continuity to what otherwise seems a fragmented, shifting, and patternless mosaic of events. In other words, this "longitudinal snapshot" of Kampuchea provides a context against which the preceding analysis may be more comprehensible.

This chronology has been constructed from a wide variety of sources. Some of the entries shown here were adapted from chronologies in books by William Shawcross, Norodom Sihanouk, François Ponchaud, Miloslav Jankovec, George Hildebrand and Gareth Porter, and Wilfred Burchett. Entries beginning in the late 1970s were mostly drawn from journalistic reports in newspapers, including the *New York Times*, the *Los Angeles Times*, the *Washington Post*, the *Chicago Tribune*, the *Christian Science Monitor*, and the *Wall Street Journal*, as well as a few others. Other miscellaneous sources include numerous government publications and a large number of scholarly and polemical tracts. This chronology has been inspired and informed by the work of many scholars, journalists, and others, most of whom must remain nameless. The author thanks them for their contributions, with apologies for not being able to name each one.

First to Twentieth Centuries

1st to 4th c.	Fou Nan Period: hydraulic economy; Indian and Hindu influences foster spread of hierarchical social relations.
5th to 7th c.	Tchen-la Period: hydraulic economy; Chinese influences.
7th to 8th c.	Javanese domination.
802 (A.D.)	Jayavarman II, the first "god-king," casts off Javanese domination and founds the Angkor Empire.
895	Yasovarman I founds new capital, Angkor.
9th to 14th c.	Angkor: Union of Fou Nan (southern Indochina) and Tchen-la (northeast of Tonle Sap).
10th c.	Buddhism is introduced; Angkor Thom is built.
11th c.	Angkor Thom ("Great City") is embellished.

230   A Chronological History of Kampuchea

12th c.	Angkor Wat ("Temple City") is built by Suryavarman II; Kingdom of Champa (present day Cochinchina or Central Highlands of former South Vietnam) taken by Angkor in series of wars.
1178 (A.D.)	Vengeful Chams sack Angkor.
1181	Jayavarman VII expells Chams, embellishes Angkor Thom.
1220	Khmers evacuate Champa on death of Jayavarman VII.
1282	Jayavarman VIII defeats Mongol invasion.
1394	Siamese capture Angkor; 100-year war follows.
1431	Capital is moved to Longvek, then to Oudong; Siamese annex the Tchen-la regions.
1626	Vietnamese annex Cochinchina.
1834	On death of Ang Chan, Vietnamese seize control of Kingdom of Angkor.
1840–1846	Territory of Kingdom of Angkor is battlefield for Vietnamese-Siamese war.
1848	Ang Duong crowned King of Angkor by joint Vietnamese-Siamese agreement; he agrees to pay tribute to both.
1863	New monarch, King Norodom, accepts a French protectorate; "Cambodge" (Cambodia) emerges.
1884–1886	French governor provokes peasant uprisings.

1900 to 1960

1907	King Sisowath of Cambodia recovers with French help the provinces of Battambang, Siem Riep, and Sisophan, previously annexed by Siamese (Thais).
3 Feb 1930	In Hong Kong, Ho Chi Minh founds the Indochinese Communist Party (ICP); ethnic Vietnamese join.
27 July 1931	Khieu Samphan is born in Cambodia.
25 April 1941	Norodom Sihanouk, age eighteen, crowned king by French.
12 March 1945	Under Japanese occupation, Sihanouk proclaims independence from France.
May 1945	Son Ngoc Thanh returns from refuge in Japan.
June 1945	Son Ngoc Thanh becomes foreign minister.
August 1945	Son Ngoc Thanh becomes prime minister.
October 1945	British, Indian, and Free French forces occupy Cambodia; Son Ngoc Thanh arrested, later deported; *Nekhum Issarak Khmer* ("Cambodian Liberation Front" or CLF) formed.
11 Nov 1945	ICP dissolves itself.
1 July 1949	Chinese Communist Party (CCP) comes to power.
8 Nov 1949	French grant limited independence to Cambodia with Franco-Cambodian Treaty; Cambodia becomes an Associate State in the French Union.

A Chronological History of Kampuchea 231

February 1951	Vietnamese communists reorganize into *Lao Dong* or Worker's Party.
3 March 1951	*Lao Dong* and CLF ally against French colonialism.
30 Sept 1951	Vietnamese reorganize remnants of ICP into three national parties, forming and dominating the Khmer People's Party (KPP).
Summer 1953	King Norodom Sihanouk launches "royal crusade for independence" from France.
9 Nov 1953	French grant complete independence to Cambodia.
7 May 1954	French garrison at Dien Bien Phu, Vietnam, falls to *Viet Minh*; next day Geneva Conference convenes.
21 July 1954	Geneva ends, orders free elections for Cambodia and Vietnam, plus a pullout of *Viet Minh* forces in Cambodia; KPP pulls out with *Viet Minh*, goes to Hanoi, to return in 1968 and 1970; a few KPP cadres stay to fight, some to form *Pracheachon* or "People's Party" to context elections.
8 Sept 1954	SEATO Treaty promulgated in Manila, Philippines.
December 1954	Sihanouk declares neutralism after meeting Nehru.
31 Dec 1954	United States announces aid to Cambodia, South Vietnam, and Laos, effective 1/1/55, to combat communism.
2 March 1955	Sihanouk abdicates to father (Norodom Suramarit) and forms *Sangkum Reastr Niyum*; he remains head of this central political institution until 1970.
April 1955	Sihanouk meets with Vietnamese, Laotian, and Chinese communists at Bandung Conference of Nonaligned Nations.
May 1955	Sihanouk signs agreement to admit a MAAG (Military Assistance Advisory Group) of thirty U.S. military men to assess Cambodian military hardware needs.
11 Sept 1955	National election returns 83 percent for Sihanouk's *Sangkum*, 13 percent for liberal Democratic Party, and 3 percent for communist *Pracheachon* Party.
13 Feb 1956	Sihanouk to Peking, signs Sino-Cambodian Friendship Treaty.
February 1956	Sihanouk refuses over-flight privileges to SEATO for joint military exercises.
22 June 1956	People's Republic of China (PRC) gives $22.3 million to Cambodia, first PRC aid ever to a noncommunist state.
Spring 1956	Sihanouk rejects SEATO membership offers; Thailand and South Vietnam impose economic blockade; U.S. CIA begins funding anti-Sihanouk rightist group, *Khmer Serei*, led by Son Ngoc Thanh; Thailand occupies northern frontier of Cambodia.

232   A Chronological History of Kampuchea

June 1958	South Vietnamese army occupies parts of Stung Treng province.
13 July 1958	Sihanouk extends diplomatic recognition to PRC.
January 1959	Sihanouk alleges "Bangkok Plot" against him.
21 Feb 1959	Cambodian General Dap Chhuon secessionist attempt with Thai, South Vietnamese, Laotian, and U.S. involvement is discovered and crushed by Sihanouk.
31 August 1959	Assassination attempt on King, Queen, and Prince.

1960 to 1967

3 April 1960	King Suramarit dies, succession crisis follows.
14 June 1960	National Assembly revises Constitution, elects Norodom Sihanouk head of state, ending crisis.
20 June 1960	Prince Norodom Sihanouk becomes head of state.
30 Sept 1960	Second KPP National Congress convenes, later to be referred to as First Congress of the Kampuchean Communist Party; twenty-one delegates opt for continued political struggle, "preparation" for armed struggle; Touch Samouth elected chairman, Nuon Chea is number two, and Saloth Sar is number three in party organization; KPP changes party name to Worker's Party of Kampuchea (WPK).
January 1962	*Pracheachon* General Secretary Non Suon plus thirteen associates arrested, imprisoned for life.
20 July 1962	WPK Party Secretary Touch Samouth disappears, presumed victim of Sihanouk, opening way for rise of Saloth Sar to party leadership.
23 July 1962	Geneva Conference calls for three-party neutralist Lao government.
January 1963	Sihanouk nationalizes banking and foreign trade.
1 April 1963	Neutralist Laotian foreign minister assassinated.
1 May 1963	Liu Shao-chi state visit to Cambodia; Sihanouk alleges CIA-*Kuomintang* attempt on Liu's life and his own.
May 1963	WPK National Congress changes party name to Kampuchean Communist Party (KCP), sends 90 percent of leadership personnel underground for infrastructural work; Saloth Sar confirmed as general secretary; he and Ieng Sary go to northeast, and later visit China.
August 1963	Sihanouk severs relations with South Vietnam, renounces U.S. military assistance.
1 Nov 1963	South Vietnam President Diem killed in *coup*.
20 Nov 1963	U.S. President Kennedy assassinated in Dallas.
December 1963	PRC begins delivery of military aid to Cambodia.
2 August 1964	Gulf of Tonkin incident between United States and DRV.

A Chronological History of Kampuchea 233

September 1964	Sihanouk meets with representatives of South Vietnamese National Liberation Front (NLF) and North Vietnamese Premier Pham Van Dong in Peking.
27 Oct 1964	Cambodian National Assembly threatens to break relations with United States if there are any further violations of Cambodia by U.S. Air Force.
November 1964	Sihanouk appeals to Vietnamese and Laotians for anti-U.S. summit conference.
7 Feb 1965	With Operation ROLLING THUNDER, United States begins bombing North Vietnam.
28 Feb 1965	U.S. announces "continuous limited airstrikes" on North Vietnam.
1–9 March 1965	Sihanouk sponsors Indochinese People's Conference in Phnom Penh; *Pathet Lao* and NLF attend.
8 March 1965	U.S. Marines land at Da Nang, Vietnam; it's war.
1 May 1965	U.S. airstrikes in Cambodia's Parrot's Beak.
3 May 1965	Sihanouk breaks diplomatic relations with United States.
June 1965	PRC agrees in principle to provide technicians and more military equipment to Cambodia.
September 1965	Khieu Thirith and Khieu Ponnary (sisters who became KCP Central Committee members and wives of Ieng Sary and Saloth Sar) go underground.
November 1965	Sihanouk sends General Lon Nol on aid-seeking mission to Peking; he returns with arms for 20,000.
Summer 1965	North Vietnamese begin using port of Sihanoukville as a supply route to South Vietnam.
11 Sept 1966	First election in Cambodia without preselection of candidates by Sihanouk.
22 Oct 1966	Rightist-dominated government emerges; Lon Nol is elected premier.
March 1967	KCP cadres organize student demonstrations.
April 1967	Massive peasant revolt in Samlaut district of Battambang Province over land expropriation and forced rice collection policy; Lon Nol sends in paratroopers, cracks down on dissent in capital.
22 April 1967	Sihanouk charges Khieu Samphan, Hou Yuon, and Hu Nim with responsibility for Samlaut rebellion.
24 April 1967	Khieu and Hou go underground via Chinese embassy; Hu Nim stays in Phnom Penh.
30 April 1967	Sihanouk removes Lon Nol (resignation "due to car accident") for failure of Samlaut pacification; Son Sann appointed as new prime minister.
2 May 1967	15,000 students demonstrate in Phnom Penh over assumed liquidation of Khieu Samphan and Hou Yuon by Sihanouk security forces.

3 May 1967	Penn Nouth appointed prime minister of emergency government.
9 May 1967	Sihanouk demands international recognition for the borders of Cambodia.
13 May 1967	NLF and Democratic Republic of Vietnam issue statement recognizing Cambodian border claims.
May 1967	United States begins Operation SALEM HOUSE, cross-border armed reconnaissance inside Cambodia.
6 June 1967	Sihanouk extends *de jure* diplomatic recognition to NLF and Democratic Republic of Vietnam (DRV).
August 1967	Samlaut rebellion stamped out by mass executions.
4 Sept 1967	Lon Nol accuses leftist Sihanouk aide, Chau Seng, of *coup d'état* plan, latter is exiled; Hu Nim goes underground.

1968 to 1970

4 Jan 1968	PRC sends new military equipment to Lon Nol, including MIG jets and artillery.
8–12 Jan 1968	U.S. Ambassador to India Chester Bowles visits Cambodia to explore resumption of relations with United States and limitation of Vietnamese border use.
17 Jan 1968	KCP's newly founded Revolutionary Army of Kampuchea (RAK) begins guerrilla operations in seventeen of nineteen provinces.
27 Jan 1968	Sihanouk declares "war" on *Khmer Rouge* (KCP); United States announces policy of "hot pursuit" into Cambodia.
29–30 Jan 1968	Sihanouk names "Government of the Last Chance": Penn Nouth is prime minister, Son Sann his deputy; PRG/NLF begin Tet Offensive in Vietnam.
20 Jan 1969	Richard Nixon sworn in as thirty-seventh U.S. president.
9 Feb 1969	General Abrams, commander of U.S. forces in Vietnam, requests airstrikes against Vietnamese bases in Cambodia.
17 March 1969	Nixon approves request for airstrikes in Cambodia.
18 March 1969	"Breakfast" airstrike against "Base Area 353" in Fishhook area of Cambodia, commencing U.S. bomb attacks designated "MENU series."
April 1969	United States agrees to respect Cambodian "sovereignty and neutrality."
21 April 1969	The KCP's front organization, the Cambodian Liberation Front, claims to have captured three provinces and partly captured three more.

24 April 1969	Summit Conference in Peking; DRV, newly founded Provisional Revolutionary Government of South Vietnam (PRG), CLF, and Laotian Front explore possibilities for unity against United States.
26 April 1969	Sihanouk announces "offensive" against Vietnamese Army in Ratanakiri Province; his army, the *Force Armée Royale Khmer* (FARK), actually attacks positions held by KCP's RAK.
2 May 1969	South Vietnamese PRG opens embassy in Phnom Penh.
9 May 1969	*New York Times* writer William Beecher reports U.S. airstrikes in Cambodia; nobody notices but Nixon.
10 May 1969	Al Haig transmits Nixon orders for wiretaps to find who leaked bombing story to Beecher.
25 May 1969	Royal Cambodian Air Force uses MIG fighters for first time against Communist positions.
June 1969	More progress, if hard-won, by RAK.
11 June 1969	U.S.-Cambodian relations reestablished with exchange of embassies.
25 June 1969	Nixon proclaims "Nixon Doctrine."
1 August 1969	Penn Nouth resigns as prime minister.
12 August 1969	Lon Nol regains the prime ministry.
1 Sept 1969	Ho Chi Minh dies, Sihanouk attends funeral.
September 1969	Lon Nol returns banking and foreign trade to private sector, then goes to Paris for "medical treatments"; Sirik Matak becomes acting prime minister.
27–29 Dec 1969	National Assembly sustains Sihanouk's rejection of banking and foreign trade denationalization.

1970

7 Jan 1970	Sihanouk, Penn Nouth plus wives and entourages go to French Riviera for annual rest and health cure.
27 Feb 1970	Sihanouk in Paris announces intent to travel to "great and friendly nations" of PRC and USSR to complain of Vietnamese occupation.
8 March 1970	Villagers in Svay Rieng Province demonstrate against Vietnamese occupation under direction of Lon Nol at order of Sihanouk in France.
11 March 1970	20,000, led by government-orchestrated troops, sack the NLF and DRV embassies in Phnom Penh.
12 March 1970	Sihanouk, in eyes-only cable, threatens heads will roll for overreaction to his anti-Vietnamese demonstration orders.
13 March 1970	Sihanouk leaves Paris for Moscow; more anti-Vietnamese riots in Cambodia; Acting Prime Minister Sirik Matak suspends government trade with PRG, announces

236 A Chronological History of Kampuchea

	FARK increase of 10,000 men; Cambodian foreign ministry notifies the PRG and DRV that all Vietnamese military forces must be withdrawn from Cambodian territory by March 15.
15 March 1970	Deadline for NVA pullout passes; Cambodia requests emergency meeting with DRV and PRG.
16 March 1970	At last official meeting between Cambodia and DRV/PRG, communists refuse to accede to troop removal; Chief of National Police Oum Manorine (Sihanouk's brother-in-law) attempts to arrest Lon Nol, but is blocked by troops loyal to Lon Nol.
17 March 1970	Oum's resignation is forced in the National Assembly.
18 March 1970	Cambodian National Assembly, voting with color-coded ballots under the watchful eye of General In Tam, deposes Sihanouk; Sihanouk leaves Moscow for Peking, informed of deposition at airport by USSR Prime Minister Kosygin.
19 March 1970	U.S. government states that Sihanouk was legally deposed, no need for new recognition of regime.
20 March 1970	Sihanouk in Peking announces intent to resist his deposition; Army of the Republic of Vietnam (ARVN) troops cross into Cambodia to harrass NVA and PRG.
22 March 1970	Hanoi Party newspaper *Nhan Dan* supports Sihanouk.
23 March 1970	Sihanouk announces formation of Khmer National United Front (FUNK); Khmer People's National Liberation Armed Forces (PFLANK) formed; Sihanouk also announces intent to form united front with Laos and Vietnam; Kratie FANK (newly renamed *Force Armée Nationale Khmer*) garrison dissolves along with numerous others.
25 March 1970	PRC's Chou En-lai endorses the "United Front of Three Indochinese Peoples"; Polish embassy in Phnom Penh offers to evacuate DRV and PRG embassy staffs.
26 March 1970	Khieu Samphan, Hu Nim, and Hou Yuon join FUNK, Khieu as vice-chairman; nonviolent pro-Sihanouk demonstrations break out in Kompong Cham.
27 March 1970	DRV and PRG evacuate embassies, break relations; FANK fires on peasant demonstrators in Kompong Cham and Takeo.
28 March 1970	Mass insurrection: 40,000 pro-Sihanouk Khmer and Cham peasants organize for march on Phnom Penh.
29 March 1970	North Vietnamese Army (NVA) initiates attacks on FANK in four of six military regions; FANK falls on column of peasants approaching Phnom Penh.
2 April 1970	In Peking, Sihanouk denounces United States as "sole culprit" in Indochina.

A Chronological History of Kampuchea

3 April 1970	NVA overruns FANK positions in Svay Rieng.
4 April 1970	PRC Premier Chou endorses Sihanouk's FUNK.
6 April 1970	NVA becomes *de facto* government, FUNK *de jure* government in Svay Rieng Province.
10 April 1970	NVA, PRG, and RAK forces drive FANK out of Parrot's Beak area of Cambodia.
11 April 1970	Pro–Lon Nol demonstrations at Phnom Penh national sports stadium.
13 April 1970	Lon Nol troops massacre 515 Vietnamese Catholics in Phnom Penh.
14 April 1970	Svay Rieng Province liberation announced on Radio Peking; Lon Nol appeals for international aid; Washington Special Actions Group (WSAG) decides to send 3,000 captured AK-47 weapons to Lon Nol.
15 April 1970	WSAG ups Lon Nol aid to $5 million plus AK-47s.
16 April 1970	NVA attacks continue all over Cambodia; Nixon orders special cache of CIA arms sent to FANK.
19 April 1970	Nixon ups Lon Nol aid to $10 million plus AK-47s plus CIA supplies and small arms.
20 April 1970	Nixon announces the withdrawal of 150,000 U.S. troops from South Vietnam.
24–27 April 1970	Summit Conference of Indochinese Peoples, to coordinate anti-U.S. struggle, meets in Peking; Chou En-lai presides with Sihanouk; DRV Premier Pham Van Dong, Laotian Prince Souphanouvong, and President of the Presidium of the Central Committee of the NLF Nguyen Huu Tho attend.
26 April 1970	Nixon: "reached my decision . . . to go for broke" in Cambodia.
28 April 1970	U.S.-ARVN invasion begins in "Parrot's Beak"; Nixon informs Laird, Rogers, and Mitchell over the strong objections of Rogers and Laird.
1 May 1970	Invasion forces advance into Fishhook area; Mao Tsetung personally endorses Sihanouk's FUNK.
4 May 1970	Kent State: National Guard kills four students.
5 May 1970	Sihanouk's FUNK forms Royal Government of National Unification of Kampuchea (GRUNK); Sihanouk is the chief of state; Khieu Samphan is vice premier and minister of defense; Hou Yuon is minister of internal affairs; Hu Nim is minister of information; and Penn Nouth is prime minister. DRV and PRC immediately recognize government-in-exile; PRC breaks relations with Lon Nol regime.
6 May 1970	North Korea breaks diplomatic relations with Lon Nol's Cambodia.

11 May 1970	Cooper-Church Amendment, prohibiting U.S. military action in Cambodia, is introduced in U.S. Senate.
13 May 1970	GRUNK is reorganized, leftists gain ground; Lon Nol's Cambodia reestablishes relations with Thailand after break since 1961.
16–17 May 1970	International Conference in Djakarta, Indonesia, seeks futilely to restore peace to Cambodia.
19 May 1970	Cambodia restores diplomatic relations with South Vietnam after break since 1963.
June 1970	North Vietnamese troops retreat from skirmish with PFLANK troops in Kompong Thom.
25 June 1970	"General Mobilization" ordered by Lon Nol.
29 June 1970	U.S. troops complete withdrawal of incursion forces in Cambodia, leaving ARVN to hold some areas.
5 July 1970	Military tribunal sentences Sihanouk to death, wife to life, *in absentia*, for treason.
20 July 1970	Son Ngoc Thanh returns to Phnom Penh, rehabilitated from *in absentia* death sentence decreed by Sihanouk, joins Lon Nol regime.
10 Aug 1970	FUNK claims liberation of half of Cambodia.
20 Aug 1970	GRUNK again reorganizes, leftists again gain.
28 Aug 1970	U.S. Vice President Agnew visits Cambodia.
12 Sept 1970	Emory Swank arrives as U.S. ambassador, first since 1965.
October 1970	Nixon administration probes for loopholes in Cooper-Church Amendment.
9 Oct 1970	Lon Nol proclaims republic: Khmer Republic born.
22 Dec 1970	Cooper-Church Amendment becomes law, prohibiting U.S. funds for military use in Cambodia.
31 Dec 1970	FUNK claims liberation of 70 percent of Cambodia.

1971 to 1974

10 Jan 1971	U.S. Military Equipment Delivery Team formed for Cambodia.
March 1971	FUNK announces claim that 80 percent of Cambodia and 70 percent of population has been liberated.
21 April 1971	Lon Nol is proclaimed marshal of the republic.
20 Aug 1971	CHENLA II offensive against communists launched by order of Lon Nol; Phase I: clear Highway Six.
20 Aug to 25 Oct 1971	PFLANK "Counter–CHENLA II Phase I": evacuate population around Highway Six, draw advancing FANK down highway with light guerrilla tactics.
18 Oct 1971	Lon Nol dissolves National Assembly.
20 Oct 1971	Lon Nol declares state of emergency, and that he will no longer "play the game of democracy and freedom."

26 Oct 1971	Lon Nol declares Phase I of CHENLA II is complete, a great victory, and that "the morale of the enemy must surely be very low"; that night, enemy blows main bridge providing access to CHENLA II column.
26 Oct to 13 Nov 1971	PFLANK "Counter–CHENLA II Phase II": battalion-sized units isolate exposed units of FANK column.
27 Oct 1971	NVA Ninth Division attacks CHENLA II column.
14 Nov to 3 Dec 1971	PFLANK and NVA "Counter–CHENLA II Phase III": division-sized attacks on FANK's CHENLA II bases.
1 Dec 1971	Surveying chaos of destroyed CHENLA II forces, Lon Nol declares operation ended; no more major FANK offenses ever again.
17 Dec 1971	Lon Nol revokes civil liberties and political rights in Khmer Republic.
29 Jan 1972	FANK's operation ANGKOR CHEY fails to take temples.
31 Jan 1972	NVA, PRG, and PFLANK troops finally drive ARVN from eastern Cambodia.
5 Feb 1972	U.S. Senate Refugee Subcommittee reports 2 million homeless in Cambodian War.
9 March to 29 March 1972	ARVN's operation TOAN THANG VIII inflicts heavy losses on NVA and PFLANK at Svay Rieng City.
10 March 1972	Chief of State Cheng Heng resigns.
11 March 1972	Lon Nol declares self president of Khmer Republic, commander-in-chief of FANK, and president of the council of ministers; Sirik Matak, prime minister.
13 March 1972	Sirik Matak is dismissed; Lon Nol takes the post of prime minister, later appoints Son Ngoc Thanh.
20 March 1972	Heavy PFLANK attacks on Prey Veng, Neak Luong, and Phnom Penh.
23 March 1972	GRUNK is reorganized third time; leftists gain.
March to April 1972	Student demonstrations in capital against Lon Nol.
4 June 1972	Lon Nol is elected President of the Republic, with 55 percent of the vote; In Tam gets 24 percent, Keo An 21 percent of a million votes allegedly cast.
7–9 Sept 1972	Food riots in capital led by unpaid FANK troops.
22 Oct 1972	Henry Kissinger goes to Phnom Penh to confer with Lon Nol for four hours.
4 Nov 1972	Richard Nixon reelected in landslide victory.
11 Nov 1972	Sihanouk rejects Lon Nol cease-fire offer.
4 Dec 1972	PFLANK attacks Phnom Penh harbor.
8 Dec 1972	Tanzania leads UN move to oust Khmer Republic.
9 Dec 1972	Khieu Samphan rejects Lon Nol call for talks.
18 Dec 1972	Nixon orders attacks on Hanoi and Haiphong, Vietnam.
27 Dec 1972	*New York Times* exposé of Lon Nol regime corruption.

240   A Chronological History of Kampuchea

27 Jan 1973	Paris Peace Accords signed; Article 20 states that all foreign troops will withdraw from Cambodia, but none do so; temporary U.S. bombing halt.
31 Jan 1973	Sihanouk in Paris offers parley with Kissinger.
5 Feb 1973	General strikes in Phnom Penh.
6 Feb 1973	DRV issues demand that United States end interference in Cambodian internal affairs.
8 Feb 1973	United States resumes bombing of Cambodia.
9 Feb 1973	Heavy fighting in Mekong River Valley.
15 Feb 1973	FANK thrust along Mekong River.
16 Feb 1973	Chou tells Kissinger in Peking that he'll ask Sihanouk if he wants to negotiate.
28 Feb 1973	Sihanouk demands an end to U.S. intervention.
3 March 1973	PFLANK shells Phnom Penh.
12 March 1973	FANK-PFLANK battle at Preahprasap.
17 March 1973	T-28 aircraft with FANK markings attacks Presidential Palace in Phnom Penh.
20 March 1973	Lon Non, Lon Nol's brother and chief of security, arrests forty-six prominent citizens, including sixteen members of royal family.
21 March 1973	Mass strikes in Phnom Penh; Sihanouk begins tour of liberated zones of Kampuchea.
31 March 1973	PFLANK uses armored units for the first time; PRG foreign minister protests U.S. carpet bombing.
April 1973	Communists begin systematic de-Sihanoukization.
2 April 1973	Petrol rationing begins in Phnom Penh.
6–9 April 1973	Very heavy U.S. air strikes against PFLANK around Phnom Penh fail to break siege.
10 April 1973	United States decides for air bridge to Phnom Penh.
11 April 1973	Sihanouk returns to Peking from tour of Kampuchea.
13 April 1973	ARVN units cross over in an attempt to relieve FANK units pressed by PFLANK offensive.
17 April 1973	Phnom Penh regime resigns *en masse*; PFLANK advances on coastal town of Kep.
20 April 1973	PFLANK-NVA-PRG/ARVN border battles rage.
22 April 1973	PFLANK advances on Phnom Penh; ARVN thrusts up the Mekong River Valley; Lon Nol, Sirik Matak, and In Tam with Cheng Heng form State council, National Assembly is suspended.
26 April 1973	PFLANK penetrates to within fifteen km. of capital.
27 April 1973	PFLANK penetrates to within three km. of capital.
28 April 1973	PFLANK opens a third front north of Phnom Penh.
10 May 1973	U.S. House attempts to block funds for U.S. airstrikes in Cambodia.

A Chronological History of Kampuchea

18 May 1973	Chou En-lai to United States: "We will approach Sihanouk on your behalf with offer of negotiations."
18–21 May 1973	Highly intense U.S. airstrikes finally begin to blunt PFLANK offensive against Phnom Penh.
29 May 1973	PRC to United States: "We will approach Sihanouk for you."
31 May 1973	U.S. Senate votes 63–17 to end Laos and Cambodia area bombing.
3–4 June 1973	Nixon rejects Sihanouk negotiation offer.
6 June 1973	Ang Snoul falls to PFLANK.
11 June 1973	PFLANK rocket attack on Phnom Penh airport.
14 June 1973	Le Duc Tho denies that he made a "tacit agreement" on Cambodia with Kissinger.
18 June 1973	PFLANK cuts all six major surface roads linking Phnom Penh with provinces.
19 June 1973	PFLANK opens new Mekong front north of capital; Kissinger proposes to Chou that he meet with Sihanouk on August 6 when he visits Peking.
30 June 1973	U.S. Congress compromises with Nixon on bombing, allows continued bombardment of Cambodia until August 15, 1973.
1 July 1973	FANK battalions destroyed near Takeo in battle.
14 July 1973	Lon Nol implements "General Mobilization"; all men aged 18 to 35 are called for military service.
16 July 1973	Sihanouk in Peking denounces "meddling" of United States.
17 July 1973	In Tam confirms that about 10,000 political prisoners are held in the Khmer Republic.
18 July 1973	Chou En-lai lets Kissinger know that deal to negotiate with Sihanouk is off.
19 July 1973	Sirik Matak becomes FANK supreme commander; Chou tells Kissinger that August 16 would be appropriate for his visit to meet Sihanouk.
19–21 July 1973	"National Congress" in liberated areas declares intent to achieve total victory against U.S. imperialism.
1 Aug 1973	PFLANK tightens siege of Phnom Penh.
6 Aug 1973	U.S. B-52s accidentally hit FANK positions.
8 Aug 1973	PFLANK units loyal to Saloth Sar enter city from east; B-52s again hit FANK at Neak Luong, causing 405 friendly casualties.
9 Aug 1973	PFLANK overruns Phnom Penh airport and radio stations, cuts phone link to Hong Kong, thus temporarily isolating Khmer Republic from world; FANK and U.S. Air Force mount counteroffensive on Highway One.

10 Aug 1973	New battles near Mukkampoul, less than twenty miles from still isolated Phnom Penh.
13 Aug 1973	PFLANK takes five more towns; U.S. Air Force intensifies area bombing in vicinity of Phnom Penh in anticipation of August 15 cutoff date imposed by Congress.
15 Aug 1973	U.S. airstrikes cease minutes before 5 A.M. CET deadline, and thus direct U.S. military intervention ends.
17 Aug 1973	PFLANK stops FANK counterthrusts south and southeast of Phnom Penh.
19 Aug 1973	PFLANK besieges Kompong Speu; relief convoy reaches Phnom Penh from Battambang.
20 Aug 1973	PFLANK attacks Kompong Cham, Mukkampoul, and near Ang Snuol.
26 Aug 1973	Phnom Penh airport again shelled; Highway Six cut again by PFLANK.
29 Aug 1973	Lon Nol declares that negotiations are no longer possible, that conflict will be decided by arms.
4 Sept 1973	U.S. Ambassador Swank leaves, not to be replaced, declares Cambodia Indochina's "most useless war."
6–11 Sept 1973	Street fighting in Kompong Cham.
12–23 Sept 1973	PFLANK holds Kompong Cham until heavy bombing on September 23 forces its withdrawal.
21 Sept 1973	Henry Kissinger is confirmed as U.S. secretary of state.
1–2 Oct 1973	FANK units revolt, refuse to fight unless meals and back pay are assured.
5 Oct 1973	FANK thrust to relieve besieged units in Vieharsuor fails.
10 Oct 1973	Prime Minister In Tam resigns.
15 Oct 1973	Lon Nol rejects In Tam resignation.
17 Oct 1973	UN General Assembly votes 68-24-29 to put GRUNK challenge to Khmer Republic UN credentials on agenda for discussion.
5 Nov 1973	PFLANK units advance to within ten miles of Phnom Penh, up east bank of Mekong to Prechang Chan.
12 Nov 1973	Hanoi Party newspaper *Nhan Dan* reports that GRUNK has transferred all offices to Cambodia.
13 Nov 1973	United States grants Lon Nol $700 million aid; FANK fails to open Highway Four.
21 Nov 1973	Nixon pledges "all-out support" for Lon Nol.
22 Nov 1973 to 5 Dec 1973	Heavy fighting reported around Takeo and Vieharsuor, continuing along Highways Three and Four.
4 Dec 1973	ARVN launches air and ground attacks into Cambodia in support of failing FANK units.
5 Dec 1973	By two-vote margin, UN upholds Khmer Republic credentials to UN General Assembly.
9 Dec 1973	In Tam resubmits his resignation as prime minister.

A Chronological History of Kampuchea 243

10 Dec 1973	Khmer Republic government resigns *en masse*; battle rages near provincial capital of Kompong Speu.
12 Dec 1973	Minister of Foreign Affairs Long Boret becomes prime minister of Khmer Republic.
25 Dec 1973	PFLANK takes Krochsoeuch and Prekampil.
6 Jan 1974	Communists open 1974 dry season offensive with bombardment of Phnom Penh.
Jan–May 1974	Mass demonstrations in Phnom Penh.
Mar–June 1974	FUNK-FANK battles level the old royal capital, Oudong, twenty-four miles northwest of Phnom Penh.
28 March 1974	GRUNK Deputy Prime Minister and Commander-in-Chief of PFLANK Khieu Samphan leads delegation including Sihanouk on tour of socialist and nonaligned nations.
2 April 1974	Mao Tse-tung is photographed with Khieu Samphan at his right hand and Sihanouk at his left.
3 April 1974	John Gunther arrives in Phnom Penh, first U.S. ambassador since Swank left seven months ago.
27 July 1974	U.S. Senate Judiciary Committee approves first Article of Impeachment (obstruction of justice).
29 July 1974	Judiciary Committee approves second Article of Impeachment (abuse of power).
30 July 1974	Article III (contempt of congress) approved and Article IV (illegal war in Cambodia) rejected by Senate Judiciary Committee.
9 Aug 1974	Richard M. Nixon resigns from the presidency; Gerald R. Ford sworn in as thirty-eighth president of United States.
28 Nov 1974	UN again rejects GRUNK challenge to Khmer Republic UN General Assembly seat, again by two-vote margin.
16 Dec 1974	U.S. President Gerald Ford and French President Valerie Giscard d'Estaing issue joint communiqué from Martinique expressing hope for peaceful negotiations among parties to conflict in Cambodia.

1975

1 Jan 1975	GRUNK/FUNK/PFLANK/KCP launch final offensive, known as the "Mekong River Offensive."
5 Feb 1975	PFLANK closes Mekong River to all traffic; Phnom Penh is now isolated from surface access.
27 Mar 1975	USSR breaks relations with Lon Nol regime.
1 April 1975	Lon Nol flees Phnom Penh for Hawaii; Neak Luong falls to PFLANK.
12 April 1975	U.S. embassy evacuated; Acting President Khoy flees Khmer Republic.

13 April 1975	Khmer New Year, ends Year of the Tiger, begins Year of the Hare.
14 April 1975	FANK HQ bombed by air; 24-hour curfew on city.
15 April 1975	Suburban Phnom Penh fuel depots burn, FANK's air base falls, defense perimeter collapses.
16 April 1975	48-hour curfew laid by Republicans; FANK troops abandon outer defense line around capital.
17 April 1975	Phnom Penh falls with only sporadic resistance; rustication of civilian population begins; FUNK says Vietnamese take Poulo Wai Island, march on Ratanakiri and Mondolkiri Provinces.
18 April 1975	Ream is rusticated.
19 April 1975	Systematic termination of military and civilian personnel of Khmer Republic begins.
20 April 1975	All Khmer nationals, including Vietnamese and Chinese, are forced out of French embassy.
24 April 1975	Rustication of Battambang, Poipet, and other cities is undertaken.
27 April 1975	Pailin is rusticated.
30 April 1975	Saigon falls; deportation of all nonnationals from French embassy in Phnom Penh begins.
3 May 1975	Khmer-Vietnamese fighting begins on contested coastal islands.
12 May 1975	U.S. container ship *Mayaguez* seized in Cambodian territorial waters; Kissinger and Ford opt to bomb Cambodia's only oil refinery.
28 May 1975	Order goes out from Phnom Penh to cease executions of those connected with the defeated regime (the order is partly disregarded, later rescinded).
21 June 1975	*Le Monde* reports fighting over Poulo Wai islands and in Ratanakiri mountains between Vietnamese and Cambodian communists.
June 1975	Saloth Sar to Hanoi for border talks; border liaison group established.
18 July 1975	Sarin Chhak (GRUNK foreign minister) and Thiounn Prasith go to North Korea, ask Sihanouk to return, he refuses.
August 1975	Khmer incursions into Vietnam increase; DRV's Le Duan to Phnom Penh for talks; Hou Yuon resigns in protest and then disappears.
19 Aug 1975	Penn Nouth and Khieu Samphan go to North Korea, offer Sihanouk position as head of state for life, he agrees.
9 Sept 1975	Sihanouk returns to Phnom Penh.
September 1975	Second round of population relocation begins.
8 Nov 1975	Vietnamese in Kroch Chmar region ordered out.

15 Nov 1975	Sihanouk goes on an eleven-nation tour on behalf of emergent state.
14 Dec 1975	Third National Congress of KCP held in Phnom Penh; arrangements for new state thrashed out.
Dec 1975	Vietnamese say Kampuchean aggression continues in Kontum and Darlac Provinces; Kampuchea alleges Vietnamese *coup* attempt in Kampuchea.
31 Dec 1975	Sihanouk returns to Kampuchea.

1976 to 1979

5 Jan 1976	Constitution is promulgated, and Democratic Kampuchea comes into existence.
Feb 1976	Abortive "*coup* attempt" in Siem Riep province alleged by Democratic Kampuchea.
20 March 1976	People's Representative Assembly chooses 150 peasants, 50 workers, and 50 soldiers for Assembly; one "Pol Pot," listed as "representative of rubber plantation workers," though previously unknown, is elected for a seat in the Assembly.
4 April 1976	Sihanouk resigns as head of state, soon put under house arrest; Khieu Samphan becomes chair of the State Presidium, new head of state.
14 April 1976	Internal shake-up in Democratic Kampuchea leadership; Pol Pot becomes prime minister.
May 1976	In Phnom Penh, Vietnamese seek summit meeting, but Khmers demur.
27 Sept 1976	Nuon Chea replaces Pol Pot as prime minister.
September 1976	Foreign minister Ieng Sary travels to Japan, buys 10,000 tons of steel (subsequently imported in January of 1977).
October 1976	Ren Fung Trading Company established in Hong Kong for trade with nonsocialist nations.
15 Oct 1976	Pol Pot regains prime minister's portfolio.
1 Nov 1976	Non Suon arrested, later executed.
25 Dec 1976	Trade agreements signed with China.
20 Jan 1977	Jimmy Carter sworn in as thirty-ninth U.S. president.
25 Jan 1977	Koy Thuon arrested, followed next day by arrest of Touch Phoem.
Feb 1977	Attempted *coup*, with apparent Vietnamese involvement; purges intensify in all areas.
14 March 1977	Phouk Chhay arrested.
March 1977	Ieng Sary on state visit to Burma, discusses possible anti-Thai and -Vietnamese cooperation.
10 April 1977	Hu Nim arrested.

30 April 1977	Vietnam says division-sized Kampuchean force attacks Ha Tien and Chau Duc regions.
May 1977	Fierce Vietnamese-Kampuchean border battle.
6 June 1977	Tiv Ol arrested.
18 July 1977	Laos and Vietnam sign a twenty-five year "Treaty of Mutual Friendship and Cooperation."
September 1977	Vietnamese General Vo Nguyen Giap leads attacks along entire 650-mile border, penetrating up to 10 miles with elements of the Ninth Division.
28 Sept 1977	CCP Chairman Hua Kuo-feng (PRC) tells Pol Pot–Ieng Sary–Son Sen–Vorn Veth delegation to PRC: you "are not only good at destroying the old world but also good at building a new one."
4 Oct 1977	Pol Pot delegation visits Pyongyang, North Korea.
November 1977	Vietnamese Ninth Division moves on Parrot's Beak area with tanks and fighter-bombers, meeting heavy resistance; Democratic Kampuchea claims that 2,000 of the 20,000 invaders have been killed in action.
December 1977	58,000-man incursion into Kampuchea to relieve the hard-pressed Ninth Division.
25 Dec 1977	Standing Committee of the Khmer People's Revolutionary Army decides for all-out war.
31 Dec 1977	Democratic Kampuchea breaks diplomatic relations with Hanoi.
Jan 1978	Vietnamese 5th, 7th, 9th, 312th, and 320th Division (or about 60,000 men) meet RAK 1st, 3rd, and 290th Divisions in Takeo and Kampot Provinces.
3 Jan 1978	Sihanouk condemns Vietnamese "aggression."
6 Jan 1978	Vietnamese withdraw from Neak Luong.
7 Jan 1978	Kampuchea claims that 29,200 Vietnamese have been killed in action since September 1977, and Vietnamese now hold only about 400 square miles of Kampuchea.
5 Feb 1978	Hanoi proposes cease-fire; Phnom Penh ignores it.
15 Feb 1978	Hanoi demands negotiations; Phnom Penh refuses.
15 May 1978	Ieng Sary proposes a seven-month cooling-off period before border talks with Vietnam.
17 May 1978	Heavy battles in Tay Ninh/Mimot regions.
4 June 1978	Ieng Sary in Tokyo alleges CIA-Vietnamese plot to destroy Democratic Kampuchea.
12 June 1978	Ieng Sary in Tokyo: "talks possible after three to four months cooling-off."
17 June 1978	Democratic Kampuchea claims that Hanoi has rejected offers to talk.
24 June 1978	Hanoi claims that two Khmer battalions were "crushed" in Tay Ninh and Kontum.

27 June 1978	Radio Hanoi on Ieng Sary's 4/6/78 charges of CIA-Vietnamese plot: "Have the Kampuchean authorities gone crazy?"
29 July to 5 Aug 1978	Defense Minister Son Sen on aid-seeking mission to Peking.
21 Aug 1978	George McGovern, before Senate Foreign Relations Committee, calls for international force to destroy Pol Pot regime.
3 Nov 1978	25-year Russo-Vietnamese Friendship Treaty signed.
November 1978	Vorn Veth leads Vietnamese-oriented *coup* attempt.
3 Dec 1978	Hanoi announces the formation of KNUFNS, or Khmer National United Front for National Salvation.
December 1978	In name of KNUFNS, Vietnam undertakes large-scale invasion of Democratic Kampuchea.
5 Jan 1979	Pol Pot in Phnom Penh predicts "certain victory" over Vietnamese invaders.
7 Jan 1979	Phnom Penh falls to Vietnamese, Pol Pot heads for the hills; "Revolutionary Council" takes power.

1979 to 1983

January 1979	Heng Samrin regime begins to settle in.
February 1979	PRC incursion into northern provinces of Vietnam with penetration up to twelve miles in places.
18 Feb 1979	Khmer-Vietnamese "Friendship Treaty" signed.
9 Oct 1979	Son Sann proclaims KPNLF on Cambodian soil.
March 1980	Leader of Kampuchean People's National Liberation Front (KPNLF), Son Sann, in Washington, D.C. for meeting with Sihanouk.
7 March 1980	Chinese begin to withdraw from northern Vietnam, after sustaining some 20,000 casualties, including an estimated 8,000 battle dead.
11 March 1980	Khieu Samphan in Peking: "all peace-loving, justice-loving countries ought to realize that it is in their interests to stop Vietnamese and Soviet expansionism."
9 April 1980	Cambodian foreign minister Hun Sen requests negotiations with Thailand on repatriation of Cambodian refugees there, but Thailand refuses.
1 May 1980	Heng Samrin convenes "International Conference on Solidarity with the Kampuchean People" (AAPSO), with delegates from twenty-one nations and four international organizations.
17–19 May 1980	Vietnamese foreign minister Nguyen Co Thach, in Bangkok for talks with Thai officials, calls situation in Kampuchea "irreversible" in response to demands for Vietnamese withdrawal from Kampuchea.

Jan 1981	Thai army command reports the defection of *Khmer Serei* leader In Sakhan, along with about 100 of his guerrillas, to Heng Samrin regime.
20 Jan 1981	Ronald Reagan sworn in as fortieth U.S. president.
9 Feb 1981	Norodom Sihanouk meets Khieu Samphan in Pyongyang, North Korea, at behest of PRC, in futile effort to form united front.
27 Feb 1981	Sihanouk announces cancellation of any plans for united front.
23 April 1981	PRC openly gives arms to noncommunist resistance movements operating out of Thailand.
26 April 1981	Son Sann meets with Al Haig, U.S. secretary of state, in Washington, D.C.
30 April 1981	Norodom Sihanouk announces plans to join united front with Son Sann; Son Sann denies it.
1 May 1981	Heng Samrin regime announces 3,417,339 eligible voters in a population of 5,746,141; electoral commission reports (one week after the fact) that 97 percent of the eligible voters participated, and that Heng Samrin was the top vote-getter.
3 May 1981	Son Sann asserts that his KPNLF commands 6,000 regular troops; he convenes 300 people for "General Assembly of the Khmer People in United States and Canada."
5–31 May 1981	Sino-Vietnamese border skirmishes continue.
26 May 1981	"Fourth" Party Congress convenes in Phnom Penh.
4 July 1981	Truong Chinh, a founder of the ICP in 1930, elected to chair both the Council of State and the National Defense Council in Vietnam.
8 July 1981	Vietnamese Ambassador Ha Van Lau, in note to UN Secretary General Waldheim explaining the Vietnamese boycott of upcoming UN Conference on Kampuchea, accuses United States and PRC of collusion "to stir up trouble"; Ieng Sary, in New York for the conference, asserts of KCP: "Our program is not ideological, not socialism, or communism." Ieng says united front still possible with Sihanouk but not with Son Sann.
13 July 1981	UN convenes Conference on Kampuchea in New York; Vietnam, USSR, and People's Republic of Kampuchea boycott the conference.
18 July 1981	UN Conference on Cambodia adopts resolution, calls on Vietnam to withdraw from Cambodia.
4 Sept 1981	With Vietnamese Communist Party Leader Le Duan in Moscow for consultations, Sihanouk announces in Singapore with Son Sann the signing of a "declaration

A Chronological History of Kampuchea 249

	for common action" against the "Soviet-backed Vietnamese."
18 Sept 1981	UN General Assembly votes 77-37-31 to retain credentials of Democratic Kampuchea, defeating the third annual attempt by the People's Republic of Kampuchea to gain UN accreditation; U.S. representative votes in favor of Democratic Kampuchea, asserting that the vote "does not imply U.S. recognition of the Democratic Kampuchean regime. . . ."
21 Sept 1981	U.S. Secretary of State Alexander Haig denounces Vietnam and USSR before UN General Assembly for "willful violations" in Kampuchea and elsewhere of 1925 Geneva Accord on Chemical Warfare.
10 Nov 1981	Association of Southeast Asian Nations (ASEAN) decides not to supply arms to Cambodian resistance groups; Singapore and Malaysia say they will supply arms independently from ASEAN.
7 Dec 1981	Kampuchean Communist Party (KCP) announces that it has dissolved itself, but that the "Government of Democratic Kampuchea" will "continue to perform its historic task of leading the Kampuchean national army, guerrillas and the entire Kampuchean people to fight the Vietnamese aggressors. . . ."
18 Feb 1982	Sihanouk meets with Teng Tsiao-p'ing in Peking.
22 Feb 1982	Sihanouk and Khieu Samphan announce tentative plan for united front; Son Sann refuses to attend.
16 June 1982	ASEAN renews call for Vietnamese withdrawal.
19 June 1982	Socialist Republic of Vietnam (SRV) Foreign Minister Thach proposes three-stage disengagement plan on visit to Bangkok.
22 June 1982	Sihanouk, Samphan, and Sann sign agreement; Sihanouk as president, Samphan as vice president, and Sonn as prime minister of the new "Democratic Kampuchea."
7 July 1982	SRV's Thach announces "significant" troop reductions.
28 Oct 1982	UN General Assembly votes 105-23-20 on a call for Vietnamese withdrawal from Cambodian territory.
21 Nov 1982	PRC prime minister tells Son Sann that Peking favors all three Cambodian resistance factions equally.
26 Dec 1982	KPNLF fighters attack Vietnamese outpost at Phum Yeang Dangkum.
5 Jan 1983	KPNLF fighters raid Vietnamese outpost at Thai border.
10 Jan 1983	Vietnamese retake Phum Yeang Dangkum.
31 Jan 1983	Vietnamese overrun KPNLF base camp at Nong Chan.
4 Feb 1983	U.S. Secretary of State George Shultz meets with Sihanouk in Peking.

23 Feb 1983	Vietnamese say that their troops will remain in Kampuchea until threats to People's Republic of Kampuchea from guerrillas and to Vietnam from PRC are ended.
9 March 1983	Nonaligned Conference in New Delhi skirts issue of who should represent Kampuchea by leaving Khmer seat empty.
23 March 1983	ASEAN nations reject SRV negotiation bid.
31 March 1983	Vietnamese Fifth Division attacks Pol Pot bases near Phnom Chat.
3 April 1983	Fighting spreads all along Thai-Kampuchean border; Vietnamese attack Pol Pot bases at Chamcar Kor and Prey Moin, Sihanouk base at O Smach, and sit poised to strike Son Sann base at Ampil Camp.
11 April 1983	Thailand receives eight 155mm howitzers from United States.
14 April 1983	PRC repeats warnings alleging Vietnamese provocations against China; SRV announces upcoming troop withdrawals in May from Kampuchea.
19 April 1983	After several days of shelling northern Vietnamese provinces, PRC warns Vietnam not to press attacks on PRC's guerrilla allies in Thai-Kampuchean border area.
20 April 1983	More 155mm howitzers delivered to Thais by United States, along with ammunition, spare parts, and vehicles.
22 April 1983	Vietnam says PRC attacks are intended to boost morale of Cambodian guerrillas; Sihanouk postpones visit to resistance bases, flies from Peking to Paris.
24 April 1983	Sihanouk meets with French President Mitterrand.
30 April 1983	Sihanouk at border resistance camp in Kampuchea, accepts credentials of ambassadors to "Democratic Kampuchea" from Malaysia, PRC, Bangladesh, North Korea, and Mauritania.
1 May 1983	Sihanouk meets Khieu Samphan at resistance base to discuss strategy for upcoming wet season rebel offensive.
2 May 1983	1,000–1,500 Vietnamese troops leave Phnom Penh on way out of PRK, and Vietnam's ambassador says that 10,000 in all will leave this month; Thai Foreign Minister Siddhi Savetsila says withdrawal "has no meaning."
3 May 1983	French President François Mitterrand, on state visit to PRC, says he will never recognize PRK, but criticizes PRC for continued support of Pol Pot faction; Thai official later charges that 2,000 Vietnamese replacements enter Kandal Province today to substitute for

A Chronological History of Kampuchea 251

1 June 1983	withdrawn troops. Sihanouk threatens to quit "Coalition Government of Democratic Kampuchea" (CGDK) over Son Sann's criticism of his plan to make a deal with PRK.
2 June 1983	Samphan letter to Sihanouk: forget any deals with PRK.
3 June 1983	Sihanouk cables resignation threat to Samphan.
8 June 1983	PRK says SRV and PRK will not negotiate with Sihanouk.
15 June 1983	SRV reportedly disarms some PRK army units.
20 June 1983	Pol Pot reported "very ill" at Phnum Malai hospital.
15 Aug 1983	PRK National Assembly report says that more than 2.7 million Kampucheans died between 1975 and 1979.
26 Sept 1983	CGDK guerrillas attack four Vietnamese bases in Pailin.
12 Oct 1983	UN General Assembly accepts credentials of Democratic Kampuchea, spurns PRK for fifth year in a row.
3 Nov 1983	TV station opens in Phnom Penh after 9-year hiatus.
12–14 Dec 1983	Vietnamese shell KPNLF base at Prati Chama.

Selected Research Bibliography

I. Introduction

A. The definitive story of Kampuchean communism has not been produced to date, and one of the most difficult challenges facing researchers in this task lies in information access and management. It is hoped that this compilation may encourage further research into the many unresolved questions touched upon in this volume, as well as those remaining unbroached as yet. This bibliography is suggestive, rather than exhaustive.

B. The plan of this Selected Research Bibliography is as follows:

I.	Introduction	253
	A. Purpose	253
	B. Plan	253
II.	Bibliographies	253
III.	Newspapers and News Serials Utilized	254
	A. Newspapers	254
	B. Official and Other News Serials	254
IV.	Articles in Journals and Edited Volumes	255
V.	Books and Monographs	261
VI.	Government Documents and Miscellaneous Sources	267
	A. U.S. Government Documents	267
	B. Miscellaneous Official Documents	270
	C. Other Sources	271

II. Bibliographies

Aschmoneit, W. *Kampuchea: Sozialhistorische Bibliographie zu Kampuchea von der Vorgeschichte bis 1954.* Munster, West Germany: SZD-Verlag, 1981.

Aschmoneit, W., ed. *Kampuchea: Sozialhistorische Bibliographies zu Kampuchea von 1954 bis 1984.* Munster, West Germany: SZD-Verlag, forthcoming.

Auvade, R. *Bibliographie critique des oeuvres parves sur l'Indochine française.* Paris, 1965.

Boudet, P., and R. Bourgeois. *Bibliographie de l'Indochine Française, 1913–1935.* 4 vols. Paris, 1929–1967.

Embree, J. F., and L. Dotson. *Bibliography of the Peoples and Cultures of Mainland Southeast Asia.* New Haven: Yale University Press, 1950.

Fischer, M. L. *Cambodia: An Annotated Bibliography of its History, Geography, Politics and Economy since 1954.* Cambridge, Mass.: Center for International Studies, Massachusetts Institute of Technology, 1967.

Hobbs, C. C., G. H. Fuller, W. D. Jones, and J. T. Dorosh. *Indochina—A Bibliography of the Land and the People.* Washington, D.C., 1950. (Typewritten.)

Marr, D. T. *Japanese Foreign Policy: A Bibliographical Essay and Annotated Bibliography.* Los Angeles, 1981. (Typewritten.)

U. N., Economic Commission for Asia and the Far East (ECAFE). *Cambodia, A Select Bibliography.* Bangkok, 1967.

University of Chicago. *Bibliography of Cambodia.* New Haven: Human Relations Area Files Press, 1956.

III. Newspapers and News Serials Utilized

A. *Newspapers*

Los Angeles Times
New York Times
Chicago Tribune
Washington Post
Christian Science Monitor
The Wall Street Journal
The Asian Wall Street Journal
Le Monde (Paris)
New Statesman (London)

B. *Official and Other News Serials*

Beijing Review (Beijing)
Nhan Dan (Hanoi)
International Affairs (Moscow)
Kambuja (Phnom Penh)
Khmer News (Washington)
Tung Padevat (Kampuchea)
Kampuchea Newsletter (Stockholm)
New Solidarity (U.S.)
The Call (Chicago)
The Economist (London)
The New York Review
Newsweek
Far Eastern Economic Review
Time

IV. Articles in Journals and Edited Volumes

Allman, T. D. "The Aristocratic Basis of the Cambodian Coup." In M. and S. Gettleman and L. and C. Kaplan, eds., *Conflict in Indochina*, pp. 362–364. New York: Random House, 1970.

———. "'Fred,' the CIA Stirrer in Cambodia." *The Bulletin* (Sydney) 21 (August 1971).

Antoshi, Y. "Democratic Kampuchea Two Years Later," *International Affairs* (May, 1977), pp. 64–69.

Asian Survey 19:8 [Special Issue on Kampuchea] (August 1979).

Barang, M. "Cambodia: In Search of Peace." *Liberation* (July–August 1971).

Barker, W. C. "Internal Developments in Kampuchea." *Australian Foreign Affairs Review* 49 (Sept. 1978), pp. 437–443.

Barnett, A. "Inter-Communist Conflicts and Vietnam." *Bulletin of Concerned Asian Scholars* 11:4 (1979), pp. 2–9.

Bartley, R. L., and W. P. Kucewicz. "'Yellow Rain' and the Future of Arms Agreements." *Foreign Affairs* 61:4 (Spring 1983), pp. 805–826.

Baudouin, S. "La Volonté de Vivre du Peuple Cambodgien." *Le Monde Diplomatique* 344 (Nov. 1982), pp. 16, 17.

Becker, E. "Murder with a Twist." *Far Eastern Economic Review*, April 16, 1982.

Brown, D. "Exporting Insurgency: The Communists in Cambodia." In J. J. Zasloff and A. E. Goodman, eds., *Indochina in Conflict*, pp. 125–135. Lexington, Mass.: Lexington Books, 1972.

Burchett, W. G. "Sihanouk and the Khmer Issarak." In M. and S. Gettleman and L. and C. Kaplan, eds., *Conflict in Indochina*, pp. 65–74. New York: Random House, 1970.

Carney, T. M. "Kampuchea in 1982: Political and Military Escalation." *Asian Survey* 23:1 (Jan. 1983), pp. 73–83.

Chandler, D. P. "Cambodia's Strategy for Survival." *Current History* (December 1969), pp. 344–348.

———. "An Anti-Vietnamese Rebellion in Early Nineteenth Century Cambodia: Pre-Colonial Imperialism and a Pre-Nationalist Response." *Journal of Southeast Asian Studies* 6:1 (March 1975), pp. 16–24.

———. "The Constitution of Democratic Kampuchea: The Semantics of Revolutionary Change." *Pacific Affairs* 49:3 (Fall 1976), pp. 506–515.

———. "Transformation in Cambodia." *Commonweal* 104:7 (April 1, 1977).

———. "Strategies for Survival in Kampuchea." *Current History* (April 1983), pp. 149–153.

Chanthou Boua, B. Kiernan, and A. Barnett. "The Bureaucracy of Death: Documents from Inside Pol Pot's Torture Machine." *New Statesman* (London), May 2, 1980, pp. 669–676.

Dassé, M. "Cambodge: la tutelle vietnamienne." *Défense Nationale* 39 (April 1983), pp. 95–106.

Devillers, P. "The Dynamics of Power in Cambodia." In M. and S. Gettleman and L. and C. Kaplan, eds., *Conflict in Indochina*, pp. 215–236. New York: Random House, 1970.

Ebihara, M. "Khmer." In F. M. Lebar, G. C. Hickey, and J. K. Musgrave, eds., *Ethnic Groups of Mainland Southeast Asia*, pp. 98–105. New Haven: Human Relations Area Files Press, 1964.

──────. "Interrelationships Between Buddhism and Social Systems in Cambodian Peasant Culture." In M. Nash, ed., *Anthropological Studies in Theravada Buddhism*, pp. 175–196. New Haven: Yale University Press, 1966.

──────. "Perspectives on Sociopolitical Transformations in Cambodia/Kampuchea: A Review Article." *Journal of Asian Studies* 51:1 (Nov. 1981), pp. 63–71.

Fifield, R. H. "ASEAN, Kampuchea and the United Nations." *Asia Pacific Community* (Summer 1982), pp. 74–88.

Finley, L. "The Propaganda War." *Southeast Asia Chronicle* 64 (Sept.–Oct. 1978), pp. 31–36.

Garrett, B. "The Road to Phnom Penh: Cambodians Take Up The Gun." In B. Garrett and K. Barkley, eds., *Two, Three . . . Many Vietnams: A Radical Reader on the Wars in Southeast Asia and the Conflicts at Home*, pp. 106–115. San Francisco: Canfield Press, 1971.

Garry, R. "Modernization of Rural Areas in Cambodia." *Civilizations* 16:4 (1966), pp. 460–472.

Girling, J.L.S. "Crisis and Conflict in Cambodia." *Orbis* 14:2 (Summer 1970), pp. 349–365.

──────. "Resistance in Cambodia." *Asian Survey* 12:7 (July 1972), pp. 549–563.

Gorden, B. K. "Cambodia: Where Foreign Policy Counts." *Asian Survey* 5:9 (Sept. 1965), pp. 433–448.

──────. "Cambodia: Shadow over Angkor." *Asian Survey* 9:1 (Jan. 1969), pp. 58–68.

Gorden, B. K., and K. Young. "The Khmer Republic: That Was the Cambodia That Was." *Asian Survey* 9:1 (Jan. 1971), pp. 26–40.

Heder, S. R. "Mistranslations in Counter-revolutionary Propaganda." *News From Kampuchea* (Waverly, Australia) 1:3 (August 1977), pp. 14–18.

──────. "Kampuchea's Armed Struggle: The Origins of an Independent Revolution." *Bulletin of Concerned Asian Scholars* 11:1 (1979), pp. 2–24.

──────. "Kampuchea 1980: Anatomy of a Crisis." *Southeast Asia Chronicle* 77 (Feb. 1981), pp. 3–11.

──────. "Origins of the Conflict." *Southeast Asia Chronicle* 64 (Sept.–Oct. 1978), pp. 3–18.

──────. "Democratic Kampuchea: The Regime's Post Mortem." *Indochina Issues* 4 (Dec. 1979).

Hiebert, L. G. and M. "Famine in Kampuchea: Politics of a Tragedy." *Indochina Issues* 4 (April 1980), pp. 1–6.

Jackson, K. "Cambodia 1977: Gone to Pot." *Asian Survey* 18:1 (Jan. 1978), pp. 76–90.
———. "Cambodia 1978: War, Pillage and Purge in Democratic Kampuchea." *Asian Survey* 19:1 (Jan. 1979), pp. 72–84.
Kershaw, R. "Cambodian National Union—a Milestone in Popular Front Technique." *World Today* 32:2 (Feb. 1976), pp. 60–68.
Khieu Samphan. "Underdevelopment in Cambodia." *Indochina Chronicle* 51–52 (Sept.–Nov. 1976), pp. 5–25.
Kiernan, B. "Cambodia in the News: 1975–1976." *Melbourne Journal of Politics* 8 (1975–1976), pp. 6–12.
———. "Social Cohesion in Revolutionary Cambodia." *Australian Outlook* 30:3 (Dec. 1976), pp. 371–386.
———. "Why's Kampuchea Gone to Pot?" *Nation Review* (Melbourne) 17 (November 23, 1978).
———. "The 1970 Peasant Uprising in Kampuchea." *Journal of Contemporary Asia* 9:3 (1979), pp. 310–322.
———. "Vietnam and the Governments and People of Kampuchea." *Bulletin of Concerned Asian Scholars* 11:4 (1979), pp. 19–25.
———. "Conflict in the Kampuchean Communist Movement." *Journal of Contemporary Asia* 10:1–2 (1980), pp. 7–74.
———. "New Light on the Origins of the Vietnam-Kampuchea Conflict." *Bulletin of Concerned Asian Scholars* 12:4 (Oct.–Dec. 1980), pp. 61–65.
———. "Origins of Khmer Communism." *Southeast Asian Affairs* (1981), pp. 161–180.
———. "Kampuchea's Choices for Survival." *Southeast Asia Chronicle* 77 (Feb. 1981), pp. 27–29.
———. "Kampuchea 1979–1981: National Rehabilitation in the Eye of an International Storm." *Southeast Asian Affairs* (1982), pp. 167–195.
Kirk, D. "Cambodia's Economic Crisis." *Asian Survey* 9:3 (March 1971), pp. 239–243.
———. "Revolution and Political Violence in Cambodia, 1970–1974." In J. J. Zasloff and M. Brown, eds., *Communism in Indochina: New Perspectives*, pp. 215–230. Lexington, Mass.: D. C. Heath, 1975.
Lancaster, D. "The Decline of Prince Sihanouk's Regime." In J. J. Zasloff and A. E. Goodman, eds., *Conflict in Indochina*, pp. 47–56. Lexington, Mass.: D. C. Heath, 1972.
Leifer, M. "The Failure of Political Institutionalization in Cambodia." *Modern Asian Studies* 2:2 (1968), pp. 125–140.
———. "Rebellion or Subversion in Cambodia." *Current History* (Feb. 1969), pp. 88–93+.
———. "Peace and War in Cambodia." *Southeast Asia* 1:1–2 (Winter/Spring 1971), pp. 59–73.
———. "Kampuchea 1979: From Dry Season to Dry Season." *Asian Survey* 20:1 (Jan. 1980), pp. 33–41.
———. "Kampuchea in 1980: The Politics of Attrition." *Asian Survey* 21:1 (Jan. 1981), pp. 93–101.

———. "The International Representation of Kampuchea." *Southeast Asian Affairs* (1982), pp. 47–59.

McCormick, G. "The Kampuchean Revolution 1975–1978: The Problem of Knowing the Truth." *Journal of Contemporary Asia* 10:1–2 (1981), pp. 75–118.

———. "Cambodia: Rationale for a Rural Policy." *Journal of Contemporary Asia* 11:2 (1982), pp. 231–236.

Marsot, A. G. "China's Aid to Cambodia." *Pacific Affairs* 2:2 (Summer 1969), pp. 189–198.

Myrdal, J. "When the Peasant War Triumphed." *Southeast Asia Chronicle* 77 (Feb. 1981), pp. 12–15.

———. "Why is there famine in Kampuchea?" *Southeast Asia Chronicle* 77 (Feb. 1981), pp. 16–18.

Nations, R. "Inside the Bitter Border." *Far Eastern Economic Review*, August 19, 1977, pp. 9–12.

Nordland, R. "Khmer Refugees: 'Reaching for Oars.'" *Indochina Issues* 30 (Nov. 1982), pp. 1–6.

Norodom Sihanouk. "Cambodia Neutral: The Dictate of Necessity." *Foreign Affairs* 36:4 (July 1958), pp. 582–586; also in M. and S. Gettleman and L. and C. Kaplan, eds., *Conflict in Indochina*, pp. 237–241. New York: Random House, 1970.

Osborne, M. E. "Regional Disunity in Cambodia." *Australian Outlook* 22:3 (Dec. 1968), pp. 317–333.

———. "Cambodia's Choices." *Current Affairs Bulletin* 47:1 (Nov. 1970).

———. "Effacing the 'God-King': Internal Developments in Cambodia since March 1970." In J. J. Zasloff and A. E. Goodman, eds., *Conflict in Indochina*, pp. 57–80. Lexington, Mass.: D. C. Heath, 1972.

———. "Norodom Sihanouk: Leader of the Left?" In J. J. Zasloff and M. Brown, eds., *Communism in Indochina: New Perspectives*, pp. 241–248. Lexington, Mass.: D. C. Heath, 1975.

———. "Reflections on the Cambodian Tragedy." *Asia-Pacific Community* 8:1 (October 1976), pp. 1–13.

Pfanner, D. E., and J. Ingersoll. "Theravada Buddhism and Village Economic Behavior." *Journal of Asian Studies* 21:3 (May 1962), pp. 341–361.

Pike, D. "Southeast Asia and the Superpowers: The Dust Settles." *Current History* (April 1983), pp. 145–148.

Poole, P. A. "Communism and Ethnic Conflict in Cambodia 1960–1975." In J. J. Zasloff and M. Brown, eds., *Communism in Indochina: New Perspectives*, pp. 249–255. Lexington, Mass.: D. C. Heath, 1975.

———. "The Vietnamese in Cambodia and Thailand: Their Role in Interstate Relations." In P. A. Poole, ed., *Indochina: Perspectives for Reconciliation*, pp. 55–69. Athens: Ohio University, Center for International Studies, 1975.

Porter, G. "Kampuchea's U.N. Seat—Cutting the Pol Pot Connection." *Indochina Issues* 18 (July 1981), pp. 1–7.

———. "Vietnam in Kampuchea: Aims and Options." *Indochina Issues* 16 (May 1981), pp. 1–7.

———. "Negotiating Kampuchea: Scenario for a Settlement." *Indochina Issues* 24 (March 1982).
Porter, G., and G. C. Hildebrand. "From Starvation to Self-Sufficiency in Cambodia." *Indochina Chronicle* 47 (Feb.–Mar. 1976), pp. 2–19.
Quinn, K. M. "Cambodia 1976: Internal Consolidation and External Expansion." *Asian Survey* 17:1 (Jan. 1971), pp. 43–54.
———. "Political Change in Wartime: The Khmer Krahom Revolution in Southern California 1970–1974." *Naval War College Review* 28:4 (Spring 1976), pp. 3–31.
Quinn-Judge, P. "Chamcar Loeu: A Gradual Recovery." *Southeast Asia Chronicle* 77 (Feb. 1981), pp. 19–26.
Rieser, E. "Red Khmer in the Jungle." *Swiss Review of World Affairs* 31:6 (Sept. 1981), pp. 17–24.
Rodman, P. "Sideswipe: Kissinger, Shawcross and the Responsibility for Cambodia." *American Spectator* 14:3 (March 1981).
Rousset, P. "Cambodia: Background to the Revolution." *Journal of Contemporary Asia* 7:4 (1977), pp. 513–528.
Roy, D. "The Coup in Phnom Penh." In M. and S. Gettleman and L. and C. Kaplan, eds., *Conflict in Indochina*, pp. 343–359. New York: Random House, 1970.
Schanberg, S. "The Death and Life of Dith Pran: A Story of Cambodia." *New York Times Magazine*, January 20, 1980.
Schell, O. "Cambodian Civil War." *The New Republic* 162 (June 6, 1970).
Scott, P. D. "Cambodia: Why the Generals Won." In M. and S. Gettleman and L. and C. Kaplan, eds., *Conflict in Indochina*, pp. 394–415. New York: Random House, 1972.
Shawcross, W. "The Third Indochina War." *New York Review of Books*, April 4, 1978.
Simon, S. W. "Cambodia in the Vortex: The Actors' Perceptions, Goals and Settlement Prospects." In M. Zacher and R. S. Milne, eds., *Conflict and Stability in Southeast Asia*, pp. 149–178. Garden City, N.Y.: Doubleday, 1974.
———. "The Khmer Resistance: External Relations 1973–1974." In J. J. Zasloff and M. Brown, eds., *Communism in Indochina: New Perspectives*, pp. 197–214. Lexington, Mass.: D. C. Heath, 1975.
———. "New Conflict in Indochina." *Problems of Communism* 27:5 (Sept. 1978), pp. 20–36.
———. "Cambodia: Barbarism in a Small State Under Siege." *Current History* (Dec. 1978), pp. 197–201+.
———. "Kampuchea: Vietnam's Vietnam." *Current History* (Dec. 1979), pp. 197–200.
———. "Kampuchea: Pawn in a Political Chess Match." *Current History* (Dec. 1980), pp. 170–174.
———. "Cambodia and Regional Diplomacy." *Southeast Asian Affairs* (1982), pp. 196–210.

Smith, H. "Nixon's Decision to Invade Cambodia." In D. M. Fox, ed., *The Politics of U.S. Foreign Policy Making*, pp. 344–353. Pacific Palisades, Calif.: Goodyear Publishing Company, 1971.
Smith, R. M. "Cambodia." In G. M. Kahin, ed., *Governments and Politics of Southeast Asia*, pp. 595–675. Ithaca, N.Y.: Cornell University Press, 1964.
———. "Prince Norodom Sihanouk of Cambodia." *Asian Survey* 7:6 (June 1967), pp. 353–362.
———. "Cambodia: Between Scylla and Charybdis." *Asian Survey* 7:1 (Jan. 1968), pp. 72–79.
———. "Cambodia: Social and Historical Background." In M. and S. Gettleman and L. and C. Kaplan, eds., *Conflict in Indochina*, pp. 39–56. New York: Random House, 1970.
Snyder, D. "Life After Death in the Kampuchean Hell." *Executive Intelligence Review*, September 29, 1981.
Southeast Asia Chronicle 64 [Special Issue on Kampuchea] (Sept.–Oct. 1978), "Vietnam–Kampuchea War: Two Views."
Southeast Asia Chronicle 77 [Special Issue on Kampuchea] (Feb. 1981), "Kampuchea Survives. . . . but what now?"
Southeast Asia Chronicle 79 [Special Issue on Kampuchea] (Aug. 1981), "The Kampuchea Debate."
Spragens, J. W., Jr. "Don't Forget the Practical Problems." *Southeast Asia Chronicle* 79 (Aug. 1981), pp. 9–12.
Stockwin, H. "Cambodia: The Continuing Catastrophe." *Worldview* 23:1 (Jan.–Feb. 1980), pp. 21–23.
Stuart-Fox, M. "Resolving the Kampuchean Problem: The Case for an Alternative Regional Initiative." *Contemporary Southeast Asia* 4:2 (Sept. 1982), pp. 210–225.
Summers, L. "The Cambodian Liberation Forces: Political and Economic Doctrine." *Indochina Chronicle* 17 (July 1972), pp. 1–6.
———. "The Cambodian Civil War." *Current History* (Dec. 1972), pp. 259–262+.
———. "Cambodia: Model of the Nixon Doctrine." *Current History* (Dec. 1973), pp. 252–256+.
———. "Consolidating the Cambodian Revolution." *Current History* (Dec. 1975), pp. 218–222+.
———. "Defining the Revolutionary State in Cambodia." *Current History* (Dec. 1976), pp. 205–208+.
———. "In Matters of War and Socialism, Anthony Barnett would Shame and Honor Kampuchea Too Much." *Bulletin of Concerned Asian Scholars* 11:4 (1979), pp. 10–18.
———. "Kooperativen im Demokratischen Kampuchea." In W. Aschmoneit and R. Werning, eds., *Kampuchea: Lesebuch zur Geschichte, Gesellschaft, Politik*, pp. 381–391. Munster: SZD-Verlag, 1981.
Szaz, Z. M. "Cambodia's Foreign Policy." *Far Eastern Survey* (Oct. 1955).
Thayer, C. "New Evidence on Kampuchea." *Problems of Communism* 30:3 (May–June 1981), pp. 91–96.

Thion, S. "The Cambodian Solution to the Third Indochina War." *Cornell Review* (Summer 1979).
──────. "The Ingratitude of the Crocodiles: The 1978 Cambodian *Black Paper.*" *Bulletin of Concerned Asian Scholars* 12:4 (1980), pp. 38–54.
Turley, W., and J. Race. "The Third Indochina War." *Foreign Policy* 38 (Spring 1980), pp. 92–116.
van der Kroef, J. M. "Political Ideology in Democratic Kampuchea." *Orbis* 22:4 (Winter 1979), pp. 1007–1030.
──────. "Cambodia: From Democratic Kampuchea to People's Republic." *Asian Survey* 19:8 (Aug. 1979), pp. 731–750.
──────. "Kampuchea: the Diplomatic Labyrinth." *Asian Survey* 22:10 (Oct. 1982), pp. 1009–1024.
Vickery, M. "Looking Back at Cambodia." *Westerly* (Perth, Australia) (Dec. 1976), pp. 14–28.
──────. "Democratic Kampuchea: CIA to the Rescue." *Bulletin of Concerned Asian Scholars* 14:4 (1982), pp. 45–54.
Weber, T. "Political Authority and Revolution: On the Messianic Tearing Down and Building Up of Structures." *Worldview* 17:5 (May 1974), pp. 27–34.
Willmott, W. E. "Cambodian Neutrality." In M. and S. Gettleman and L. and C. Kaplan, eds., *Conflict in Indochina*, pp. 242–254. New York: Random House, 1970.
──────. "Analytical Errors of the Kampuchean Communist Party." *Pacific Affairs* 54:2 (Summer 1981), pp. 209–227.
──────. "The Two Battles for Kampuchea." *New Zealand International Review* 6:5 (Sept.–Oct. 1981), pp. 7–9.
Winnacker, M. "In the Name of Independence." *Southeast Asia Chronicle* 79 (Aug. 1981), pp. 6–8.

V. Books and Monographs

Ampter, J. A. *Vietnam Verdict: A Citizen's History.* New York: Continuum, 1982.
Armstrong, J. D. *Revolutionary Diplomacy.* Berkeley: University of California Press, 1977.
Armstrong, J. P. *Sihanouk Speaks: Cambodia's Chief of State Explains His Controversial Politics.* New York: Walter and Company, 1954.
Aschmoneit, W., and R. Werning, eds., *Kampuchea: Lesebuch zur Geschichte, Gesellschaft, Politik.* Munster: SZD-Verlag, 1981.
Babbit, I., trans. *The Dhammapada.* New York: New Directions, 1965; and Oxford University Press, 1936.
Barron, J., and A. Paul. *Murder of a Gentle Land: The Untold Story of Communist Genocide in Cambodia.* New York: Reader's Digest Press, 1977.
Berman, P. *Revolutionary Organizations: Institution-Building in the People's Liberation Armed Forces.* Lexington, Mass.: Lexington Books, 1974.

Briggs, L. P. *Ancient Khmer Empire*. Philadelphia: American Philosophical Society, 1951.
Brodrict, A. H. *Little Vehicle: Cambodia and Laos*. London: Hutchinson, 1947.
Burchett, W. G. *Mekong Upstream*. Hanoi: Red River Publishing House, 1957.
———. *The Second Indochina War: Cambodia and Laos*. New York: International Publishers, 1970.
———. *The China-Cambodia-Vietnam Triangle*. Chicago: Vanguard Press, 1981.
Burchett, W. G., ed. *My War with the CIA: The Memoirs of Prince Norodom Sihanouk*. New York: Random House, 1972.
Buttinger, J. *The Smaller Dragon: A Political History of Vietnam*. New York: Praeger, 1958.
———. *Vietnam: A Dragon Embattled*. 2 vols. New York: Praeger, 1967.
Butwell, R. T. *Southeast Asia Today—and Tomorrow: Problems of Political Development*. 2nd ed. New York: Praeger, 1969.
Cady, J. F. *The Roots of French Imperialism in Eastern Asia*. Ithaca, N.Y.: Cornell University Press, 1954.
———. *Southeast Asia: Its Historical Development*. New York: McGraw Hill, 1964.
———. *Thailand, Burma, Laos and Cambodia*. Englewood Cliffs, N.J.: Prentice Hall, 1966.
Caldwell, M. *Cambodia in the Southeast Asian War*. Belfast, Me.: Porter, Bern, 1979.
Caldwell, M., and Lek Tan. *Cambodia in the Southeast Asian War*. New York: Monthly Review Press, 1975.
Carney, T. M., ed. *Communist Party Power in Kampuchea: Documents and Discussion*. Cornell University Southeast Asia Program, Data Paper no. 106. Ithaca, N.Y.: Cornell University, 1977.
Chaliand, G. *Revolution in the Third World*. New York: Penguin Books, 1978.
Chandler, D.P. *The Land and People of Cambodia*. New York: Lippincott, 1972.
———. "Cambodia Before the French: Politics in a Tributary Kingdom." Ph.D. dissertation, University of Michigan, 1973.
———. *The Early Phases of Liberation in Northwest Cambodia: Conversations with Peang Sophi*. Melbourne: Center of Southeast Asian Studies, Monash University of Australia, 1976.
———. *A History of Cambodia*. Boulder, Colo.: Westview Press, 1983.
Chandler, D. P., et al., eds. *Revolution and Its Aftermath in Kampuchea: 8 Essays*. New Haven: Yale University Press, 1983.
Chomsky, N. *Two Essays on Cambodia*. Nottingham: Bertrand Russell Peace Foundation, 1970.
Chomsky, N., and E. S. Herman. *After the Cataclysm: Postwar Indochina and the Reconstruction of Imperial Ideology*. Boston: South End Press, 1979.
Coedes, G. *The Making of South-East Asia*. Berkeley: University of California Press, 1967.

Selected Research Bibliography 263

―――. *The Indianized States of Southeast Asia*. [W. F. Vella, ed., and S. B. Cowing, trans.] Honolulu: East-West Center Press, 1968.
Debré, F. *Cambodge: La Révolution de la Forêt*. Paris: Flammarion, 1976.
Delvert, J. *Le Paysan Cambodgien*. Paris: Mouton, 1961.
Dudman, R. *Forty Days with the Enemy*. New York: Liveright, 1971.
Elliot, D.W.P. *The Third Indochina Conflict*. Boulder, Colo.: Westview Press, 1981.
Ester, H. *Vietnam-Thailand-Kampuchea: A First Hand Account*. Canberra: The Australian Council for Overseas Aid, 1980.
Falk, R. *The Vietnam War and International Law*. 4 vols. Princeton: Princeton University Press, 1968–1976.
Fall, B. B. *The Viet-Minh Regime, Government and Administration in the Democratic Republic of Vietnam*. New York, 1956. (Mimeograph.)
Fifield, R. H. *The Diplomacy of Southeast Asia: 1945–1958*. New York: Harper, 1958.
―――. *Southeast Asia in United States Foreign Policy*. New York: Council on Foreign Relations, 1963.
Fried, J.H.E. *United States Military Intervention in Cambodia in the Light of International Law*. A paper presented to the International Conference of Lawyers on Vietnam, Laos, and Cambodia. Toronto, May 22–24, 1970. A revised version, dated Feb. 1971, appears on pp. 100–137 in Richard A. Falk, ed., *The Vietnam War and International Law*, Vol. 3, *The Widening Context* (Princeton: Princeton University Press, 1972).
Gettleman, M. and S., and K. and C. Kaplan, eds., *Conflict in Indochina: A Reader on the Widening War in Laos and Cambodia*. New York: Random House, 1970.
Giap, V. N. *People's War, People's Army*. Hanoi: Foreign Languages Publishing House, 1961; and New York: Bantam Books, 1968.
―――. *People's War against U.S. Aeronaval War*. Hanoi: Foreign Languages Publishing House, 1975.
Girling, J.L.S. *People's War: Conditions and Consequences in Southeast Asia*. New York: Praeger, 1969.
Grant, J. S., et al., eds. *Cambodia: The Widening War in Indochina*. New York: Simon and Schuster, 1970.
Groslier, B.-P. *The Art of Indochina*. New York: Crown Publishers, 1962.
―――. *Indochina*. [J. Hogarth, trans.] New York: World, 1966.
Hall, D.G.E. *A History of Southeast Asia*. London: Macmillan, 1955.
Hammer, E. J. *The Struggle for Indochina*. Stanford: Stanford University Press, 1954.
Heder, S. R. "Kampuchean Occupation and Resistance." Chulalongkorn University, Asian Studies Monograph No. 27. Bangkok, Thailand: Institute of Asian Studies, Chulalongkorn University, 1980.
Heine-Geldern, R. *Conceptions of State and Kingship in Southeast Asia*. Cornell University Southeast Asia Program, Data Paper no. 18. Ithaca, N.Y.: Cornell University, 1956.

Hering, B., and E. Utrecht, eds. *Malcolm Caldwell's South East Asia.* James Cook University of Queensland, Southeast Asia Monograph Series No. 5. Townsville, Australia: Committee of Southeast Asian Studies, 1979.

Herz, M. *A Short History of Cambodia from the Days of Angkor to the Present.* New York: Praeger, 1958.

Hildebrand, G., and G. Porter. *Cambodia: Starvation and Revolution.* New York: Monthly Review Press, 1976.

Honey, P. J. *Communism in North Vietnam: Its Role in the Sino-Soviet Dispute.* Cambridge, Mass.: M.I.T. Press, 1963.

Hou Yuon. "Le Paysannerie du Cambodge et Ses Projets de Modernisation." Ph.D. dissertation, Faculté de Droit, Paris, 1955.

Imbert J. *Histoire des institutions khmeres.* Tome II of the Annales of the Faculté de Droit de Phnom Penh. Phnom Penh, 1961.

Jankovec, M. *A Chronology of Events in Indochina: January 1, 1973–December 31, 1973.* Prague: International Organization of Journalists, 1974.

Johnson, C. *Autopsy on People's War.* Berkeley: University of California Press, 1973.

Jorden, A. A., Jr. *Foreign Aid and the Defense of Southeast Asia.* New York: Praeger, 1962.

Jumsai, M. L. *History of Thailand and Cambodia.* Paragon, 1970.

Kahin, G. M. *The Afro-Asian Conference: Bandung, Indonesia, April 1955.* Ithaca, N.Y.: Cornell University Press, 1956.

Kahin, G. M., ed. *Governments and Politics of Southeast Asia.* 2nd ed. Ithaca, N.Y.: Cornell University Press, 1964.

Khieu Samphan. *Cambodia's Economy and Industrial Development* [L. Summers, trans.] Cornell University Southeast Asia Program, Data Paper no. 111. Ithaca, N.Y.: Cornell University, 1979.

Kiernan, B. "Khieu Samphan: Cambodia's Revolutionary Leader." North Melbourne, Australia: Dyason House Papers, 1975.

_____. *The Samlaut Rebellion and Its Aftermath: 1967–1970. The Origins of Cambodia's Liberation Movement.* Monash University Center of Southeast Asian Studies, Working Papers 4 and 5, Parts I and II. Melbourne, Australia: Monash University, 1976.

Kiernan, B., and Chanthou Boua, eds. *Peasants and Politics in Kampuchea, 1942–1981.* London: Zed Press, 1982.

Kissinger, H. A. *White House Years.* Boston: Little, Brown and Company, 1979.

_____. *Years of Upheaval.* Boston: Little, Brown and Company, 1982.

Kosut, H., ed. *Cambodia and the Vietnam War.* Facts on File, 1971.

Lancaster, D. *The Emancipation of French Indochina.* New York: Octagon, 1961, 1974.

Leifer, M. *Cambodia: The Search for Security.* New York: Praeger, 1967.

Ling, T. *Buddhism, Imperialism and War: Burma and Thailand in Modern History.* London: George Allen and Unwin, 1979.

Majumdar, R. C. *Kambuja-Desa or An Ancient Hindu Colony in Cambodia.* Philadelphia: Institute for the Study of Human Issues, 1980.

Mao Tse-tung. *Quotations from Chairman Mao Tse-tung.* Peking: Foreign Languages Press, 1976.

Moise, E. E. *Land Reform in China and North Vietnam: Consolidating the Revolution at the Village Level.* Chapel Hill: University of North Carolina Press, 1983.

Morice, J. *Cambodge, du Sourire à l'Horreur.* Paris: Editions France-Empire, 1977.

Myers, C. *Derrière le sourire Khmer.* Paris: Plon, 1971.

Myers, R. J. *Cambodia: The Struggle for Survival.* Watts, 1980.

Nixon, R. M. *The Memoirs of Richard Nixon.* 2 vols. New York: Warner Books, 1978.

Norodom Sihanouk. *Kambuja.* Phnom Penh: Preah Kanta Bopha Villa, 1966.

_____. *L'Indochine vue de Pekin: Entretiens avec Jean Lacouture.* Paris: Seuil, 1972.

_____. *The Cambodian Resistance.* Auckland, New Zealand: The Auckland Vietnam Committee, 1973.

_____. *Chroniques de Guerre et d'Espoir.* Paris: Hachette/Stock, 1979.

_____. *War and Hope: The Case for Cambodia.* [M. Feeney, trans.; W. Shawcross, intro.] New York: Pantheon Books, 1980.

Osborne, M. E. *The French Presence in Cochinchina and Cambodia: Rule and Response (1859–1905).* Ithaca, N.Y.: Cornell University Press, 1969.

_____. *Politics and Power in Cambodia.* Victoria: Longman Australia, 1973.

_____. *Before Kampuchea: Preludes to Tragedy.* Sydney, Australia: George Allen and Unwin, 1979.

Pike, D. *Viet Cong: Organization and Techniques of the National Liberation Front of South Vietnam.* Cambridge, Mass: M.I.T. Press, 1966.

_____. *Cambodia's War.* Southeast Asian Perspectives No. 1. New York: American Friends of Vietnam, 1971.

Pin Yathay. *L'Utopie meurtrière; un rescapé du génocide cambodgien témoigne.* Paris: Robert Laffont, 1979.

Pomonti, J.-C., and S. Thion. *Des Courtisans aux Partisans: Essai sur la crise cambodgienne.* Gallimard, 1971.

Ponchaud, F. *Cambodia: Year Zero.* New York: Holt, Rinehart and Winston, 1978.

Poole, P. A. *Cambodia's Quest for Survival.* New York: American-Asian Educational Exchange, 1969.

_____. *The Expansion of Vietnam in Cambodia: Action and Response by the Governments of North Vietnam, South Vietnam, Cambodia and the United States.* Athens: Center for International Studies, Ohio University, 1970.

Purcel, V. *The Chinese in Southeast Asia.* London: Oxford University Press, 1951.

Pym, C. *The Ancient Civilization of Angkhor.* New York: NAL/Mentor, 1968.

Quinn, K. M. "The Origins and Development of Radical Cambodian Communism." Ph.D. dissertation, University of Maryland, 1982.

Reddi, V. M. *A History of the Cambodian Independence Movement 1863–1955.* Tirupati, India: Sri Venkateswara University, 1970.
Rejai, M. *The Comparative Study of Revolutionary Strategy.* New York: David McKay Co., 1977.
Robequain, C. *The Economic Development of French Indochina.* London: Oxford University Press, 1944.
Rowman, R. *The Four Days of Mayaguez.* New York: Norton, 1975.
Sak Sutsakhan. *The Khmer Republic at War and the Final Collapse.* Washington, D.C.: U.S. Army Center for Military History, 1980.
Sar Desai, D. R. *Indian Foreign Policy in Cambodia, Laos and Vietnam, 1947–1964.* Los Angeles: University of California Press, 1968.
Schier, P., and M. Schier-Oum. *Prince Sihanouk on Cambodia: Interviews and Talks with Prince Norodom Sihanouk.* Hamburg: Institut fur Asienkunde, 1980.
Shawcross, W. *Sideshow: Kissinger, Nixon, and the Destruction of Cambodia.* New York: Simon and Schuster, 1979.
Simon, S. W. *War and Politics in Cambodia: A Communications Analysis.* Durham: Duke University Press, 1974.
―――. *The ASEAN States and Regional Security.* Palo Alto, Calif.: Hoover Institution Press, 1982.
Smith, R. M. *Cambodia's Foreign Policy.* Ithaca, N.Y.: Cornell University Press, 1965.
Soutrelle, G., and J.-C. Fontan. *Avec les Maquisards: du Cambodge Interdit.* Mercure de France, 1977.
Steinberg, D. J. *Cambodia—Its People, Its Society and Its Culture.* New York: Taplinger Publishing Co., 1959.
Taylor, J. *China and Southeast Asia: Peking's Relations with Revolutionary Movements.* New York: Praeger, 1976.
Thompson, V., and R. Adloff. *Minority Problems in Southeast Asia.* Stanford, Calif.: Stanford University Press, 1955.
Tran Dinh Tho. *The Cambodian Incursion.* Washington, D.C.: U.S. Army Center for Military History, 1979.
Turner, R. F. *Vietnamese Communism: Its Origins and Development.* Stanford, Calif.: Hoover Institution Press, 1975.
van der Kroef, J. M. *Communism in South-East Asia.* Berkeley: University of California Press, 1980.
Vannsak, K. *Aperçu de la Révolution Khmer Rouge.* Montmorency, France, March 2, 1977.
Williams, M. *The Land in Between: The Cambodian Dilemma.* New York: William Morrow and Company, Inc., 1970.
Willmott, W. E. *The Chinese in Cambodia.* Vancouver: University of British Columbia Press, 1967.
Wittfogel, K. *Oriental Despotism: A Comparative Study of Total Power.* New Haven: Yale University Press, 1957.

Zasloff, J. J., and M. Brown, eds. *Communism in Indochina: New Perspectives.* Lexington, Mass.: D. C. Heath, 1975.

Zasloff, J. J., and M. Brown. *Communist Indochina and U.S. Foreign Policy: Postwar Realities.* Boulder, Colo.: Westview Press, 1978.

Zasloff, J. J., and A. E. Goodman, eds. *Conflict in Indochina: A Political Assessment.* Lexington, Mass.: D. C. Heath, 1972.

VI. Government Documents and Miscellaneous Sources

A. U.S. Government Documents

Agency for International Development. *Fact Book for Asia.* Washington, D.C.: U.S.G.P.O., 1967.

Choinski, W. F. *Country Study, Cambodia.* Washington, D.C.: Military Assistance Institute, Department of Defense, 1963.

Munson, F. P., et al. *Area Handbook for Cambodia.* Washington, D.C.: U.S.G.P.O., 1968.

U.S. Comptroller General. *Report on the Payment of Phantom Troops in the Cambodian Military Forces.* Report of July 3, 1973. Washington, D.C.: U.S.G.P.O., 1973.

U.S. Congress. House of Representatives. *Military Activities with Regard to South Vietnam, North Vietnam, and Cambodia.* February 27, 1975. Washington, D.C.: U.S.G.P.O., 1975.

_____. *Use of U.S. Military Forces in the Evacuation of U.S. Citizens and Others from Cambodia: Message from the President.* April 14, 1975. Washington, D.C.: U.S.G.P.O., 1975.

_____. *Use of U.S. Military Forces in the Recovery of the SS Mayaguez, Communication from the President.* May 15, 1975. Washington, D.C.: U.S.G.P.O., 1975.

U.S. Congress. House of Representatives. Committee on Foreign Affairs. Subcommittee on Asian and Pacific Affairs. *Hearings* of May 9, 10, June 6 and 7, 1973 on *U.S. Policy and Programs in Cambodia.* Washington, D.C.: U.S.G.P.O., 1973.

U.S. Congress. House of Representatives. Committee on Foreign Affairs. Subcommittee on National Security Policy and Scientific Developments. *Hearings* of June 18, 23–25, 30, July 1, 9, 23, 30, and Aug. 5, 1970 on *Congress, the President, and the War Powers.* (Pp. 497–563 and July 28 testimony.) Washington, D.C.: U.S.G.P.O., 1970.

_____. *Geneva Convention Relative to the Treatment of Prisoners of War, with Reservations, If Any, by Governments Participating in Hostilities in Vietnam, Cambodia and Laos.* Washington, D.C.: U.S.G.P.O., 1970.

_____. *Mekong Project: Opportunities and Problems of Regionalism.* Congressional Research Service Report, May 1972. Washington, D.C.: U.S.G.P.O., 1972.

U.S. Congress. House of Representatives. Committee on Government Operations. Subcommittee on Foreign Operations and Government Information. *Hearings* of Feb. 17 and 24, 1972 on *Economy and Efficiency of U.S. Aid Programs in the Khmer Republic*. Washington, D.C.: U.S.G.P.O., 1972.

―――――. *U.S. Economic Assistance to the Khmer Republic*. Report of June 16, 1972. Washington, D.C.: U.S.G.P.O., 1972.

―――――. *Hearing* of Nov. 12, 1973 on *U.S. Nonmilitary Assistance to Southeast Asia*. Washington, D.C.: U.S.G.P.O., 1973.

U.S. Congress. House of Representatives. Committee on International Relations. Subcommittee on Asian and Pacific Affairs. *Hearings* of Feb. 11, May 1 and 6, 1980 on *1980, The Tragedy in Indochina Continues: War, Refugees and Famine*. Washington, D.C.: U.S.G.P.O., 1980.

―――――. *Hearing* of Dec. 12, 1979 on *Use of Chemical Agents in Southeast Asia Since the Vietnam War*. Washington, D.C.: U.S.G.P.O., 1979.

―――――. *Vietnam-Cambodia Conflict*. Report prepared by Douglas Pike of the Congressional Research Service. Washington, D.C.: U.S.G.P.O., 1978.

U.S. Congress. House of Representatives. Committee on International Relations. Subcommittee on International Organizations. *Hearing* of May 3, 1977 on *Human Rights in Cambodia*. Washington, D.C.: U.S.G.P.O., 1977.

―――――. *Hearing* of July 26, 1977 on *Human Rights in Cambodia*. Washington, D.C.: U.S.G.P.O., 1977.

U.S. Congress. House of Representatives. Committee on International Relations. Subcommittee on International Political and Military Affairs. *Hearings* of May 14 and 15, 1975 on *Seizure of the Mayaguez, Part I*. Washington, D.C.: U.S.G.P.O., 1975.

―――――. *Hearings* of June 19, 25, and July 25, 1975 on *Seizure of the Mayaguez, Part II*. Washington, D.C.: U.S.G.P.O., 1975.

―――――. *Hearings* of July 31 and Sept. 12, 1975 on *Seizure of the Mayaguez, Part III*. Washington, D.C.: U.S.G.P.O., 1975.

―――――. *Seizure of the Mayaguez, Part IV*. Report of Oct. 4, 1975. Washington, D.C.: U.S.G.P.O., 1975.

U.S. Congress. House of Representatives. Committee on International Relations. Subcommittee on International Trade and Commerce. *Hearing* of June 4, 1975 on *U.S. Embargo of Trade with South Vietnam and Cambodia*. Washington, D.C.: U.S.G.P.O., 1975.

U.S. Congress. House of Representatives. Committee on the Judiciary. *Hearings* of July 24–27, 29, and 30, 1974 on *Debate on the Articles of Impeachment*. Washington, D.C.: U.S.G.P.O., 1974.

―――――. *Impeachment of Richard M. Nixon, President of the United States*. Report of August 20, 1974. Washington, D.C.: U.S.G.P.O., 1974.

―――――. *Statement of Information, Book XI: Bombing of Cambodia*. Impeachment Inquiry Staff Report of May–June, 1974. Washington, D.C.: U.S.G.P.O., 1974.

U.S. Congress. House of Representatives. Special Subcommittee on Investigations. *Hearings* of March 6, 11–13, April 9, 14–16, 18, May 7, 8, 1975,

Jan. 27 and May 5, 1976 on *Vietnam-Cambodia Emergency, 1975, Parts I–IV*. Washington, D.C.: U.S.G.P.O., 1976.

U.S. Congress. Senate. *Documents Relating to the War Powers of Congress, the President's Authority as Commander-in-Chief and the War in Indochina.* Washington, D.C.: U.S.G.P.O., July 1970.

———. *"Mayaguez"; Communication from the President.* May 15, 1975. Washington, D.C.: U.S.G.P.O., 1975.

U.S. Congress. Senate. Committee on Agriculture, Nutrition and Forestry. Subcommittee on Foreign Agricultural Policy. Hearing on April 4, 1974 on *Foreign Food Assistance*. Washington, D.C.: U.S.G.P.O., 1974.

———. Hearing of Nov. 19, 1979 on *Food Aid to Cambodia*. Washington, D.C.: U.S.G.P.O., 1979.

U.S. Congress. Senate. Committee on Armed Services. Hearings of July 16, 23, 25, 26, 30, and Aug. 7–9, 1973 on *Bombing in Cambodia*. Washington, D.C.: U.S.G.P.O., 1973.

U.S. Congress. Senate. Committee on Foreign Relations. *Background Information Relating to Southeast Asia and Vietnam.* 7th rev. ed. Washington, D.C.: U.S.G.P.O., Dec. 1974.

———. *Cambodia: May 1970.* Staff Report of June 3, 1970. Washington, D.C.: U.S.G.P.O., 1970.

———. *Cambodia: December 1970.* Staff Report of Dec. 14, 1970. Washington, D.C.: U.S.G.P.O., 1970.

———. Hearings of March 5, 16, 18, 22, and 26, 1971 on the *Geneva Protocol of 1925*. (Contains State Department report on defoliation in Cambodia, pages 247–254.) Washington, D.C.: U.S.G.P.O., 1971.

———. Hearings of April 11 and 12, 1973 on *War Powers Legislation, 1973*. Washington, D.C.: U.S.G.P.O., 1973.

U.S. Congress. Senate. Committee on Foreign Relations. Subcommittee on Arms Control, Oceans, International Organizations and Environment. Hearing of Nov. 8, 1979 on *Cambodian Famine and U.S. Contingency Relief Plans*. Washington, D.C.: U.S.G.P.O., 1979.

U.S. Congress. Senate. Committee on Foreign Relations. Subcommittee on East Asian and Pacific Affairs. Hearing of Aug. 21, 1978 on *Indochina*. Washington, D.C.: U.S.G.P.O., 1978.

———. Hearing of Sept. 27, 1979 on *Southeast Asia Refugee Crisis*. Washington, D.C.: U.S.G.P.O., 1979.

U.S. Congress. Senate. Committee on Foreign Relations. Subcommittee on U.S. Security Agreements and Commitments Abroad. *Thailand, Laos and Cambodia: January 1972.* Staff Report of May 8, 1972. Washington, D.C.: U.S.G.P.O., 1972.

———. Hearing of April 27, 1973 on *U.S. Air Operations in Cambodia: April 1973*. Washington, D.C.: U.S.G.P.O., 1973.

———. *Thailand, Laos, Cambodia and Vietnam: April 1973.* Staff Report of June 11, 1973. Washington, D.C.: U.S.G.P.O., 1973.

U.S. Congress. Senate. Committee on the Judiciary. Subcommittee to Investigate Problems Connected with Refugees and Escapees. Hearing of January

27, 1975 on *Humanitarian Problems in South Vietnam and Cambodia: Two Years After the Cease-Fire*. Washington, D.C.: U.S.G.P.O., 1975.

———. *Hearing* of May 9, 1972 on *Problems of War Victims in Indochina, Part II: Cambodia and Laos*. Washington, D.C.: U.S.G.P.O., 1972.

———. *Hearing* of April 16, 1973 on *Relief and Rehabilitation of War Victims in Indochina, Part I: Crisis in Cambodia*. Washington, D.C.: U.S.G.P.O., 1973.

———. *Hearing* of Jan. 27, 1974 on *Relief and Rehabilitation of War Victims in Indochina: One Year After the Cease-Fire*. Washington, D.C.: U.S.G.P.O., 1974.

———. *Hearing* of May 3, 1972 on *War Victims in Indochina*. General Accounting Office Report on "Problems in the Khmer Republic Concerning War Victims, Civilian Health, and War-Related Casualties," pp. 81–112. Washington, D.C.: U.S.G.P.O., 1972.

U.S. Department of the Army. *Psychological Operations: Cambodia*. Washington, D.C.: Special Operations Research Office, American University, April 1959.

U.S. Department of Commerce. Bureau of International Commerce. *Basic Data on the Economy of Cambodia*. Overseas Business Reports, OBR 65-19. Washington, D.C.: U.S.G.P.O., 1965.

U.S. Department of Defense. Office of the Secretary of Defense. *United States–Vietnam Relations, 1945–1967*. 12 vols. Report prepared for the House Armed Services Committee. Washington, D.C.: U.S.G.P.O., 1971.

U.S. Department of State. *Background Notes: Cambodia*. Publication 7747. Washington, D.C.: U.S.G.P.O., 1977.

———. *Chemical Warfare in Southeast Asia and Afghanistan*. Report to the Congress from Secretary of State Alexander M. Haig, Jr. Special Report No. 98. March 22, 1982.

———. *Chemical Warfare in Southeast Asia and Afghanistan: An Update*. Report from Secretary of State George Shultz. Special Report No. 104. November 1982.

———. *Foreign Relations of the United States, 1950—Volume VI: East Asia and the Pacific*. Washington, D.C.: U.S.G.P.O., 1976.

Whitaker, D. P., et al., eds. *Area Handbook for the Khmer Republic*. Washington, D.C.: U.S.G.P.O., 1973.

B. *Miscellaneous Official Documents*

Burstein, D., ed. *Kampuchea Today: An Eyewitness Report from Cambodia*. Chicago: Call Pamphlets, 1978.

Department of Press and Information. Democratic Kampuchean Ministry of Foreign Affairs. *Black Paper: Facts and Evidences of the Aggression and Annexation of Vietnam Against Kampuchea*. September 1978.

Dossier Kampuchea I, II, et III. Hanoi, Le Courrier du Vietnam, 1978. (Also published in English under the title *Kampuchea Dossier I, II, and III*.)

Fighting Cambodia: Reports of the Chinese Journalist Delegation to Cambodia. Beijing: China Books, 1975.

Kobelev, E. V., comp. *Kampuchea: From Tragedy to Rebirth*. Moscow: Progress Publishers, 1979.

National United Front for Kampuchea. "The Political Program of the National United Front for Kampuchea." *Beijing Review* no. 23, 1970.

Simonov, V. *Kampuchea: Crimes of the Maoists and Their Rout*. Moscow: Novosti Press Agency Publishing House, 1979.

Vietnam, Socialist Republic of. *The Vietnam-Kampuchea Conflict: A Historical Record*. Hanoi: Foreign Languages Press, 1979.

C. *Other Sources*

1. Official radio broadcasts are monitored, translated, and reprinted by the following two sources:
    a. British Broadcast Corporation, Summary of World Broadcasts, Far East [BBC SWB, FE].
    b. U.S. Foreign Broadcast Information Service [FBIS].
2. The reference departments of many major university research libraries offer access to the "DIALOG" automated bibliographic retrieval system, based in Palo Alto, California. DIALOG retrieves citations from a very large data base, containing a number of files of particular interest to the study of the Kampuchean revolution, including:
    a. Congressional Information Service (File 101)
    b. U.S. Political Science Documents (File 93)
    c. Social Scisearch (File 7)

Index

ADKW. *See* Association of Democratic Khmer Women
Agrarian reform, 204–206
Alliance of Communist Youth of Kampuchea (*Sampoan Yuvachun Kommunis Kampuchea*) (Yuv.K.K.), 161, 169
Alliance of Democratic Khmer Youth (*Sampoan Yuvachun Kampuchea Pracheathibodey*), 161
Angkar, 159–160, 162, 179
 cruelty of, 216
 See also Kampuchean Communist Party
Angkar Loeu, 78(figure), 79, 159, 186, 188, 192, 193, 195, 196, 206, 207, 210, 211, 215
 debate within, 179
 repression of, 196
Angkor Empire, 6–7, 10, 150
Angkor Wat, 6, 115, 153, 199
ARCLIGHT, 99, 100(map), 101
Army of the Republic of Vietnam (ARVN), 64, 97
 attacks on NVA sanctuaries, 76, 89, 90, 106–107
 tactics of, 119
ARVN. *See* Army of the Republic of Vietnam
ASEAN. *See* Association of Southeast Asian Nations

A Soa, 150
Association of Democratic Khmer Women (ADKW), 167, 169, 173
Association of Southeast Asian Nations (ASEAN), 200, 203

Battambang, 8, 11, 16, 68, 69, 70, 71, 74(n35), 85, 130, 145, 160
Berlin Youth Festival, 49–50, 55
Black Book, 66, 67, 68
Bou Meng, 179
Boun Oum, 87
Brzezinski, Zbigniew, 31
Buddhism, 152–153
 influence on ideology, 27, 28, 37(n6), 152
 as reactionary, 158
 revival of, 199
 spread of, 10–11
 Theravada, 142(n91), 151
Burchett, Wilfred, 187–188, 196

Cadres
 importance of, 125
 and people, 157
Cambodge. *See* Cambodia; Democratic Kampuchea
Cambodia, 197
 border disputes of, 186
 civil war sources, 97–98
 deaths in, 148(table)

demographic trends, 13(figure), 14–15, 16, 17, 18(table), 148, 149
diplomatic relations with U.S., 85–86
economy of, 16, 19–21, 22(table)
empires of, 6–8, 12
ethnic differences in, 16, 17, 24(n21), 62
and French colonialism, 8, 42
guerrilla warfare in, 79–86, 130
homogeneity of, 40
idyllic image of, 11–12
land use and ownership, 14(table), 15(table), 16–17
1970 coup, 103–107
political instability of, 10
protests against U.S. bombings, 98–99
terms for, 23(n4)
territorial violation of, 75–76
See also Democratic Kampuchea; Khmer Republic
Cambodian Committee for National Liberation, 46–47(figure)
Capital markets, 17
CCNL. *See* Cambodian Committee for National Liberation
CCP. *See* Chinese Communist Party
CECUF. *See* Central Executive Committee of the United Front
Central Executive Committee of the United Front (CECUF), 46–47(figure), 56
Central Intelligence Agency (CIA), 10, 36, 87, 88, 92, 147
Central Office for South Vietnam (COSVN), 91
Chandler, David P., xiv, 12, 178
Chau Seng, 57
CHENLA I, II. *See* Force Armée Nationale Khmer

China. *See* People's Republic of China
Chinese Communist Party (CCP)
radicals in, 175–176
support for KCP, 203
See also People's Republic of China
Chou Chet, 167
Chou En-lai, 44, 57, 133
as Sihanouk supporter, 174–175
on socialist development, 201–202
CIA. *See* Central Intelligence Agency
CIDG. *See* Civilian Irregular Defense Group
Civilian Irregular Defense Group, 88, 106
Classless society, 200–212
Cochinchina, 50, 189
Colby, William, 87, 88
Communist Party of the Soviet Union (CPSU), 162, 163
Constitution of Democratic Kampuchea. *See* Democratic Kampuchea, Constitution of
Cooper-Church Amendment, 93
COSVN. *See* Central Office for South Vietnam
CPK. *See* Kampuchean Communist Party
CPSU. *See* Communist Party of the Soviet Union

Dangkor district, 147
Dap Chhuon, 87
Democratic Kampuchea
agrarian reform in, 205
autarky of, 208
and consciousness transformation, 157–162
Constitution of, 151, 171, 172–173, 207, 212, 213, 215, 221–227
external policies of, 174

fall of, 196
finance in, 209
food priority of, 213–214
individual disorientation in, 158
new, 199
ownership in, 210–211
postregime stage, 185–200
privilege in, 214
revolutionary slogans of, 159–160
social structure in, 211–212, 215–216
and technology, 209
as truly revolutionary, 216
and Vietnam, 177, 186–191
as weak state, 195
See also Cambodia; Kampuchean Communist Party
Dulles, Allen, 87
Dulles, John Foster, 44, 87
Duryavarman II, 154

FANK. *See Force Armée Nationale Khmer*
FARK. *See Force Armée Royale Khmer*
Finance, 208–209
"Fishhook" area, 76, 91, 108, 196
FLLPK. *See* Kampuchean People's National Liberation Front
Food
  prices of, 19(figure)
  shortages of, 17–18, 213, 214
Food for Peace Program, 93, 95, 139(n45)
Force Armée Nationale Khmer (FANK), 90, 93, 95, 106, 139(n46), 190
  CHENLA I offensive, 110, 111, 134
  CHENLA II offensive, 111–115, 134, 195–196
  after defeat, 145–146
  defense strategy of, 109(map)
  demoralization of, 117

deterioration of, 121
growth of, 108
and Phnom Penh defense, 115
tactics of, 119, 135
See also Khmer Republic; Lon Nol
Force Armée Royale Khmer (FARK), 84
Ford, Gerald, 123, 145
France
  Cambodian students in, 49
  colonial rule of, 7, 11
  Franco-Cambodian Treaty of 1949, 42–43
Free Khmer (*Khmer Issarak*), 10, 42, 164, 166, 168, 190, 193
French Communist Party (PCF), 50
  Cambodian members of, 37–38(n12), 49
  and de-Stalinization, 32
French Revolution
  ideals of, 7
  and KCP, 32
FUNK. *See* National United Front for Kampuchea

Geneva Conference (1954), 43, 189
Geneva Convention (1955), 43
GRUNK. *See* Royal Government of Khmer National Unification

Heder, Stephen, 178, 187, 207, 211
Helms, Richard, 89
Heng Samrin, 193, 200
Hieu Seng, 164
Hildebrand, George, 1
Historical myth, 149–150
Ho Chi Minh, 35, 39, 45, 194
Ho Chi Minh Trail, 76
Hou Yuon, 28, 29, 31, 48(table), 68, 125, 130, 131, 155, 164, 167, 170–171, 178, 189

alleged assassination of, 71
on peasantry, 201
purge of, 171
return from France, 56
and Sihanouk, 50, 60
theories of, 51, 144, 201, 212
Hu Nim, 12, 15, 28, 48(table), 56,
  64, 125, 130, 131, 155, 164,
  167, 174, 178
  arrest of, 177
  confessions of, 179
  dissertation of, 51–52

ICA. See Indochinese Communist
  Alliance
ICC. See International Control
  Commission
ICP. See Indochinese Communist
  Party
Ideology
  characteristics of, 33–35
  personal-social function of, 81
  and political behavior, 125
Ieng Lin, 190
Ieng Sary, 28, 48(table), 56, 57,
  125, 132, 142(n92), 166, 173,
  174, 182(n45)
  as anti-Vietnamese, 189
  on armed resistance, 55–56, 58
  covert positions of, 59
  European tour of, 132
  on leadership, 124
  on rustication, 198
  as Stalinist, 49–50, 164
Ieng Thirith (Mrs. Ieng Sary), 162,
  167, 173, 201. See also Khieu
  Thirith
Indochinese Communist Alliance
  (ICA), 46–47(figure)
Indochinese Communist Party
  (ICP), 35, 39, 40, 45, 46–
  47(figure). See also Khmer
  People's Party (KPP)
Indochinese People's Conference,
  65

Industrial development, 206–208
Infant mortality rates, 61
In Tam, General, 86, 135
Intelligence Identities Protection
  Act (U.S.) (1982), 138(n19)
International Control Commission
  (ICC), 43
Internationalists, 164, 166, 168,
  176, 177, 190, 193
  liquidation of, 189
Issarakists. See Free Khmer
Ith Sarin, 153–154

Jayavarman I, 154
Jayavarman II, 6
Jayavarman VII, 10, 154

Kambuboth College, 56
Kambuja. See Cambodia
Kampot, 192
Kampuchea. See Cambodia;
  Democratic Kampuchea
Kampuchean Communist Party
  (KCP)
  and Angkor Wat, 153
  authority of, 155–156, 169
  behavior stages of, 35–36
  Central Committee of, 124–125,
    166–171
  class policy of, 146–147
  as complete state, 2, 128
  deindustrialization by, 207
  de-Sihanoukization campaign,
    132, 133, 153–154
  dissolution of, 199
  establishment of, 35
  evolution of, 78–79(figure)
  first congress of, 57–58
  and French culture, 31–32
  and guerrilla warfare, 69
  "High Organization" of, 159
  historical continuity of, 152
  identity of, 55–61
  ideology of, 27–34, 179, 216
  intellectual foundation of, 51

internal power struggle in, 98, 162–180
isolation of, 83
leadership of, 48(table), 124–125, 185
lineage of, 46–47(figure)
and Lon Nol, 134–135
major players in, 163–166
and Marxist theory, 29–31
mass support for, 126–127
and Montagnard tribes, 85
name adopted, 59
and nationalism, 33
organization of, 127–128, 169(figure)
Paris group of, 60
party history, 67
and peasantry, 149–150
and People's Republic of China, 82, 174–177
and population compliance, 80
as pure Khmer society, 28
purges in, 177–179
revolutionary strategy of, 66–69, 135–136
and Sihanouk, 128–133
as socialist development model, 200
and traditional value systems, 129
and U.S. incursion, 97, 117
victory components, 124–136
and Vietnamese, 133–134, 190
Western press condemnation of, 147
See also Angkar; Democratic Kampuchea; Pol Pot; Revolutionary Army of Kampuchea; Stalinists
Kampuchean People's National Liberation Front (KPNLF), 78–79(figure), 197
Kbal Damrei, 145
KCP. *See* Kampuchean Communist Party

Keo Meas, 164
Keo Moni, 164
KFF. *See* Khmer Freedom Front
Khieu Ponnary, 125, 167. *See also* Pol Ponnary; Saloth Ponnary
Khieu Samphan, 12, 21, 28, 29, 31, 36, 48(table), 51, 115, 118, 121, 122(photo), 125, 130, 131, 132, 149, 153, 155, 164, 166, 167, 178, 187, 188, 195, 196, 198, 199, 201
on death estimates, 149, 181(n11)
dissertation of, 52, 212
on KCP organization, 128
and nationalization, 64
as presidium president, 173
repression of, 59, 71, 72(n10)
return from France, 56
in Sihanouk government, 60
on Vietnam, 189
Khieu Thirith, 50, 125, 167, 189. *See also* Ieng Thirith
Khmer Freedom Front (KFF), 46–47(figure)
Khmer Issarak. See Free Khmer
Khmer Loeu, 10, 85
Khmer National Liberation Committee (KNLC), 46–47(figure), 78–79(figure)
Khmer National United Front for National Salvation (KNUFNS), 78–79(figure), 193, 196, 199
Khmer People's Liberation Committee (KPLC), 46–47(figure)
Khmer People's Party (KPP), 35, 40, 41, 45, 46–47(figure), 59, 78–79(figure), 189
emergence of, 45–52
revolutionary role of, 68
Second Congress of, 57–58
weakness of, 40–41

278 Index

See also Indochinese Communist Party
Khmer Republic, 134–135. See also Lon Nol
Khmer Rouge. See Kampuchean Communist Party
Khmer Rumdo, 10, 77, 131, 164, 166. See also Norodom Sihanouk
Khmers Blancs, 10
Khmer Serei, 10, 36, 64, 86, 87, 88, 135
Khmer Students' Association (KSA), 49, 55, 78–79(figure), 189
  disbanded, 51
Khmer Students' Union (KSU), 46–47(figure), 51, 55, 78–79(figure)
Kissinger, Henry, 77, 88, 92, 95–103, 133, 134, 139(n50)
  on Cambodian incursion, 89
  criminal conduct charge against, 96
  errors of, 98–101
KNLC. See Khmer National Liberation Committee
KNUFNS. See Khmer National United Front for National Salvation
Kompong Cham, 106, 111, 118, 196
Kompong Thmar, 110
Kompong Thom, 111, 118, 190
Kosygin, Alexei, 86
Koy Thuon, 167
KPLC. See Khmer People's Liberation Committee
KPNLF. See Kampuchean People's National Liberation Front
KPP. See Khmer People's Party
Krang Ta Chan, 179
Kratie, 91
  as communist operations headquarters, 107
  liberation of, 130
Krom Pracheachon. See Khmer People's Party
KSA. See Khmer Students' Association
KSU. See Khmer Students' Union

Land
  agricultural, 15, 17, 204–206
  appropriation of, 70
  changing use of, 14(table)
  cultivation of, 15(table)
  ownership of, 15(table)
  redistribution, 205–206
Landlords, 62, 203–205, 211
Le Duan, 190, 194
Le Duc Tho, 134
Lenin, Vladimir, 30, 162, 163, 200
Lin Piao, 29, 30–31
Lon Nol, 35, 66, 134, 135, 153, 211
  ascension to power, 76
  defense strategy of, 108
  flight from Cambodia, 123
  regime corruption, 95
  in Samlaut rebellion, 70
  with Son Ngoc Thanh, 86
  U.S. dependency of, 92
  See also Force Armée Nationale Khmer; Khmer Republic
"Lon Nol Line," 108, 109(map), 111, 115
Lon Non, 134
Lovek Logistic and Training Facility, 121

MAAG. See Military Assistance Advisory Group
MACV. See Military Assistance Command, Vietnam
Manila Conference (1954), 43, 44
Maoists, 164, 168, 176, 177, 190
Mao Tse-Tung, 29, 30, 55, 157, 201, 202
MAP. See Military Assistance Program

Marx, Karl, 27–28, 29, 200
Mass motivation, 126
Meak Sam Hon, 132
Mekong Delta, 7, 16, 189
Mekong River, 90, 91
Mekong River offensive, 121–122, 134
Men Suon, 45
MENU, 99, 102(map)
Military Assistance Advisory Group (MAAG), 231
Military Assistance Command, Vietnam (MACV), 96
Military Assistance Program (MAP), 93, 94(table)
Mit Deuch, 170, 178
Monarchy, 129, 153
  as "Defender of the Faith," 129, 150
  demystification of, 155
Mondolkiri, 85, 107, 190
Moneylenders, 62

National Assembly, 65–66
Nationalism, 33, 79, 80, 208, 211
National Liberation Front (NLF), 76
National United Front for Kampuchea (FUNK), 36, 47, 78–79(figure)
  collapse of, 133
  founding of, 129–130
  Political Program of, 213
Neak Luong, 123, 130
Nekhum Issarak Khmer (NIK), 46–47(figure)
NEZ. *See* Vietnam, New Economic Zone
Nguyen Co Thach, 187
Nguyen Thanh, 107
Nhim Ros, 173
NIK. *See Nekhum Issarak Khmer*
Nixon, Richard, 92
  on Cambodian incursion, 89–90
  and coup against Sihanouk, 87, 88, 89
  criminal conduct charge against, 96
  impeachment of, 99
  on Vietnamization, 77
NLF. *See* National Liberation Front
Non Suon, 59, 164
Norodom Monissara, 106
Norodom Sihanouk, 41–44, 199, 201
  abdication of, 9, 43
  on anti-Vietnamese aggression, 187
  Buddhist socialism policy of, 60–61
  coup against, 86–89
  crusade for independence, 43
  economic reforms by, 64
  and external communists, 63
  and government debt, 21
  GRUNK role of, 131–132
  on Hou Yuon, 50
  and KPNLF, 197–198
  as leadership symbol, 129–130
  on Lon Nol, 130
  as nationalist, 211
  policy of nonalignment, 43, 44, 53(n6)
  power loss of, 62–63
  and RAK confrontation, 83
  renunciation of U.S. military aid, 64
  repression by, 59, 71, 74(n35)
  resistance to coup, 103
  right to rule, 8
  and U.S. relations, 65
  on Vietnamese, 194
  See also Khmer Rumdo
Norodom Suramarit, 43, 62, 153
North Vietnamese Army (NVA)
  attack on FANK, 106
  in Cambodian territory, 76, 84

Counter-CHENLA II, 114–115, 134
weapons for PFLANK, 107
Nuon Chea, 58, 66, 173, 176
NVA. *See* North Vietnamese Army

Observateur, L', 56
Oddar Meanchey, 145
Oum Manorine, 70, 236
Ownership, 210–211

Paris Peace Accords, 133, 134
"Parrot's Beak," 65, 76, 191, 196
Pathet Lao, 77
Patriotic Youth Association (PYA), 161
PCF. *See* French Communist Party
Peang Sophi, 160
Peasantry
  alienation of, 158, 159, 195
  debt of, 16, 24(n18, n19)
  economic position of, 12, 62, 64–65, 69–70
  health conditions of, 61
  land ownership of, 15–16
  nationalism of, 80
  productivity, of, 17
  revolutionary attitudes among, 71, 78, 126–127
  in socialist development, 201
  support for Sihanouk, 103–106
  values of, 129
People's Liberation Central Committee (PLCC), 46–47(figure)
People's National Liberation Armed Forces of Kampuchea (PFLANK), 47, 78–79(figure), 92, 106
  command of, 146, 165
  Counter-CHENLA II, 114–115
  growth of, 108, 119
  as independent force, 115
  leadership of, 122(photo)
  Mekong River Offensive, 121–123

1974 dry season offensive, 121
Phnom Penh assault of, 118
regional military commanders, 168
solo offensive, 117–119
strategy of, 110–111
U.S. bombing casualties of, 117–118
victory of, 195–196
See also Revolutionary Army of Kampuchea (RAK)
People's Party. *See* Khmer People's Party
People's Representative Assembly (PRA), 172–173, 214, 215
People's Republic of China (PRC), 77, 151, 174, 214
  agrarian reform in, 205
  armaments to Sihanouk, 82
  capitalist enterprises of, 16–17
  distrust of Vietnam, 197
  finance in, 208
  industrialization in, 206
  ownership in, 210
  as socialist development model, 202, 203
  social structure in, 211, 212
  and technology, 209
  See also Chinese Communist Party
People's Republic of Kampuchea (PRK), 197, 198, 199, 200
PFLANK. *See* People's National Liberation Armed Forces of Kampuchea
Phnom Penh, 86, 88, 90, 106, 107, 108, 110, 114, 117, 163, 165, 166, 167, 196
  assault on, 118, 121–123, 134
  "liberation" of, 170
  rustication of, 144–145
Phouk Chhay, 164, 174
PLCC. *See* People's Liberation Central Committee
Pochentong airfield, 110, 111, 122

Pok Doeuskomar, 167
Pok, 192
Politbureau. *See* Stalinists
Political power, 150
Pol Ponnary (Mrs. Pol Pot), 173
Pol Pot, 198
  ambitions of, 50, 51, 177, 187
  as anti-Vietnamese, 189
  on armed struggle, 66–67
  atechnical orientation of, 210
  on class structure, 211–212
  as prime minister, 173, 176
  on revolutionary tasks, 216
  social model of, 212
  tactical error by, 196
  See also Kampuchean Communist Party; Saloth Sar; Stalinists
Pol Pot faction. *See* Stalinists
Ponchaud, François, 1–2, 55
Popular Socialist Community (*Sangkum Reastr Niyum*), 9, 10, 43, 56, 65, 86
Population
  explosion, 14–15
  rural density of, 18(table)
  trends, 13(figure)
  See also Cambodia, demographic trends
Porter, Gareth, 1
PRA. *See* People's Representative Assembly
Pracheachon. *See* Khmer People's Party
Pracheachonists, 164, 166, 168, 176, 190, 193. *See also* Khmer People's Party
PRC. *See* People's Republic of China
PRG. *See* Provisional Revolutionary Government of South Vietnam
Private property, 27, 205, 210
PRK. *See* People's Republic of Kampuchea

Provisional Revolutionary Government (PRG) of South Vietnam, 76, 85, 91
Pu Kombo, 150
Purchasing power, 20(table)
PYA. *See* Patriotic Youth Association

RAK. *See* Revolutionary Army of Kampuchea
Ratanakiri, 85, 190
Rath Samoeurn, 49–50
Reddi, V. M., 17
Religion, 151–152. *See also* Buddhism
Revolution
  aims of, 157
  defined, 2, 217
  as metapolitical activity, 1
  power in, 150, 151
  problem of, 149
  psychological research on, 80–81
  social conditions for, 124
  at victory, 143
Revolutionary Army of Kampuchea (RAK), 165
  founding, 69
  growth of, 81–82, 108, 137(n12)
  recruitment by, 84
  refounding of, 170
  Vietnamese support of, 82
  as warrior-caste, 214–215
  war with Vietnam, 191, 192
  See also Kampuchean Communist Party; People's National Liberation Armed Forces of Kampuchea
Rice cultivation, 29
Rogers, William, 88, 89
Royal Government of Khmer National Unification (GRUNK), 47, 78–79(figure), 118, 165
  de-Sihanoukization campaign, 132–133

founding of, 129
  segregation in, 131
Rubber plantations, 7
Rumdo. *See* Khmer Rumdo
Rustication, 144–145

Sak Sutsakhan, 90–91, 110, 115, 123, 145
Saloth Ponnary, 167
Saloth Sar, 28, 48(table), 55, 125, 127, 128, 153, 158, 166, 168, 171, 190
  on armed resistance, 58
  and Central Committee members, 167
  covert positions of, 59
  as deputy party secretary, 60
  name change, 172
  party supremacy of, 144, 171
  return from France, 56
  as Stalinist, 49–50, 164
  troops of, 118, 123, 198, 215
  on victory, 124
  visited PRC, 174
  See also Kampuchean Communist Party; Pol Pot; Stalinists
Saloth Sar, Mrs., 173
Saloth Sar faction. *See* Stalinists
Samlaut rebellion, 66–67, 68, 69–71, 81
Sampoan Yuvachun Kampuchea Pracheathibodey, 161
Sampoan Yuvachun Kommunis Kampuchea, 161, 169
Sam Sary, 87
Sangkum Reastr Niyum. *See* Popular Socialist Community
Saukham Khoy, General, 123
Schanberg, Sydney, 1
SEATO. *See* South East Asian Treaty Organization
Second Indochina War, 75
Self-criticism, 198

Shawcross, William, 12, 95–103
Siem Riep, 8, 60, 68, 118
Sien An, 49, 50, 179
Sieu Heng, 41
Sirik Matak, 35, 76, 77, 85–86, 106, 135
Sisophan, 8
Sisowath Monireth, 42
Si Votha, 150
Sneuer, 159
Socialist development, 201–212
Socialist Republic of Vietnam (SRV), 186, 202
Social structure, 211–212
Sok Thouk, 167
Son Ngoc Minh, 41
Son Ngoc Thanh, 42, 49, 64, 135
  and *Khmer Serei*, 64, 86
  U.S. support for, 87
Son Sann, 70, 197, 198, 199. *See also* Kampuchean People's National Liberation Front
Son Sen, 48(table), 57, 122(photo), 125, 164, 166, 173, 201
  covert positions of, 59, 60
  in Sihanouk government, 56
Son Sen, Mrs., 173
Son Thai Nguyen, 86
So Phim, 173, 193
SORYA operations, 117
South East Asian Treaty Organization (SEATO), 44, 53(n7), 87, 96, 137(n17)
Soviet Union, 82, 162–163, 197, 203, 206, 208, 209, 214
Speculators, 20–21
Spragens, John, 193–194
SRV. *See* Socialist Republic of Vietnam
Stalin, Joseph, 29, 30, 32, 50, 162–163, 201
Stalinists, 45–49, 133, 164, 190, 191

cadres loyal to, 118
divisions within, 57
interrogation centers of, 178–179
perseverance of, 197
as politbureau, 167–169
purges by, 171, 192–193
support from China, 198
triumph of, 136, 177–180
young cadres' role in, 162, 170
See also Kampuchean Communist Party; Pol Pot; Saloth Sar
Stung Treng, 85, 107
Suryavarman II, 6
Svay Rieng, 191, 196. See also "Parrot's Beak"

Takeo, 106, 118, 127, 179, 192
Ta Mok, 155, 164, 170
Tax collection, 70
Technology, 209
Teng Hsiao-p'ing, 175, 176
Tet Offensive, 84–85
Thioun Mum, 49, 50, 51, 55
Thiounn Chhum, 209
Third Indochina War, 186–187
Thouch, Deputy Commander. See Vorn Veth
Tim Niang, 130
Tiv Ol, 167
TOAN THANG 43, 91
Touch Phoen, 164
Touch Samouth, 41, 58–59, 72(n11), 164
Trade, 208
Tuol Sleng, 178, 179
Tuol Svay Chrum, 106

UFTIP. See United Front of the Three Indochinese Peoples
UN. See United Nations
United Front of the Three Indochinese Peoples (UFTIP), 36, 78–79(figure), 189

collapse of, 133–134
as facade, 77–78
United Nations (UN), 96, 98, 132, 140(n53), 198
United States
bombing programs of, 81, 99–102, 145
Cambodian incursion of, 65, 77, 89–95, 96, 107–108
diplomatic relations with Cambodia, 65, 85–86
Food for Peace Program, 93–94
House Subcommittee Hearings on Human Rights in Cambodia, 147, 180(n4)
imperialism of, 77
and Lon Nol support, 92–93
military assistance program, 63, 64, 92, 93, 94(table)
Operation Phoenix, 75
and Sihanouk coup, 87–88
in South Vietnam, 75
Urban elite
economic position of, 12
and Lon Nol support, 108
nationalism of, 79–80

VC. See Viet Cong
VCP. See Vietnamese Communist Party
Victory, 156
Viet Cong (VC), 111, 114
Vietnam
agrarian reform in, 205
attitudes toward Kampuchea, 188–189, 190
capitalist enterprises in, 16–17
distrust of China, 197
finance in, 208
industrialization in, 206
invasion into Democratic Kampuchea, 193–194, 197
New Economic Zone (NEZ), 193–198

ownership in, 210
as socialist development model, 203
social structure in, 211
support for KCP, 77
and technology, 209
Vietnamese Communist Party (VCP), 39, 46–47(figure)
Vietnamese Revolutionary Youth League (VRYL), 46–47(figure)
Voeun Sai, 107
Vo Nguyen Giap, 29, 30, 194, 196
incursion into Kampuchea, 191
organizational model of, 37(n7), 108
Vorn Veth, 122(photo), 164, 173

unsuccessful revolt of, 193
VRYL. *See* Vietnamese Revolutionary Youth League

White Khmers. *See Khmers Blancs*
Worker's Party of Kampuchea (WPK), 46–47(figure), 57, 58, 78–79(figure)
WPK. *See* Worker's Party of Kampuchea

Youth, revolutionary role of, 160–162
Yukanthor, Prince, 27
Yuv.K.K. *See* Alliance of Communist Youth of Kampuchea